Acknowledgements

Nothing For Something would not have been possible without the continuing support of Keith Whittles, Whittles Publishing Ltd, and the following organisations and resources:

North Wales Archives, Harry Thomas, Boderw Restaurant and Hotel, Penmaenmawr Museum, Suryiah Evans, the Bank of England, the National Archives Kew, www.arthurlloyd.co.uk, Highland Archives Inverness, Northern Meeting Group Archives, London Metropolitan Archives, British Film Institute, Library of Congress USA, *North Wales Life*, Buckinghamshire County Council Archives, Glasgow Council Archives, *Daily Mirror*, Bureau of Aircraft Accidents Geneva, Derby Library Services, Staffordshire County Council Archives, Reach Publishing, Welsh Newspaper Archives, Trove Australia, Calne Heritage Centre, Rhyl Library, British Methodist Churches Archive, Tuck Postcard Archive, Newspapers.com, FindMyPast, Ancestry UK, UK Census, Peter Higginbotham, Mull History and Archaeology, Matthew Lloyd, Rhyl in Days Gone By, London Stock Exchange, Drive Archive, British Motor Museum, DVLA, Wexford Archives.

Thank you to the following organisations for granting permission to reproduce images:

Daily Mirror and Mirrorpix, British Newspaper Archive, Mary Evans Picture Library, North Wales Archives, Calne Heritage Centre and Matthew Lloyd (www.arthurlloyd.co.uk).

All other images are in the public domain, or their original copyright has expired or is unknown.

Author's note

To enable you to truly appreciate the extraordinary scale of Violet's fraud, I have in many places added today's approximate equivalent of the various sums mentioned.

This account is based on painstakingly researched evidence. All conversations featured are based on statements, newspaper reports, and trial transcripts. Some of Violet's probable movements and decision-making process is inferred, based on witness sightings and interviews.

Nothing For Something:

Violet Charlesworth

The Edwardian Con Artist Who Fooled The World

Mark Bridgeman

Whittles Publishing

Whittles Publishing Ltd,

Dunbeath,

Caithness, KW6 6EG,

Scotland, UK

www.whittlespublishing.com

© 2025 Mark Bridgeman

ISBN 978-184995-597-3

Printed and bound by CPI Group (UK) Ltd, Croydon, CR0 4YY

Contents

Introduction

'First find someone who wants something for nothing, then give them nothing for something.'

The con artist's mantra, first attributed to Joseph 'Yellow Kid' Weil

Historian and writer Simon Heffer described the Edwardian era as the Age of Decadence. An age in which life (for the wealthy élite, at least) was one of over-indulgence in art, architecture, achievement, apparel and accumulation. Not surprisingly, in a society with such political and financial imbalance, it became a golden era for crime, too.

In the year 1887 *A Study in Scarlet,* the first Sherlock Holmes story by Arthur Conan Doyle, was published. He was perhaps the first writer to truly capitalise on the public's insatiable appetite for crime stories, both imagined and true. Soon, serialised tales of master criminals filled the pages of newspapers, periodicals, and penny dreadfuls which sold at bookshops and railway station news-stands throughout the length and breadth of Britain. Fiction or non-fiction, they quenched the public's thirst for entertainment, thrills, and gossip in the days before television, movies, radio and social media. The Whitechapel murders, the Thames torso killings, and the Frederick Bailey Deeming story, among many others, shocked the nation. The readers of the new Victorian middle classes were horrified to learn of the brutal murders that permeated Britain's streets.

During the 1890s and early 1900s, almost by way of light relief, tales of confidence tricksters and fraudsters seeped into the nation's newspaper columns. Such stories provided entertainment for the nation – and continued profits for the newspaper owners – without the shock value generated by a gruesome murder. From the gaslit safety of the parlour, the newspaper coverage of these intrepid tales might even garner a secret and a begrudging admiration among the readers for the fraudster's bravado and ingenuity – while publicly disapproving of such unlawful behaviour, of course.

The story of the beautiful and intriguing Violet Charlesworth is one such tale. Growing up, Violet was a voracious reader and would, no doubt, have read with lurid fascination the newspaper accounts of George Appo, David Lamar, William Thompson, Joseph Weil, and other infamous confidence tricksters. Little did she realise that, in one aspect of the con at least, she would soon eclipse them all.

During 1909 and 1910 Violet's painstakingly established fraud fascinated the English-speaking population of the world. Had she lived in the age of the internet and of the tawdry reality TV shows of the early 21st century she would have undoubtedly been a huge star, a celebrity, an influencer. Yet, even in an era when news could only be spread by word of mouth, by newspaper, via the quips of a music hall variety act, or the beginnings of the Pathé News reels in the cinemas, she achieved a fame and notoriety only dreamt of by politicians and entertainers of the period. Two decades later, many still spoke of her crimes. Indeed, at that time, any woman suspected of a similar confidence trick was accused of 'Doing a Violet'. Directly as a result of her escapades, three further phrases entered the English language: – 'Violet's Leap' and 'Violet's Gap' – both meanings now largely forgotten – and 'Did she jump or was she pushed?' – a lurid newspaper headline describing the events you are about to read. Its original usage is also now long lost. Nevertheless, Violet's legacy would live on in other forms. She even had a racehorse named after her. And although many have tried to emulate her – with varying degrees of success – few have succeeded, and certainly not with quite as much style.

Yet a generation later her story was largely forgotten.

Violet is known to have perpetrated three long cons. Her first was highly effective, but with one significant error. Her second was rushed, panicked, and ill-executed. However, her final trick was so well implemented that even today it still leaves us with more questions than answers. The final move in a three-card trick, if you will.

Nonetheless, Violet's story is not merely another morality tale of a criminal's wrongdoing and their inevitable just desserts, but is also a study of the changing age that bridged the gap between the death of Queen Victoria and the outbreak of the Great War. In an era so often nostalgically pigeon-holed as 'the long and leisurely sunlit afternoon', the establishment hoped that the old order could continue for ever as the new century dawned and the new king took the throne. However, those in the country who existed outside the bubble of country house parties and croquet on the lawn were displaying a new willingness and desire to challenge authority. Arguably, without that determination women might never have achieved universal suffrage, nor Ireland gained its freedom from British rule.

In the Edwardian era, when the domestic lens focused on the fight for women's suffrage in a world of male privilege, Violet Charlesworth found a very different way in which to make her indelible mark on a man's world, simultaneously shattering the glass ceiling of the Edwardian class system. She was a charlatan and a callous confidence trickster who lived life like a pampered princess in an era when the average working family survived on less than £1 a week. Yet she won the adoration of countless admirers and suitors, and of the hordes of reporters encamped outside her door. She fascinated, shocked, and enthralled a nation. All of which she achieved with the panache of a movie star – and all before the age of 25. This, then, is Violet's tale. The story of a beautiful and seemingly rich young woman who fooled the affluent, the gentry, and – above all – the system.

After all, the next best thing to wealth is the perception of it.

Mark Bridgeman

www.markbridgemanauthor.co.uk

The Language Of The Fraudster

As defined in *Confessions of a Confidence Man:
A Handbook for Suckers* by Edward H. Smith, 1923.

Confidence trick

An act of cheating or tricking someone by gaining their trust and persuading them to believe something that is not true. British English. Also known as a scam, fraud, grift or hustle.

The long con

Sometimes called the 'long game', is a scam that unfolds over a period of weeks, months, or even years. it may involve the use of accomplices, and even props such as forged documentation, costumes and scripted lines. It aims to rob the victim of huge sums of money or valuables, often by getting them to empty their banking accounts or borrow from family members.

Foundation work

Preparations made in advance of the fraud, including the hiring of any assistants required and studying the background knowledge needed for the role.

The approach

The victim is approached or contacted.

The build-up

The victim is given an opportunity to profit from participating in a scheme. The victim's greed is encouraged, such that their rational judgment of the situation might be impaired.

The extras

Refers to the unexpected peripheral benefits of the fraud, or to extra accomplices brought in to help make the scam more convincing.

The pay-off or convincer

The victim receives a small payout as a demonstration of the scheme's purported effectiveness. This may be a real amount of money, often 'borrowed' from another victim. In a gambling con, the victim is allowed to win several small bets. In a stock market fraud, the victim is given fake dividends.

The hurrah

A sudden manufactured crisis or change of events forcing the victim to act or make a decision immediately. This is the point at which the 'con' succeeds or fails. With a financial scam, the con artist may tell the victim that the "window of opportunity" to make a large investment in the scheme is about to suddenly close forever.

The in-and-in

A conspirator (someone else working for the con artist, but assuming the role of an interested bystander) puts an amount of money into the same scheme as the victim, to add an appearance of legitimacy. This can reassure the victim; and give the con artist greater control when the deal has been completed.

The melon drop

The melon drop is a scam in which the fraudster intentionally bumps into their intended victim and drop a package containing already broken glass. The damage is then blamed on the victim's clumsiness. The trick's name originated when con-artists discovered that the Japanese valued watermelons at a high price; and would pay handsomely if they believed they had accidently [sic] damaged one.

The getaway

The point in the fraud at which the perpetrator makes their escape, usually hoping to never meet the victim again. If the scam has worked effectively, the fraudster will have taken the victim's funds, without the victim even knowing that they have been robbed.

The mark

Another name to describe the victim or intended target of an attempted fraud.

The three-card trick/find the lady

Also known as Three-card Monte, is a confidence trick in which the victim, or 'mark', is tricked into betting a sum of money, on the assumption that they can find the "money card" among three face-down playing cards. By extension, it has come to mean any form of trick in which the victim is given the illusion of choice but is actually deceived into making the decision that the fraudster originally intended them to.

The Spanish prisoner

The fraudster claims that a family member, usually of an upper class or wealthy status, has been imprisoned abroad. The con artist then claims that he or she is penniless and unable to help their family member. The 'mark' is then encouraged to loan money in order to secure the release of the prisoner, who will then be in a position to pay a huge reward. It is usually followed by repeated requests for money, which the victim is reluctantly obliged to loan, over fears that they will lose their original investment.

Reading the room

The ability to judge the mood, personality, and susceptibility of the intended victim or victims, in any given situation.

A CONFIDENCE TRICK.

PROFESSOR KITCHENER: "Ladies and Gentlemen, I have here an empty bag, capable of containing £100,000. As I am wanting that amount, I merely place the bag upon the table, whisper the magic words 'Gordon,' 'Khartoum,' when, hey presto! we shall find the bag is full."

1: The Bait

This story begins with a mystery and ends with a riddle.

Illuminated only by the bright moonlight of a chilly January night, a young man dressed in a slightly dishevelled chauffeur's uniform, and a well-dressed young lady about 35 years of age staggered from the scene of a motor-car accident and lay down on the side of the empty highway, momentarily gathering their thoughts. The New Year festivities had recently passed; it was now a few minutes before 9 pm on 2 January 1909, a crisp, still, and crystal-clear Saturday evening. Seemingly still dazed, the pair glanced first left, then right, into the bluish hue of the moonlit night. They were quite alone. No streetlights illuminated that isolated stretch of road. A light was shining from a window of the Ship Inn, a few hundred yards to the east of them.

Penmaenbach Point, as it appeared in 1909

The narrow, twisting, and lonely coast road in North Wales on which the accident had occurred that evening ran like a thin, flat ribbon chiselled into the side of an otherwise dangerously steep cliff face, 50 feet above the rocks and sea below. The only protection for road users from the sleep drop and the jagged rocks beneath was afforded by a low stone wall approximately 18 inches thick and no more than 3 feet in height.

Above and behind the roadway, which had been carved, then levelled, from the craggy hillside, the moonlit hills and snow-frosted mountains of North Wales loomed ominously, casting a shadow across any passers-by, and thoughtlessly shedding the occasional loose shard of rock, allowing it to cascade downwards onto the surface of the road.

The accident had occurred close to the small community of Penmaenmawr, on the Bangor to Colwyn Bay road, at a sharp bend in the highway called Penmaenbach Point. This notoriously dangerous curve in the road sits close to an oddly shaped rock nicknamed the Devil's Thumb which, protruding from the base of the cliff, resembles a giant digit pointing portentously towards the sky. It appeared that the wheels of the unfortunate automobile, which had been motoring north-eastwards towards Conwy, had skidded, then hurtled into the low boundary wall that protected road users from the serrated rocks and tide-washed sands that sat threateningly below the road. At the precise point at which the motor car had come to rest, there was a two-foot-wide gap in the wall (designed to offer pedestrians a haven from traffic at the dangerous bend in the road). The car was sitting motionless with its engine still running, sandwiched at an angle inside this space; one of its narrow front wheels dangled precariously close to the edge of the precipice. The vehicle's rear wheels sat resting against the kerb, which had acted as a chock, preventing the motor car from rolling any further forward.

It was an extraordinary piece of bad luck that the driver of the motor car on that fateful evening had succeeded in skidding and crashing into the only point in the low, 18-inch-thick, stone sea wall in which there was a gap, and at which a vehicle would be least protected from the rocks and sea below. Nevertheless, the expensive imported Minerva motor car had somehow managed to wedge itself into the only gap on that particular stretch of road. Considering the damage sustained to the wall, the motor car did not appear to be too badly affected, and it had also miraculously avoided a collision with one of the many thick telegraph poles positioned at intervals of 50 yards or so along the side of the roadway.

Despite the relative quietness of the highways in 1909, driving was a much more trying occupation for the individual than it is today. Country roads were not often metalled. Nor were they helpfully lined with reflective white paint, or adorned with cats' eyes. No streetlighting illuminated the driver's journey, and vehicle headlights were little more than the oil-lit carriage lights that had previously adorned horse-drawn modes of transportation. Steering was cumbersome and unresponsive (compared to that on a modern vehicle) and braking systems relied on the external 'cable and drum' method, which was susceptible to the vagaries of extreme weather. The Bangor to Colwyn Bay stretch of road has since been widened and altered, to become the modern A55 North Wales Expressway, and is barely recognisable when compared to its appearance in 1909. In the 1980s the Ship Inn was demolished to make way for the expressway, with tunnels – one of them bypassing Penmaenbach Point – blasted through the cliff face to accommodate four lanes of traffic. Now a busy dual carriageway, the modern road is complemented by crash barriers and streetlighting. It is hard to imagine the much narrower and unmetalled road surface that would have challenged the Edwardian motorist. Coupled with the absence of any warning signs, far less powerful headlights, and the extreme darkness, driving conditions in the Edwardian era would seem exacting indeed to any modern motorist.

Back then, automobiles were still a comparatively rare sight, certainly in North Wales, and particularly such an expensive and fine example of the motor car as the imported Belgian Minerva 1908 Landaulette. With its double-sleeve valve motor engine developed by Charles Yale Knight in the United States to run almost silently, even if the road had been busy that night it is unlikely that anyone would have heard the car or witnessed the accident.

Yet earlier in the day the shiny, bottle-green Minerva, registration number LB 6709, had certainly turned heads as it sped from St Asaph, through Colwyn Bay, Conwy, and onwards to Bangor, as it conveyed its three occupants on their Saturday afternoon excursion. If you were affluent enough to own a motor car, it was a toy of pleasure, to be used for driving as fast as possible, for feeling the wind in your hair, and for attracting the envious (and frequently disapproving) glances of pedestrians as you sped by. With its removable landau cover, the Minerva offered its owner the perfect driving experience, a chance to see and be seen in pleasant weather, yet providing a modicum of protection from the elements. The Minerva marque also offered its owner a high level of build quality; at that time it was considered second only to Rolls Royce as the ultimate in motoring status symbols. Vehicle prices in 1909 reflected this, the cost of an average motor car matching that of a small house. Recent purchasers of the Minerva marque in 1908 had included the kings of Belgium, Sweden, and Norway, the American business tycoon Henry Ford, and the Belgian Impressionist artist Anna Boch.

On that chilly but clear January day in 1909, this gleaming example of the Minerva motor car had left St Asaph carrying its three occupants for a day's excursion to Bangor, followed by afternoon tea at the Castle Hotel, concluding with a 20-mile nocturnal return drive. In the car were the chauffeur, 25-year-old Albert Watts, and his employers, Lillian and Violet Charlesworth. Lillian was 35 and a little reserved. Her sister, Violet, was 24 (in fact, that evening's motor-car accident would occur just a few days prior to Violet's 25th birthday), and the more flamboyant of the two siblings. Violet was dressed luxuriously; she regularly purchased lavish outfits from the high-class Brook Street fashion houses in London. She adorned herself in expensive jewellery and sported a large and very noticeable full-length crimson motor coat of the type to keep stylish young ladies warm while they travelled the country in their motor cars. Violet's fashion sense was keen, as was her wit and sense of business. Yet within the strict social order of Edwardian England, with its limited opportunities for unchaperoned liaisons, Violet Charlesworth still managed to attract many admirers and much comment (some complimentary, some derogatory). Not only did she live an active and public love life; she also dabbled in stocks and shares on that strictly male preserve, the London Stock Exchange, for which she retained the services of her own broker.

Despite employing not one but two chauffeurs, Violet generally insisted on driving her own motor car, particularly during the hours of darkness. She enjoyed the exhilaration of night-time driving. Although in 1903 the national speed limit had been increased from 14 to 20 mph, courtesy of the Motor Car Act, this was not sufficient for Violet, who preferred to drive much faster whenever the situation allowed. In truth, there was little chance of being apprehended or prosecuted on the quiet country roads of Britain, and the speed limits, largely unenforceable, were generally ignored. Her desire to be seen behind the wheel often saw her suffer the sharp backlash of local opinion and comment (perhaps tinged with a little jealousy too) as she powered along the highways and byways of Britain. It was widely thought in 1909 that women did not possess the correct temperament for driving, a skill much better suited to the logical and more rational male mind. Indeed, the driver's position in the car was often the most uncomfortable, frequently exposed to the elements, and not considered suitable for the 'more delicate' sex. The attitude to female motorists of the Edwardian era can be perfectly summed up in a commonly used disparaging remark of the time, often shouted by male bystanders to a lady motorist in her vehicle – 'Woman at the wheel!'

It was not long, however, before the rigorous social etiquette of the era caught up with the new trend for female motoring, and instruction was given to ladies, informing them how to dress appropriately when inside a motor car. And if they insisted on taking the wheel themselves, 'helpful' advice was readily provided.

Published in 1909, and certainly read by Violet, was the influential *The Woman and the Car: A Chatty Little Handbook for All Women Who Motor or Who Want to Motor*, by pioneering female driver Dorothy Levitt. An adventuress, who in 1906 had set the land speed record for a female motorist (91 mph), Levitt would doubtless have been the archetypal role model upon which Violet modelled herself. Yet even Levitt was forced to comply with the conventions of the day, as shown by her advice to other lady motor car owners:

An all-important question is dress. Automobilists are nowadays more careful in the choice of their attire, but there are still a goodly number who seem to imagine it is impossible to look anything but hideous when in an automobile:

As regards a frock – the plain "tailor-made" with a shirt blouse of linen, silk or "Viyella" is without a doubt the most comfortable – and the wearer has the advantage, at the end of the day's run, of appearing trim and neat. Under no circumstances wear lace or "fluffy" adjuncts to your toilette— if you do, you will regret them before you have driven half a dozen miles.

The little drawer under the seat of the car is the secret of the dainty motorist. What you put in it depends upon your tastes, but the following articles are what I advise you to have in its recesses. A pair of clean gloves, an extra handkerchief, clean veil, powder-puff (unless you despise them), hair-pins and ordinary pins, a hand mirror – some chocolates are also very soothing, sometimes!'

Surprisingly, knowing the conventions of the time, Dorothy Levitt was allowed to publish the following advice on the dangers of motoring for the lone female driver:

If you are going to drive alone on the highways and byways it might be advisable to carry a small revolver … While I have never had occasion to use it on the road … it is nevertheless a comfort to know that should the occasion arise I have the means of defending myself. If you are driving alone a dog is great company. The majority of dogs like motors and soon get into the habit of curling up on the seat by your side, under your coat.

Perhaps Violet's love of dogs (her constant companions) arose from this advice. Thankfully, she is not known to have taken a revolver with her during her nocturnal sojourns. However, she did become one of the first female applicants for the new Licence to Drive a Motor Vehicle, as required under the terms of the 1903 Motor Car Act.

Meanwhile, at the scene of the accident at Penmaenbach Point on 2 January 1909 the slightly dazed and confused Lillian recovered her composure first, and helped Albert to his feet. She staggered the few hundred yards along the road in her full-length dress and coat, and threw open the door of The Ship. Obviously distressed, she blurted out the terrible news: 'There has been a dreadful car accident! My younger sister has been catapulted into the sea.'

The occupants of the Ship Inn, mostly quarrymen and fishermen, followed her outside into the cold night air. One of the fisherman ran along the Morfa to Penmaenbach Cottages to request help, while the rest made their way quickly westward, towards the scene of the accident.

In addition to the occupants of The Ship, it was not long before a small crowd of people gathered, all curious and anxious to help. Albert explained that Lillian's sister Violet had wanted to drive – in fact, he claimed, she had insisted on doing so. After the trio had departed the Castle Hotel in Bangor for their return journey to St Asaph, Albert had climbed into the passenger seat, and Violet had taken the wheel. However, as the car had rounded the sharp bend in the road next to the Devil's Thumb, it had struck a loose stone and skidded violently through 90 degrees, before colliding with the wall. According to Lillian's version of events the violent and sudden jolt had catapulted a screaming Violet over the open-top glass windscreen down the cliff face, and into the sea

SCENE OF THE MOTOR-CAR ACCIDENT IN NORTH WALES.

Scene of the motor-car accident near Llandudno, when a lady named Miss Charlesworth was killed. The vehicle suddenly swerved and ran into a recess between the rocks. The force of the impact flung Miss Charlesworth through the screen in front of the car and over the precipice into the sea, sixty feet below. The small picture is of the late Miss Charlesworth, while the cross shows the actual spot where the accident occurred.

below. In the Minerva, it was only the rear passenger compartment that was protected by the landau cover; the front seats were exposed to the elements.

The cliff road and protruding ledge where Violet's motor-car came to rest

As the small group listened in horror to Albert's story, Lillian frantically implored them to help her search for Violet. In the pitch-black of the night, Lillian said, she had heard her sister scream, before the sickening sound of a splash as Violet had hit the water. In just a matter of moments, Lillian explained, she feared that Violet's body might have been washed away.

The locals knew only too well the potential dangers on that particular stretch of carriageway, notorious for its damp and slippery road surface, acute bend, falling rocks and low guard wall. The likelihood of a serious motor-car accident was only too real. Despite a railway tunnel having been forced through the nearby rockface in 1848, little by way of improvements had been made to the roadway by 1909 (the first road tunnel was finally constructed in 1932, with an additional parallel tunnel added in 1992).

Increasingly, more people arrived, including Dr Moreton Roberts, who had cycled from Penmaenmawr in the moonlight, and Mr R.J. Hughes, the borough

[Photo. Topical.

THE SLOPE DOWN WHICH, ACCORDING TO THE CHAUFFEUR'S FIRST STATEMENT, MISS CHARLESWORTH FELL AFTER BEING THROWN THROUGH THE WIND-SCREEN OF THE CAR.

surveyor, until quite a sizeable crowd had gathered. The local police constable, PC Evans from Penmaenmawr, was called, and an initial search for Violet was organised. Meanwhile, Superintendent Rees and Sergeant Evans from the Conwy and Penmaenmawr police stations were summoned. After hastily requisitioning a horse and cart they soon arrived at the scene to join the worried group, who were all perched by the low wall, peering down to the reflection of the moonlight on the shoreline below. In 1909 serious motor-car accidents were still a rare occurrence on Britain's roads; accidents involving a stray horse and cart were still a far more frequent occurrence. On the rare occasion that collisions involving motor cars did occur, the low speeds attainable at that time usually reduced the chance of any serious injury. In fact, during the whole of the previous year there had only been a total of 16 motor-car accidents recorded on Britain's roads. Violet Charlesworth's accident was the first such incident ever investigated by the Conwy Police.

Dr Moreton Roberts was asked to examine the two survivors. At this point Lillian Charlesworth was now lying in a slumped and incoherent manner on the ground near the location of the accident; she seems to have regressed into this strange pattern of behaviour despite having been well enough to run to The Ship a few minutes earlier. Albert was at that moment leaning against the low wall and attempting to describe the events of the evening to PC Evans.

After examining Lillian and Albert, Roberts described them both as appearing to be 'cold, bruised and almost insensible, and not able to offer a coherent explanation'.

Lillian, he explained later, 'was not injured, only apparently suffering from shock. Both she and the chauffeur were in much distress; however, they are in no worse plight than that. I then went in search of her sister's body with the others.'

Albert only constantly repeated the same question: 'Where is the lady? Where is she?'

Instead of proceeding with their questioning, the police decided to escort the pair to the nearby Gwynfa Lodging House, a large property on the hilly Paradise Crescent in Penmaenmawr, in order that they might rest for the night. The landlady had spare rooms available, and lit a fire for the pair.

'Interviewing can resume in the morning,' explained Rees, first making sure he had obtained some identification from the two survivors.

When asked by a local newspaper reporter to comment, Rees replied,

> After my arrival at Penmaenbach on Saturday night I found Miss Lillian Charlesworth and the driver in such a frenzied state that I thought it advisable not to question them too closely as to what had occurred, as the crowd there would have thought it cruel to do so. But after some trouble I gathered from their incoherent statements that the lady in the motor car with them had gone over the rocks. I thought the next thing was to ascertain where they belonged to, and at last, after a good deal of trouble, they told me, and then I sent them in the charge of a policeman and Dr Moreton Roberts in my own cart to Penmaenmawr to make them comfortable for the night.

Superintendent Rees
of Conwy Police

Although hampered by the darkness, the police conducted as thorough a search as was possible of the rocky shoreline below the site of the crash, but were still unable to locate Violet's body. This appeared to confirm the survivors' story that Violet had been 'catapulted' into the waters of the Menai Strait and ultimately to her death. The decision was taken to postpone any further search until the morning of 3 January, when daylight would better suit their efforts. The local police were mindful of a similar incident that had occurred a year or so earlier at the nearby Great Orme's Head, by Llandudno, when a child had fallen from the headland in the dark. The authorities had searched for the child in vain on the shoreline at the foot of the cliffs below, only to find his body days later, suspended on a narrow ledge near the top of the cliffside just a few feet from where he had initially lost his balance. Their rushed search in the dark had failed to spot the unconscious child on the rocks above them. He had subsequently died of dehydration, because nobody had thought to lower a searcher by rope from the spot where the child had fallen. This time, the police had no wish to make the same mistake.

2: The Tease

Nevertheless, as the sun rose the following morning and illuminated the scene of the previous evening's accident, instead of yielding answers to the strange incident it simply raised more questions.

Police officers and volunteers from Penmaenmawr and Conwy combed the rocks below the gap in the retaining wall at the point where they calculated that the trajectory of Violet's body from the motor car was most likely to have thrown her. To their horror they uncovered two pieces of evidence lodged on the jagged rocks, which were later identified as belonging to Violet. A black suede notebook (in which Violet had meticulously recorded all her motor-car journeys), and a grey tam o' shanter hat, a fashionable driving bonnet for discerning Edwardian ladies. The discovery of these items seemed to confirm that Violet had indeed been washed out to sea, yet with more than twelve hours now having passed between the accident and the daylight recommencement of the search along that stretch of coast, the identification of the probable location of Violet's body presented several problems. At low tide along that stretch of coast a great sandbank is exposed, which forms a large shelf reaching out almost half a mile into the Irish Sea, and which is clearly visible from the road all the way around the bay and north to the Isle of Anglesey, offering excellent visibility should a body come to rest anywhere along its length. However, at high tide there are often conflicting and fierce currents from the Menai Strait to the west and from the Conwy estuary to the east. These currents often converge, and tend to push any object floating there outward into deeper waters, then sweep them in a northerly direction; in the years before our story commences, several victims of drowning had eventually washed ashore as far north as the Lancashire coast. In addition, tidal swells and rough weather could cause the sea level to rise by up to 30 feet, and these might have carried Violet Charlesworth's body far out into the Irish Sea.

Yet several of the local fisherman remained puzzled. Local volunteers, including Mr Parry from Penmaenmawr, searching for Violet's body, descended the rough cliff paths leading from the road above down to the rocky outcrop below. He soon discovered that the rocks beneath the road had remained dry all night, meaning the tide had not risen to a level high enough to sweep away a body that might have been lying there. In fact, knowledgeable locals reported that the high tide at that particular point seldom covered the rocky shoreline at a level high enough to carry anything away. This observation was confirmed by the discovery of Violet's tam o' shanter and notebook from the rocks; both items were dry, and had clearly been neither covered by any rising tide nor washed away. How could an object as heavy as a body be swept away yet an item as light as a notebook remain there? In addition, the weather on the night of the incident had been clear, still, and settled. There had been no storm or heavy wind to even momentarily dash the water onto the rocks. In fact, the sea had remained noticeably calm and serene all night. At the reported time of the accident (believed to be sometime before 9 pm) high tide was still almost an hour away, meaning that Violet and her possessions could have landed on dry rocks only to then be carried away as the waters rose. However, even when the tide attained its maximum height that night, around 10 pm, the waves had still not managed to wash away Violet's hat or black notebook. This presented a puzzling paradox.

On the following day (Sunday 3 January), the sun rose around 8.30 am, and a renewed search effort was coordinated to coincide with sunrise and low tide. If the body of Violet Charlesworth had lain close to her recovered hat and notebook, then it almost certainly would also have remained both visible and dry, clearly well above the waterline. If that was the case, the police surmised, why had the moonlight search on the preceding evening not managed to locate it? In fact, the previous evening had been reported as one of the lowest tides of the year, with only 15 inches of water at the foot of the cliffs. Yet there was still no trace of a body. Several boat owners from Conwy volunteered to row along the shoreline, but

A Tam o' Shanter hat of the type worn by Violet, popular with Edwardian Lady 'Automobilists'

were then unable to locate any trace of Violet's body. Even a local 16-year-old boy, a strong swimmer who knew the coastline well, waded chest-deep into the icy waters, but reported nothing. The only additional clue yielded in the second search was a folded pocket map thought to belong to Violet. But this too was dry.

Next came a shock for the police as they continued their investigation into Violet's disappearance. When Rees returned to Gwynfa Lodging House in Penmaenmawr on the morning of 3 January, to continue his interview with Lillian and Albert, he was dumbfounded to find that despite his instructions to the couple to remain there they had vanished. It turned out that a motor car driven by a Mr Joseph Gratton, a friend and lodger of the Charlesworths, together with a neighbour, Mr Buxton, had arrived at 4 am (having travelled the 23 miles from the Charlesworths' family home, Boderw in St Asaph) had spirited Lillian and Albert away.

One of the other lodgers at Gwynfa, a local nurse, had been entrusted by the police to look after the two survivors. Later she reported that when Albert and Lillian had attempted to leave, she had indignantly reminded them that the police had insisted that they remain there for an interview to be completed.

Boderw, the Charlesworth family home in North Wales

However, Joseph Gratton had ignored her request, explaining: 'Lillian's aged and feeble parents need their sole surviving daughter with them at this time of such deep sorrow.' It is worth pointing out that Violet and Lillian's 'aged and feeble' parents were aged only 63 and 58 at the time, and that they actually had another adult child, their son, Frederick. The nurse also told Rees, 'I never saw a woman so calm after such a terrible accident.'

It is worth noting at this stage that Boderw (meaning Oak Place in English) was a substantial Victorian villa in the pleasant cathedral city of St Asaph, contained within its own walled – and inaccessible – grounds. The house would play a crucial part in the unfolding story, and we shall return to this later.

Meanwhile, Rees addressed the waiting newspaper reporters:

> I intended on Sunday morning to take the first opportunity of interviewing them, but to my great surprise I found that they had left Penmaenmawr at four o'clock this morning in a motor car containing two gentlemen who had driven over from St Asaph in response to their telephone message. They left without communicating with me in any shape or form as to the best means of recovering the body of Violet Charlesworth, and up to the present I have heard no word from them. Many people, boatmen and others, have been searching at the expense of a considerable amount of exposure and fatigue for the missing lady, but her relatives do not seem to have given any instructions whatever regarding the search.'

Rees had no intention of allowing the matter to die down. The following day, Monday, he requisitioned a motor car for the journey to Boderw in order to interview Albert and Lillian. The pair seemed somewhat reluctant to be interviewed by the superintendent, claiming that they were too ill and upset, and had been confined to bed.

Nonetheless, Rees persisted, and Albert eventually gave an official statement, which seemed to differ somewhat from his initial version of events:

> Before reaching Penmaenmawr, something went wrong with the engine, and I had to get out to see it. Then, after passing Penmaenmawr, Miss Violet decided to drive, and I then got down out of the motor car and extinguished the acetylene head lights, leaving only the oil lamps burning. It was bright moonlight at the time.
>
> After turning the point at the top of the hill the gear was changed to top speed. Then a stone must have been struck and the car turned right into the wall. When the car struck the wall, I pulled Miss Violet towards me. After going through the wall the car stopped with a sudden jerk which threw me off. I left Miss Violet on the footboard doubled up. I could not say whether she was seated or not. I heard her give one scream, then she was gone, then I was dazed for a while.
>
> When I came to myself, I saw a boy passing me and going down the rock. Afterwards some men and a woman came back with Miss Lillian. Miss Violet was nowhere to be seen. She was wearing a long scarlet motor coat, trimmed with squirrel-coloured fur.

Lillian corroborated Albert's statement, adding:

> We were driving on the right side of the road, when all of a sudden I felt a terrible jerk and heard my sister scream. I got hold of the handle of the door, and after opening it, jumped out and shouted for help. I was feeling stunned and fell to the ground. When I came to myself I was lying on the ground and a

Violet's Minerva motor-car, photographed after the accident

> dog was licking my face. I shouted for help, then ran down the road to the Ship Inn at Penmaenbach Point and told them of the accident. I was very upset, and I don't remember anything more.

Rees then visited Mr Buxton, the neighbour who had travelled with Joseph to collect Albert and Lillian on the previous evening. Unlike the occupants of Boderw, Buxton seemed willing to cooperate with the authorities, and gave the following statement:

> I have lately been appointed manager of the motor department of Messrs Thorneycroft. I was awakened from my bed on Sunday morning (3rd January). I have a residence at St Asaph, about half a mile from Boderw, where the Charlesworths live. On the night of the occurrence the police, receiving news of the accident, went to Boderw, and after conveying the news suggested that some of the family or the friends should go to the spot. It was then explained that Mrs Charlesworth, the girls' mother, was dangerously ill from heart disease. Presently the police sergeant suggested that as I was the only person with a motor car near at hand my help should be sought. At one o'clock in the morning, Mr Gratton, a friend of the family, and Heywood, who is the chauffeur to Miss Lillian Charlesworth, arrived at my place and roused us up with a violent ringing of the bell. The servants got up, and eventually I went to the door. Mr Gratton and the chauffeur informed me that there had been a terrible motor accident at Conwy, and that one lady had been killed, while her sister and the driver were severely injured. They asked me whether, since Heywood was an experienced driver, I would lend them my car to get to the scene. I said I could not do that but in the circumstances I would drive them myself. I added that I would come along as quickly as I could and would pick them up at the house. When I got along towards Boderw I found them a hundred yards away from the place. The young chauffeur said, "Don't drive down to the house; their mother will hear us, and will be upset."
>
> They got into my car, an 18-h.p. Thorneycroft, and I drove them to Conwy. Blowing my horn at the police station, I got the Superintendent out, and had a talk with him. He explained that the survivors were now in a nursing home about two miles from the scene of the occurrence, at a house which, I think, was called Gwynfa. We set off along the road to find it. Penmaenbach Point, where the affair occurred, is two or three miles out of Conwy, and about twenty-five miles from St Asaph. It was a bright moonlight night, and when we came to the gap in the wall that skirts the road, one could see it quite plainly. With a view to finding out whether this was actually the spot,

Nothing For Something

I pulled up.

At last we found Gwynfa. It was on a hill, and I pulled up at the foot, and Mr Gratton and the chauffeur got out and walked on up. They were gone so long that I eventually went up to see what they were doing, and I found the landlady of the place lighting a fire. Mr Gratton and Heywood, I was told, had gone to the doctor, who lived near, to get permission to awaken Miss Charlesworth and Watts, the chauffeur, in order to take them home. When they returned Mr Gratton said that the doctor had told him he was of opinion there was nothing at all wrong with them except shock, and that there would be no harm in taking them home, and in as much as the mother of Miss Charlesworth was ill. When the chauffeur Watts was awakened and came out I examined his face closely, and there was not a scratch on him. I noticed his gold-braided motor-coat had white limestone on the back of it.

In conversation with him I said, "Was the lady driving?"

"Yes, she was," he replied.

"It is almost an impossibility," I said, "for her to have been thrown out from behind the wheel, considering there is an arm between the two seats."

"As soon as the car struck the wall," he said, "I made a jump and dragged Miss Lillian with me. Then I remembered nothing more."

That was all Watts said. When I saw Miss Lillian Charlesworth, I did not bother her with questions, thinking she would be very much upset and agitated by what had occurred. I said, "I am very sorry to hear of your terrible experience."

She replied, "Yes, it is horrible, isn't it?"

I went down to the foot of the hill to back my car up towards them, thinking to spare the lady as much walking as possible in her agitated state. But she took Mr Gratton's arm instead and walked down without apparent effort or disturbance.

All got into the car. Heywood, Miss Lillian's chauffeur, took his place beside me. The other three, Miss Charlesworth, Mr Gratton, and Watts, got into the back of the car.

We travelled back by the road we had come. The time was about four o'clock when we passed the gap in the wall, and the moon was shining brightly. None of the three said anything, or asked me to stop, as we passed the gap in the wall. The moon was shining brightly, as we passed the spot. I noticed they did not look over down the cliff. Heywood, the young driver by my side, said, "Don't stop the motor car, it will frighten them again."

When we reached Boderw, Mr Gratton gave Miss Charlesworth his arm, and they went into the house without saying a word to me. The young chauffeur, however, gave me a word of thanks. Early this morning (Monday 4th January) I went and saw the injured car at the garage in Penmaenmawr, to which it had been taken. The windscreen had nearly all the glass gone from it.

Rees then asked Buxton for his opinion regarding the probability of a driver being thrown from a motor car as the result of an impact with some object. Buxton stated:

I have been a driver for fifteen years and have driven various cars over all kinds of roads at home and abroad. In my judgment it is impossible for anybody sitting in the driver's seat to be thrown out by impact with any object without the smashing of the steering column and wheel. As a matter of fact, in this case, the steering column and wheel were in their proper position and uninjured.

Next to be questioned by Rees was Dr Moreton Roberts from Penmaenmawr, who had attended the crash scene that night:

Doctor, did you sanction the removal of the patients from the Gwynfa Lodging House at Penmaenmawr on Sunday morning?'

Roberts replied:

Not as such, Superintendent. My advice to Mr Gratton and the second chauffeur, Heywood, when they knocked me up between two and three o'clock in the morning, was to let Miss Lillian and the driver rest for the night. I then said that I would call round to see them between nine and ten o'clock in the morning.'

Rees enquired:

'Did you examine Miss Lillian Charlesworth and the driver, Albert Watts, to ascertain their injuries?'

Roberts answered:

'No. They were all right. The driver complained of his knee, but I saw him walking, and as there was nothing of consequence wrong with him I did not bother myself.'

'Did the lady complain of any injury, Doctor?

'No; no injury at all. There was no concussion or anything of that kind. When I got them into my trap and was driving them to Penmaenmawr they were both in great distress.'

'Did you think it was genuine?'

'If you had asked me at the time I would have said "yes". I certainly did not detect anything to the contrary, though the driver was making rather convulsive movements and fidgeting with his fingers, and I thought there was no need for it. I tried to get some information from him, but failed. He kept crying out, "Where is the lady?" and, "Have you found her?"'

"And Miss Lillian Charlesworth, Doctor?"

'I could understand Miss Charlesworth being frightfully upset, but why should the driver be more so? I should have thought he would have gone to find his mistress's body. He seemed to be more keenly distressed than Miss Lillian. She just kept saying, "Oh, why did I let her drive?"'

'And, Doctor, what is your expert opinion in the matter?'

There was a moment's silence, while Dr Roberts gave the matter some careful consideration, before finally stating:

It is my personal opinion that the missing woman was not driving the car at the time of the occurrence. If she had occupied the driver's seat, it was, in my opinion, a physical impossibility for her to have been pitched out in the way alleged. In front of her, and close in, would be the steering wheel, on the right side, the driving apparatus, and on the left the other occupant.'

'And, Watts, the chauffeur?'

Roberts responded:

'He did not pretend to me that Miss Charlesworth was pitched out through the windscreen. He told me that she bumped to the side, and, to prevent her from falling, he had caught hold of her, but he fell, and she fell beside him. When he got out of the motor car on to the rock she had gone over.'

Another question occurred to Rees:

'Do you think, judging from the damage done to the car, that the impact would be sufficient to project a heavy person either through or above the screen and over the shelf of the rock?'

'I do not think so. I think the driver, as I have said, would have kept fast in his seat. The front of the car, when I saw it, was about a yard from the verge of the rock ledge, and the back wheels were against the kerb of the road. The tyre on one of the wheels had been torn as though it had skidded, and the car was at right angles to the road.'

'Do you think, doctor, that the young lady may have been put into the water in a different way?'

'I cannot say, Superintendent, but a drowned body, if it is not caught upon something or washed away, may take nine days to float to the surface. And, I understand, the lady was wearing a heavy fur coat and shawl, which might weigh a body down. It may be weeks until a body is found, if it ever is.'

'Thank you, Doctor.'

Already, in just the first 24 hours of the investigation into Violet's disappearance, the police had encountered differing opinions and statements. Rumours were already beginning to circulate in North Wales – financial embarrassment, a jilted lover or a clandestine marriage, and even stories of a secret locked room at Boderw.

Rees instantly realised that it would not be long until the presshounds had sniffed out the story and would quickly descend on Boderw. What he needed was answers, not more questions.

Rees then returned to the scene of the accident at Penmaenbach Point. Despite the Conwy Police's lack of experience in forensic car crash investigations, Rees showed remarkably advanced insight into his collection of evidence at the scene. First, even a cursory examination of the car's windscreen showed that it was only the glass on the passenger side that appeared to be broken. Yet it was Violet, according to her two fellow passengers, who had been in the driving seat at the time of the incident.

In addition, Rees' opinion concurred with that of Moreton Roberts: surely the large steering wheel would have prevented someone from being thrown out from the driver's side.

Nor were any telltale traces of blood visible, either on the windscreen or inside the vehicle. The low wall and the rocky cliff below also yielded no evidence of trauma. In fact, despite an extensive search, the only evidence located so far had been Violet's hat, map, and notebook.

1909 advertisement for the 35h.p. Minerva

The accident also presented further anomalies. If the Minerva had skidded and stopped abruptly with enough force to propel Violet's body over the edge of the cliff, then why was the vehicle itself largely undamaged?

As it turned out, other than a partially shattered windscreen, the motor car was easily driven away from the scene following the accident. Secondly, why had the two survivors not been more seriously injured, when the impact had been (according to Albert's first statement) sufficiently violent enough to 'catapult' Violet headlong into the water? That night, even at high tide, any object propelled from the road above would have needed to travel at least 30 feet outward in a horizontal direction to miss the rocky outcrop and land directly in the water. This would have required the Minerva to have collided with the wall at considerable speed.

MISS VIOLET GORDON CHARLESWORTH, THE MISSING MOTORIST.

This was clearly impossible, since the only logical scenario in which such an incident could occur would require a vehicle to have smashed into the wall head on while travelling in a straight line and at very high speed, then coming to an abrupt stop. Only this chain of events could create the required catapult-like effect required to hurl a body into the water. But on such a narrow and winding road, the only collision likely to occur would be a glancing blow against the wall – a blow hardly likely to propel an object at the correct angle, or over the required distance, to allow it to sail over the outcrop of rocks below and land directly in the water. Rees also conjectured that if a person had merely fallen from their motor car onto the rocks and then tumbled down them, it was unlikely that the body would have maintained enough momentum to reach the water. Even if it had done so, there would surely have been some traces of blood or torn clothing on the rocks.

Also, it seemed curious to the superintendent that at the spot where the car had pierced the gap in the retaining wall the rocks behind it protruded several feet outward in a shelf-like formation, providing a perfectly safe resting place for the motor car. So it could not fall directly to the shoreline below. Had the crash taken place just a few feet either side of that exact location, the motor car could have easily careered 40 or 50 feet down onto the rocks at the bottom.

Next, he pondered the strange behaviour of the crash survivors – if that was indeed what they were. When first questioned, despite being interviewed separately, they had both used the identical and somewhat unusual term, 'catapulted', to describe Violet's ejection from the motor car.

Yet, when Albert had next been spoken to, he had explained that he and Violet had clung to each other as they desperately tried to scramble clear from the motor car, fearing that it would career over the edge onto the rocks below. According to Albert at that point in the questioning, it was only when Violet had managed to climb from the motor car onto the low sea wall that she had slipped and fallen over the edge. This fundamentally different version of events clearly raised suspicions, especially as a mere slip from the sea wall could never have propelled a body far enough horizontally for it to have fallen into the sea and been washed clean away.

The demeanour of the two witnesses also sounded alarm bells. At first they had both seemed incoherent and distressed. However, this had soon subsided. They had quickly become calm and lucid, not appearing to exhibit any strain or upset whatsoever, even managing to surreptitiously telephone Boderw that same night in order to organise their swift exit from the Gwynfa Lodging House at 4 am.

Meanwhile, news of the shocking events of 2 January soon reached the local newspapers, then the national press, as reporters sensed an extraordinary story with which to grip their readers. Sensational headlines soon began to appear in Britain's press:

MOTOR-CAR MYSTERY

THE WELSH CLIFF TRAGEDY

THE CRIMSON CLOAK MYSTERY

YOUNG LADY'S SUPPOSED TERRIBLE DEATH

TRAGEDY BY MOONLIGHT

AN EXTRAORDINARY ACCIDENT!

THE LADY VANISHES!

VANISHING VIOLET

And, perhaps the most enigmatic of all, a tagline that would soon enter the lexicon of popular culture – one that still prevails to this day:

DID SHE JUMP, OR WAS SHE PUSHED?

Or the more sinister angle hinted at by this headline in the *Liverpool Echo*:

WAS THERE A MOTIVE?

The Daily Mail even posed the question:

WOMEN MOTOR DRIVERS: DO THEY LOSE THEIR NERVE MORE EASILY THAN MEN?

A leading London physician responded by stating, 'Women should not drive cars. They are unsuited physically and temperamentally, easily tired, nervous and highly strung, and prone to follow their instincts without thinking.'

In order to fully understand the immense public curiosity in the incident and the resulting macabre interest in the story by the nation's newspapers, it is important to appreciate both the prevailing attitudes during that pre-war era and the limited alternative forms of entertainment (other than the huge number of daily newspapers) available at that time.

First, the printed media reigned supreme both as a source of amusement and as virtually the only source of information. Television and broadcast radio did not yet exist. The moving picture was in its infancy. Although single-reel films had begun to appear, Wales did not yet have its first recognisable cinema; the occasional (silent) film would be shown in hastily converted town halls or in circus-like tents. In fact, the people of Wales would have to wait until 1911 to see the nation's first permanent cinema, when the market hall building in Brynmawr was converted to allow moving pictures to be shown. Even then, the building still doubled as a market hall, with several rows of seats removed weekly to enable food stalls to be erected; following the market each day, the stalls were removed and the wooden floor disinfected in time for the matinée. Patrons, however, still complained about the smell of discarded produce that lingered in the auditorium.

In Britain, newsreels would only start to accompany films in 1910, meaning that until then the cinema was mainly a source of entertainment, not information. Newspapers, on the other hand, provided a cheap source of up-to-date news, entertainment, and information, affordable by almost all classes. In turn, the papers naturally reflected the interests of their readership. Popular news stories of the era included the exploits and outrages of the suffragette movement (both nationally, and locally at Colwyn Bay), the Liberal reforms of Asquith and Lloyd George, the passing of the Children's Act, the Incest Act, and the Prevention of Crime Act. Locally, the *Colwyn Bay and North Wales Weekly News* reported on a series of rather turgid and depressing local cases of child neglect, abandoned wives, and fiancées seeking compensation for breach of promise, together with stories of petty theft and drunkenness. But holidays, restaurants, and motor cars were beyond the means of the ordinary working person, whose limited leisure time was spent drinking, reading newspapers, watching a variety show, or perhaps – for those slightly more affluent –purchasing one of the many new books published at the time, such as *Scouting for Boys*, or G.K. Chesterton's novel *The Man Who Was Thursday*, or E.M. Forster's *A Room with a View*, or Kenneth Grahame's children's tale *The Wind in the Willows*.

When daily life tended to be a monotonous routine of long working hours for men and domestic drudgery for women, what better than to live your life vicariously through the scandalous news stories of the day? Fuelled by the popularity of the Sherlock Holmes detective stories, the case of Oscar Slater, Evelyn Nesbit and, within living memory, Jack the Ripper, it was no surprise that public interest would reach a climax as news of the seemingly unfathomable mystery surrounding the disappearance of Violet Charlesworth reached the noses of the newshounds.

Before long, intrepid reporters from across the country had been despatched to North Wales to uncover the truth behind the mystery of the expensive motor car, the strange disappearance of a glamorous and beautiful lady, and the gossip that was inevitably circulating.

The first reporter to arrive at the Charlesworth household said to the fractionally opened front door: 'Good afternoon. To whom am I speaking?'

The young man who then peered around the door refused to identify himself (it was presumably either Albert or Heywood, Lillian's chauffeur), before saying, 'Please leave!' He even refused to accept the reporter's business card.

A second journalist who attempted contact did so by telephone. 'Good day,' he began. 'Can you tell our readers, have you yet made sworn statements to the police that Miss Charlesworth's body is lost, so that the administration of her estate can begin?'

A gruff male voice barked out a terse response: 'There is no information to give you, and we do not want to hear what you have to say!'

The task of discovering exactly what the Charlesworth family really knew as against what they were concealing was clearly not going to be a straightforward one. In fact, even the brilliant fictional detectives of the day, Sherlock Holmes or Dr Thorndyke, might have struggled to piece together this intriguing puzzle.

Eventually it would take a rural police constable and several eagle-eyed witnesses, together with a baker's shop assistant and a dedicated newspaper reporter, to slowly piece together the life story of Violet Charlesworth and the increasingly complicated chain of events that would eventually lead to the mysterious car crash on that fateful evening.

This, then, is the strange tale of Violet May Gordon Charlesworth and what really happened on the night of Saturday 2 January 1909.

3: The Switch

It was 1870, the 33rd year of Queen Victoria's reign. The Post Office had recently introduced postcards, the first undersea telegraph cable link to India was established, and among the British poorer classes the fight to legalise trade unions continued.

An engineer named David Charlesworth, a hardworking young man from the town of Stockport in Cheshire and an ardent campaigner for the legalisation of shop floor trade unions, was introduced to a spirited young lady from the town of Newport in Shropshire, while attending a town hall dance in the county. He could not help but notice how elegantly she danced. He was 25 at the time, and the girl, Miriam Davies, was 21. She lived with her elder sister Eliza at Marsh Farm, at Edgmond in Shropshire. It had been rumoured locally that Miriam was descended from an aristocratic family fallen on hard times, although the only evidence of this seems to have been elicited from a neighbour who had once remarked, 'Miriam Davies has seen better days, but they were clearly a family of superior appearance.'

David was immediately taken in by her charms, and within months the couple were married. Miriam then gave birth to three children: Frederick, born in 1871, a year after their marriage; Lillian, born in 1873,[1] and Miriam (junior), who arrived in 1875. Two further children were born, but sadly died in infancy. Interestingly, Lillian at age eight was listed on the 1881 census as a cousin, not a sister, although as a daughter on the baptism records and later census reports. Yet another mystery in this unfolding story.

As his family grew, David found employment with the recently formed Dorman & Walker Engineering Company in Foregate Street, Stafford.

The Charlesworths moved to accommodate their expanding family and Miriam's growing social aspirations, renting a compact cottage in Izaak Walton Street, at Tillington in Stafford, a narrow row of red-brick terraces named after the Stafford-born writer. With just three small bedrooms in the house, the children all slept in one of the rooms, while the third was let out to a boarder, a work colleague of David's named Alfred Toddington, in order that the weekly bills might be met.

---

1   It seems that as Lillian was originally listed as the Charlesworths' cousin she may have been the daughter of David's sister, Priscilla Birch. However, Lillian appears to have been brought up by David and Miriam Charlesworth as their daughter.

Another daughter was born, on 13 January 1884, by which time the family had moved half a mile away to a slightly larger bay-fronted property, in Lovatt Street in Stafford. This road of slightly larger, although still uninspiring, terraced houses was better suited to the growing family. Although the weekly rent was affordable there would be little room for extras. If the family wanted any luxuries, they would need to find a supplementary source of income.

Mrs. Coulson, or "Miss Lilian Charlesworth," as she called herself, photographed by her missing sister.

The newly arrived daughter would be christened May, although later in life she would claim that this was a mistake and subsequently take to calling herself Violet (for reasons which will become apparent). The practice of changing names without any official documentation such as a deed poll declaration was fairly common practice during the 18th, 19th, and early 20th centuries; many people desired to disassociate themselves with an unfortunate family reputation, or perhaps to give the impression that they were married. Should an individual wish to

Mrs. Charlesworth, the mother of Miss Violet Charlesworth and " Miss Lilian Charlesworth."

advertise their new moniker, they might simply make an announcement in their local newspaper. However the name change was often a purely private arrangement, one in which the individual fervently wished to distance themselves from their previous title.

May was a sickly and delicate child; many family friends had given her little chance of living beyond childhood. In fact, although never quite blossoming into full health, May did surprise her elder siblings and survive into adulthood, although she was always blighted with a less than robust constitution. It was said by unkind neighbours that she was often veiled by her mother because of recurrent attacks of an undiagnosed illness which occasionally left her with a brown spots on her face, bloodshot eyes, and a rather sallow complexion. Perhaps it was poor nutrition, or perhaps Addison's disease (a kidney infection similar to that suffered by Jane Austen), or possibly even an attack of scarlet fever. In any case, her mother frequently kept her away from school during her formative years (choosing to educate her at home instead), although May was recorded as sporadically attending Rowley Street Church of England School in Stafford.

Despite May's poor health, family life continued in a similar vein to that of many working-class Victorian families. Further siblings were born and did not survive. Although by the 1880s infant mortality rates had improved,

25 per cent of children did not survive beyond their fifth birthday. Scarlet fever also claimed the lives of a huge number of children between 1840 and 1890, particularly in the Midlands, most succumbing to the disease within 48 hours of infection.

For the majority of working-class households, with many mouths to feed, life was challenging. Hundreds of thousands lived below the poverty line and the average family's diet consisted of bread, potatoes, jam, sugar, and vegetables. Meat was the exception, not the rule. In sharp contrast, the wealthy dined on a selection of game, a choice of meats and exotic fish, extravagant desserts, all washed down with a selection of fine wines. Inevitably, poor diet was a source of childhood illness and deaths among the poorest 50 per cent of the population. The Charlesworths were better off than many working-class families – but never wealthy enough for their driven matriarch, Miriam, to be satisfied.

Sadly for the Charlesworth family, only Lillian, Frederick, and May (Violet) would survive into adulthood. Meanwhile, their father, David, continued to work diligently, becoming a union official for the Amalgamated Society of Engineers. When an economic downturn forced him to leave his engineering job at Dolman's he became an assistant superintendent for the Prudential Insurance Company – a job far more suited to his wife's middle-class pretentions.

Miriam, meanwhile, who continued to daydream of her imagined noble lineage, was clearly less than satisfied with her own lot in life. She invested her frustrations and aspirations in her children, who would probably have grown up fantasising of a wealthy and titled long-lost ancestor who might one day magically reappear at their door. In stark contrast, her husband's lack of ambition and imagination would have been a constant frustration to Miriam's social pretensions. Her powerful personality would be a future source of friction between the couple.

Meanwhile, the world looked on in wonder as the construction of the Eiffel Tower was completed in Paris, in time for the 1889 World's Fair. Many thought the structure too tall and unsafe and likely to collapse after a short time. Its foundations were strong, however. Two decades later, as the Eiffel Tower celebrated its twentieth anniversary, it was Violet's foundations that would be crumbling.

By 1891 the family had moved to Granville Terrace in Stone, 8 miles north of Stafford, and shortly afterwards to King Street in Whittington, Chesterfield, where May was recorded as having briefly attended school. Her elder brother, Frederick, had recently enrolled as a theology student, and her sisters were employed as seamstresses at a local factory. The family now seemed to be the model of working-class – or even lower middle-class-- respectability.

Around the turn of the century, as the country mourned the passing of Queen Victoria, the Charlesworth family moved to 34 Joseph Street in Derby, and shortly afterwards to a terraced house in Jackson Street. In the era before mass motor-car ownership, long-distance commuting was not practicable, and it was not uncommon for families to move home on a frequent basis, following the man of the house who took employment wherever he could find it. Neither was it unusual for a family to decamp in a moonlight flit, to avoid unpaid bills or rent arrears.

It seems that by the time the family had settled into Jackson Street, May's elder siblings had moved out; Lillian had married an assistant at a Derby jewellers, and Frederick was pursuing his new career as an engineer in the Georgian city of Bath. Although Jackson Street was a road of unpretentious, flat-fronted, brick-built terraced cottages opening directly onto the street and with little in the way of social status, it was to be the springboard from which Miriam would debut her daughter May on the Derby social circuit. By exploiting May's obvious charm and gregarious nature, Miriam would have hoped that the strategy would reap considerable rewards for the family.

In the meantime, she helped supplement the family's income by giving children's dancing lessons at a nearby Derby hotel, charging participants 15 shillings (now about £100) a term. Young May often took part too, gaining a reputation as an excellent dancer.

Life seems to have been enjoyable for May in Derby. She attended Sunday School at the Wesleyan Methodist Chapel in King Street in a centrally heated hall large enough to accommodate 500 children. It was here that she was given her first Bible, which she read from cover to cover. The prestigious building, with its fine, stately Greek façade – a Doric porch, and upper floor with Ionic pilasters and large arched windows – must have impressed May and her family, as they attended on a regular basis. The chapel also attracted many well-to-do Derby families, all immaculately attired for Sunday service. May and Lillian would

Violet posing for an oil painting which she commissioned

watch and admire the ladies' fashionable dresses and expensive hats, and dream of mixing in such circles. Lillian would eventually choose the chapel for her own wedding.

General Charles George Gordon

The King Street Methodist Chapel, which was demolished in 1966

Not only was a keen observation of Derby's wealthiest families, socialising and laughing as they entered their ornate carriages upon leaving the chapel, May's first experience of such opulence and grandeur; it also served to highlight to her the obvious class divides in Edwardian society. May's admiration for the finer things in life would certainly remain with her for the rest of her days.

Sadly, this magnificent venue, in which May had first observed the opportunities that wealth might offer an aspiring young woman, no longer exists. The King Street Methodist Chapel was demolished in 1966.

Meanwhile, despite her frequent absences from school caused by her weak constitution, May developed a voracious enjoyment in reading. Romantic novels, magazines, periodicals, and music all fuelled her imagination for the events to follow. She would soon mature into diverting and interesting company, with a keen sense of fun and the ability to hold her own in conversation. May showed some musical progress too; she was chosen to perform a solo at the Methodist Chapel and later would compose several songs. Her enjoyment of literature also continued into adulthood, which helped compensate for her lack of formal education. She was able to discuss the novels of William Morris, H.G. Wells, Mark Twain, E.M. Forster, and Rudyard Kipling in any social circle, always managing to leave a favourable impression. I imagine she would have been not a little inspired, too, by Thackeray's *Vanity Fair*, in which he foregrounds the extravagant and careless lifestyle of his opportunist protagonist, Becky Sharp, in the chapter entitled 'How to live well on nothing a-year'.

As May matured into an attractive young woman, she also developed her own individual sense of eye-catching style. Always as fashionable as her budget would allow, she favoured the new 'silhouette' style of long shaped skirts and fitted blouses designed to highlight her attractive figure. This would garner her much attention from the male population of Derby.

One young newspaper reporter who met her on several occasions would later vividly describe her as

A tall, elegant lady, of splendid figure, with soft, wavy brown hair parted in the middle, her tiny face with the small splash – like an acid mark – on the left temple. Her broad white forehead and fine white teeth, and above all, her eyes. Her beautiful eloquent brown eyes that could melt icebergs and soften stone.

It would not be long before she began to utilise her easy-going charms for her own ends.

Derby at the beginning of the twentieth century possessed many fine public buildings and private homes. The many affluent silk mill owners in the county demanded suitable restaurants, theatres, clothiers, and jewellery shops in which they might display their newly acquired wealth. It was the perfect setting for May's mother to debut her daughter onto the Derby social scene.

It was now the 1903 social season, and the British Empire was at its zenith. The class values of the Mother Country were as strong and as rigid as ever.

Following the frightening experience of the Derby earthquake in the spring of 1903, in which chimney pots and tiles were shaken from the roof of the Charlesworths' home, Miriam took her daughter May on a shopping trip into the centre of Derby; it was felt that May, who was referred to at the time as 'delicate', needed a distraction. Miriam decided that she would experiment with what would now be labelled re-inventing yourself. Miriam intended to create an aura of wealth and sophistication around her daughter, in the hope that the effect would attract attention, gifts, and money.

It seems that Miriam's idea had first originated three years earlier, on 15 June 1900, when she, in conversation with a wealthy Derby general practitioner, Dr Barrett, had unsuccessfully attempted to persuade him to temporarily loan her a sum of money on the promise that she would repay it from a potential future windfall which she might be inheriting. Referring to her deceased daughter (who had also been named Miriam), she informed Barrett, 'What a pity it is that Miriam [junior] did not live, because when May is 21 there would have been a fortune for both of them.'

The ploy did not seem to impress Dr Barrett, who laughed off Miriam's attempt to secure a loan from him based on her declaration.

Nevertheless, May was not disheartened by Miriam's failure to secure any financial benefit from her declaration to Dr Barrett. Instead, May would embrace and polish her mother's scheme to such an extent that she would soon become an almost unstoppable force of nature.

By 1903 May had now taken to calling herself Violet May Gordon Charlesworth. The Christian name May had, she claimed, been given to her at birth by mistake. Perhaps the newly named Violet thought her personal reinvention deserved a rather grander and longer epithet, in a similar vein to the king's third daughter, Princess Louise. In January that year, King Edward VII had been declared Emperor of all India, and he had made his eldest daughter, Princess Louise, the Duchess of Fife and the Princess Royal. The idea of a Scottish royal title, with all its proud history, seemed to especially appeal to May, who could only imagine the riches and respect that might accompany it.

Whatever Violet's public pretensions, in private her family referred to her simply as Vi.

The name Gordon was deliberately chosen by Violet to hint at some Scottish ancestry. On a visit to a draper's shop in Derby her mother explained to the shopkeeper that Violet was in fact the goddaughter of the famed war hero General Charles George Gordon, and might one day inherit his fortune. Known affectionately to the British public as Chinese Gordon or Gordon of Khartoum, the general, having fought in the Crimean War as a young man, was much admired by the British public. He then consolidated his military reputation in China, where he was given command of the Ever Victorious Army (an army of Chinese soldiers led by European officers). Under Gordon's command the army was instrumental in quashing the Taiping Rebellion, frequently defeating much larger forces.

Gordon, a man of the highest principles, was then appointed Governor-General of Sudan by Queen Victoria. His heroic defence of Khartoum during the year-long siege by the Mahdi in 1884/5, in which he managed to arrange the evacuation of 2,500 women and children, earned him much praise and admiration. Unfortunately (although, conveniently for Violet's story) he was killed at Khartoum by three khalifahs of the Mahdi. His death would ultimately be heavily and powerfully romanticised as a symbol of British and Christian values against the 'heathen' forces opposing the Empire. A painting by George William Joy – 'General Gordon's Last Stand' – painted in 1893 helped to establish this image. His reputation was later reinforced in the 1966 blockbuster film *Khartoum*, starring Charlton Heston.

Violet Charlesworth could not have chosen a more symbolic, admired, and trustworthy figure with whom to claim a family relationship. In addition, as General Gordon had been killed some 20 years earlier, there was little chance of anyone ever disputing her claim. Strangely enough, Violet was not the first person to employ General Gordon's name in a money-making fraud; it had already been used in 1898 to inspire confidence in a fraudulent scheme to raise money for a new college building in the Sudan, even though he had passed away 14 years previously.

General Gordon is not the only possible inspiration for Violet's choice of name, however.

4: The Foundation

The pseudonym Violet Gordon might have also been inspired by the name given to the heiress daughter of American millionaire retail magnate Harry Gordon Selfridge. Violette Gordon Selfridge would go on to live the kind of effortlessly glamorous and wealthy lifestyle that Violet Charlesworth could only dream of, with the Selfridge family frequently appearing on the society pages of the newspapers. Violette Gordon Selfridge, who coincidentally also called herself Violet and bore a passing resemblance to Violet Charlesworth, would go on to marry Comte Jacques Blaise de Sibour, a French aristocrat, aviator, and adventurer.

Whilst the names General Gordon and Violette Gordon Selfridge may have provided the inspiration for the characters in the fantasy life Violet was creating for herself, it is almost certain that the original inspiration for her scheme came from an unfolding newspaper story she read sometime between 1900 and 1902. The similarities are too many to be coincidental (the full details are revealed in Appendix G). It seems that while the front pages concentrated on the 'Fenian outrages' in Ireland, or the aftermath of the second South African (or Boer) War, Violet was content to pore over the smaller stories and the gossip columns, searching for valuable nuggets that might help embellish her yarn.

Society girl, Violette 'Violet' Gordon Selfridge, daughter of American retail magnate Harry Gordon Selfridge. It is possible that Violet 'borrowed' both Violette's name and lifestyle

Whatever the origin of Violet's tall tale, the ploy seems to have been a hugely successful one for her among the shopkeepers of Derby. She rapidly became an effective *raconteuse*, learning to 'read the room', enabling her to quickly adjust her story when required. To her great surprise, she managed to elicit a number of elegant silk dresses on credit, including a fashionable crimson motor cloak lined with musquash fur, designed to be worn whilst driving in an open-top luxury motor car. Everyone, it seems, wanted to win the favour of the (apparently) well-connected young lady, due to inherit a fortune, described by many as 'prepossessing' and as 'the angel in white'.

It appears that during 1903 and 1904 Violet repeated the charade on several more occasions, acquiring dresses, hats, and jewellery from several Derby merchants. She occasionally modified the version of her fairytale inheritance story, depending on her chosen audience, sometimes exaggerating the story even more. Violet's confidence and sincerity in delivering her fabricated story never wavered. She became ever more polished, and by virtue more credible, with each passing day. In October 1903 she created an even more outrageous adaptation, in which she claimed to have nursed an elderly gentleman back to health, who in return had bequeathed his entire estate to her, valued at some £800,000 (now £122 million). Violet's mother, Miriam, would then explain that despite her daughter only currently receiving a small quarterly allowance from the wealthy gentleman's estate, she was constantly pestered by cads and fortune hunters. According to Miriam, 'These unprincipled rogues have even propositioned my daughter in the street.' This version of the story was used as justification for Violet to acquire two large and expensive pedigree St Bernard dogs as a form of protection, no doubt purchased with money offered to her by a well-meaning acquaintance, taken in by the cunningly woven tale.

However, this particular variation of Violet's yarn appears to have been dropped after a short period. Perhaps it was unsuccessful, or perhaps the astronomical sum involved seemed too outrageous? After all, the success of a confidence trickster rests on two simple principles: first, the ability to inspire enough confidence in their mark, in order that the truth of the proposed transaction is not questioned. And secondly, that the success of such of a scam depends not on the con artist's ability to prove that their claim is true but instead on the inability of anyone else to prove that it isn't. A legacy of that size, already made, would surely have been too easy to disprove.

Soon a new, and more romantic, adaptation of Violet's inheritance story was debuted at social gatherings. Much to their delight, mother and daughter found themselves invited to afternoon teas in Derby and as far afield as Wolverhampton. These much-loved Edwardian social occasions offered the participants every chance to embellish their position in society. Miriam seized these opportunities with relish, explaining to the group that her daughter had become engaged to a wealthy Scottish gentleman, colonial, and soldier named Alexander MacDonald, after the pair had met at the Caledonian Hotel in Edinburgh (which had recently opened to much acclaim). Miriam explained that the young man was 'serving in the ranks, but a gentleman by birth'. This important and outwardly trivial detail added by Miriam made it virtually impossible for anyone to check the validity of her claim, as it was only the officers' postings, but not those of the rank and file, that were reported in the *London Gazette* and other newspapers' social columns. According to Miriam Charlesworth, Alexander MacDonald had left South Africa by steamer on a return voyage to England with the intention of marrying Violet. Tragically, however, during the voyage home, he had lost his life while in the Bay of Biscay, and had been buried at sea somewhere along the western coast of France, close to the Spanish border. The young man, Miriam explained earnestly, was so enamoured of Violet that he had bequeathed his entire fortune of £75,000 (now £12 million) to her. The money, Miriam added, was held in a form of trust fund, which she would receive on her 21st birthday. This enormous sum of money did not seem to raise any degree of suspicion among her social circle. Instead, her new acquaintances became rapt in Violet's tragic tale of lost love and tantalising fortune.

With the audience taken in by her every word, Miriam would then explain the ongoing tragedy of the situation. Violet, distraught with grief, wished to visit the exact spot in the Bay of Biscay at which her fiancé's body had been laid to rest, in order to cast a wreath upon the waves. Unfortunately, the cost of the journey was currently beyond the family's budget. Although Violet

Caledonian Hotel, Edinburgh

knew that she would inherit the huge bequest within the next twelve months, she was inconsolable in the meantime. Broken-hearted, she could not wait a moment longer to pay her final respects to her lover. If only some kindly person could finance the trip for her, Violet promised she would pay them back with interest – just as soon as she received her inheritance.

The tale was, of course, an elaborate confidence trick then known colloquially as 'the Spanish Prisoner'. In the con's original form, the fraudster told their intended quarry that their wealthy lover or family member had been imprisoned in Spain. Supposedly, the prisoner could not be released without a vast sum of money being raised to secure their freedom. The trickster, of course, could not raise the required funds without help. Gullible marks were persuaded to assist, with the promise of a greater monetary reward by the grateful prisoner upon their release. Often the con artist would then require further payments, and further ... until the unfortunate victim had been stripped of all their assets. Adding an element of time pressure, in which the fraudster would emphasise the urgency in which payment was required, together with a helpful dollop of emotion, usually helped ensure the trick's success. The scam had existed for at least

80 years and been made popular in the memoirs of French criminalist Eugène François Vidocq, who in turn had influenced the work of Victor Hugo, Edgar Allan Poe, Sir Arthur Conan Doyle, and Honoré de Balzac. The trick had been employed in New York to great effect during 1898, in a case which had been widely reported in all the British newspapers and was no doubt known to Miriam and Violet. Today this form of fraud still exists, in the form of the Nigerian 419 scam.

Miriam and Violet's personal twist on this elaborate fraud was probably partly inspired by a popular sea shanty regularly sung in the music halls that the family visited:

> **The Bay of Biscay, Oh!** (1901)
> Ye gentlemen of England
> Who live home at your ease,
> It's little do you think
> Of the dangers of the seas;
> When we receive our orders
> We are obliged to go
> On the Main to proud Spain.

And also by an intriguing news story reported in 1901, in which the schooner *Wildfire* had been mysteriously lost with all hands in the Bay of Biscay during a storm. The fate of the *Wildfire* only came to light several weeks later, when a message from the beleaguered vessel was found floating in a corked bottle off the port of Felixstowe. (Incidentally, the use of a message in a bottle may well have inspired another chapter in Violet's tale, which we shall come to later).

It is probably unfair to criticise the gullibility or intelligence of Violet and Miriam Charlesworth's intended victims in this elaborate scam. It appears that Miriam and her daughter were both well-rehearsed, extremely convincing, and totally adept at manipulating all those around them. Far from appearing avaricious and callous, the pair exuded warmth and charm, appearing endearing and extremely emotional as they busily separated their neighbours and acquaintances from their hard-earned savings.

An early victim of their fraud (although there were doubtless many others who never came forward) was a wealthy widow and neighbour, Mrs Martha Smith of 57 Victoria Terrace, Macklin Steet, in Derby. The Charlesworths had befriended her while living in Jackson Street. Violet, on being invited inside Mrs Smith's house, would have given an impeccable performance, only lifting her veil rather than removing it. She would have drunk daintily from her teacup, the handle pinched correctly between her thumb and forefinger, and dabbed the corner of her mouth delicately with her napkin. In fact, this haughty demeanour had been so well practised that she was often rather ironically referred to by her neighbours as 'the duchess'.

To the kindly widow, Violet was every inch the heartbroken upper-class heiress temporarily fallen on hard times. Violet had even told Mrs Smith that she had promised to use some of her inheritance to found a rest home for discharged soldiers.

Mrs Smith was clearly completely seduced by Violet's carefully woven deception and the earnest way in which it had been presented to her. Being a patriotic and warm-hearted lady, she agreed to lend Violet a substantial sum of money – £80 (now £12,000). Violet and her mother gratefully informed Mrs Smith that she would be fully repaid as soon as Violet reached the age of 21, which would fall on Friday 13 January 1905 – the date an omen that Mrs Smith obviously failed to notice. When the sum was returned, Violet assured her, it would include a 4 per cent dividend to compensate for any loss of interest she might have otherwise received.

The arrangement seemed so amenable and so well thought out. How could Mrs Smith possibly refuse to help such a sincere young lady? During 1903, 1904, and into early 1905, Mrs Smith lent Violet varying sums of money on several occasions. The initial amount of £80 taken by Violet from Mrs Smith was a substantial figure at the turn of the century – more, indeed than the average pay-packet for an entire year; typical annual salaries at that time were approximately £50–£75. It seems that Violet approached Mrs Smith several times during the next few weeks, usually asking for a payment of £20 on each occasion. Mrs Smith was so assured of Violet's honesty that despite remonstrances from her relatives she made regular visits to the Co-operative Society and Compton's Bank in Derby to withdraw funds on Violet's behalf.

It appears that Violet may have also played on the poor health she had suffered as a child, and, as Mrs Smith would later explain: 'Violet said her young man was injured in the South African war and was drowned in the Bay of Biscay when he was coming home. She also said that if only she lived long enough, she would go to the Bay of Biscay to drop a wreath in the water near the spot where he was drowned.'

These handsome advances to Violet enabled her to enjoy the luxuries she had always longed for. She began to indulge herself more and more. There soon followed trips to the fashion houses of London, the lush jewellers and diamond merchants that lined Bond Street and Hatton Garden, and the beginnings of an interest in the stock market. Whenever her funds diminished she made another heartfelt plea to Mrs Smith – and, presumably, other gullible innocents who had fallen for the persuasive charms of Violet and her mother. To facilitate her purchases, Violet opened several deposit accounts at various banks and credit institutions. Her ability to inspire trust and confidence in others seems to have been second to none, with retailers appearing anxious to gain favour with the charming heiress. Violet's usual tactic was to first purchase goods with cash, to create an aura of ease and confidence, then make any subsequent purchases by cheque. However, she would make a special point of asking the retailer not to present the cheque immediately, for two reasons:

Bond Street, London. C1910

First, she claimed that the trustees of her inheritance would not approve of the transaction, and secondly, she assured the merchant that if they would hold onto the cheque uncashed, she would simply replace it with cash – plus interest – immediately on receipt of her inheritance.

Violet's charms must have been considerable. Rather than causing alarm bells to ring among London's upmarket stores, this tactic had exactly the effect she desired, resulting in her being offered an extended period of time before she received the inevitable demand for the cheque to be honoured. One such firm was the prestigious Messrs J.W. Benson & Co., Jewellers. The company had enjoyed the patronage of Queen Victoria and it occupied prominent premises in Ludgate Hill, in the Royal Exchange, and in Bond Street. Not intimidated by the jeweller's royal appointment, Violet purchased almost £2,000 (now £300,000) worth of diamonds from the company, in several transactions over a period of eight months. Perhaps to avoid embarrassment, J.W. Benson would later claim that they held a perfectly legitimate cheque from Violet, totalling £1,500, which they confidently expected to be honoured, leaving them 'only £500' (now £75,000) out of pocket.

Indeed, following the motor-car accident in 1909, J.W. Benson & Co. went as far as issuing a statement, claiming, 'Miss Charlesworth's liabilities to the firm are around £500, and not the sums speculated in the press. While Miss Charlesworth has made large purchases of jewellery, she has paid a considerable amount towards those purchases herself by a cheque which we still hold.'

It seems that J.W. Benson & Co. must have found both Violet and her promise to return incredibly persuasive – they continued to hold Violet's uncashed cheque for many years, apparently expecting that she would one day walk through their door carrying a large amount of cash and a profuse apology. This raises an important question: how many other merchants, no doubt too embarrassed to come forward, continued to retain cheques and promissory notes from Violet, in the vain hope that she might one day return to exchange them for cash and finally settle her outstanding account?

Herein lies the difficulty in establishing the true extent of Violet's widespread deception. It seems unlikely that her bank balance would have allowed her to purchase such large sums of jewellery legitimately. She had no visible means of income and was not employed. Her father was not wealthy. Instead, it is far more likely that the many companies duped by her kept silent, more interested in preserving their own reputation – and, in the case of J.W. Benson, in maintaining their royal patronage by keeping Queen Victoria's name at a distance from an unsavoury scandal.

However, it would not be long until Mrs Smith (and undoubtedly others) began to grow impatient for some repayment of their kindness. In the summer of 1905 she wrote to Violet expressing her concern, and pressing her for payment, exclaiming, 'you must have surely received your inheritance by now'.

Soon, Violet's creditors began to receive official letters of correspondence from the young heiress's appointed trustees, explaining that there had been an obscure legal complication in the administration of her inheritance from Alexander MacDonald following his death in the Bay of Biscay. This complication had resulted in the delay of the payment due to Violet, and she explained that she would now need to wait until her 23rd birthday (in January 1907) to receive her endowment. The letters were always eloquently written, expressing deep regret at the inconvenience and, in the letter received by Mrs Smith, wishing her 'every kind of happiness', and mentioning the divine guidance of God. At Christmas Mrs Smith also received an elaborately illustrated seasonal calendar from the Charlesworths, entitled 'Moonlight on the Wye' and inscribed 'To wish you every joy and happiness this Christmastide, and all good fortune throughout the coming year, from Miss Violet Gordon Charlesworth, London E.C.' – the letter having no doubt been written during one of Violet's many stays at one of London's finest hotels.

Each time Violet contacted Mrs Smith, she assured her that 'recompense will be made as soon as it is possible', yet each time a further excuse was made. Meanwhile, despite undoubtedly feeling frustrated, Martha, it appears, still firmly believed she would eventually be paid back.

Sadly – and, with the benefit of hindsight, predictably – this failed to happen. Instead, in 1905, the Charlesworth family precipitately moved house. Violet's father, David, announced his retirement as an assurance agent for the Prudential, and the family decamped to the seaside resort of Rhyl in North Wales, 120 miles away from Derby. This move dumbfounded the Charlesworth's neighbours and friends in Derby. David was only 59 years of age at that time, and the Old Age Pensions Act had yet to be introduced. The benefit of an old age pension was still three years away and, even then, the Act initially provided an income of only 5 shillings per week, limited only to those above the age of 70. So Mrs Smith and the Charlesworths' other neighbours in Derby were at a loss to understand how the family could possibly afford such a sudden – and financially challenging – move.

The Charlesworths rented a spacious villa named Foryd Lodge on the west bank of the River Clwyd, close to Rhyl harbour. The house, which incurred an annual charge of £30 (now £4,500), was rented from the Gratton family, who lived in the farmhouse next door. In addition to David Charlesworth's retirement being given as a reason for the sudden move, it was also explained that an urgent change of air was needed to assist with Violet's asthma. In 1905 Foryd Lodge was certainly in an isolated and windswept location, ideal for fresh sea breezes. The large detached house was a far more expansive property than their Jackson Street home, and its rent at least double the six shillings a week they had previously paid, notwithstanding the additional costs of furnishing and running such a spacious home. Rhyl had recently become a popular destination, largely due to its convenient rail links, and it is probable that the location would have already been well known to the Charlesworths, who had travelled there for family holidays in 1903 and 1904.

Foryd Harbour, Rhyl

There is one obvious question. Just how were the Charlesworth family able to finance this rapid and unexpected leap in their social standing, from a three-up, three-down street-fronting terraced house at six shillings a week, to a large detached Victorian villa costing more than double that amount? *And* managing to accomplish all this without Violet's father, David Charlesworth, remaining in gainful employment? This surprising and sudden change in fortune was explained by David as an unexpected windfall in the form of an inheritance from his recently deceased brother in Canada. Again, as with all well-rehearsed confidence tricks, such as Violet's story of the fiancé buried at sea, the story was more difficult for anyone else to disprove than it was to verify. David claimed to have received a settlement of £7,000 (now £1 million) from his brother, who had emigrated to Canada many years earlier and made a fortune in business. There is no evidence whatsoever to substantiate this unlikely tale; nevertheless, it does seem to support the theory that Violet and her mother had already become highly proficient in separating unsuspecting neighbours and friends from their life savings, and that the whole family were complicit in this undertaking. The annual lease of Foryd Lodge alone equated to almost a year's income for the average working-class family, before even considering the family's additional living costs, which now included expensive furnishing, a maid, a cook, and a gardener. The extra burden of a larger rent on the family's budget does not, however, seem to have curbed their spending. Miriam arranged for cannons to be fired along the Rhyl coastline, complemented by a fireworks display, to celebrate Violet's 22nd birthday.

Rhyl, although fashionable among holidaymakers, was perhaps a little vulgar for Violet's expensive tastes and pretensions. Nevertheless, it was an important rung on the Edwardian social ladder – a ladder which Violet intended to climb as quickly as possible. She was now a shapely young woman in her early twenties. Portrayed by many as slim, elegant, beautifully dressed, 'demure, quiet, with a soft voice' and 'tall'. Later records would reveal that she was around 5' 5" in height; hardly tall, but above the average height of 5'2" for a woman in the Edwardian era –. Her predilection for boots with heels and flattering fitted outfits may have given admirers the impression that she was taller than her actual height. Violet began to appear at fashionable social occasions, and was variously described in the society press, and by acquaintances, as 'mature beyond her years, but appearing not more than 20 or 21, always heavily veiled', by others as 'quick-witted, poised, charming, and humorous', and – perhaps most important of all – with 'the scarce gift of inspiring confidence'.

Violet in Highland dress

And so the pattern was set. With increasing confidence and audacity Violet and Miriam spun their series of well-rehearsed yarns to a staggeringly wide range of merchants, jewellery dealers, shopkeepers, and grocers from North Wales, through the Midlands, and down to London. After at least two years of practice their well-honed tale of a future huge inheritance had been polished and improved to such a degree that Violet almost believed it herself, and virtually all those who crossed her path fell immediately under her spell. The elegant 'heiress' now confidently informed all that met her, 'I will inherit a fortune when I'm 25.' The incantation worked its magic.

Although the public's voracious appetite for crime stories undoubtedly reached its zenith in 1905, in no small part thanks to the triumphant return of Arthur Conan Doyle's fictional detective, Sherlock Holmes, from the dead, it seems that no one suspected that Violet was telling anything but the absolute truth. At every social occasion where the opportunity arose, Miriam would earnestly explain that her grief-stricken daughter had 'met a handsome army officer and colonial named Alexander

MacDonald at a Highland ball', emphasising Violet's supposed noble heritage to cement the story. He had proposed marriage, then been tragically lost at sea on his return trip from India – or South Africa – or in some versions, died after injuries inflicted during the Boer War. If only Violet could raise the required funds, Miriam would implore, she would finally be able to travel abroad and pay her final respects at his resting place.

Violet in Highland dress

The story barely ever failed; and the money, it seems, just kept rolling in.

5: The Convincer

Whenever Violet's newest victim failed to be sufficiently impressed by her tearful and tragic tale of a lover lost at sea, she returned to the story in which she claimed to be the goddaughter of General Gordon of Khartoum.

With growing confidence, Violet now added more detail and authenticity to the story in which she portrayed her 'godfather', General Gordon, as a wealthy hero in the best British Imperialistic sense. This version of the fraud perpetrated by Violet and her mother gradually became more sophisticated during the years 1905–1908, requiring her to employ the services of a highly respected (but unsuspecting) London firm of solicitors, James & James, whom she had no doubt stumbled across during her shopping sojourns in the capital. Violet engaged the firm to uphold her interests by acting on any instructions that they might receive from a Mr James Robert Gordon of Olivier Street in Derby who, she informed them, was the trustee of General Gordon's estate. As a result, greater authenticity was added to every layer of the elaborate story she wove.

The prestigious James & James, Solicitors, Ely Place, Hatton Garden, London, EC. began to receive a series of letters headed 'From Mr James Robert Gordon Esq, Trustee to the estate of General Gordon of Khartoum, Derby', in which he instructed the solicitors to write to each of Violet's financial sponsors offering their personal thanks for supporting her. They were also instructed to send all of Violet's creditors a receipt for the money they had given her, and even the occasional small gift of appreciation, to which was added – 'On the instruction of Mr James Robert Gordon Esq, Official Trustee'.

James Robert Gordon was, of course, entirely fictitious. The letters and telegrams of instruction sent to the solicitors, and purporting to have come from the trustees of General Gordon had been written by Violet herself, then mailed anonymously by her collaborator in Derby. It would later be discovered that her assistant in this deception was a Mr Sidney Baker of 13 Olivier Street, who not only mailed letters on Violet's behalf, supposedly written by Mr J. Robert Gordon, but also acted as an unofficial PO Box for her imaginary trustees. He would receive the correspondence from James & James addressed to The Trustees of General Gordon – and, later, many other concerned individuals chasing monies owed by Violet – then simply redirect the letters to her. It also appears that Baker knowingly (and without question) allowed Violet to send and receive mail from his address in the names of Charlesworth, MacDonald, Gordon, and probably many other pseudonyms. In order to transact this underhand business, Violet was known to regularly visit Baker's home unchaperoned, sometimes even staying overnight – an unusual, not to say eyebrow-raising, circumstance in Edwardian England. Baker was married, a French polisher by trade, and ten years Violet's senior, yet his wife does not appear to have objected to the close relationship between her husband and Violet, nor to her regular overnight stays at their home.

Whatever Baker's unknowing complicity in Violet's deception, he appears to have been easily influenced, and completely deceived, by her. He was to escape prosecution for his unknowing part in her fraud, later stating, 'She was a girl well worthy of a good man's love. I took her at her word. I believed her entirely.'

Violet was undoubtedly an extremely bright and cunning woman, who had researched and prepared her fraudulent scheme exquisitely. Clearly, she had carefully considered every aspect of her plan. At that time, her declaration that 13 Olivier Street was the fictitious address of her trustees was not technically illegal; to misrepresent an address for fraudulent purposes did not become an offence until after certain loopholes were tightened by The Post Office Act 1908, which did not then come into force until May 1909 – at which point any criminal proceeding for postal fraud could not be retrospectively applied.

The headed notepaper belonging to Messrs James & James Solicitors added a certain legitimacy to Violet's endeavours and added a convincing element to her fraud, deceiving a whole series of victims over a long period of time. If Messrs James & James had taken the trouble to travel to Derby to check the validity of Mr J. Robert Gordon, they would have quickly discovered that the office of General Gordon's Trustees was a modest terraced house in a narrow residential street. A simple enquiry at the local post office would have also revealed that it was not the mysterious J. Robert Gordon who regularly mailed handfuls of letters to their office, but Violet herself. In fact, she was well known to the clerk there, who later commented, 'She sent an extraordinary number of letters and telegrams, which sometimes numbered fifty or sixty words in length!'

Unbeknownst to Violet, her extravagant word usage while composing her telegrams had attracted the attention of other post office users, causing that pointed remark to be made. At a time when telegrams were charged at a flat rate of 6d (now £3.50) for up to twelve words, customers took great pains to limit the number they used so as not to incur the excess charge of a ha'penny for every additional word. It seems that Violet was content to spend today's equivalent of £11 in order to send a 60-word telegram. In comparison, a 60-word letter sent by normal mail would have cost her no more than a penny (now £1). Speed, it appears, was more important to her than thrift.

Among the various interpretations of the inheritance story spun by Violet, one extraordinarily detailed version seems to stand out above all others. It may well be that there was at least some element of truth contained within it, since she did not attempt to gain any sort of financial reward when explaining this variation on the theme to a close friend. Always aloof and reserved, Violet seldom revealed any of her innermost thoughts.

However, following the motor-car accident in 1909, a friend of Violet's named Margaret was interviewed by a reporter and recalled a story Violet had once told her regarding an incident which had taken place three years earlier.

'I must tell you about a concert,' Margaret began, 'which Violet told me took place on Wednesday, October 24th, 1906, in Edinburgh at the residence of Mrs M.A. Edwards-Dalgleish. It was given by Mr and Mrs J.R. MacDonald, on the departure for Australia of four brothers, named Donald MacDonald, Kenneth MacDonald, Clive MacDonald, and Hector MacRae MacDonald.

'The programme of this concert, of which I still have a copy, consists of eight pages and a cover, and states that the concert commences at 7.30 pm. The first item is the "MacDonald March", which was composed by Miss Violet Gordon Charlesworth. She has written several songs, and one, "Come Back to Scotland", she sent to the King. She also presented a copy to Harry Lauder (a popular Scottish music hall entertainer of the era).

'Did you ever hear how Violet became possessed of her funds?' the reporter asked Margaret.

'I understood it was by the will of a young soldier. Violet has told me that she was engaged to an Imperial Yeoman named Taverner, and she has shown me his photograph. She told me he met with a motor accident in South Africa, and died on his way home to England, about five or six years ago. He was supposed to be connected with the Clan Gordon, and that is why she assumed the name of Gordon Charlesworth. But she appeared reluctant to talk about the matter. When I mentioned it once, she said: "Oh, please don't talk to me about him, it makes me feel so miserable".'

Violet in Highland dress

That evening's concert had been a genuine one, not a figment of Violet's imagination. A photograph of Violet in full Highland dress was taken during the event. Her friends also seem to have been most grateful for her contribution to the evening's entertainment, as she was photographed holding a large basket of laurels, tied with satin, on which was printed,

Presented to Miss Violet May Gordon Charlesworth ("Chummy") by an admiring circle of friends and acquaintances, Edinburgh Oct. 24 1906.

The Path of Duty is the Way of Glory.

Violet was also presented with a cushion embroidered with the word 'Chummy'. A cushion which she valued enough to keep – and which would, following the motor-car accident in 1909, be used to identify some of her possessions.

Meanwhile, returning to the story, evidence of Violet's all-encompassing ambitions soon became apparent. In early 1907 the family moved from Foryd Lodge to a substantial eight-bedroomed detached property within its own grounds at St Asaph, a few miles inland from Rhyl. The large house, known as Boderw, was surrounded with a large walled garden and had a sweeping carriage driveway, which enabled Violet to park her own motor car in front of the house, much to the envy of neighbours. In 1907 Boderw occupied a quiet and secluded spot on the outskirts of the small but pleasant ancient cathedral diocese of St Asaph, which ideally suited the Charlesworth family. Today, however, the property operates as a restaurant and small hotel sitting next to the North Wales Expressway, and although the building has changed very little, it is now very difficult to imagine the peaceful solitude it would have once offered the family.

Away from the slightly brasher surroundings of Rhyl, which the family had found too noisy, mainly due to the number of large vessels that constantly steamed along the shipping channels to and from the docks in Liverpool, they would have hoped to enjoy their newfound wealth in peace. David Charlesworth was now referred to by the family as a retired doctor (not an insurance consultant) who had suffered a stroke. Meanwhile, Lillian, who had been married to a Mr Coulson, a Derby jeweller, had, on the failure of her marriage, returned to live with the family (although the reason was never discussed with acquaintances or visitors).

St Asaph was a respectable and genteel, if slightly quiet, community noted for its 14th-century cathedral, quaint streets, and pleasant Victorian villas. The arrival of the Charlesworths in St Asaph probably created much interest locally, and undoubtedly suited Violet's desire to climb the social rungs of the Edwardian class ladder. She even organised a Scottish pipe band concert on the lawn of Boderw. Unfortunately, the small community in St Asaph offered her limited scope for excitement and entertainment. Violet wished to see and be seen. However, before her upwardly mobile ambitions could be accomplished, she required yet another source of income from yet another benefactor. Luckily, a new opportunity had recently presented itself. One which was far too good for her to miss.

In December 1906, shortly before moving to Boderw, Violet had been taken ill with an attack of 'weak nerves, high temperature, and exhaustion', which was blamed on her delicate disposition. The family called in a local doctor from Rhyl, Dr Edward Hughes Jones, to attend to her. He was escorted upstairs by the family's new maid to find Violet draped on her bed, immaculately dressed, with her long hair cascading over the pillows, resembling a pre-Raphaelite painting. The heavy curtains were partially drawn and the newly installed electric lights dimmed, to present Violet in a more flattering light. Although every effort had been made to ensure she appeared as attractive as possible, outwardly, she seemed pale and lethargic.

Meanwhile, her mother and sister were busying themselves attending to her every need, as any concerned family might do.

There had been a recent outbreak of meningitis across the cities of Britain, and Dr Hughes Jones was perhaps concerned that Violet had contracted the illness during one of her many jaunts around the country. However, his fears were soon forgotten, as he was instantly taken by her beauty. During the course of his visit, Violet casually introduced the story of the vast fortune: 'I am due to inherit on my 25th birthday from Mr MacDonald, a Scottish colonial.' She explained to Dr Hughes Jones that she had been made a Ward in Chancery, meaning that due to her young age the large sum of money left to her, £150,000, was controlled by trustees who advanced her an annual income of only £240 (now £35,000). Despite this seemingly generous amount being more than three times the average person's salary in 1907, it appears that Dr Hughes Jones immediately took pity on her – even waiving his fee of one shilling. Violet wove an elaborate tale explaining that her agent, Mr J. Robert Gordon of Derby, was acting on behalf of her trustees (whom she named as Colonel Williamson, Francis Williamson, and Mr Harrison) who, in turn, completely controlled her access to any funds.

Incidentally, the name of Colonel Williamson may have been suggested to Violet by a wealthy and well-known Scottish laird and magistrate of the same name. The real Colonel Williamson was eminently respectable, and this small detail added a great deal of authenticity to Violet's account. It must also be remembered that in 1907 it would have been a great deal more difficult for anyone to check the validity of Violet's claims than it is today. During the Edwardian era, matters of business were usually taken on trust and based on honour, first impressions, letters of introduction, and the convincing nature of the business acquaintance. In fact, it had for several centuries been seen as normal for aristocrats and other obviously wealthy families to run up bills with their suppliers and other businesses, payment being made late, if at all. Suppliers were often simultaneously proud of their prestigious client whilst being terrified to press for the payment of outstanding accounts, for fear that their client's custom would instantly be removed – and without payment, to boot, as punishment for having the effrontery to even ask.

Dr Hughes Jones was 42 years of age, greying at the temples, slightly overweight, and with a kindly face. He was a well-respected and generous man, from a well-known medical family. Together with his brother John, he lived and operated a lucrative practice at an eight-bedroom villa, Medeor House, at 3 Elwy Street, Rhyl. Having qualified as a medical professional in 1890, he was experienced, too. However, his medical experience seems to have been completely clouded by his attraction to Violet and, despite being nearly twice her age, he was instantly smitten. No doubt, like many middle-aged and older men, he was flattered by the attention that the much younger Violet had given him.

Violet explained to the doctor that the Charlesworth family were currently embroiled in a long running battle with a marine salvage company named Robert Jones & Co. The company had recently purchased an obsolete and rusting warship, the 1,600-ton cruiser HMS *Fearless*, from the Royal Navy. *Fearless* had been abandoned in the sea channel close to their home at

Foryd Lodge, and the salvage company intended to break up the vessel using dynamite. 'The potential noise of the explosions caused by this activity coupled with the risk of catapulting metalwork,' Violet informed the good doctor, 'has been too much for my frail nerves, and I have been told is likely to cause a relapse in my condition.'

HMS *Fearless*

On 22 March 1907 David Charlesworth managed to obtain a court injunction against Robert Jones & Co, temporarily preventing any salvage operations. This despite the family having already moved to Boderw by that time. However, according to the Charlesworths' claims, these operations continued unabated throughout April and May, with the dynamite used by the salvage company causing the coastline to be showered with dangerous shards of metal. Violet signed an affidavit claiming that she had seen debris from the salvage operations scattered on nearby farmland, and her father testified that large pieces of iron had embedded themselves in their back door, in their larder window, and across their garden.

Joseph Gratton, the Charlesworths' neighbour and landlord at Foryd Lodge, also seems to have become embroiled in the court proceedings, and may well have been persuaded to testify by Miriam and Violet. Nevertheless, despite their earnest performance in the witness box at the resulting hearing, the magistrate was unhappy with Violet, Miriam, and David Charlesworth, clearly believing that the family had manufactured their evidence. He refused to accept that their injunction against the salvage operations had been violated. Following a lengthy summation, in which he expressed his forthright opinion regarding the Charlesworths' motivations in bringing the case, he awarded substantial costs against the family.

At any rate, this was the version of the story which Violet told Dr Hughes Jones as she lay on her sickbed.

Violet explained to him that her family could not possibly afford to pay such exorbitant legal costs, and that the judge had been vindictive towards her in bringing such a ruling against the family. Already completely under Violet's spell, Dr Hughes Jones duly lent her the required funds, 'to tide you over your little difficulties'. Violet, of course, promised to repay the money – with interest – as soon as she received her inheritance.

Despite this story appearing to be both outrageous and improbable, it was swallowed whole by the infatuated medical man. A few days after advancing Violet the required sum of money, Hughes Jones received a gift of two gold scarf pins together with a letter on the headed notepaper of Messrs James & James Solicitors, thanking him for his generosity and assistance. The letter intimated that Violet had 'personally chosen the scarf pins', and was signed, 'Mr Gordon, on behalf of Miss Violet Charlesworth and her trustees'.

Not only had the doctor fallen for such an unlikely tale, the ingenious letter and gift had also helped Violet achieve two further aims. First, the 'personally chosen' gift hinted at a degree of intimacy and affection, and secondly – and perhaps more crucially – it appears that Hughes Jones now fully believed the legitimacy of Violet's position as a potentially wealthy heiress.

Ironically, despite the apparently improbable nature of Violet's story regarding the HMS *Fearless* salvage operation, it was in fact true. Ironically, it would be virtually the only truthful thing Violet would ever tell the poor besotted Dr Hughes Jones. Meanwhile, using his loan, the Charlesworths were able not only to pay their outstanding legal costs relating to their overturned court injunction, but also to have been successful in preventing the use of explosives in any future salvage operations.

Whether Violet had been genuinely ill or had cynically targeted the wealthy doctor as a potential victim is not known. In 1906 Miriam had used the Welsh newspapers to announce that Violet's 'coming-of-age' celebrations[2] were being postponed following advice from the family doctor. Likewise, during April of 1908, Violet, who had been asked to open a bazaar at St Asaph National School, was 'unavoidably absent through illness'. Her brother Frederick performed the duty on her behalf. The following month Violet was shaken up after she swerved in her motor car while avoiding oncoming traffic, and crashed into a horse and cart. Luckily it was a minor accident, and no one was hurt. It does not appear to have discouraged Violet from motoring, as the upcoming events will demonstrate.

It is entirely conceivable, of course, that Violet's bouts of ill health may have been ruses to lay the foundations of the family's attempts to obtain their high court injunction against the salvage operation. By claiming that the constant noise from the shipping channel had caused Violet's health to worsen considerably, her reported bouts of illness may have helped to strengthen the family's case, as well as prepare the ground for Violet's seduction of Hughes Jones. Certainly, the newspaper announcements regarding her health appear to be suspiciously convenient and coincidental, especially as, despite her apparent ambitions to climb the social ladder, she had been practically invisible on the Welsh newspaper society pages at that point.

Whatever her reason or motivation, it seems that Violet was fully prepared for Dr Hughes Jones' initial visit to her sickbed. She had clearly rehearsed her tale well, and was fully able to prey on his generous nature. Over the coming years, it is certainly not unfair to say that Violet's health would be conveniently utilised by the family when a necessary degree of sympathy was required.

There was mutual benefit in the financial arrangement, nevertheless. Now seen as sympathetic to Violet's supposed short-term financial difficulties – and, no doubt, hoping to win her affections by agreeing to loan her additional sums of money – the doctor now had a genuine reason to make further house calls on Violet.

The blossoming relationship between the pair continued, with the doctor calling regularly to pay his respects. Now feeling comfortable that Violet's requests to borrow money were genuine, the doctor lent Violet a staggering £1,000 (now £150,000) in January 1907, despite having known her for only four weeks. The good doctor, although much older than Violet, fell deeply in

---

2   Violet would in fact have been 22 in January 1906, not 21. The reason for postponing her coming-of-age celebration until her 22nd birthday is not known, although she may have been ill.

love with her and earnestly believed his feelings were reciprocated. Violet must have callously encouraged his affections. The couple became engaged in May 1907, Violet clearly convincing him that marriage was to quickly follow. A few days after their betrothal Violet's new fiancé lent her a further £100. On this occasion, to add further authenticity to Violet's claim of future wealth, Dr Hughes Jones received £30 in £5 notes via Messrs James & James Solicitors, apparently on behalf of Violet's trustees, once again thanking him for his help in assisting her.

During the course of the next 18 months the doctor advanced Violet an eyewatering £4,000 (now £600,000). Throughout this period he must have firmly believed that Violet still intended to marry him and that she was only a matter of months away from becoming a woman of great wealth (which he, as husband, would then – despite the comparative freedom created by the Married Woman's Property Act of August 1907 – still have considerable control over). The pair exchanged intimate and affectionate letters in which she often asked for a small loan to 'tide me over my temporary difficulties'. If Violet noticed any reluctance in the doctor's answers, this was assuaged with responses such as 'Ye ken, laddie, that all my fortune will be yours as well as mine one day.'

If Violet did notice any wavering in the doctor's affections, she had a contingency plan in place. She now informed Dr Hughes Jones that her inheritance was in fact worth not £150,000 but £250,000 (now £38 million). When asked by the doctor why she had not revealed the full amount of the inheritance to begin with, Violet replied that she had not wished to boast.

To add validity to her story, on every occasion the doctor advanced Violet an additional sum, he immediately received an IOU from Colonel Williamson (the fictional trustee). Using some of the funds loaned to her by Dr Hughes Jones, she then repaid a small portion of the money she had borrowed from Mrs Smith in Derby (£5 in April 1907 and £10 in March 1908). This subtle move, like those employed by all great con artists, was carefully designed to keep Mrs Smith on the hook, once again reinforcing the legitimacy of Violet's inheritance story.

Meanwhile, Violet continued to ingratiate herself into polite society. She donated a silver cup to the local rifle club, which she named the Gordon Cup, and presented it to the winner of their 1907 short-bore competition. She also contributed another silver trophy, the Gordon Charlesworth Cup, and eleven silver and gold medals for the Easter Monday St Asaph football competition.

However, by November 1908, with her 25th birthday now fast approaching, the story of her supposed inheritance was about to unravel. Dr Hughes Jones, although blinded by Violet's charms in matters of the heart, was astute in the sphere of finance, and he fully expected to see his money returned with interest on that date. The subject of their marriage was also a source of contention between the couple, with the doctor anxious to name a date at the earliest possible juncture. Violet, quick-witted as ever, hit on an ingenious solution to delay matters.

One morning in early November 1908, Dr Hughes Jones was sitting alone at Medeor House in Rhyl, when his maid brought in his breakfast tray and the early post. Among his morning correspondence was a handwritten letter in a white envelope, adorned with a red one penny Edward VII stamp, franked with a London postmark, and marked 'URGENT'. He immediately recognised Violet's handwriting. She had travelled to London earlier the previous day, intending to visit the first Ideal Home Exhibition at Olympia, and must have posted the letter almost immediately upon her arrival in the capital. This conveniently allowed her to present the following awkward news by letter, rather than in person:

> Eddie,
>
> I have terrible news. My trustee, Colonel Williamson, has his own personal feelings for me and is refusing to allow me to receive any of my inheritance, unless I first break off my engagement to you. He is determined to win me yet ...
>
> I shall not get a penny unless I break our engagement. I, who will one day have £7,000 a year and an estate. All my fortune would have been yours. It is cruel, bitterly cruel, laddie, but our engagement must be over. But it is all for love's sake, laddie, laddie.
>
> And now, Eddie, my own, please be assured of my deepest affection, ever your devoted and someday wife,
>
> Violet.

She enclosed a promissory note for the outstanding debt, to remove any suspicion that her decision had been purely financial. And, with that sudden and savage swish of Violet's pen, her association with the heartbroken doctor was over.

In turn, Dr Hughes Jones would later state, 'I was deeply in love with her. I wanted to marry her because I loved her, not because I wanted to marry an heiress.'

Between first meeting Violet in December 1906 and the breaking of their engagement in November 1908, Dr Hughes Jones had loaned Violet a total of £5,430 (now £810,000). In return he had received two scarf pins, £30 in £5 notes, and a handful of worthless IOUs.

The monetary, as well as the emotional, loss was no doubt a deep one for the doctor. There was a note of desperation in his final note to Violet: 'I have done all I can for you, my love.'

Violet outside The Plough in St Asaph. Motor-cars were still a comparative
rarity and attracted a great deal of interest.

6: Salting The City

Even before Violet received her first large injection of cash from Dr Hughes Jones in early 1907, she certainly appears to have lived in a manner far beyond that made possible solely by the initial payments made to her by Mrs Smith in Derby.

In total, she had by 1908 acquired around £400 from Mrs Smith, but by the time the Charlesworth family moved to North Wales she had certainly received no more than £250 from that source. And despite his largesse, Dr Hughes Jones had not lent Violet the majority of the £5,430 that he was to be eventually deprived of until after May 1907. How, then, did Violet and her family afford their extravagant lifestyle prior to May 1907?

It is almost certain that Violet, using the story of her fictional inheritance, must have persuaded other people to part with their life savings – and at a scale that will probably never be known. Perhaps these poor, unwitting victims were too embarrassed to ever concede publicly to being so easily deceived. Conceivably, there were married men among the number, or other rich suitors, humiliated by the easy way in which they had succumbed to Violet's obvious charms. There may also have been other wealthy widows like Mrs Smith, who later passed away penniless, feeling too ashamed and foolish to ever come forward.

Violet, possibly in the garden at Boderw

Whatever the true number of victims, or the actual amount of money acquired by Violet Charlesworth during the period 1906–1908, she managed to finance and maintain a lifestyle matching that of the wealthiest, most titled ladies in England. To Violet this must have seemed a perfectly correct and justifiable state of affairs. All around her, the cream of Edwardian society embraced an extravagant lifestyle in their London houses and country shooting estates, involving banquets, dancing, wine, cigars, and illicit affairs. Seemingly, Violet truly believed it was possible for her to match the conspicuous consumption of the wealthier classes without any financial foundation at all. Her world was, however, a house of cards – and one built on quicksand and IOUs. Meanwhile, perpetually ticking in the background, lurked the invisible stopwatch counting down the days until her 25th birthday.

During her two-year association with Dr Hughes Jones, Violet spent an inordinate amount of time away from Rhyl, no doubt searching for other potential benefactors while simultaneously indulging her tastes for the finer things in life. Clearly, she held no genuine affection for the doctor, and appears to have spent as little time with him as possible. It seems that he provided no more than a convenient solution to the complications that Violet caused herself through her rapidly accelerating overindulgences. The root of these difficulties can be traced back to January 1906, at which time Violet had initiated yet another money-making scheme – one that showed a great deal of intelligence and imagination, and would probably have yielded her enough funds to maintain her extravagant lifestyle had it not been for events across the Atlantic during 1907–08.

To fully appreciate the bold nature of Violet's plan, it is important to first paint a picture of life in Edwardian Britain and to understand the place of women in society. In 1906, with the foundation of the Women's Social and Political Union (WSPU) by Emmeline Pankhurst, the struggle for universal suffrage was formally begun. However, in an attempt to mock and denigrate the validity of the movement, a correspondent from the *Daily Mail* created the term 'suffragette' to describe the WSPU's members. The term was derived from the word 'suffragist', and the WSPU, rising to the challenge, used the term as the title of their newspaper, thereby quashing the implied criticism. Meanwhile, Violet had her own ambition for female emancipation – by conquering another strictly all-male preserve, the London Stock Exchange.

The beginning of 1906 also marked a high point at home in the certainty and validity of British imperialism. The Liberal party, led by Henry Campbell-Bannerman, swept to power in February's general election, with a large majority. King Edward VII, embracing the arts, placed British culture at the centre of a world dominated by the Empire. The Second Boer War had resulted in victory for the British army. Britain's long-held naval superiority seemed assured with the launch of the multi large-gunned battleship HMS *Dreadnought*, and the first Rolls Royce motor car to be driven in Britain turned heads on the nation's highways.

The class system in Britain seemed as permanent as ever. Although by working hard a man might hope to get on, he could never rise above his station in life. For the majority of women opportunities were even scarcer, an advantageous marriage being the only realistic escape from a life of domestic drudgery. During the Edwardian era a quarter of women in the country were employed in domestic service, attending to the needs of their 'betters'. At the same time, the working-class man knew his place. Social relationships were strictly defined, and interaction between the classes was governed by a strict set of complex and rigid rules – what we would now call manners or etiquette. Edwardian gentlemen never, for example, shook hands. Ladies never removed their gloves in public. Men would raise their hat in the presence of an equal or a superior, but not to a member of the lower classes. The lives of the rich revolved around grand social occasions and lavish dinner parties. And those who attended these gatherings were impeccably dressed gentleman – or ladies, draped in flawless diamonds – with high-society manners and polished behaviour. There was a sense of certainty and optimism in the air. The sun never set on the British Empire, everyone knew their place, and provided that the old order could be maintained everything would carry on – wouldn't it? – much as it had done under the reign of the recently departed Queen.

Violet, like a child with her nose against a sweet-shop window, yearned to join this upper-class world, but it seemed that this would never be possible in a country restricted by Edwardian social mores. The only route to this exclusive club was to do what she did best – pretend. All that she required to pull off this deception would be the necessary courage, backed by a healthy bank balance. If she could beg, borrow, or swindle enough money, Violet reasoned, not only could she become part of the Edwardian establishment, but she might also take on those pillars of male preserve – motoring, playing the stock market, controlling her own bank account, and achieving financial independent for herself.

Yet, as 1906 reached its conclusion (at the time when Violet first met Dr Hughes Jones), it became clear there had been a noticeable change in the air. A succession of fatal train crashes on the nation's rail network had knocked confidence in the reliability of British engineering and ingenuity, and a summer heatwave had stretched the population's patience. Sylvia Pankhurst led a high-profile WSPU suffragette march in London, demanding voting rights for women and disrupting the state opening of Parliament. Female anti-vivisection campaigners clashed violently with the police, and eloquent advocates for female equality such as Millicent Fawcett ensured that the atmosphere for change continued; indeed the very presence of HMS *Dreadnought* would spark a naval arms race between Britain and Germany, eventually leading – by a somewhat roundabout route, admittedly – to the Great War.

It had been during 1906, in this changing atmosphere of struggle for greater female freedoms, that Violet Charlesworth had embarked on her next money-making masterplan. It seems, however, that she was a different kind of feminist. While Violet was certainly never satisfied with the limitations of either her sex, or the working-class environment into which she had been born, her emulous personality led her to desire the lifestyle of the society ladies she read about in the newspaper gossip columns, and enviously witnessed dining at the best West End restaurants.

Yet she had no intention of achieving this rise in her social status through hard work. Violet had realised that to succeed in the male-dominated world of the London Stock Exchange (an institution which did not allow women access until 1973), she would require money, charm, bravado, and confidence – topped off with a stylish outfit, a diamond tiara, and – to add that finishing touch – the latest motor car.

Thanks to the elderly Mrs Smith and other unnamed benefactors, Violet's well-stocked deposit account ensured that she possessed more than enough capital to begin her flirtation with the stock market. Her clear intention was to secure sufficient dividends to allow her to repay those who had advanced sums to her – such as Mrs Smith – before they became suspicious. Violet hoped to achieve this all before her 25th birthday and the inevitable exposure of the story regarding her fictitious inheritance.

The London Stock Exchange

Violet appears to have entered the markets not on a whim but following a period of detailed research and investigation. Investment in the exponential growth of American Railroad and associated freight businesses was at the time an attractive proposition to many British investors, and Violet fully intended to follow suit, hoping to reap some of the rewards on offer. Indeed, in the first decade of the twentieth century, three quarters of the shares in the Illinois Central Railroad were held outside of the USA, and half of the Pennsylvania Railroad stock was owned by overseas investors, all reaping handsome returns.

The opportunity to earn seemingly infinite dividends, without graft, must have seemed like manna from heaven to the 22-year-old Violet. In 1906 the London Stock Exchange was the largest in the world, and New York the second. The Stock Exchange buildings in both cities were designed both to impress and to inspire confidence. The British and American markets operated on stable exchange rates, using the classic gold standard. However, the close links between the two exchanges meant that any securities traded in either London or New York might lead to an equal exposure to risk, as well as reward, on the other side of the pond.

In January 1906 Violet wrote a carefully worded letter of introduction to the firm of Fenton, Dale & Company, Stockbrokers, at 65 Basinghall Street, in heart of the City of London. She explained in her handwritten note that she wished to 'play the markets and speculate on a small scale'. Her knowledge of the share trading seems to have impressed Fenton, Dale & Co, who assumed her to be a much older lady, with some experience of the markets; Violet was familiar with many of the terms used on the trading floor and she seemed to possess a remarkable business acumen. She outlined the story of her vast inheritance and further explained 'I wish to speculate without the knowledge of my trustees, who would not approve of such a thing. If they found out that I had been speculating on the Stock Exchange, they might delay the granting of my fortune.'

Violet opened her trading account under the name Miss Violet Talbot, which seems to indicate that she had no difficulties in providing references and bank account details under that name (she may have also possessed another trading account, under the name of Miss Trevor).

Solicitor's and banker's references for Miss Violet Talbot were obtained, the London & Provincial Bank kindly providing her stockbrokers with a recommendation, stating 'Miss Violet Talbot's account can be relied upon up to a fair amount'. This proved to be adequate, and Violet was duly granted a trading account with Fenton, Dale & Co. She immediately made an ongoing arrangement with the company, informing them, 'I will forward any buying and selling instructions to you via letter or telegram. See that you carry out my instructions to the letter.' With that, Violet began her career as a stock market speculator.

Initially, her investments were in small amounts, usually for the purchase of American Railroad stock. Violet possessed a great deal of intelligence in financial matters, and had maintained a keen eye on the Dow Jones Index since obtaining her first advance from Mrs Smith in 1905. The price of American Rail shares had risen steadily, with the Dow Jones Industrial Average reaching a high of 103 on 6 January 1906. A modest correction in share prices followed the uncertainty caused by the San Francisco earthquake in April 1906, but this did not seem to deter Violet. Instead, she spread her investments across a wider portfolio, showing a good deal of financial acumen, and managed to achieve respectable profits.

Union Pacific Railroad shares

The stock market appeared to offer the answer to all Violet's problems. Dividends were regularly paid to her via her brokerage account. There seemed to be little or no risk. After all, even the money she had originally invested was not hers. As time went by Fenton, Dale & Co. became more and more comfortable with Violet's reliability and increased her credit limit, allowing her to trade in larger and larger unit transactions. The opportunity had arrived for her to become a player on the stock markets, enabling her to finance the lifestyle she desired without resorting to the tale of her fictitious inheritance. It all seemed too good to be true.

And, of course, it was. Little did Violet know that her bubble was about to burst.

During the summer heatwave of 1906 she instructed Mr Percival at Fenton, Dale & Co. to purchase 1,550 Union Pacific shares, in the full expectation that the market would rise rapidly, thus enabling her to extract a quick profit. This type of speculation relied on a rapid rise in the market – a bull market – resulting in an instant return. At that time Violet needed funds quickly and could ill afford to see her investment tied up for a long period.

Although American Railroad stocks were generally seen as a sound purchase, the price having risen by approximately 150 per cent since 1890, the scale of Violet's investment surprised even her brokers. Nevertheless Fenton, Dale & Co. proved to be as easily persuaded by her as both Dr Hughes Jones and Mrs Smith. In fact, Mr Percival would later say, 'she had the scarce gift of inspiring confidence'. In 1906 Violet's purchase of 1,550 Union Pacific shares at $29.30 each amounted to $45,415 or approximately £10,000 (now £1.5 million).

Violet confidently expected to earn a huge dividend within a matter of weeks. The Union Pacific share price had increased by 30 per cent between 1904 and 1905 and even in the more difficult market between 1905 and 1906 it had still risen by 7 per cent. In the anticipation of a return of 10 per cent, Violet hoped to achieve a dividend of £1,000 (now £150,000) by the end of the year, more than enough to help finance further trading speculations and keep her creditors at bay – temporarily, at least. Buoyed by optimism from her new money-making venture, Violet hired her first motor car and began to take a keen interest in motoring. She often took long runs, sometimes with a friend, sometimes alone.

However, the events of late 1906 and 1907 were about to shake the leaves from Violet's seemingly evergreen money-making tree.

It was in January 1906 that she had purchased that sizeable wedge of Union Pacific shares. Her timing could not have been worse. It turned out to be the company's high point. The April 1906 earthquake that then devastated San Francisco contributed to a general instability in the New York stock market, and prompted a flood of money from the USA's east coast to the west, to aid reconstruction. Further stresses occurred in late 1906, when the Bank of England raised its interest rates (partly in response to UK insurance companies paying out huge amounts to US policyholders). This created a more attractive market for investors in London. By July 1906 US stock values had declined 18 per cent from their January peak. From September 1906 to January 1907 the stock market slid a further 7.7 per cent, then a further 9.8 per cent by the end of March 1907. Within that month alone, the period known as the 'rich man's panic', Union Pacific shares seemed to the worst affected, falling a whopping 50 points. Violet was, in stock market parlance, wiped out.

Almost all of Violet's investment had been made utilising credit from Fenton, Dale & Co., who now expected immediate repayment. But the stock market was in jitters, and she had no prospect of raising enough funds to repay her debt. Steady declines in share values continued during the summer of 1907, until the hope that the fall might be a short-lived one had completely evaporated.

At this stage Violet had yet to receive her proposal of marriage from Dr Hughes Jones, and had not yet been the recipient of his misplaced generosity. Instead, in order to repay her huge debt to Fenton, Dale & Co. she decided to enter the bear market by beginning a strategy of short selling. This was a simple concept in theory, but relied on deep pockets and nerves of steel. She would commission Fenton, Dale & Co. to borrow, and immediately sell, a block of shares on her behalf, in the anticipation that their value would drop. Once they had done so she would buy them back at their new lower price and pocket the – hopefully substantial – difference between the two transactions. However, in practical terms it was an advanced strategy usually only undertaken by experienced traders. Short selling was (and still is) considered far riskier than 'going long' on a stock, as without a stop-loss strategy in place there was no limit to the amount the investor could lose. With a huge slice of luck an individual might make a substantial sum of money very quickly. Without it, an even larger amount could be lost.

Nevertheless, to Violet it must have seemed, in this fraught and falling market, to be the only money-making option available. First, however, she would need to persuade Fenton, Dale & Co. to increase her level of indebtedness to an even larger degree. Astonishingly, considering the already huge amount of paper debt owed by her to the firm, Mr Percival seemed happy to entertain Violet's proposal to extend her credit even further. First, though, he insisted on meeting her in person to discuss her proposition. Presumably wishing to conceal her address, Violet invited him to meet her not at Boderw, her impressive eight-bedroom property in North Wales, but at the fictitious address of her trustees, the tiny two-up, two-down cottage in Olivier Street, Derby, belonging to Mr Baker. Again, despite Baker's involvement, he does not seem to have ever been brought to account for his part in Violet's deception.

Upon Mr Percival's arrival at the modest house in Olivier Street, he was astonished to discover a far younger woman than he had expected. Violet's level of understanding of the markets thus far, coupled with her perceived business acumen, had given the broker an impression of a middle-aged and wealthy woman rather than the attractive young lady he would later describe as: 'A simple, reserved little lady of 23, who wore quiet village-made frocks and lowered her eyes demurely when she talked about the price of Unions or suggested a large loan.'

Violet, despite her outward modesty, was ruthlessly determined to borrow yet more money from her stockbrokers by impressing them with her supposed creditworthiness and social status: 'Mr Percival, I find myself short at the moment, but it ought not to be difficult for me to raise money, seeing what fine estates, jewels, and motor-cars I have. My furs are worth hundreds of pounds, my trustees are buying me an estate in both Scotland and England, and I have much jewellery. My fortune, with accumulated interest, will amount to half a million. You could lend me the money on the security of my jewellery alone.'

It seems the stakes were so high for Violet that she chose that moment to increase the value of her pretend trust fund to £500,000 (now £75 million).

As a form of collateral she offered her opulent jewellery collection, which included a fabulous diamond tiara purchased in Bond Street for £700 (now £100,000).

Fenton, Dale & Co. offered her a derisory £400 on the strength of it, on condition that they retain the jewellery in their London office as a form of security.

In response, Violet, using all her charm, smiled seductively at Mr Percival, said, 'Come, Mr Percival, whatever use is it to you? You don't really want it. I will keep it for myself.'

And, sure enough, like putty in her hands, the stockbroker, allowing her to keep the jewels, promptly handed over £400 in banknotes to Violet by way of a short-term loan. She even reached an agreement with the company which allowed her to borrow further funds by presenting them with a series of post-dated cheques.

On Violet's request Fenton, Dale & Co. also agreed not to cash these cheques until 15 January 1909, at which point they clearly firmly believed her inheritance would be paid.

'That I might have a run of investing in stocks and shares,' Violet explained to Mr Percival, 'without being called on, for any case, in the event of losses. If I am lucky enough to win on any deal I would then receive a supply of ready cash, and repay you most handsomely.'

Using her new bear market trading account, Violet sold 375 Pacific Union shares, which on being repurchased made her a rapid and not inconsiderable profit of £400 (now £60,000). She hoped to withdraw this dividend in cash, but Fenton, Dale & Co. were understandably unwilling to accede to this request. Violet then offered to secure the withdrawal of these funds by offering a guarantee of repayment, which she claimed was 'backed up by a responsible gentleman in the medical profession of splendid position'.

Using this method Violet managed to secure further cash advances from Fenton, Dale & Co. (and two further London stockbrokers) of £225 in October 1907, £500 in November 1907, and a whopping additional £2,500 (now £380,000) from Fenton, Dale & Co. during early 1908. For all of these payments she wrote promissory notes: 'As security against my last outstanding balance, and for further small investments, interest, brokerages fees, and for services in getting the bills discounted.'

She further explained, 'My quarterly allowance, furniture, diamonds, motor-cars, furs and trustees are excellent security, even if I fail to take up these bills, there is my inheritance due on my twenty-fifth birthday ... please excuse me for not giving the name of my trustees, on the grounds that that they would be angry and might seriously injure me.'

To put these huge amounts into context today, it must be remembered that in 1907 £400 was a vast sum of money, more than five times the average yearly salary at that time. Indeed, a recent vote at Westminster had increased MPs' salaries to £400 per annum, a move that had outraged the general population who believed it would result 'in a chamber filled with

self-serving fat-cats and an end to integrity among Members of Parliament!'
Not that such trivialities concerned Violet, of course. Yet again, she had
acquired ample funding to allow her to keep even the most persistent
creditors at bay while still allowing her lavish lifestyle to continue.

In her efforts to impress Fenton, Dale & Co. Violet had mentioned the
purchase of two large country estates in England and Scotland. She had
clearly realised that if she expected to mix with the wealthy Edwardian
upper classes, she would need to acquire a country pile with which to
impress them.

And so in May 1907 Violet accepted Dr Hughes Jones' proposal of
marriage. He was blissfully unaware of her colossal stock market losses
and, still thinking that she was less than two years away from a huge
inheritance, continued to lend her large sums of money. Some she used to
feed small crumbs back into her brokerage account, thus allowing her to
continue cashing cheques from it. The rest she intended to spend on a new
country residence to match her imagined social status. Occasionally, as if in
delicious anticipation of this significant step up the social ladder, she would
call herself Lady Violet Charlesworth.

Had she been able to maintain this precarious balance of robbing
Peter to pay Paul, she might have been able to delay her (now, seemingly
inevitable) demise for a great deal longer. Unfortunately for Violet, her pig-
headed insistence in continuing to gamble on the stock market during such
a volatile period would result in even heavier losses, due primarily to the
Knickerbocker Crisis in late 1907.

During October of that year the stock market collapse worsened
considerably, effectively ending Violet's chance of ever repaying the
increasing sums she now owed to both Dr Hughes Jones and Fenton, Dale
& Co. As a result of a failed bid by various investors in New York to corner
the market on stock belonging to the United Copper Company (in which
Violet had also invested), panic ensued. This created a huge run on banks
and financial institutions as thousands of customers desperately attempted
to withdraw their funds in cash, ultimately resulting in the collapse of the
Knickerbocker Trust Company, the third-largest banking corporation in the
US at that time. A seismic financial shock reverberated around the globe,
wiping out any gains Violet had made and simultaneously plunging her into
even further debt.

The complete collapse of Violet's investment portfolio, coupled with her
ever-increasing and ever more decadent expenditure, should have been
the red flag she needed. Surely the end of her adventure had been reached.
Nevertheless, it seems that she had other ideas. Her insatiable desire for
the finer things in life was still to be completely fulfilled, and for Violet there
was to be no turning back.

7: Dressing The Part

In truth, the small, provincial community of St Asaph was never likely to satisfy the ambitions of a would-be socialite like Violet for long. She wished to throw lavish parties, and be extravagantly entertained in return. She yearned for elegant restaurants, glittering balls, expensive motor cars, and nights in luxurious hotels.

She bought an expensive ticket for the Goldsborough Hall Ball at Knaresborough in Yorkshire. It seemed that her social climbing was at last making waves, as she spent the evening in the company of Britain's élite, including Lady Gunter, Lady Garnock, and Lady Mountgarret. Violet, in a gown of white *crêpe de chine* topped with a white satin robe and silver draperies, turned heads. There could be no stepping back for her now.

In November 1907 she visited Bailey's Garage in Lichfield Road, Stafford, and purchased a second-hand 15-horsepower Humber motor car. However, during a return trip to London it broke down. Violet, taking it back to Bailey's, not only persuaded the garage to exchange the car for a brand-new one, she also left' with a cheque for £60 in compensation (to 'cover the difference', as Violet explained). Her persuasive powers must have been considerable – she had yet to pay for the first car! As a result, her total outstanding account with Bailey's Garage stood at £360 (now £50,000). A few weeks later she returned to the garage, accompanied by her solicitor, and settled a small portion of her outstanding bill in cash. She then persuaded the owner, Mr Bailey, to open a second credit account for her. This, she explained, was to be used for petrol, repairs, and sundries, as she did not wish to carry money with her when out motoring.

Bailey's Garage, Stafford

After she had impressed Bailey with the story of her inheritance, her next task was easily achieved. Violet ordered a brand-new Daimler, for which she persuaded Mr Bailey to pay the £127 deposit on her behalf by offering to repay him, with interest, as soon as she received the allowance from her trustees. (That deposit, paid by Bailey to the Daimler Motor Company, was of course never recovered.)

Soon after ordering the Daimler, Violet persuaded Mr Bailey to allow her to borrow a Minerva motor car as a stop-gap while she waited for her new Daimler to arrive. However, Violet then found the 25hp Minerva underpowered and not large enough for her beloved dogs. Instead, she visited the main Daimler showroom in London and wrote a cheque for £1,200 (now £180,000) for a larger 35hp Daimler straight four (an identical model to that recently ordered by King Edward VII). Whilst writing the cheque she casually enquired if 'Daimler would be kind enough to recommend a good chauffeur to me. It is so hard to find one these days'.

Albert Watts (driving), photographed by Violet

The company duly did so: Albert Watts, a handsome, dark-haired man of about Violet's age, who happened to be a Daimler employee. Watts first accompanied Violet on test drives and then as part of her arrangement with the Daimler Motor Company, who clearly considered her an extremely valuable customer. She felt instantly at ease in Watts' presence and offered him a job as her own private chauffeur. It appears that he accepted. In contravention of the social etiquette of the era, he would spend many hours in her company and his duties seem to have extended far beyond those of a chauffeur. He would be employed as a permanent member of Violet's household staff until the fateful night of the car crash in January 1909.

After dark, Violet would often take one of her motor cars and drive at breakneck speed along the quiet and winding country lanes, disappearing for hours at a time, exhilarated by the thrill. Sometimes, on a whim, she would check into a quiet country hotel or stop at a seaside restaurant. Sometimes her sister Lillian or her friend Margaret would accompany her, and the pair would travel to London for lavish shopping weekends. Violet spent extravagantly in upmarket West End shops such as Peter Robinson's in Oxford Street. She would select a number of valuable articles without ever asking the price, and often pay the bill using a £100 note (now £15,000).

Not content with merely shopping, Violet would indulge her weakness for Danish pastries and Bath buns in cafés and patisseries, then conclude her weekend breaks with a visit to the music halls and restaurants of the capital.

Inns of Court Hotel 267 High Holborn

Afterwards, she would take rooms at the Curzon Hotel in Mayfair at £2 per night, or at the Inns of Court Hotel in Holborn, where she took a liking to the hotel's boots,[3] George Campbell. Eventually, after a few days at the hotel, she offered the young man a position on her staff at Boderw as footman and handyman. George accepted and promptly left his employment at the hotel to go to North Wales with Violet. Although he would of course have been fed and housed, he does not appear to have ever received his agreed salary from the Charlesworths.

As the ease with which she seemed able to obtain silk dresses, tiaras, and expensive furs increased, so did her ambition. She welcomed male company, flattering them, perhaps even seducing them, and never failing to mention the story of the vast inheritance she was soon to receive. Men fell over themselves to win her attentions, some rather foolishly, and others undoubtedly without the knowledge of their wives. It seemed that Violet had almost everything she desired. All she needed to complement her extensive wardrobe, motor cars, pedigree dogs, and jewellery, was a palatial country estate.

In early 1908 the country keenly awaited news from Ernest Shackleton's voyage to Antarctica aboard the *Nimrod*, and wondered if Prime Minister Henry Campbell-Bannerman would step down following a series of heart attacks. Violet, however, had no time for these pedestrian concerns. She was enthusiastically occupied in motoring along the leafy country lanes of England in search of a new country residence. Not only did she desire somewhere suitable to reflect her rapidly rising social status, but she also wished for a substantial garden, somewhere to construct large breeding

---

3   The 'boots' boy, whose position was the lowest among the male staff members of a hotel or household, was employed to perform such menial tasks as collecting and polishing the shoes left in the corridors outside guests' bedrooms. Interestingly, this rather mundane task formed an important plot point in the Arthur Conan Doyle novel, *The Hound of the Baskervilles*, first published in 1902.

kennels, for the twelve pedigree dogs now in her possession, including five St Bernards – four of them named Bruce, Second to None, Imp, and Rose – and Wolverton Lady, her collie.

The Hall Calne (picture taken prior to demolition in 1983)

Violet also yearned for a home that more conveniently enabled her to visit the shops, theatres, banks, and stockbrokers of London. Instead of seeming to be troubled by her heavy losses in the 1907 stock market collapse, Violet instead agreed to take a £189 per annum lease on an elaborate Italianate mansion known as Woodlands in the quiet Wiltshire market town of Calne. The property may have been suggested to her by her brother Frederick, who had been working nearby, in Bath. Now, in addition to Boderw in St Asaph, her staff, her extravagant shopping habit, motor cars, travel, hotels, stock market trading, and pedigree dogs, Violet had a second property to maintain. Her annual living costs in 1908 were estimated to be well in excess of £4,000 (now £600,000), and may even have been as high as £9,000 (now £1.4 million).

Woodlands House and grounds had been constructed in around 1869 by Charles Harris, a local business tycoon and owner of the largest bacon curers in the country at the time. However, following his death in 1872, followed by that of his widow, the house was let to tenants. In 1908 Violet signed a five-year lease at the annual rent of £189 (now £30,000). Once again, she provided a letter of introduction from her fictitious trustees, a solicitor's letter, and a reference from her London bankers. Violet assured the Harris family that the rent payment would present her with little difficulty, as she was due to inherit £250,000 on her 25th birthday (at that point less than one year away).

She immediately ordered that the house be renamed The Hall, which she felt better

Violet commissioned an oil painting of herself with one of her beloved St Bernards

reflected her imagined status. She commenced an ambitious programme of redecoration at a cost of more than £400 (now £60,000), including repainting, refurbishing, and wallpapering all the main reception rooms, enhancing the ornamentation of the entrance gates in gold leaf, relacquering all the brass fittings, and landscaping the substantial gardens. She opened accounts with local tradesmen and shopkeepers, ordering furniture and furnishings from them, as well as employing three gardeners and a housekeeper, plus a carpenter to construct elaborate kennels in the garden. The ornate pillars and grand proportions of the building rather lent themselves to the impression of wealth and title that she wished to portray. It seems that she succeeded admirably, as she had little trouble in obtaining credit and deflecting creditors. Her fable of an inheritance due imminently seemed to provide the necessary degree of comfort required for her to persuade tradesmen – and even her landlords – to wait for lengthy periods of time for payment.

But Violet found that she could not bear the noise and upheaval caused by the building work, so never spent more than an hour or two at The Hall, preferring to reside at the nearby Lansdowne Hotel or drive overnight to London. During the summer of 1908 she also frequently visited the London lodgings of her chauffeur, Albert Watts, in Chiswick. The liaisons were reputedly for afternoon tea; however the arrangement seems a highly unusual one. Generally, if Albert's landlady was at home Violet would remain in the Daimler outside, and Albert would carry out a laden tray so that she might partake of afternoon tea from the comfort of her car. This scene was a source of great amusement to the children playing in the street, who began to recognise Violet's distinctive appearance with her veiled face, crimson motor cloak, and expensive motor car. Despite her seemingly louche lifestyle, Violet was occasionally invited indoors, and she appears to have made a favourable impression on Albert's landlady, who thought her to be a lady due 'to the gentle way she greeted me'.

Violet also took a liking to the landlady's daughter, and promptly asked to come into service at The Hall in Calne as a maid. The girl was flattered *by* the offer and Violet promised to write confirming the details. However, a few days later Violet wrote to her explaining that she was 'sorry that I cannot engage you yet, but when the estate is handed over by the trustees I will send for you'.

Rumours did circulate that Violet and Albert were lovers, or even married. There was certainly a closeness between the pair which may explain Albert's strange behaviour on the night of the motor-car accident a few months later, in January. In fact, following that crash, a Daimler employee and friend of Albert, interviewed by the *Morning Leader* newspaper, declared:

> Watts was always a very respectable and intelligent man and, as far as we know, there was nothing whatever against his character. We put him in charge of the cars bought by Miss Charlesworth, and together they used to drive on touring expeditions to many parts of the country. Whenever Watts came back to the garage he used to speak in enthusiastic terms of the lady, and seemed quite "gone" on her, as the saying is.
>
> When Watts became her own personal chauffeur, he told us that he never wished for a better mistress, and he hoped he might keep the job. Miss Charlesworth herself was extraordinarily keen on motoring and would drive about at all hours of the day and night. She came in here many times and behaved in a quiet, ladylike way.
>
> The other chauffeurs who knew Watts used to chaff him about his young mistress, and it was evident that the lady was very sweet on him.

To further accentuate her social status, Violet also ordered expensive monogrammed headed notepaper, envelopes and cards for The Hall. These all incorporated an expensive die-cut family crest, matching those she had already purchased for Boderw. She had designed the crest, which she seems to have 'borrowed' from the wealthy family of a Yorkshire mine owner named Joseph Charlesworth (no relation). Perhaps she hoped that anyone with a heraldic interest might assume she was a descendant of this well-established family. The family crest was adorned with the strangely apt motto *Mors potius Macula* – 'Death before Disgrace'. When personally supervising the intricate die-cut of the cockerel's head atop a ducal coronet at a local printing factory in Calne, Violet had explained 'It is the family crest of my Scottish ancestors.'

She also donated a trophy to the yearly Calne Show, and offered to present it on an annual basis. Not surprising, the newly named Gordon-Charlesworth Challenge Cup was awarded to the pedigree dog class. Violet graciously debarred her own dogs from entering for that cup, although she did exhibit her new St Bernard puppy, Gordon, in one category at the event, winning first prize. She claimed to have paid a breeding fee of over £1,000 (now £150,000) for the puppy, and clearly relished mentioning this in conversation to her wide-eyed audience, explaining that she wished to recuperate some of her outgoings via her own breeding programme. To help publicise her success, Violet designed, financed, and produced a circular featuring a picture of the Gordon-Charlesworth Challenge Cup; 300 copies were printed at a cost of £30 (now £4,000) and circulated in the district. She also commissioned an artist to paint portraits of her beloved St Bernards, and entered several other horticultural and country shows in Calne and the surrounding villages. She clearly enjoyed her role as the mysterious and apparently wealthy new tenant at The Hall.

Stories of her huge financial legacy and enormous wealth were whispered jealously among the ladies of the town, but rather than be irritated by this, Violet clearly relished being mistakenly referred to as 'the Honourable Violet' or even 'Lady Violet'. Dressed in cream and white silks and expensive furs, wearing her Bond Street jewellery and Paris *haute couture* hats, Violet was every inch the society heiress and lady. But pride, as they say, comes before a fall.

Meanwhile, Violet's dangerous obsession with motor cars continued unabated. She studiously recorded all her journeys in her black suede motoring diary, which she carried with her at all times. The notebook contained a detailed account of her trips across England, to North Wales, Scotland, and back to London; in 1908 alone she drove an astonishing 60,000 miles. Many of her trips were undertaken at night, solo, with just one of her beloved St Bernards for company. Considering the lower speed limits in force at the time, the high cost of petrol, tyres, and spare parts, and the lack of decent road surfaces, her mileage is quite simply staggering. An average of 164 miles per day means that Violet spent on average at least four to five hours every day behind the wheel.

An approximation of her annual petrol bill goes some way in helping to understand just how profligate Violet was. With petrol costing around one shilling a gallon, and her Daimler or Minerva probably returning approximately 18 miles per gallon at most, her annual fuel cost was conceivably in the region of £160 (now £26,000) – although, knowing Violet as we now do, we can safely assume that the majority of this huge total was obtained on account. Credit which she almost certainly never repaid.

Miss Violet Charlesworth
as a motorist

During one of her visits to Chiswick with Albert, she stopped at another motor-car showroom, in Shaftesbury Avenue, and attempted to negotiate the purchase of yet another motor car. Violet's eyes had been drawn to a large second-hand vehicle that had previously belonged to a millionaire. This seemed to please her, as she promptly strolled past the potted aspidistras and the moustached salesmen at their wooden desks, to address the showroom manager directly, 'My name is Miss Violet Gordon Charlesworth. I live at St. Asaph and I need that motor-car for taking parties to balls during the winter.'

Violet insisted that her family crest, together with the initials V.G.C., be hand-painted in gold leaf on the side of the vehicle. When asked to pay for the motor car, she replied, 'I have a quarterly allowance of £1,500, and I have already exceeded it, so I cannot get any more now. But in January next year I shall be coming into a fortune of a quarter of a million, on January 13th.'

Despite her assurances, the manager had some reservations and was not happy to offer credit without a banker's reference. This was duly taken, but was not deemed satisfactory. As a result, Violet was told she would be required to pay the full balance on collection. Unsurprisingly, despite repeated communications from the garage during the next few weeks she never returned to collect the motor car. On this occasion, Violet's well-rehearsed yarn proved to be her downfall. It so happened that the showroom manager was well acquainted with the St Asaph district and later told newspaper reporters that:

> What puzzled me was as to where the "wealthy" people giving the round of balls and entertainment could live in St Asaph? There was another curious thing – Miss Charlesworth's readiness to pay the advertised price without troubling to ascertain whether the car was really worth it. She simply took a fancy to it because it was a flashy car.
>
> She was always very quietly dressed, and her voice was unusually soft. She had not a good complexion, but her eyes were very fine. It was easy to see that she was not well educated, the grammar in her letters was faulty, and she had a way of repeating herself, which is what a highly educated woman does not do. She was not particularly dainty in her appearance. Her hands were rough – probably from attending to motor cars herself. While she gave good references, I formed the opinion that she was posing as a person of a higher rank than that to which she really belonged. In fact, she had a "large" way of talking that I thought she must be weak mentally.

Violet even wrote to the garage and demanded that her deposit be returned! The garage wrote back, refusing, and explaining that they had already gone to a great deal of expense, preparing the vehicle for collection. On this one – extremely rare – occasion, Violet had failed to seduce someone with her virtuoso performance.

However, it does seem that almost everyone else was deceived by Violet. Nevertheless, perhaps on this occasion the increasing strain of her lifestyle was beginning to affect her judgement and her ability to convince others so easily. This failure was no doubt on her mind as she drove back to North Wales. Once again, she was driving far too quickly as she sped through Abergele towards Colwyn Bay. As she rounded a corner in the road, close to the local school, she was unable to stop in time as she encountered two carts heading towards her from the opposite direction. She veered violently to the right to avoid an impact – but skidded and careered into a large coal cart on the side of the road. The collision was so violent that the cart was smashed into pieces, sending cascades of coal across the road like a black landslide. The momentum then caused Violet's car to swerve uncontrollably into a stone wall near the fire station. The bonnet of the motor car was completely destroyed, but remarkably Violet escaped – shaken, but without a scratch on her. Perhaps it was an omen of things to come. One thing was for certain; this incident would necessitate yet another trip to the motor-car showrooms of London.

Undaunted by her previous failure to obtain credit, and clearly unfazed by her accident, Violet returned to London two days later, to visit the Minerva Motor Co. in North Crescent, Bloomsbury. She entered the grand building, passing under the statue of the goddess Minerva, and insisted on dealing only with Mr William Chard Hamilton, the managing director. With him she reached an agreement to hire a luxurious Minerva Tourer for a monthly fee and after making a down payment on the car she drove it to a vehicle upholsterers to have sumptuous carpeting fitted. Next, she visited a custom coachbuilders to have a landaulette roof section added.[4]

Minerva House

Violet wrote further cheques to both companies, which she faithfully promised to honour at a later date. Her collection of cars might now be called a fleet, as the number

---

4   In 1908, cars were not manufactured on the production line system, with the option of factory-fitted extras available, as they are today. Car owners, then known as 'enthusiasts', customised their vehicles at their own expense.

soon increased to four, then six. Although part of her automobile collection was leased, Violet was more than happy to give any admirers the impression that she owned all the vehicles outright.

Was Violet a cynical manipulator, callously playing on the generous nature of her victims, or a Walter Mitty-esque character – a listless, romantic daydreamer who seemed to float from one fantasy to the another, never really understanding the true consequences of her actions? It is certain that every new purchase and acquisition in Violet's life became progressively more ostentatious and increasingly unnecessary, yet, like a rabbit trapped in the headlights, she does not appear capable of changing direction. Each new pleasure was financed by even more borrowing. Every new adventure seemed to risk collapsing her financial house of cards. Yet at each turn Violet's new pleasure appears to have satisfied her for an ever shorter period of time. Like any addict, she appeared hellbent on continuing her self-destructive search for the next high.

8: The Extras

As spring turned to summer in 1908 the winds of change blew across Britain. Herbert Henry Asquith had become Liberal prime minister, the suffragette movement was planning its first large-scale rally in London, and the Franco-British Exhibition (which Violet visited with her sister Lillian) opened in London to celebrate the Entente Cordiale between Britain and France. Meanwhile the euphemistically entitled Irish Question – the debate over Home Rule in Ireland – continued to fracture the nation.

With the arrival of better weather Violet was able to increase the frequency of her visits to Scotland. The days were lighter and the road surfaces less rutted, making her gruelling motor-car journeys much easier. She claimed ecstatically that she had uncovered some proof of her Gordon Clan Scottish ancestry and was anxious to learn more. Perhaps she sincerely believed there was some truth behind the tale she had woven so elaborately for the past five years – or, more probably, she desperately needed to put some distance between herself and the growing number of creditors in England pressing her for repayment.

In any case, Scotland must have seemed like a haven from her troubles. She headed immediately for the west coast, and boarded the MacBrayne steamer *Clansman* from Oban across the Firth of Lorn to the Isle of Mull. Throughout her Scottish excursion she took great pleasure in the jealous glances that her fashionable London wardrobe attracted from the more traditionally dressed ladies of the Highlands and Islands. Violet's pillar-box red dress, her crimson motor cloak, furs, hats, and expensive diamond jewellery turned heads along the Esplanade in Oban, then in Main Street, Tobermory. But Violet, whilst no doubt enjoying the attention she received, would later learn to regret her eye-catching sense of fashion. Mull would remember her.

Tobermory c1908

Once back on the Scottish mainland, Violet relished the empty roads of the Highlands on which she could indulge her love of motoring. Those to whom she owed ever-increasing sums of money would now have a great deal of difficulty in locating her. Here in Scotland, Violet must have thought to herself, she would be free to invent an even more ostentatious persona with which to impress her next target.

Violet had clearly enjoyed the attention she had received on her previous visits to Edinburgh and must have yearned to be part of the social set in Scotland, envisaging grouse shoots, balls, and lochside picnics in the Highlands, just as Queen Victoria had done.

Violet travelled the Highlands extensively in her motor car and eventually engaging the services of R. Noble, the leading Inverness house agent, stated her desire to lease a Scottish shooting estate for the summer season: 'One that will be ideal for parties, shoots, and entertaining,' she added.

Violet did not have long to wait. Her agent recommended a suitable property, Flowerburn House – complete with excellent shooting rights – situated in a beautiful location near Fortrose, in the Black Isle, just north-east of Inverness. Violet immediately fell in love with the grand house. She could imagine the shooting set gathering on the driveway, her fleet of motor cars lined up outside to impress would-be suitors, against a backdrop of dolphins and seals playing in the Moray Firth, all under the wide-open crystalline skies of Scotland's north-east. To Violet's delight, the house was available for immediate lease. The handsomely proportioned granite-built villa, with its ornate Victorian glass conservatory entrance, was ideal for her pretensions, and at the beginning of June 1908 she signed a seven-year lease at a rent of £250 (now £40,000) per annum. She took immediate possession of the property.

But despite a promise made to the owners, the Sutherland family, Violet failed to provide the first rental payment for the property when it became due. Unusually for Violet, she was unable to convince the astute owners to wait any longer for this first instalment and was forced to part with £250 when a writ threatening court action was presented to her. This large sum must have placed an unbearable strain on Violet's already fragile finances. Perhaps, like Cinderella, she knew that at the stroke of midnight on her 25th birthday her enchanted surroundings would evaporate. However, her desire for the trappings of the Edwardian upper-class set appears to have blinded her to the precipice she was heading inexorably towards. She seemed determined to enjoy herself while she could. Violet was well-read and intelligent, despite her lack of schooling as a child, and it is certain that she was fully aware that following the passing the Debtors Act in 1869, a person could no longer be sent to a debtors' prison simply for owing money. And although she would have no doubt been aware that fraud was a far more serious matter, her extravagant expenditure continued, despite the continuing threats of legal action.

Violet in Welsh national dress

Nothing For Something

Ironically, it was a charitable act on Violet's behalf that first sowed a seed of doubt among the shopkeepers of St Asaph, who until that point had been more than happy to extend generous lines of credit to her. In May 1908 she had written a cheque in support of a fundraising campaign towards the construction of a new chapel building, which she hoped would be named after her.

In an embarrassing moment for Violet, the cheque bounced.

On 23 June 1908 the Daimler Motor Company in London wrote to Violet, stating their intention to take further action against her. Violet responded with this extraordinary letter,

> Dear Sir,
>
> Upon my return to home in Scotland to-day I was deeply sorry to find a letter awaiting me from your solicitors pressing payment of your account. Please don't for a single second think that there was any desire on my part that I did not send you the account. I have never done such a thing, and never would. It is only that have been lately pressed as I have never been in life before, and through illness, and of all the expenses it has entailed.
>
> Please, please don't take proceedings. I could never, in my position, hold up my head again if such a fearful thing happened. I have never owed a penny before to anyone; you are the only one. Please instruct your solicitors to hold the matter over until 7th July – only a fortnight hence. I enclose you a post-dated cheque for July 7th for £107 5s. Please accept £5 more, then, as interest, and for the trouble I have given you in this matter. The cheque will without fail be honoured by my Rhyl bank on that date, after receiving my quarterly allowance.
>
> Please wire me at the Westminster Hotel, at Chester, before tomorrow afternoon saying that you will postpone until 7th July. Do, please, do. I have never had cause for this trouble before. Don't take any proceedings, please don't. It would break my heart – the disgrace! Oh, do wait! Please wire to me; I enclose a 6d. stamp.
>
> Do not fail me. Wait until the 7th. I know you can withdraw the letter from your solicitors until then. Please do. Please accept cheque until the 7th. Please, for pity's sake, don't fail me.
>
> Yours, faithfully, and thanking you very much in anticipation,
> (Miss) V. Gordon Charlesworth

Despite her financial woes Violet continued, outwardly at least, her hedonistic lifestyle. She attended her first Inverness ball in June, the Military Ball hosted by Sir Hector Munro, at which she referred to herself as Lady Violet. Once again, she spun the story of the young heiress on the verge of inheriting an immense fortune. She was now just six months from her 25th birthday.

Violet frequently left Flowerburn at midnight to take long motor runs along the deserted roads of the Highlands. Her trips often lasted several hours, during which time she would regularly travel as far as Perth, more than 100 miles away, not returning until the early hours of the morning. She was a daring driver who frequently took risks on the narrow and twisting roads. It may be that the worry of her encircling creditors was slowly proving too much for Violet; or perhaps the plan for the car crash and a very public death was already forming in her troubled mind? One way or another, Violet's day of reckoning was fast approaching.

Flowerburn House

In order to credibly present herself to any would-be visitors as a titled lady with a Scottish shooting estate, Violet first needed to play the role convincingly. She urgently needed a new and generous benefactor, because her London stockbrokers were now threatening legal action over her unpaid trading account, and Dr Hughes Jones in Rhyl was quickly losing patience with her constant pleas for money and her procrastination over their wedding plans – the doctor had eventually been assured by Violet that they would marry in January 1909, after she had postponed the date of their nuptials on several occasions.

First, Violet went to a traditional Highland outfitter in Dingwall and purchased a set of bagpipes and an outfit in the dark green, navy blue, black, and yellow Gordon tartan. She

Flowerburn House

Violet at Flowerburn House

left a small deposit and promised to pay the balance of £60 immediately upon receipt of her inheritance. She then commissioned a photographer to take her portrait, posing in her Highland dress. Violet claimed to her inquisitive friends that she had posed for the portrait in the grounds of her new Highland estate (or 'shooting box', as she casually referred to it). However, the photograph is clearly a studio-based one.

Violet wished to furnish the house not only for shooting weekends but as a homage to her imagined links with the Gordon clan. Having purchased lengths of Gordon tartan fabric, she made enquires for a suitable interior furnisher. She was given a copy of *The Highland Association Bazaar Handbook* by her house agent, in which the following recommendation was given:

The selection of Furniture in Messrs A. Fraser & Company's warehouse is sufficiently fashionable to please the most exacting aestheticism of this epicurean age, including Queen Anne, Chippendale, Hepplewhite, Sheraton, Adams, Italian, Renaissance, Karly English, etc. Gems of the Mercantile Age. The Visitor to Inverness at this season will not regret an hour spent in the big Warehouse in Union Street, where several of the departments, with their stock of quaint and beautiful articles of all periods from four hundred years ago to the present day, have the aspect of a museum – A. FRASER & CO., Showrooms: UNION STREET INVERNESS (near the Railway Station).

She visited Fraser & Co. at their Union Street showrooms in the second week of July, and obtained £800 worth of antique furniture, curtains, and upholstery velvets, entirely on credit, even though the company had never met her before. Frasers also specialised in the furnishing of shooting lodges for the summer market. Violet, it appeared, would leave no stone unturned in her desire to craft the perfect Scottish country weekend experience for her guests. Fraser & Co were persuaded by Violet that her imminently due inheritance would be able to cover her entire bill of sale in just a matter of weeks. She was also able to convince the firm that immediate delivery of the goods to Flowerburn House was essential (despite her account being unpaid), due to the impending arrival of several important and wealthy guests. The company duly delivered her furniture and were given a small deposit cheque by Violet. The balance, amounting to the equivalent of more than £120,000 today, was never paid.

Violet left a team of decorators at Flowerburn to complete the transformation of the property into that of a perfect Highland retreat. They were instructed to decorate many of the rooms entirely in Gordon tartan. She then journeyed to London on another shopping excursion, this time for rugs, porcelain, silver, and other accessories. On Saturday 25 July 1908, the final day of the London Olympics at the White City Stadium, Violet checked into a suite at the Inns of Court Hotel, at 267 High Holborn in the City, for an extravagant shopping weekend. After visiting Gamages Department Store (at that time a leading London supplier of furniture and high-class décor), Violet arranged an appointment with Mr Henry Denniss and Mr Harold Hampton, two representatives of the company, asking them to bring samples to her hotel. The two salesmen carefully laid out samples on the floor of Violet's suite. She agreed to purchase several pieces of furniture that she thought suitable for her Highland estate, along with some glassware, porcelain, silver, and a collection of handmade tiger, polar bear, and leopard skin rugs. The total bill amounted to £243 (now £37,000)., including carriage. Violet promised Mr Denniss a cheque for £100 upon delivery of the goods to Flowerburn

Violet outside Flowerburn House

Fraser & Co.

House, and promised to pay the balance 'at the end of September, when I expect to receive a large sum. I am having a shooting party on the 12th August at Flowerburn, and the goods must be delivered there before that date.'

The salesmen immediately realised the importance of the Glorious 12th to a lady of Violet's obvious wealth and social standing. Mr Dennis was further impressed by Violet's palatial hotel suite, manner, and bearing, and assured her that they would do their 'very best to meet your delivery expectations; however, our firm's usual terms are cash on delivery.'

Gamages, London

Violet, as perceptive as ever, quickly realised that her story promising payment by September was unlikely to persuade Gamages to part with such a valuable order and deliver it as far away as the north of Scotland without first obtaining full payment. She informed Mr Denniss and Mr Hampton that she was favoured with not one but two expectations of money in September 1908. First, she informed the two men that her fiancé, Dr Hughes Jones, 'has from time to time given me money, and I am expecting more in September'.

She further embellished her tale by adding, 'The other amount I am due to receive is a gift I am expecting from a gentleman friend, a Mr Alex MacDonald, who belongs to Melbourne, Australia. I met him seven years ago at a party when I was eighteen. He proposed marriage to me – several times – but I declined. Ultimately, he said he would never forget me, and when I reached the age of 25 he would present me with a gift of £250,000. It is a promise that I can rely upon. Mr MacDonald has visited England several times since then, and I have seen him each time. He is about 33 years of age, a gentleman with no profession, and I believe he is very rich. Should you wish to seek a reference from him, the only address I have is c/o Menzies' Hotel, King William Street, Melbourne.'

The fable seems to have impressed Gamages sufficiently for the company to arrange immediate transportation of the goods over the considerable distance of 580 miles from their Holborn Circus showroom to Flowerburn House in Ross-shire. No mean undertaking in 1908. Once again, Violet had been extremely well prepared; Menzies Hotel had an excellent reputation throughout the Empire and was regularly used by colonials, thus providing a credible address for Violet's fictitious lover. However, had Gamages taken the simple step of messaging the hotel via the newly established international telegraph system, which had revolutionised communication with the colonies, they might have saved themselves a great deal of time and money. There was no Alex MacDonald resident at the Menzies Hotel – nor had there been, either before or after that period (so research would suggest).

Following the meeting, Violet wrote to Gamages on her new Flowerburn House crested notepaper, confirming the order. Again, had the two salesmen shown a little more diligence, they might have checked with their employer's accounting department. In December 1907 Violet had previously visited their Holborn Circus department store and opened a credit account for the purchase of a gramophone with a number of records, and some ornaments and vases. The account, for £75 5s 4d, was never paid, despite Violet having at the time provided an excellent reference from the London and Provincial Bank.

But, just how did she manage to get away with it?

In 1909, when the story of her motor-car accident first emerged, journalists began to piece together the story of Violet's life. A reporter for the *Daily Sketch* interviewed an unnamed employee of Gamages, who rather poetically declared, 'If you looked into the lady's eyes, you would believe everything she told you.'

After completing her business with Gamages, Violet rang the bell and informed the hotel's bellboy to say that she would be checking out shortly. As her bags were being carefully placed in her motor car, the manager of the Inns of Court Hotel presented Violet with her outstanding bill, amounting to nearly £50 (now £7,500) and insisted that she settle it immediately. Violet, thinking quickly, replied, 'I must return to Scotland urgently now, but I will be visiting again soon, and will settle it then. I would be most grateful if you would hold it over, please.' The manager agreed ...

Violet's journey back to Scotland was clearly a frenetic one, as both she and Albert were summoned for 'Driving a motor-car at a dangerous speed which was highly dangerous to the public', on Nantwich Road in Crewe. Despite being waved down by PC Walley as they passed the Egerton Arms at 30 mph, Albert failed to stop. The police officer was unable to read the car's registration number as it was covered in mud, and was forced to give chase in what was probably one of the county's first such incidents. He eventually caught up with the speeding motor car at the railway station. Violet and Albert were fined a total of £2 with an additional £1.11s.6d in costs. One witness to the events, Mr Edward Gittens, a taxicab driver, told the police, 'The car approached the station like a flash of lightning. If something had been coming the other way, nothing could have averted a serious accident.'

It was yet another lesson for Violet (she had been fined for speeding at Dunstable in 1907) – but again, one that she apparently did not learn from.

Back in the north of Scotland, and away from her anxious English creditors, Violet intensified her efforts to ingratiate herself onto the Highland social scene. She offered to donate and present a silver cup at the Northern Meeting Highland Games. However, much to her chagrin, the offer was refused.

Nevertheless she was delighted to receive a note from a member of the Northern Meeting Highland Ball Committee – perhaps in placation – recommending that she be added to the Late List for the ball, giving her the opportunity to attend the prestigious event. The Late List made tickets available to those not formally invited, provided they had been recommended and approved by a committee member. According to the official minutes of the Northern Meeting Committee, Violet and her sister Lillian, having been 'vouched for by Mr Charles D. Stewart', were allocated ticket nos. 332 and 333. Stewart, the owner of Brin House, a shooting estate close to Flowerburn House, was a well-known and successful Inverness solicitor. It seems that Violet had already made a favourable impression on her new and influential neighbour.

An invitation to the Northern Meeting Ball in Inverness was an exciting step up in social circles for Violet, and she was both pleased and flattered. The 1908 ball, to be held on Thursday 17 September, would be the leading social event in the Highlands that year, and the climax of both the Northern Meeting Highland Games and the summer season. Extra zest and importance had been added to the Highland summer season in 1908, with the presence of His Majesty the King at nearby Moy Hall. Violet, desperate to enter Highland society, quickly accepted the invitation to the ball, hoping that the event might afford her an introduction to a new and worthwhile acquaintance among the lairds and nobility expected to be in attendance – perhaps even a prospective (and wealthy) suitor. One to whom she could spin the tale of her expected inheritance.

At no little expense, Violet engaged Mr and Mrs George Rowe, the Edwardian era's leading society dance instructors, for a series of ballroom dancing lessons and calisthenic exercise classes. With her already trim figure toned to perfection, Violet clearly intended to turn heads, as well as loosen wallets, as she entered the ballroom.

At the ball she was introduced to many of the distinguished guests present, including the baronet Sir John MacPherson-Grant of Ballindalloch Castle and official convenor of the ball, and Prince Albert Edward, the Prince of Wales and second child of Queen Victoria and Prince Albert. Lady Violet May Gordon Charlesworth (a title that she delighted in giving herself) must have finally felt part of Edwardian society. The sickly child of a factory worker, the working-class girl from a small terraced cottage in Stafford, had finally become Cinderella at the ball. Violet, her taste as exquisite as ever, had ensured that her costume would reflect that season's vogue for satin and diamonds. Gone were the fussy frills and ruched gowns of 1906 and 1907. Instead, she chose a closely fitted gown of white chiffon with a high-waisted bodice adorned with Gordon tartan, telling of her (imagined) proud heritage, topped by her diamond tiara. To the outside world, Violet perfectly projected the image of a young lady and wealthy heiress, naturally blessed with impeccable taste. With her expensive motor car parked outside, her sister Lillian as chaperone, and her ample charm and poise, Violet was the quintessence of a lady. How could anyone at that year's ball possibly realise it was all just a façade?

No expense had been spared to ensure that the spacious Northern Meeting Ballroom in Church Street, Inverness, looked resplendent. One section of the hall had been converted into a drawing room with casual tables and chairs. Extravagant flower arrangements adorned the room. The supper tables

Ferguson & Forrester

for the 600 guests were tastefully decorated, each containing an ornate floral centrepiece. A grand supper had been supplied by Messrs Ferguson & Forrester, the eminent Edinburgh and Glasgow-based 'restaurateurs, caterers, purveyors and confectioners', who supplied a seven-course *spécialité diner du jour*. Expensive wines flowed, all supplied by Thomas G. Henderson's Wine Merchants in Inverness, and an 'excellent and up-to-date programme of dance music' was presented by the Mr David Logan

Orchestra. Prize-winning pipers from across Scotland played the most popular Highland reels and strathspeys, and Violet danced enthusiastically.

Outwardly Violet was calm, poised, and serene. Inwardly, however, she realised that her situation was a precarious and desperate one. More than ever, she needed a rich and generous suitor. Time was running out.

She spent the evening chatting to the Countess of Cawdor, Lady Eleanor Brodie, the Marchioness of Salisbury, the Countess of Cardigan, and Lady Hermione Cameron of Lochiel among others. It appears, however, that Violet spoke rather too freely of her country houses and fleet of motor cars, to the distaste of the genuine ladies present. Adeline Louisa Maria, the elderly and rather eccentric Countess of Cardigan, when writing her memoirs the following year, recalled of her encounter with Violet: 'Money shouts, while birth and breeding whisper.'[5]

After supper, Violet was introduced to several unattached young men, all immaculately attired in traditional Highland formal dress, white tie and tails, or military uniform. She took a special interest in any potential admirers, and made every effort to appear demure and charming. Violet now added a further twist to her fairytale of impending fortune, telling any would-be suitors that she was in the process of securing yet another country estate, this time to the value of £80,000 (now £12 million). She chatted enthusiastically about her recent visit to the battlefield at Culloden, her interest in Jacobite history, and a proposed trip to Australia. For Violet, the Northern Meeting Ball might be the culmination of her dreams and aspirations, an opportunity to impress a potential lover, who could rescue her from her creditors and satisfy her extravagant tastes.

Would she meet Mr Right? Right for romance, or ripe for fleecing? In her desperate financial straits, would circumstance present Violet with the ideal mark?

---

5   This statement includes an unspoken condemnation of Violet's dialect and accent. These would have instantly revealed her as being nouveau riche (at best), and the countess on meeting her would have doubtless made a swift escape.

9: The Mark

Sadly, the evening was to end in disappointment for Violet. The thrill of happiness and the sense of hope she had experienced on entering the ballroom soon changed from joyous expectation to gloomy despair. Violet swiftly realised that the men to whom she had been introduced were essentially male versions of herself – young men who had spent virtually their last few shillings on a ticket and a hired costume in a desperate attempt to meet a wealthy and unattached lady. The most callous breed of gold-diggers, these young men spent the evening surveying the attendees at the dance, fervently hoping to be introduced to the daughter of a lord or lady, a wealthy spinster, or even an eligible widow, to whom they might serve up ladlefuls of insincere flattery. Had Dr Hughes Jones, Mrs Smith, Fenton, Dale & Co., or any of Violet's many creditors been able to witness her increasing desperation that night, they might well have experienced a wicked sense of *schadenfreude* from the irony of her situation. Violet had been dealt a cruel hand in the game of poetic justice at what was for her the most crucial time.

Eight years later, in a newspaper article celebrating the 95th birthday of Mrs Kennedy, a noted society figure in Inverness, she recalled meeting Violet at that ball. The fearsome old lady, who had as a young girl met Sir Walter Scott, had obviously been less than impressed by Violet, claiming, 'I was the first person in the north to doubt the credentials of Violet Charlesworth.'

Among the many hobbies of the missing Miss Charlesworth was the leasing of residences. In the top picture is Flowerburn, Inverness-shire, which she took last summer, on a long lease. The lower picture shows another of her homes, Bod Erw, which is at St. Asaph, North Wales.

Meanwhile, Violet's creditors grew ever more impatient. Solicitors acting on behalf of the owners of Boderw in North Wales, and The Hall in Calne, were instigating bankruptcy charges against Violet, citing unpaid rent. Legal summonses were issued, and the house agents were instructed to place To Let signs outside both properties. Despite Violet's pleas, the owners refused to wait

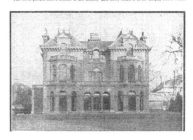

It would not be long until the newspapers published pictures of Violet's country houses

another moment for payment. Violet knew that she could not return to Boderw or The Hall without awkward questions being asked of her. But having already paid the first year's rent in advance for Flowerburn House, she had at least a short period of grace before her creditors would begin tracking her down in the Highlands.

She began to hatch her plan – a scheme which must have seemed to be her only way out; she placed an advertisement in several Scottish newspapers asking for 'Gentlemen Boarders to reside at the house'.

But unfortunately for Violet, this strategy did not yield any additional income; it merely served to alert her chauffeur and maid at Flowerburn to her financial woes. They soon informed the local tradesmen and shopkeepers in and around Inverness to whom Violet already owed large sums of money. Sure enough, several Inverness and Fortrose merchants soon began to call at Flowerburn, each demanding immediate payment of their overdue accounts. At first, Violet's maid refused to grant them admission, informing them: 'Miss Gordon Charlesworth is far too ill to receive visitors.' Violet thanked the girl for helping her avoid a potentially awkward situation, and promptly gave her grateful maid the night off, instructing her, 'Please do not wake your mistress on your return tonight, but wake me in the morning at the usual time. I am sure I shall feel better then.'

As domestic staff were only usually permitted one afternoon off a fortnight, the maid jumped at the chance. Sadly, it appears that she too was to be duped by Violet. The following morning, on entering Violet's room with a breakfast tray, the maid was astounded to find the room empty. Violet had packed her belongings and vanished during the night. Taking her favourite pictures, jewellery, clothes, rugs, and other valuables, she had crept out of her home in the dead of night and driven like the wind down the Great North Trunk Road towards England. The maid, of course, never received her wages.

South Street, Perth

Violet broke her long journey south in the Fair City' of Perth. She visited two pawnbrokers, W.M. Fyfe's in South Street, where she pledged several small items including a watch, and Herraughty's in Mill Street, where she pawned a valuable brooch for £14 (now £2,000). Described by the pawnbroker as 'energetic, self-reliant, and ready conversationalist', she had little trouble in persuading him to part with such a large sum of cash. Now, armed with some spending money, Violet headed towards the English border.

Before leaving Scotland, Violet had written to a friend in Liverpool describing her money difficulties and explaining that taking her own life might be the only option left to her. Violet's friend, distressed, and naturally worried, reminded her of Mr B. Samuel, a sympathetic Leicester financier and diamond merchant, who Violet had communicated with by letter on previous occasions in an attempt to borrow money.

So Violet, once back in England, decided to call in person on Mr Samuel at his London Road premises, hoping to obtain a loan against her collection of valuable diamonds. After introducing herself, Violet opened her jewel case and revealed to the dumbstruck dealer a studded diamond tiara, a large diamond star, two half-hoop diamond bracelets, a large diamond brooch, two beautiful cluster rings, a large marquise ring, a French-made diamond pendant, a dainty necklet, and a diamond-encrusted hair ornament. Each beautifully set individual gemstone had been perfectly cut in Brilliant cut, best displaying its numerous facets and revealing the piece's exceptional quality by maximising the effect of the light passing through the head of the diamond.

Samuel, flushed with excitement, examined the jewels closely with his loupe. As he had guessed from his first glance, he saw that the gems were flawless blue-white diamonds of the finest quality. Characterised by the lack of impurities in the stone's crystal structure, the gems exhibited the perfect bluish-white body colour that gave them their name. Violet was clearly a woman of exceptional taste.

He realised that these diamonds were among the rarest and finest known to exist (only 1 per cent of the world's diamonds fall into the flawless category) and privately guessed their value to be in the region of £5,000 (now £7,500,000), and that this was probably the most valuable private collection anywhere in the country at that time. The stones would almost certainly have been mined in South Africa, and their cutting, cleaving, and polishing would most probably have been undertaken by Joseph Asscher & Co. of Amsterdam,[6] the world's leading diamond craftsmen.

Samuel exclaimed, 'Miss Charlesworth, what glorious diamonds! I have never seen such lovely stones. They look to be worth thousands. They are of a higher quality than even that of the Cullinan diamond.'[7] Knowing the

---

6   It was Asschers who undertook the cutting of the Cullinan diamond.

7   The Cullinan had recently been presented to King Edward VII by the Transvaal Colony government, and at the time of writing is still the largest and most valuable gemstone ever discovered.

value of the gems, Mr Samuel looked up from his loupe and enquired, 'Can you produce any receipts?'

Violet replied, 'When my fiancé presented me with these tokens of respect and esteem, he did not present me with a receipted bill! Perhaps you would have him ask him for one! I fear that would not do.'

Instead, she provided a certificate valuing the gems at just £1,600 (now £245,000) and asked for an advance of £1,000 using the collection as security. Samuel realised that the valuation was hugely inaccurate, which only served to raise his suspicions further. Why would Violet produce a certificate which so clearly undervalued the gems?

In addition, despite being impressed by the magnificent jewels and their obvious worth, he was surprised to find someone as young as Violet in possession of such valuable diamonds, and in such a new display case, since it was likely that the gemstones had been mined several years earlier. Cautiously he questioned her, 'How are ornaments so fine in your possession? Why is the case so new, and why are the settings so modern?'

Violet, unfortunately, was unable to satisfy Samuel's natural caution. So, on hearing that she intended to visit London next, he referred her to a merchant in Oxford Street, who he thought might be more willing to assist her.

Violet visited the merchant immediately after arriving in London, but even after obtaining another expert's independent valuation he too, became suspicious of such a high-value collection of jewels owned by such a young woman – presented, moreover, in a jewel case that did not provide any clue as to their origin. Although, as mentioned earlier, Violet had in fact acquired much of her impressive diamond collection from J.W. Benson & Co. in 1905 and 1906, she clearly had no intention of allowing this merchant to uncover that fact. The truth behind her ability to purchase such an expensive collection remains an enigma. It seems doubtful that she had been able to afford such costly gems by using the money loaned to her by Dr Hughes Jones alone. Possibly she had yet another lover willing to loan her vast sums, or lavish her with extravagant gifts. Or did she have other lines of credit which have never emerged? Indeed, it is certain that the collection of ornate jewellery would have been well beyond the purse strings of Dr Hughes Jones and the widow Mrs Smith. It would later also emerge that Violet had purchased at least part of this jewellery collection under the name of Miss Mackenzie. The reason for this also remains a mystery. Perhaps she wished to keep the name of a benefactor secret, or to prevent the gems from ever being traced back to her. Violet's excuse, however, was far more prosaic. She merely claimed that Mackenzie 'was a chance name that came into my head'.

Returning to Violet's attempts to persuade the London merchant to grant an advance against the security of the gems, Violet even offered him one of her motor cars as a further surety, for which she was able to prove ownership by producing an invoice, dated 22 February 1908. Nevertheless, on this rare occasion her charms proved ineffective. She was unable to convince the wily merchant and she left empty-handed, with the weight of her crippling debt still pressing down on her.

Would the story of her fictitious inheritance now finally catch up with her? Or could she find another route out of her predicament? Apart from her jewellery, Violet had few possessions that could be readily exchanged for cash. Yet, with some money in her purse and her cheque book in hand, there was still hope of obtaining a loan to pay her creditors. She had no intention of giving up just yet.

Despite these pressing worries, Violet made little effort to rein in her extravagant lifestyle. She returned to London in October and once again booked into the Inns of Court Hotel in High Holborn. Although her outstanding bill was still unpaid, she managed to persuade the manager to offer her a suite of rooms on the first floor. The manager, still apparently convinced by the tale of her inheritance, might have anticipated that the hotel's sizeable overdue account would be settled in the near future. Once safely ensconced in her room Violet wrote the letter to Dr Hughes Jones in Rhyl, informing him that her trustee, Colonel Williamson, was still threatening to withhold her inheritance if they continued their relationship. She realised the doctor would be both furious and heartbroken, but she could not conceive of any other way to both break her promise of marriage and still prevent him from uncovering the truth regarding her fraudulent inheritance.

On Tuesday 3 November 1908, during her stay at the Inns of Court Hotel, Violet noticed an advertisement in the *London Evening News*. Placed by a firm of London accountants, Messrs Webb and Company of Wellington Street, in The Strand, the advertisement read: 'For anyone in financial difficulties, private arrangements are effected, and extra capital introduced.'

Under the impression that Messrs Webb & Co. would be able to help resolve her financial problems, Violet picked up a sheet of the hotel's headed notepaper and wrote to them,

> Sirs,
>
> I am sorely in need of assistance, and a chance to square everything up, and the wording of your advertisement has led me to think that you might be able to give me the chance I so much need, and would be so grateful of.
>
> The facts, in short, are these. I am requiring about £2,000 to clear off my debts, and having lost all my money, I have no

means on which I could give you security, only this, that you would own all the goods on which you paid the debts, excluding a Daimler motor-car, which has cost over a thousand pounds, and as I could not take delivery, the Daimler Company have obtained judgement against me for over £900. The car has never been put on the road.

I am starting on my own in a good way in the motor business, and have the promise of several car orders now, and would pay you any interest and also the full amount back, if only you will grant the loan?

Will you please wire me to 'Poste Restante', Stafford, to-morrow, saying if you are likely to do it?

(Miss) V. Gordon Charlesworth.

P.S. I could give you full particulars almost at once, if you think you would do it.'

Messrs Webb & Co. duly responded, suggesting that she call at their office to discuss the matter further.

Violet was quick to act and arrived in The Strand by hansom cab the following morning, to plead personally to Mr Webb, 'Sir, I currently have no prospects and am not entitled to any money. I had £2,000 left to me, but I have spent all that. I owe the firm of Frasers of Inverness £700 for the furnishing of Flowerburn House. My parents have nothing to say to me about the matter, owing to me having taken the lease on Flowerburn House. I need to borrow £2,000 or £3,000 for the purpose of starting a motor business.'

'Miss Charlesworth,' explained Mr Webb, 'we are not moneylenders, but accountants.'

'Then perhaps, Mr Webb, you might come to Inverness and help arrange matters with my creditors?'

'I could,' Webb replied, 'on the condition that my charges and expenses are paid.'

'Very well', Violet answered, 'I will bring the money for the purpose of your expenses tomorrow morning at 11:30.'

She thanked Mr Webb politely and left.

Unsurprisingly, the following morning she did not return. Instead, the firm received a handwritten letter on the notepaper of the Royal Automobile Club, Pall Mall, of which, Violet was a member. The brief note declared: 'I regret being unable to call on you at 11:30 as arranged. I have mentioned the matter to my solicitors, and now await their advice in my affairs. I am anxious to have my affairs put straight a little. If I can arrange matters suitably, I will let you know my intentions as early as possible.'

That terse communication bore only the address of the RAC and no other contact information. Messrs Webb & Co. did not hear from Violet again; then a few weeks later they, like many others, were shocked to see a report of her death in the motor-car accident.

Meanwhile, Violet continued to visit theatres, music hall shows, and West End restaurants, using the money she had obtained against her pawn shop pledges. Perhaps now she fully understood the gravity of her situation. She could not continue to evade her creditors for ever. Time seemed to be running out for her.

It seems that it was by acting on pure impulse that Violet decided to pay a visit to Derby on 14 November 1908. Fresh from her trip to the first Ideal Home Exhibition in London, she had once again spent excessive amounts of money and needed a soft mark from whom to extract some ready cash. After stopping en route in Stafford to have four new tyres fitted on her motor car (for which she wrote a cheque) Violet arrived in Derby and called unexpectedly for afternoon tea at Dr Barrett's home. The doctor, who had been acquainted with Violet and her mother since the family had first moved to Derby, was surprised, as Violet appeared to be in great distress.

With reddened eyes, she pleaded with the doctor: 'I have been awfully extravagant, but I was left with no choice, when my car broke down. As an old and dear friend, could you lend me two or three hundred pounds?'

She had been left with no option but to purchase that new set of tyres for her motor car, which had been subjected to a series of lengthy journeys along the length and breadth of Britain's highways. The cost of tyres, coupled with their fragility and short lifespan, gives us another valuable insight into Violet's expenditure at that time. Tyres in 1908 were little more than glorified bicycle tyres, costing on average around £15 each (now £2,250). They were expected to last only 2,500 miles. Violet's mileage for the year 1908 was recorded in her black motoring diary as being in excess of 60,000. Therefore, we can confidently estimate that she would have required a complete new set of tyres on around 24 occasions during 1908, at a cost of £60 each time – a staggering total of approximately £9,000 (now £1.4 million) – and, indeed, higher than her average petrol bill, mentioned earlier. Once again, it is probable that she obtained a great deal of this on credit, or by post-dated cheque. To place this in context, in 1908 her spend on tyres alone was more than 20,000 times the average person's annual salary.

Using every weapon in her arsenal, Violet begged Dr Barrett to lend her the money, promising to repay him on her 25th birthday. However, the doctor had never believed the fanciful stories spun by the Charlesworths. Despite later saying that Violet was a 'very charming girl who could interest one without effort', he refused to loan her a penny. Violet implored him once more, but he replied emphatically, 'Oh, Lord, no. I don't think so.' Subsequently, when the full extent of Violet's fraud became public knowledge, Dr Barrett would repeat these words to anyone that might care to listen. It seems he took great pleasure in being one of the very few people not to be seduced by Violet's entrancing demeanour.

Violet left the doctor's house and immediately called on Mrs Smith, from whom she had already extracted £381. Mrs Smith, glancing through her net curtains and seeing a motor car drawing up outside her home, might well have been somewhat comforted to notice Violet climbing down from a new Daimler tourer, aided by the two chauffeurs who had accompanied her. The car carried the Scottish registration plate ST 148, which Mrs Smith mistakenly understood to mean that Violet had journeyed especially from Scotland to pay her a visit.

Violet greeted Mrs Smith and immediately explained that £200 in cash had been stolen from her motor car and she was both frightened and distraught. 'If my trustees find out I have lost £200,' she explained to Mrs Smith, 'they may well withhold the rest of my inheritance.'

Unlike Dr Barrett, Mrs Smith had been completely taken in by Violet's story. The sight of the new car had comforted her; surely it meant that Violet's inheritance had now been paid and her money would soon be returned. She readily agreed to loan Violet some but not all, of the money she needed.

What happened next was probably the single most contemptible action of Violet's life, and one for which there can be no sympathy. Mrs Smith apologised, explaining to Violet that she had already loaned her almost all her entire savings of £400. At that moment Violet might have been overcome with guilt and let the matter drop. Instead, she insisted that Mrs Smith withdraw every penny she possessed from her Co-operative savings account. Mrs Smith, utterly taken it by Violet's story, went immediately to the Co-operative Stores and despite the protestations of her relatives, withdrew her final £20 (now £2,800). Her entire remaining life savings. Violet, rather than suffering any pangs of guilt, was clearly unsatisfied; she begged Mrs Smith to search the drawers and empty jars of her home, in the hope that she might locate just a few more pounds. Mrs Smith was able to find just a single sovereign coin (£1), which she duly handed to Violet. Having divested Mrs Smith of her entire savings, Violet thanked her and left.

Now growing increasingly desperate, Violet wrote to Fenton, Dale & Co. begging that they see their way to either loaning her a large sum of money so that she might earn back some of her stock market losses, or at least delay any legal action against her. This time the company refused outright. Violet then contacted a financier in the city and attempted to obtain an advance on a £3,000 life insurance policy she had opened. She hoped that even a loan of just a few hundred pounds would tempt the financier. However, he refused, stating that the policy was of little value due to her youth; the wait to receive any annuity would be too long, he felt.

Violet replied sharply, and with a tone of desperation in her choice of words, 'Well, I really cannot die to order, can I?'

Somewhat ironically, Fenton, Dale & Co., the stockbrokers to whom she now owed more than £10,000, had themselves recently approached Lloyd's of London and taken out a large insurance policy of their own against Violet's life. They rightly feared that an outright loss of £10,000 would have been too large a strain for even their capacious coffers. Following Violet's car crash in January 1909, Mr Percival from Fenton, Dale & Co. explained to investigators:

> Her life has been covered by three or four different parties, of which I am one, and in each instance the amount insured is a substantial one.
>
> It was only within the last month or so that precautions were taken against the failure of Miss Charlesworth to meet her liabilities. This was due to the doubts which were cast on her story as to the large fortune she was to inherit.
>
> More than one financial firm with whom she has done business has made secret enquiries as to her social status and the amount of money she had at her command, with the result that the insurances were effected.
>
> We, at Fenton & Dale, are covered on her life to the extent of several thousands of pounds, and one or two others have secured insurances for stiff sums. Miss Charlesworth was young and healthy and there was no difficulty in getting the underwriters to take the risk.
>
> Without any knowledge of the total amount, which has not been officially supplied to me, I can state with certainty that the insurances come to at least £15,000 (now £2.2 million).

Meanwhile, Violet remained registered at the Inns of Court Hotel in London until Thursday 17 December 1908, although she was seldom there. However, on that date she was forced to check out; pressure from the hotel's manager regarding her unpaid account had made matters too uncomfortable. There had also been unsubstantiated reports regarding visits paid to Violet at the hotel by several unnamed men. In an era of strict marriage laws, high moral values (at least, publicly), and chaperoning of unattached ladies when entertaining in their hotel rooms, the hotel management felt obliged to show their displeasure at Violet's alleged behaviour. Rumours would later circulate that she had entertained several married men at the Inns of Court Hotel, with newspapers even speculating that this may have included Members of Parliament and even of the Lords. If the rumours were true, this may help account for Violet's continuing ability to finance her decadent lifestyle. However, following her motor-car accident in January 1909 not a single well-connected gentleman came forward, claiming to have been duped into loaning her money.

Violet managed to slip away from the Inns of Court Hotel during the night. Meanwhile, letters addressed to her continued to arrive there, as they had done for several days. In any case, she had ignored all of the previous correspondence sent to her at the hotel, perhaps having already guessed the contents. After her moonlight flit, Violet drove to Stafford in her Minerva Landaulette before travelling on to North Wales. She arrived to be greeted by several demands for money, including the threat of legal action by Dr Hughes Jones.

The desperate situation required even more desperate action. Violet realised that only her most audacious plan to date could possibly save her from discovery, ruin, and disgrace. We are lucky enough to still have a record of her increasing frantic movements during those last few days before the motor-car accident on 2 January 1909, thanks to an enterprising reporter from the *Nottingham Evening Post* who, following the car accident, managed to obtain two pages from Violet's notebook which had been discovered on the rocks underneath the crash site. Handwritten in pencil under the heading 'Mileage Register', they bear witness to a women's final frenetic attempts to put her house in order while avoiding her creditors. During the period 10–27 December 1908, Violet travelled a total of 2,731 miles. Her notebook entries were as follows:

December 10th	Stafford to St. Asaph and back.
	Stafford to Calne and return.
December 11th	Stafford to Derby and back.
December 12th	Stafford to London.
December 13th	In town.
December 14th	London to Stafford.
December 15th	Stafford to Newport[8] and back.
December 16th	Stafford to London.
December 17th	In town, and London to Stafford.
December 18th	Stafford to St. Asaph and back.
December 19th	Stafford to Kendal and back; to Wales.
December 20th	St. Asaph to Edinburgh.
December 21st	Edinburgh to Fortrose.
	(Flowerburn House).

8 Newport in Shropshire was the home of Violet's mother's family.

December 23rd	Fortrose to Wick and back on 24th.[9]
December 25th	Fortrose to Inverness and return.
December 26th	Fortrose to Glasgow.
December 27th	Glasgow to ----'

The entry for Christmas Day is a reflection of the severe weather in Scotland that thwarted Violet's efforts to drive south again. The desperate nature of her situation is made all the more obvious by her endeavours to even attempt the journey in such dangerous driving conditions. Again, the same enterprising reporter for the *Nottingham Evening Post* described her difficulties:

> Though the destination of the last journey is not stated, it is now known that it was Perth, for on the following day, in the blizzard which snowed up railway trains and made highways impassable, Miss Violet actually motored south to Wigan, using a stock of petrol she obtained with a portion of the proceeds of a diamond brooch pledged with a pawnbroker. Accompanied by an elderly gentleman, who has not been identified, and her chauffeur, she was on the road during the terrible day and nights of December 28th and 29th. The car was forced at top speed through snowdrifts, but several times it became embedded and had to be pulled out by teams of horses. After procuring more petrol at Wigan, where she left the pawnticket as security, the party went on to Liverpool, and on the afternoon of 30th she reached the Welsh coast at Prestatyn. Here another drift was encountered. A rush was made at it with the motor-car, but the mass of snow was so great that the machine almost buried itself and stopped. Again, horses were obtained to extricate the car, and after taking tea at a local hotel, Miss Charlesworth was driven to the station, and returned to St. Asaph by train.

After being forced to spend most of the Christmas holidays travelling in a blinding blizzard, Violet finally reached Boderw in an obviously distracted state of mind, but in time for Friday's New Year's Eve celebration and to see in 1909.

She was not idle on her arrival back in North Wales, however. On New Year's Eve she received a visit at Boderw from Mr D.G. Thomas, a representative of Messrs Price & Co., Grocers, of St Asaph. Mr Thomas, was persistent, and refused to leave until he had seen Violet. She finally agreed,

---

9   During this journey Violet stopped at Helmsdale railway station in Sutherland, to dispatch two metal chests to be 'collected when called for' at the offices of the Midland Railway Company in Birmingham.

whereupon he presented her with a summons for non-payment of her outstanding account. The following day he was presented with a visiting card from Violet, on which she had written, 'With regard to both the actions and words of Messrs Price and Co., Miss Gordon Charlesworth refuses to see them on any subject whatever. They must deal directly with her solicitors.' It also appears that Violet found time to engage a removals company, who took several large boxes from Boderw on the afternoon of New Year's Day on her behalf. This seems to have been the last known independent sighting of Violet prior to the day of the motor-car accident.

On New Year's Day 1909, the day that the new National Old Age Pension Scheme finally came into force, the weather improved and Violet's Minerva motor car was returned to her. That day, then, saw her busily preparing to initiate a new scheme of her own. It was a dangerous strategy, fraught with hazards, but there was not a moment to lose.

On Saturday 2 January 1909 the weather was particularly fine and dry. According to the version of events given by Lillian and Albert Watts following the accident, Violet had decided to go for an afternoon drive, and the party of three had set out from St Asaph around 3.30 pm. However, as the weather was so pleasant, the trio decided to extend their trip and take afternoon tea at the Castle Hotel in Bangor. Then, as described in the opening chapters of this book, Violet decided to take the wheel on the return journey, resulting in the accident at Penmaenbach Point and Violet's body being catapulted into the sea, before being washed away.

But what really happened on that brilliantly moonlit night? And what *did* become of Violet Charlesworth? After painstakingly piecing together all the known clues, reading and rereading all the witness statements and newspaper reports, poring over archives, and uncovering Violet's own handwritten memoirs, and then by visiting the location of the accident, scrutinising railway and ferry timetables, travelling the length and breadth of the country, and carefully studying Violet's movements, I am now able to reveal the probable course of events on that January evening in 1909.

Castle Hotel, Bangor.
Where Violet plotted her escape

10: The Melon Drop

The chill of first light meant that only the birds were awake in the early morning of 2 January 1909. The majority of St Asaph's residents were grateful to remain in their beds on that Saturday morning, sleeping off the New Year exuberances of the previous two days.

Meanwhile, in the driveway at Boderw Albert quietly loaded Violet's luggage into the Minerva motor car: two steamer trunks, a tin chest, and a large monogrammed portmanteau, cleverly designed with one half arranged to hang full-length dresses and the other with drawers to store accessories. The trunks and chest contained a selection of Violet's more valuable jewellery, furs, rugs, photographs, and other items. The portmanteau was filled with Violet's extensive travelling wardrobe, including her treasured corset-free outfit created by French designer Paul Poiret. After Albert had closed the motor car's doors as quietly as possible, Violet silently checked that all her luggage was securely on board, counting each piece with her gloved fingers. Albert cranked the starter as noiselessly as he could, before the pair exited the driveway and drove to Conwy railway station in the morning mist. Once there, they despatched the trunks and chests, with instructions that they were to be stored until collected at the left luggage office of a large railway station in the Midlands. (Violet was in the habit of sending baggage to be stored at various left luggage offices around the country.) While Violet transacted this business with the clerk, a railway porter noticed her distinctive crimson motor cloak. Meanwhile, the portmanteau, remaining in the Minerva motor car, was concealed as best as possible. In the late morning the pair returned to Boderw for an early lunch. By that hour, the bright winter sunshine had transformed the chilly January morning into a crisp and clear day.

At 3.30 pm Violet, together with her sister Lillian and Albert, left Boderw in the Minerva. Violet sat in the passenger seat, wrapped up against the winter chill in her warm crimson motor cloak, gloves, and tam o' shanter driving bonnet. Lillian, who sat in the rear, was also snuggly wrapped in a long dark motor cloak. Albert (with whom Violet might, or might not, have been engaged in an affair) took the wheel. As they departed, Violet informed the staff that they intended to take advantage of the fine, dry weather and take the Minerva for a short spin in the countryside. The family, it seems, knew otherwise; the trio had something very different in mind.

They drove westwards through Colwyn Bay towards Conwy. Lillian would later inform the police that only when they reached Conwy did they made the impulsive decision to extend their day out due to the fine weather. However, in reality, it appears that their eventual destination was in fact a secret and pre-planned arrangement known only to the three of them. Instead of returning to St Asaph the two sisters and Albert pushed on along the winding coast road, through Penmaenmawr and finally to Bangor. Once there, Albert pulled up in the narrow High Street and parked opposite the cathedral, outside the entrance to the Castle Hotel. He opened the car doors for Violet and Lillian, who walked up the steps into the hotel. Albert, perhaps conscious of the conspicuous nature of the large and expensive Minerva, drove around the corner, through the arch at the rear of the hotel and into the covered garage area. He remained there, sitting in the motor car.

Violet and Lillian were shown into the hotel's oak-panelled lounge, where they ordered afternoon tea. It was a busy Saturday afternoon, with many other visitors taking advantage of the fine weather and the New Year holiday. Soon an appetising arrangement of tea, sandwiches, and fancy cakes were brought to the table by a uniformed waitress. As she left, Violet asked if the hotel, 'might have a copy of Bradshaw's?'[10] The waitress smiled and returned with a large copy of the guide, which she placed on the lacy tablecloth next to Violet. It was now just after 4.30 pm.

Violet and Lillian bent their heads in concentration as they pored over the railway timetables. Bangor station was just a few hundred yards away. It would have been obvious to anyone sitting close by that the pair were carefully planning a railway journey. Soon, the waitress returned. The sisters seemed to be in no particular hurry, and Violet ordered fresh tea. Darkness had now descended outside, save for a brilliant moon that gradually illuminated the sky. Meanwhile, Albert remained in the adjacent undercover garage and car park, grateful for the hotel's foresight in installing heating there.

Violet and Lillian smiled, as they carefully thumbed the timetable until they finally located the train service that suited their carefully thought-out plan. However, they would now need to pass a little time, as the train was not due to depart for at least another two hours. So they sent a message to Albert, who was still patiently waiting in the hotel garage. He went to the nearby Rowland's Commercial Temperance Hotel (more suitable for someone in service) and ordered a hot meal, leaving the Minerva in the hotel car park. It seemed clear that the trio did not wish to be seen together in public.

By 6.15 pm the afternoon tea customers had mostly drifted away and

---

10 The railway timetable listings.

the staff at the Castle Hotel began to clear the lounge ready for the dinner service. Violet and Lillian realised they could delay no longer and, paying the one shilling and sixpence bill, left the hotel. They were witnessed leaving by several other customers and members of staff, who put the time of their departure at between 6.15 and 6.30 pm. When asked later, everyone remembered Violet's distinctive red motor cloak.

There were no reported sightings of either the Minerva or its three occupants anywhere in Bangor from 6.30 pm until shortly after 8 pm, when it was seen pulling up outside the two-storey red-brick railway station. It is clear the trio had no wish to be observed during that time, and it is most probable that Violet and Lillian had sat in the motor car in the hotel's garage until the streets were quieter. The trio then departed at 8 pm and proceeded down the High Street towards the railway station. It was now dark, although the shiny green Minerva motor car was observed by a railway inspector as it pulled up among the horses and carts waiting outside the station's entrance. He noticed a young lady sporting a distinctive crimson motor cloak, engaged in a protracted goodbye with the other occupant of the motor car, before being assisted by a young, dark-haired man wearing a chauffeur's uniform. The man enquired about the mailboat sailings from Holyhead, before engaging a porter to wheel the young lady's large portmanteau through the arched entrance and into the main station concourse. She tipped him and said, 'Thank you' in a quiet, soft voice. She then purchased a ticket for the 8.30 pm slow service to Holyhead, walked past the bookstall without stopping to browse, and made her way into the waiting room. The station was quiet and there were no further confirmed sightings of Violet there.

It is worth pointing out that in Albert's original statement following the accident (see Chapter 1), he affirmed that Miss Violet and Miss Lillian had taken afternoon tea at a hotel in Bangor (he claimed that he could not remember the hotel's name) which advertised 'afternoon tea for cyclists available', and that they had stayed for one hour while he had waited in the car outside, then driven straight back to St Asaph.

His version of events seems unbelievable for three reasons. First, no witnesses remembered seeing the shiny bottle-green Minerva outside the hotel – this, in an era when fewer than 3,000 cars were registered in the whole of Britain and any car, let alone that highly conspicuous one, was still unusual enough to be remarked upon. Secondly, it is hard to believe that Albert would have sat outside the hotel for an hour directly underneath a large sign saying, 'Castle Hotel', and forgotten that fact by the following day. Finally, the drive from Bangor to the eventual scene of the accident at Penmaenbach Point would, even in 1909, have only taken only a maximum of 30 minutes, meaning that the car – if Albert's version is to be believed – should have arrived at the site of the accident at around 6 pm, and not 9 pm as he would later claim.

In addition, if, in contrast to his account, the 'accident' really had occurred just before 9 pm, this seems to coincide with the evidence of the railway porter, who had noticed the Minerva pulling away from outside Bangor railway station at around 8.15–8.30 pm. Importantly, the porter reported that he had been unable to see how many people were in the motor car.

Meanwhile, Violet, having purchased a ticket for that Saturday night's London and North-Western service from Bangor to Holyhead, boarded the passenger carriage. The train departed Bangor just before 9 pm – meaning she cannot have been in her motor car at that time.

Bangor Railway Station

The Bangor–Holyhead rail connection was mostly utilised in the collection and delivery of packages to and from the mail steamer RMS *Connaught*, which plied the route across the Irish Sea from Holyhead to the port of Kingstown (now Dún Laoghaire), 8 miles to the south of Dublin city centre. That night the train had just one passenger carriage coupled, which contained a handful of travellers making their way to Holyhead. At least one other passenger clearly remembered seeing a young lady, whom she described as 'wearing a long crimson cloak reaching to her feet, and covering up the whole of her dress'.

At the very moment that Violet's train departed Bangor railway station, the Minerva motor car containing only Lillian and Albert was heading through Penmaenmawr towards the bend in the road. Later, a cyclist in Penmaenmawr distinctly remembered noticing the car speeding past him in the bright moonlight. He swore there were only two occupants in the car, a young man and a woman. Another definitive sighting was that by PC Owen, who recalled seeing the motor car driving past him at around 8.50 pm. He was certain that the car was being driven by a man. PC Owen also remembered part of the car's registration number, LB, and that the tail light was broken (indeed, Albert had accidentally broken one of the tail lights during a recent visit to Stafford).

Meanwhile, Albert raced away from Penmaenmawr towards Conwy, around the sharp bend at Penmaenbach Point, where the Devil's Thumb juts ominously skywards. A few yards after the bend, when Albert reached the gap in the wall – the point where Violet was supposed to meet her tragic death – he abruptly brought the car to a standstill and switched off the engine. First making sure the highway was deserted, illuminated as it was by the bright moonlight, he turned the steering wheel to the left, released the handbrake, and gently pushed the car towards the low wall intended to prevent motorists and pedestrians from falling to the rocks below. As he pushed the car through the gap in the wall, there was a slight crunching sound as it knocked a few stones from the edge of the wall onto the rock shelf below. The car came to rest with its rear wheels wedged against the kerbstones (preventing it from rolling any further forward), and its front wheels precariously close to the edge; however, at that point the rocky outcrop on the far side of the wall protruded horizontally, preventing the car from crashing into the sea below. Albert and Lillian then quickly set about preparing the scene of the make-believe accident. Albert kicked some loose stones from the wall, to give the impression that the car had struck it with a greater force than it actually had, while Lillian carefully tossed Violet's black suede notebook and tam o' shanter motoring hat onto the rocks below, taking care not to throw them too far, in the hope that they would be recovered the following day. Meanwhile, Albert picked up a loose stone and smashed the windscreen on the passenger's side, to add authenticity to the idea that Violet had been thrown from the vehicle. Foolishly, however, he smashed the glass on the wrong side, forgetting that their story relied on the idea that Violet was supposed to have been in the driving seat, and not the passenger seat, at the time of the accident.

Conscious that another road user could pass at any moment, Lillian, carefully mimicking the gait and persona of someone in a state of panic, staggered the few hundred yards along the road towards the Ship Inn to raise the alarm. She threw open the door to the Inn and blurted out in a convincingly distressed tone, 'There has been a dreadful car accident! My younger sister has been catapulted into the sea!'

Meanwhile Albert remained at the scene of the supposed crash, preparing himself for the inquisition to come; desperately attempting to create as persuasive a crash scene as possible. Having found a pocket roadmap in the footwell of the Minerva, he tossed that over the edge too. One of the headlamps had been slightly damaged during the motor car's collision with the wall. This pleased Albert, although he would have harboured an inbuilt aversion to destroying such a lovely example of the automobile. He realised that for their story to be believed the Minerva would need to appear a great deal more damaged than it was. Perhaps he had intended to create a more credibly broken windscreen; however, the crowd from the Ship Inn were now heading quickly towards him. There was no more time, and he needed to prepare himself for the inevitable questioning. He knew that he must appear simultaneously dazed, traumatised, and anxious about the disappearance of Violet. However, Albert and Lillian had rehearsed their story well. He must not panic. He must remember the line he had practised as they prepared for the grand deception – 'Miss Charlesworth was catapulted into the sea. Where is she? Where *is* the lady?'

The police were summoned and the frantic search for Violet began, as volunteers scrambled down the rocks to the sea below, all desperately scouring the shoreline for a glimpse of her body or a vital clue that might help locate her. Meanwhile, sitting on the edge of the wall above in the moonlight, Albert and Lillian answered Superintendent Rees's questions as plausibly as they could. Despite their obvious nerves and apprehension, they appear to have been convincing, and were soon spirited away to Gwnyfa Lodging House in Penmaenmawr, so that the questioning could be resumed in the morning. This development was probably a surprise to Albert and Lillian, who had no doubt expected to be returned to the safety of Boderw that night.

Meanwhile, 36 miles away in Holyhead, the 9 pm London and North-Western steam locomotive pulled up alongside the gently curving platform, the billows of steam trapped under the roof helping to conceal Violet as she alighted with the other passengers. However, she did not exit the station immediately, but lingered in a shadowy corner of the platform, waiting for most of the passengers and employees to clear, before returning to her now empty compartment in the passenger carriage. Alone, Violet then pulled down both the window and the door blinds. Clearly, her desire was to remain on board undetected. This was not indecision, regret, or panic, but part of a carefully thought-out plan.

THE CLIFF NEAR LLANDUDNO OVER WHICH MISS CHARLESWORTH WAS "THROWN INTO THE SEA"

The cliff near LLandudno

The train idled at the station (a ticket inspector remembered seeing a lone lady inside one of the compartments in the passenger carriage and pulling down the blind – presumably not wishing to be seen, he had thought at the time). When the station clock reached 11.30 pm the train edged forward, travelling the short distance to the Admiralty Pier, to coincide with the arrival of the mailboat RMS *Connaught* from Ireland, due to dock there a few minutes later. The carriages were mostly empty, save for a scattering of passengers and a few railway employees.

Numerous postcards were printed showing Violet and the scene of her car crash

Onlookers survey the scene of the 'accident'

There seems little doubt that Violet was one of those few still on board the train for that short journey towards the pier; Inspector Johnson of the London and North-Western Railway's platform staff also noticed 'a well-dressed lady at Holyhead station just after the arrival of the 9 pm service from Bangor'

Later he observed the same lady at 11.30 pm, 'riding in an otherwise empty carriage to the Admiralty Jetty'. When asked later to describe the lady, he informed newspaper reporters that she was 'more than middle-height and wearing a red cloak. It was the same lady.'

Once the train was alongside the harbour, mail and other provisions were loaded and unloaded from it onto the *Connaught*, together with the few passengers wishing to travel across to Ireland at that late hour.

In 1909, due to increased tensions over the Irish Home Rule question, and the formation of agitating groups (as they were seen by the government in Westminster) such as Sinn Féin and the Irish Republican Brotherhood, it was not unusual to see a strengthened police presence at the dock. Detective Dunney, stationed near the Admiralty Pier by the Royal Irish Constabulary, noticed 'a lone lady alight from the train and walk towards the mailboat's berth.' The detective also remembered a youth, perhaps 14 years of age, standing close to her. Dunney was not sure if the two were together, but assumed that the youth might have been tipped by the lady to assist with her luggage.

Violet was next seen by Sergeant Hughes from the Board of Trade Police, as she was walking under the Admiralty Arch in the direction of the lighthouse, onto the jetty and towards the mailboat's berth. Sergeant Hughes, shown a portrait photograph of Violet a few days later, stated, 'I clearly recollect a lady coming from the train, heading towards the boat, who bore a striking likeness to this portrait of Miss Charlesworth.'

Neither Detective Dunney, Sergeant Hughes, nor anyone else, witnessed the lady returning and reboarding the train, which was being loaded with the Irish mail, ready for a 12.20 am departure from Holyhead for the return journey to Bangor, meaning she must have boarded the *Connaught*. Both men, who were experienced observers trained to spot the movements of 'Irish agitators', were certain that the lady had boarded the RMS *Connaught*, ready for its return voyage to Kingstown in Ireland.

It appears that the lady first waited patiently, her face lowered, while the remaining passengers disembarked from the ship, before boarding the now almost empty vessel. Although the *Connaught* was not due to set sail for a couple of hours, it was not unusual for passengers to board early. No doubt, in Violet's case, to escape the cold of the January night, and to secrete herself in a quiet corner of the ship.

There seems little doubt that it was Violet who boarded the mail steamer that night. There were no sightings of anyone matching her description returning to Bangor on the 12.20 am service either on the train or at the station. In addition, the stewardess on the *Connaught*, Miss Hughes, described witnessing a lady on board the vessel: 'There was a strange lady passenger travelling alone on that trip, who clearly wished to keep herself to herself. She was young, of slender build, rather pretty, fair, and well dressed. She was travelling in a long red coat, with a monogrammed portmanteau. She joined the steamer from the local train and left the boat immediately on arrival at Kingstown in Ireland.'

Why did she wish to travel to Ireland? A young lady sailing unescorted for Ireland in the middle of a dark January night … What did Violet have planned next?

Kingstown Harbour

11: The Ticking Clock

It may be that Violet, by choosing to stage the accident late on the evening of Saturday 2 January, displayed a great deal more cunning than might at first be realised. She would have been fully aware that all Welsh telegraph offices were open for only a very restricted period on Sunday mornings. With very few telephones available, this would present both the authorities and any journalists with a significant obstacle in swiftly circulating either the news of the story, or a description of Violet, providing her with a useful time advantage in making her escape. In fact, the problem was raised in the House of Commons a few months later by the Member of Parliament of Oswestry, William Bridgeman.[11]

There also appear to be two plausible reasons for Violet choosing to flee North Wales at such a late hour on that Saturday night, and to set sail for an island she had never visited before.

Conceivably, she hoped to hide on the Emerald Isle and ride out the storm of publicity caused by her apparent death in the motor-car accident and more probably she intended to catch the Sunday morning departure of the New York-bound Cunard Liner SS *Campania* from Queenstown (now Cobh) in County Cork. If Violet did intend to steam for New York, embarking from Ireland would have seemed a much safer choice, avoiding the risk of being recognised at a UK mainland port, where news of her motor-car 'accident' might have already been received. Clearly, Violet was also prepared to risk attracting the unwanted attention that a young female travelling without a husband or chaperone might arouse; in the Edwardian era this was, after all, an unusual circumstance.

Her cunningly envisioned plan was finally beginning to materialise.

It is most likely Violet had gambled that following an unsuccessful search of the coastline around Conwy she would be assumed to have been drowned and eventually be officially declared dead, thus enabling her family to claim her life insurance policy

SS *Campania*

---

11 No relation to the author!

(valued at several thousand pounds), simultaneously wiping away her debts and any allegations of fraud. After all, a dead person cannot face trial. Then, after a suitable length of time had elapsed, the Charlesworths, together with Violet's ample life insurance annuity, could relocate to another part of the country, one in which they were not known. Eventually, Violet could return under a pseudonym and begin a new life. Remember that she had already used many different names during her various money-making schemes, and that she possessed several bank accounts under different aliases. Perhaps the family as a whole even intended to move abroad; Violet had previously mentioned travelling to Europe, or to the Americas, or even as far as Australia.

If this was Violet's ultimate intention, then it seems almost certain that she would have planned to evade both justice and her creditors by beginning a new life overseas before slipping back into England once the sensation of her death had slipped from the headlines. In 1909 Ireland was part of the United Kingdom thus subject to British law, so it seems logical that Violet would have intended to place as much distance as possible between herself and the long of arm of the law. It is also highly probable that she proposed to travel under a false name. This was a considerably easier undertaking in 1909 than it is today. Little in the way of identification was required (the first official passports were not issued until eleven years later), and an immaculately attired lady like Violet would have been judged very much on her impeccable appearance.

The next step in the chain of events can only be surmised. There appear to be two possible alternatives. Perhaps Violet, alone in a strange land for the first time, and given the time to contemplate the enormity of her actions during the lonely and dark Irish Sea crossing, simply changed her mind and decided to return to the mainland. This seems unlikely, however. What almost certainly happened next was nothing more than a combination of unfortunate timing, poor planning, and bad luck.

The RMS *Connaught*, after battling headwinds and adverse currents in the Irish Sea, arrived at Kingstown a few minutes after 6 am on Sunday 3 January – well behind schedule. As the vessel, sounding its foghorn, squeezed through the narrow gap between the breakwaters, Violet knew she would be facing a race against time to catch a train south to Queenstown, enabling her to reach the New York-bound *Campania* in time. She collected her luggage and hurriedly crossed Harbour Road to the connecting railway station on the Dublin, Wicklow and Wexford Line. But unfortunately for Violet, the *Campania* was due to sail from Queenstown for New York at 10.30 am, and according to the timetable her rail journey there would be almost four hours, involving many stops. On starting her journey, it quickly became clear to Violet that the carriages would be crowded with workmen, soldiers, farmers, and families, all returning home after the New Year festivities, and all jostling for seats.

Nevertheless, it appears that Violet did leave Kingstown by train in a desperate attempt to reach Queenstown before eventually giving up. There is evidence to support this. First, from a passenger on the platform at Bray[12] railway station, nestled under the shadow of the Wicklow Mountains, who later recalled noticing, 'A pretty lady in a long red motor cloak' that morning, and, secondly, another witness, who said he had spotted, 'A distraught young lady in a long red coat alighting the train at Wexford, and then seeming to change her mind and waiting for the return train to Kingstown.' Both witnesses confirmed that the lady was carrying a handbag monogrammed with the initial C.

It seems, then, that Violet abandoned her journey at Wexford, when she realised the awful truth – she could not reach the *Campania* in time. Her dream of escaping her crippling debts was over.

Bray Railway Station

'What next?' Violet thought to herself. 'Remain in Ireland and wait for the next sailing to New York?' This would, however, necessitate a wait of at least a month, with limited financial resources, in a country she had not visited before, and with every chance of being discovered. Violet quickly realised that a swift return to the mainland was her only option, and that she must achieve this before newspaper reports reached Ireland and inevitably matched description of the lady from the Welsh motor-car accident with the woman seen boarding the ferry at Holyhead, to cross the Irish Sea.

Ironically, the American mail steamer *Snowdon* had departed Admiralty Pier at Holyhead en route for Kingstown two hours prior to the *Connaught*, and had Violet been aboard that vessel she would have had ample time to catch an earlier Cork connection and reach Queenstown Harbour in time for the *Campania*'s departure. It may be that she was unaware of the *Snowdon*'s earlier sailing time. However, it is more probable that she had ruled out the *Snowdon*, instead favouring the *Connaught*, on which public travel was readily permitted and on which her appearance would be far less conspicuous. Private individuals were not permitted to sail on the *Snowdon*, as it was a special service, chartered solely for the purposes of mail transportation. So, even if Violet had been granted special dispensation to board, her presence would have been evident in the extreme.

---

12 Bray would later be renamed Daly, to commemorate the 1916 Rising, and in honour of Edward Daly, a commandant with the Irish Volunteers.

Now, on that Sunday morning, as she sat on the windswept and open platform at Wexford station, sheltering as best she could from the chilling January breeze, Violet realised that if she returned to England questions would need to be answered. Her creditors might even be waiting at the Admiralty Pier in Holyhead or – even more terrifying – the police might be there too. There was also the prospect of public humiliation, a sobering thought in any era but especially so during the gilded Edwardian age. Momentum seemed to have shifted, and fate now appeared to be against Violet. Could she wrestle back control of her own destiny once more?

The next instalment in Violet's saga is a somewhat bizarre one, although it does demonstrate her ability to think on her feet and to improvise.

While Violet waited at Wexford railway station for the return service, that would take her north to Kingstown Harbour and back to the RMS *Connaught*, she was witnessed by a passer-by who noticed her exiting Wexford station and then turning left along the path to the shoreline.

Why had she chosen to leave the station?

Violet, separated from her family by the choppy waters of the Irish Sea, had of course no idea whether or not the intended outcome of the staged motor-car accident had been believed. Or even if Lillian and Albert had plucked up the required courage and resolve to keep their end of the bargain. Were the authorities searching for her body? How many witnesses had seen her? At least, Violet speculated as she made her away along the Wexford shoreline, it would take the police several days before they gave up the search for her body. And at this point it was still less than 24 hours since she had said goodbye to Lillian at Bangor station. So the story of her disappearance was unlikely to reach the Irish newspapers for a day or so. Even if the other passengers on the *Connaught*, or even on the train south from Kingstown, had noticed her, surely they would not be able to connect the story of a tragic motor-car accident in North Wales with the sighting of a young woman on board an Ireland-bound mail steamer, or on a railway platform in Wexford?

Violet, quick-witted, had realised that she had just a few precious hours in which to return to England before the readers of the *Wicklow People*, the *Wexford Newsletter*, or the myriad of Dublin newspapers learned the tragic tale of the lady in the red motor cloak. It would not be long before she was recognised, Violet conjectured. But what if the Kingstown–Holyhead steamer service was already under surveillance?

An idea had suddenly crossed her mind, as she sat waiting shivering in the morning mist on the railway platform at Wexford station. It was time for a little insurance. She wrote a note in pencil on a scrap of paper and carefully rolled it tightly before pushing it into an empty mineral water bottle and sealing the cork tightly. She glanced at the station clock, hid the bottle containing the message under the folds of her cloak, and left the station. She made her way along the shoreline until she found a quiet spot near the supports of the Wexford Bridge. Checking she was not overlooked, she left the bottle on the shoreline and hastily retreated to the railway station.

Several years earlier Violet had read the tragic tale of the vessel *Wildfire* lost at sea, and of the poignant message that had floated ashore. That story had formed part of the inspiration for her fictional inheritance. Ever resourceful, she had now found a way to utilise another part of that narrative. Inside the tightly sealed bottle Violet's carefully rolled scrap of paper read:

> To the press, police, and public of Ireland. Miss Violet Charlesworth presents her compliments and hopes she has not caused them any worry. Her journey from Cork to Rosslare has been very pleasant indeed, and she hopes to visit Ireland again soon. Au Revoir. This bottle was thrown through the porthole as our fine steamer was passing the great Tuskar Lighthouse. How powerful are these lights – V.G.C.

The message was designed to throw the authorities off the scent by creating the impression that she had boarded a different ferry, the Rosslare–Fishguard route, to disembark in South Wales. The bottle was sure to be discovered, Violet thought to herself, and it might have the welcome effect of redirecting the police's search in the wrong direction.

Unknown to Violet, however, just a few minutes earlier, another witness had noticed, 'A pretty lady in a long red coat', by the waterfront, close to the western side of the Wexford Bridge.

A lady closely matching Violet's description was then seen by the manager of a local hotel in Wexford, who noted: 'I served her breakfast at 10.50 am. I then saw the young lady return to Wexford Railway Station and board the northbound train to Kingstown.'

Tuskar Lighthouse

Once back in Kingstown, Violet must have booked a passage on the *Connaught*'s evening sailing to Holyhead. She then sheltered in the warmth of the shipping office waiting room for the remainder of the day, before making the return voyage to North Wales, arriving at Holyhead around 11.30 pm on the night of Sunday 3 January 1909. She disembarked, then made her way back along the Admiralty Pier and into Holyhead railway station. She had been away for a fraction under 24 hours. The station was quiet; there was no service until the early train on Monday morning. Violet warmed herself as best she could in the austere waiting room and closed her eyes.

It seems that Violet must have then made the return rail journey to Bangor station early on that Monday morning, as a lady exactly matching her description was witnessing purchasing newspapers at the station's bookstall during the morning of Monday 4 January. The kiosk attendant would later identify Violet from a newspaper photograph recalling: 'I had the strong impression that the lady wore a long red coat, and seemed to behave in a furtive manner, clearly not wishing to be noticed.'

Was Violet frantically scouring the early editions looking for any news of the accident? It is highly probable. She may have already telephoned Boderw to speak to her family. We know that her home in St Asaph was one of the first in the town to have an electric telephone connected; it had been installed in 1907. We can only imagine her trepidation as she nervously picked up the receiver in Holyhead and asked the operator to connect her to 'St Asaph 10, please'. If Violet did telephone, her mother Miriam would have surely been shocked, expecting her daughter to be en route to the Americas, with no means of communicating with her until she had disembarked in New York. However, Miriam would also have been able to inform Violet that the motor-car accident had been successfully staged, that Lillian and Albert had given the police a statement explaining how her body had been thrown into the sea, and that she must now lie low until the police gave up searching and public interest had subsided. Only then would the family be able to claim Violet's life insurance.

Violet, hoping that it would still be possible for her to slip away from North Wales unnoticed, carefully studied the newspapers at the station's bookstall that Monday morning. The headlines told the painful story of the Bradford unemployed who had recently left the town on a hunger march; many of them had taken part purely for the gift of free corned beef and a new pair of boots offered to all participants. Violet, not used to such privations, visibly winced at the thought. She scoured each page meticulously for any indication of her supposed death. Finally, despite the waves of fatigue, her spirits were lifted by a sketchy report in the first edition[13] of the *Welsh Evening Express and Evening Mail*. There, tucked away on page 4, between an analysis of the forthcoming Wales v. England rugby match at Cardiff Arms Park and a New Year greeting from the Maypole Tea Company ('the best tea, now only one shilling and fourpence!'), was nestled this short article:

---

13 In 1909 five editions of the newspaper were published every day, their stories updated continuously with each new edition.

OVER A PRECIPICE !
LADY FLUNG FROM A MOTOR INTO THE SEA

A shocking motor-car accident, involving the death of one lady and injuries to another and to a chauffeur, occurred near Llandudno on Saturday night. At nine o'clock a large car, containing the two Misses Charlesworth, of Boderw, St. Asaph, was going round Penmaenbach Point on the coastline, when it suddenly swerved aside and ran into a recess between the rocks. The force of the impact flung one lady through the glass front of the car and over a precipice into the sea 60ft. below, causing her death. The body has not yet been recovered, having been washed out to sea by the tide. The other Miss Charlesworth and the chauffeur were injured, but not dangerously. The car was scarcely damaged.

Evening Express and Evening Mail, 4th January 1909

Although the report would soon be syndicated to many other newspapers across Britain (a system commonplace at that time), it would only begin to appear outside Wales over the following days. First in the English newspapers and then, in the weeks that followed, further afield. Violet realised the importance of this point. No one would as yet be searching the English countryside looking for her, and providing that she was not seen, it would be assumed that she had drowned following the accident.

Violet conjectured that she probably had up to 48 hours to place as much distance as possible between herself and the scene of the 'accident'. At this stage, and from the tone of the newspaper report, she had no reason to believe that the story of her death in the motor-car accident was already being questioned by the authorities. To Violet, it was imperative that she was not spotted by anyone. Thinking as quickly as ever, she secreted herself in a quiet corner of the railway station, thumbed a copy of Bradshaw's Railway Guide, and carefully planned her next move.

She had several hundred pounds remaining from the pawning of her jewellery and her travelling trunk, and she had a few precious hours in which to escape unnoticed. To keep warm on that cold January morning, she pulled up the fur collar of her distinctive crimson motor cloak, grateful for the warmth it provided.

12: The Shut-Out

Although Violet would later offer a different version of the days that followed the motor-car accident (ostensibly to imply that her actions were instinctive, rather than pre-planned), it is most probable that the actual chain of events unfolded as follows.

After her return to Bangor railway station from Ireland, early on the morning of Monday 4 January 1909, she boarded a train to Conwy. On her arrival there, she did not visit the ticket office to purchase a ticket for her onward journey – presumably to avoid being noticed in her distinctive red motor cloak. Instead, she swiftly crossed to another platform and found an empty carriage on the connecting train to Chester, where she purchased a ticket on board, which would have attracted far less attention. On arriving in Chester, Violet boarded yet another service, and made the 80-minute journey to Snow Hill station in Birmingham. Again, she felt safer knowing that the carriages were quieter than usual; many people had yet to return to work following the New Year break.

Once at Snow Hill, Violet alighted and made her way across the extensive concourse to the left luggage office. Snow Hill station in 1909 was a much grander affair than it appears today, rivalling New Street as Birmingham's main transport hub. At the time of Violet's visit it was being rebuilt and refitted, to incorporate a new large booking hall with an arched glass roof, and

Birmingham Snow Hill (early 1900s)

lavish waiting rooms fitted with oak bars. The main platform area was protected from the elements by a large glass and steel overall roof, with a concourse leading to two large island platforms containing four through platforms and four further bay platforms. Although Snow Hill station was far busier than the quiet branch lines from North Wales, this suited Violet; the hustle and bustle of the ongoing building work coupled with the thronging population of Birmingham going about their daily business meant she could easily blend into the crowd.

Violet enquired at the luggage office for a large box she had forwarded a few days earlier to be collected by a Mrs Miller, from Craven Arms in

Shropshire. The clerk eyed her up and down and asked for the name on the box. Violet repeated, 'Mrs Miller.' She was informed by the official that there was nothing there for her, and was referred to New Street station instead. Violet, annoyed at this inconvenience, made her way from the relative warmth of the station into the cold January air and hastily made her way through Cathedral Square to New Street station. It was now late morning, and the lamplighters had extinguished the gas street lights in the square. Without her tam o' shanter hat (which had been left in the Minerva) she had only the silk mackintosh hood from her motor cloak to keep her hair dry and her ears warm. Once inside New Street station she made enquiries for her box at the left luggage office. The clerk requested that she sign the receipt book while he retreated to the rear to locate her package. This time, the clerk was successful, and returned to the desk, carrying a box. In the meantime, Violet had signed the receipt book in the name of Mrs Miller. However, she refused to give the clerk either an address or the required letter of instruction authorising her to collect the box. He then apologetically informed her that it was railway policy that without such a written instruction he could not release the box to her. She responded impatiently, 'The box belongs to my brother, to whom I must telegraph to gain his permission before I can give you an address.'

This stance seemed to have little effect on the railway official and Violet left, announcing to the clerk, 'I will need to go to the telegraph office.' After her departure, he glanced at the receipt book and noticed that she had crossed out the name 'Mrs Miller' before leaving. Violet never returned to collect the box, which would remain in storage at the station until her description, coupled with the story of her motor-car accident and her disappearance, had reached the Birmingham newspapers.

Thwarted in her efforts and clearly distressed at being unable to reclaim the contents of her box, Violet boarded a train northbound towards Crewe. She would later claim (in an attempt to appear contrite and remorseful) that at this point in her adventure she had considered returning to Boderw and confessing everything: 'You can clearly imagine my feelings of distress. As I reached Crewe I felt an impulse to go back, but I had not the courage.'

On arrival at Crewe she asked a porter for details of trains to Scotland. After deliberating between Edinburgh and Glasgow, she booked a third-class ticket on the 1.04 pm service to Glasgow, and settled into an empty carriage where she drifted into a fitful sleep, broken by the occasional jolting of couplings and the noise of passengers boarding the train and alighting at various stops on the route. From Wigan northwards, the carriages were busy and Violet could not rest, despite her extreme fatigue. Eventually she gave up any attempt to sleep, her mind racing, filled with potential scenarios and possible strategies through which she could extradite herself from this tricky situation, entirely of her own making.

The train – a slow one with many stops – finally arrived at a bustling Glasgow Central Station around 8 pm on Monday 4 January. Violet left the station with her suitcase and checked into the nearby North British Hotel on the north side of George Square. The luxury hotel, previously known as the Queen's Hotel, had been acquired by the North British Railway Company in 1903 and renamed accordingly. Violet, who had been a guest there during her last visit to Scotland, was made welcome once again. In fact, she had left some luggage there in 1908, and she gratefully collected it from the concierge. Violet then took some refreshment in the hotel's restaurant before retiring to her bedroom for the night.

Interestingly, for the entire length of her journey from Conwy to Chester, to Birmingham, to Crewe, and on to Glasgow, Violet was not witnessed by anyone as being in possession of the large portmanteau which she had taken to Ireland and back. The most likely explanation is that she had contacted someone at Boderw in advance, arranging for it to be collected from her

North British Hotel, Glasgow

on her arrival at Conwy, and swapping it for a more practicable carrying case. A few days later, following the public revelation of her staged accident and subsequent disappearance, a handful of witnesses came forward, all claiming to have seen Violet loitering at Conwy railway station that morning. It was widely thought by many locals at the time that she had simply returned to Boderw and was in hiding there, with the full complicity of her family. Later events would, however, prove that this was not the case.

Meanwhile, now feeling a little more at ease, Violet awoke in her Glasgow hotel room early on the morning of Tuesday 5 January. Her mind was clearer after the fatigue of the past three days. At breakfast she sat reading *The Scotsman* newspaper. Fortuitously, she noticed, the front pages seemed to be preoccupied with the Messina earthquake in Italy, and with the arrest of Oscar Slater in New York for the Glasgow West End Murder. Perhaps, Violet reasoned, the story of her accident and apparent death would not be deemed interesting enough for the Scottish press? Then as she thumbed the pages, her heart sank. She saw, buried at the bottom of page 5, a small Stop Press announcement:

THE WELSH MOTOR FATALITY: A Penmaenmawr telegram states that the body of Miss Charlesworth, reported to have been thrown over a cliff in a motor accident on Saturday, has not been recovered. No further information regarding the occurrence could be obtained, as the other occupants of the car left Penmaenmawr on Sunday.

Perhaps even Scotland would not be far enough away. Violet looked furtively around her. Suddenly her eyes were drawn to her red motor cloak on the chair beside her. The distinctive nature of the coat, coupled with its colour and style (which often drew admiring glances) suddenly dawned on her. She hurriedly finished her breakfast and, after making enquiries at the hotel reception, made her way to the Glasgow agent for Pullar's.

A sign in Pullar's shop window advertised exactly the service Violet had been hoping for:

PULLAR'S DYERS

Daily parcels delivered when necessary. Items returned by special arrangement within a week, cleaning or dyeing. Drapery, Dressmaking and Millinery.

Violet passed her crimson motor cloak across the counter to the sales agent, requesting that it be dyed blue. The young man asked for her name, Violet responded, 'Mackay, Miss Mackay.' When asked if she wished to collect the coat or have it forwarded, Violet requested that the newly dyed item should be forwarded to Oban Post

Edwardian Lady's Motor Cloak

Office, marked 'To be collected by Miss Mackay'. After leaving the store, she purchased a few more items, before checking out of the North British Hotel leaving an unpaid bill of £2, which she promised to return and pay later. Following a consultation of Bradshaw's Railway Guide, she quickly made her way along a busy Buchanan Street to the railway station that bore its name. This station, which served the connecting routes to the north, was the lesser known of Glasgow's main stations, so Violet hoped it might be less busy. However, as she made her way through the large iron gates and into the station concourse, the platforms and ticket office were already filled with passengers. The station clock outside the entrance showed the time to be just past 1 pm.

Buchanan Street Station

Violet approached the narrow opening in the ticket office window and requested a single third-class ticket on the 2 pm service to Oban. The attendant informed her that she would need to change at Stirling, and that there would not be much time to make the connection. Violet nodded and made her way to the platform.

The service was late in departing due to the recent adverse weather which had necessitated some clearance of snow from the lines around Dunblane. This did indeed result in Violet missing her connection at Stirling. Nevertheless, she felt that a huge weight had been lifted from her shoulders. She was away from the hurly-burly of the busy city. There was now significantly less chance of being recognised or noticed, she thought to herself. So, unperturbed by the slight delay, she booked into the adjacent Station Hotel for the night.

After a more restful night, she awoke early and returned to Stirling station before the sun had risen on the morning of Wednesday 6 January. It was dark and bitterly cold, but Violet did not mind. The station was empty, save for a handful of horse carts loading and unloading produce aboard the waiting wagons, and her 5.20 am train to the west coast was empty too. Violet boarded it, and secreted herself in an empty compartment. By 9 am, as the watery winter sun was at last beginning to rise above McCaig's Tower and Battery Hill, the train pulled into Oban railway station, and Violet, virtually unnoticed on that quiet January morning, took the short walk from the station to the harbour. Once there, she boarded the new motorised mailboat, *Lochinvar*, destined for Craignure and Tobermory on the Isle of Mull, and soon she was sailing westward, away from the shores of the British mainland, for the second time in just four days.

Violet clearly intended to ride out the inevitable media interest in her disappearance by concealing herself in a quiet backwater, hoping that any public speculation and official scrutiny into the story of her disappearance would quickly wane. However, the early morning editions of the northern newspapers all carried the following piece, which already seemed to hint at some doubt in the authenticity of her cover story:

WELSH MOTOR TRAGEDY

THE SEARCH FOR THE BODY OF MISS CHARLESWORTH.

£20 REWARD OFFERED.

The remarkable motor-car accident which occurred at Penmaenbach, on the coast road of North Carnarvon [*sic*], and which resulted in a wealthy young lady named Miss Violet Gordon Charlesworth being thrown from the vehicle over the cliff into the sea, continues to attract attention throughout the country. Her social position, the fact that the body has not yet been recovered despite prolonged search, and that some unusual incidents occurred subsequent to the accident, have invested the circumstances with an unusual degree of interest. A lad scrambled down to the beach, and waded through the water, which was then not very deep (the tide was ebbing), but still could find no trace of the unfortunate lady. The only thing discovered was her hat at the foot of the cliff …

A reward of £20 has been offered by Mrs. Charlesworth for the recovery of the body of her daughter.[14] The motor-car was removed from Penmaenmawr last night. The springs are bent, and the steering gear would work, but was slightly bent. The switch was turned on and the brakes had not been applied.

Meanwhile, at the Charlesworths' family home in St Asaph, Miriam and Lillian refused to entertain any callers. Any person knocking at the

---

14 The story that the Charlesworths had offered a reward seems to have been erroneous, and was soon replaced with perplexed newspaper speculation questioning why this outwardly well-to-do family had not offered any reward at all, or indeed, shown any apparent concern, on behalf of their missing family member. According to one news reporter, they appeared 'to be remarkable in their inaction or grief'.

door of Boderw was greeted by the family's maid, who would inform them tersely that 'Violet's mother and sister are far too ill to receive visitors'. Any attempts to access the grounds at Boderw without permission were met with the ferocious barking of Violet's dogs. When Superintendent Rees called to question Lillian the maid even refused to accept his business card, claiming that she did not recognise him.

It seems that the intense public interest in the case had taken the family by surprise. Although in 1909 the grounds of Boderw were surrounded by a high wall, thick shrubbery, and a heavy gate, this did not deter an ever-increasing throng of spectators from gathering outside on the corner of the Bodelwyddan and Rhuddlan roads. From the comparative safety of the upstairs windows, Miriam could see that a sizeable number of those assembled beyond the walls were newspaper reporters (both local and national), and that others were anxious St Asaph merchants and shopkeepers, all with outstanding accounts in the name of Violet Charlesworth. The remainder were members of the public, all eager for an early look at the potential stars of a sensational story.

ALL THE PEOPLE IN THE WONDERFUL CHARLESWORTH CASE.

Group showing all the people in the wonderful Charlesworth case. (A) Miss Violet Charlesworth. (B) Mrs Coulson ("Miss Lilian Charlesworth"). (C) Mr. Gratton, who, with "Miss Lilian," went to Scotland to identify the lady calling herself Miss Macleod. (D) Mr. Charlesworth. (E) Mrs. Charlesworth. (F) Dr. Miller, a friend of the family. The small photograph, which was taken by Miss Violet Charlesworth, shows Watts, the chauffeur. The large photograph is by D. Whyte.

The whole family

According to the *Northern Chronicle*, at an unknown point between the morning of Sunday 3 January and Tuesday 5th, Albert had managed to slip away from Boderw under cover of darkness and post a letter to a Mr Sydney Charles Holloway, an employee of the Minerva Motor Company, in Tottenham Court Road, London. It appears that the letter was designed to help strengthen the Charlesworths' version of events on the night of the accident, should awkward questions be asked. On the strength of that letter from Albert, and under instruction from the Minerva Motor Company to assess the damage to the motor car – which, of course, had only been hired by Violet, and on which a large outstanding bill remained – Mr Holloway set off for North Wales immediately. He was also instructed by his employers to visit Superintendent Rees at Conwy Police Station following his examination of the motor car.

Holloway and Albert had previously become friends through Albert's associations with the London motor trade, and Holloway now informed Rees that the Charlesworths had all been unwell since the day of the accident, and also averred that after seeing the motor car in question, he could now testify to the events of 2 and 3 January.

This seemed to placate the police, in the short term at least. Holloway then issued a statement to the gathered pressmen,

> I am Mr Sydney C. Holloway of Tottenham Court Road, London. I called upon Superintendent Rees at Conwy last night, respecting the singular motor accident at Penmaenbach. From information I gave him, the Superintendent is now inclined to accept the original account of what occurred. Mrs Charlesworth, her husband, and surviving daughter have all been ill since the accident. These facts explain the apparent indifference of the family regarding the missing lady's fate.

Although Holloway's statement to the police may have temporarily persuaded the authorities that the accident was a genuine one, it seems that others were not so easily convinced. More ominous for Violet and her family was the rapidly increasing newspaper speculation regarding Violet's extravagant expenditure and lifestyle. The newshounds, it seems, had picked up the scent of a good story.

Meanwhile, the local boatmen in the Conwy estuary searched the waters again on Monday 4 and Tuesday 5 January, but to no avail. However, with no reward offered by the Charlesworth family for the recovery of Violet's body and the police refusing to guarantee any recompense from the public purse, the number of boatmen willing to participate rapidly dwindled.

In addition, suspicions had been aroused regarding the seemingly trivial damage to Violet's vehicle. and after reading the sensational details of the horrific accident in the newspapers, Holloway fully expected the vehicle to be undrivable, and had already arranged to have it transported to London by goods train. However, on inspecting the Minerva, he was able to give the following description of the surprisingly light damage sustained:

> The front axle of the offside wheel is set back two inches. The front windscreen is smashed. So far as I can see at present, there is no damage to the machinery of the car and, although the steering is little stiff, the vehicle is quite driveable, and I have just driven it back here from Penmaenmawr. I intended to put it on the train for London, but have decided now to drive it to London instead.

Holloway, like many of the locals, concluded that the damage to the vehicle simply did not reflect the alleged ferocity of the accident. The apparently indecent haste in which Albert had contacted the Minerva Motor Company to arrange for Holloway to travel from London to North Wales in order that the car could be inspected and collected, also puzzled many onlookers. Although according to the Charlesworth family, Albert was supposedly too ill and too distraught over the loss of Violet to speak to either the police or press, he was clearly rational enough to contact a garage in London regarding something as trivial as minor damage to a motor car. Suspicions grew that the family wanted the Minerva removed from the scene as quickly as possible in order that the rather superficial damage would not be questioned.

The young boy who had waded out into the cold water to search for Violet was also perplexed. He too struggled to conceive how anyone could either drown or be washed away in such shallow water. Yet, for the time being at least, Superintendent Rees appeared to be satisfied with the Charlesworth family's explanation. It seemed that the enterprising newspaper reporters who were gathering in the area would need to dig a little deeper themselves, if the truth was to be unearthed.

On Tuesday 5 January the *North Wales Times* was among the first to cast doubt on the likelihood of the crash being a legitimate accident,

> Another point worth noting concerns the spot where the smash occurred. It is very remarkable that it should have happened exactly where it did. If the sudden swerve into the wall had been taken a few yards higher up or a few yards lower down the road, and if the protecting wall had given way, the car would have inevitably fallen forty or fifty feet over the retaining wall on to the beach below, and would have been smashed to splinters, whereas by a mysterious chance it went through the wall at a point where it could conveniently come to rest on the ledge at the top of the rock.

In the days that followed, pressure mounted on the family as the gathering reporters probed deeper and deeper into the circumstances of the accident and the strange behaviour of the Charlesworth family. On 6 January, the *North Wales Times* again questioned the unusual comings and goings at Boderw immediately following the crash:

> The various conflicting statements attributed to the chauffeur Watts, which do not tally with Miss Lillian Charlesworth's version, are much commented upon. In addition, there are many other circumstances which increase the difficulties of accepting the published accounts of the accident as accurate.

The *Morning Leader* newspaper was undoubtedly the most proactive in seeking to uncover the truth behind the strange motor-car accident and the supposed death of Violet. The paper quickly determined that

> during the last twelve months Miss Violet Gordon Charlesworth has incurred liabilities running into thousands of pounds, and … quite recently a London tradesman obtained a judgement against her in the County Court for a considerable sum. A fortnight ago, bailiffs were put in at Boderw, St Asaph, where Miss Charlesworth has recently been living, where goods were removed by order of a London solicitor.

Meanwhile, despite being supposedly consumed with grief and shock, Violet's father, David, had not been idle. By 7.45 am on the morning of Monday 4 January he had already managed to wire the following telegram to several tradesmen with whom his daughter held outstanding accounts:

> 7.45. 4th January.
> Miss Violet Gordon Charlesworth killed in motor accident near Conwy on Saturday night. D. Charlesworth.

The strange relationship between Joseph Gratton and the Charlesworth family provided the assembled newshounds with another angle of interest. As mentioned previously, Joseph had been the Charlesworths' neighbour and landlord at Foryd Lodge when the family had first relocated to Rhyl. However, by 1908 he had become a widower and had moved into Boderw as a tenant of the Charlesworths. This may have been in lieu of monies owed to him by Violet, who had also borrowed a considerable sum from him during the previous three years. He appears to have been easily influenced by the family, having become embroiled in their attempts to file a dubious court injunction against the maritime salvage operation in the Rhyl estuary during 1906/7, and removing Lillian and Albert from Gwynfa, against police instructions, on the night of the car crash. No doubt Joseph had a strong affection for Violet, as he often accompanied her on long motoring trips around the country. He was 15 years Violet's senior, and was in all probability flattered and charmed by her attentions (as were Dr Hughes Jones and no doubt many others).

Joseph's possible motives towards Violet will be explored later in this book; however, at this stage he seemed content to act as the family's unofficial spokesman at Boderw in the face of the numerous journalists that had gathered outside like vultures.

An impromptu press conference was reluctantly agreed to by the Charlesworth family for the afternoon of 5 January, three days after Violet's disappearance. Joseph presented himself at the gates of Boderw, appearing rather uncomfortable and looking much older than his 40 years. He spoke through the bars in the locked gates to a clutch of impatient of newspapermen, angry tradesmen (all with overdue accounts), and the many curious members of the public who had assembled outside. They, no doubt, would have noticed the To LET sign which had already been placed at the entrance of Boderw by the house agents The conclusion was obvious – either the Charlesworths could not afford the rent or they intended to leave in haste, or both. Would Joseph Gratton be able to calm their growing hostility?

13: The Flaw

The dialogue between Joseph Gratton and the various reporters, recorded verbatim, appeared in numerous newspapers across the land during the following days:

> Q: How do you know the family, Mr Gratton?
> A: I am a friend of the family, and my home at present is at Boderw.
> Q: When can we speak to Miss [Lillian] Charlesworth and Albert?
> A: Miss Charlesworth and Watts are very ill in bed presently.
> Q: Is it possible that they have serious injuries?
> A: No, only a slight bruise on the inside of one of Watts' legs.
> Q: How old is the missing lady?
> A: Miss Violet Charlesworth would have been 25 years of age next week.
> Q: Why have instructions not been given for a search for the body?
> A: Instructions have been issued this day, asking the Rhyl Police to print handbills detailing a description of Miss Violet Charlesworth, and offering a reward of £20 for the recovery of her body.
> Q: Mr Gratton, why did you travel to Penmaenmawr at four o'clock on Sunday morning to take the young lady and the chauffeur away?
> A: In consequence of a telephone message from the local police, and out of consideration, both for Miss Charlesworth and her aged parents, both of whom are in feeble health. Mrs Charlesworth suffers from a diseased heart.
> Q: By taking Miss Charlesworth away at such an early hour, did you not prevent Superintendent Rees from making the inquiries he had arranged to make as to how the accident really occurred?
> A: They were too dazed to give a proper account.
> Q: Did Dr Moreton Roberts sanction their removal?

The question was repeated several times, until Joseph reluctantly responded:

A: No, he did not exactly sanction their removal.

Q: Have they given any account of how the accident happened? [*Pause*] Mr Gratton, have they given any account of how the accident happened?

The question was put to Joseph three times, but he did not reply.

He then raised his hand into the air abruptly, signalling that the interview was at an end. With that, he hastily retreated into the sanctuary of the house. Several of his answers had been misleading, although how far he had been taken into the Charlesworths' scheming may never be fully known.

Over the next 48 hours the British public and press clamoured for more answers. Frustratingly, the police appeared to be inactive (perhaps hoping that the discovery of a body might vindicate their inertia). In the interim the newspapers were not cautious in filling the vacuum by revealing the true extent of Violet's extravagant lifestyle:

> Miss Violet Charlesworth took a five years' lease of The Hall at Calne, in March last, but never resided there. Extensive alterations to the house were carried out at her orders, and those who did the work have pressed of late unsuccessfully for payment. One tradesman whose bill was about £200 obtained a writ of County Court Judgement in the High Court. This writ was served on Miss Charlesworth at the Inns of Court Hotel, London, last week. The Hall is now in possession of the bailiffs.

The story of Violet's disappearance – far from remaining contained, as she might have hoped, as merely a strictly local tale of tragedy – began to spread to the London, Irish, and Scottish newspapers, and from there across the Atlantic to the Americas, even prompting editorial comment from an anonymous 'North Wales source' who stated in the *London Evening News*:

> As a result of inquiries made yesterday, I find that the missing young lady was financially embarrassed to quite an exceptional degree, and that a short time ago, when in Liverpool, she wrote to a friend intimating her intention of leaving the country this month. Indeed, she was to have been a defendant at the Rhyl County Court this month in an action for the recovery of £500 in which she was indebted.

The British press, now sensing a different story, had begun to speculate that the young lady was missing, not dead. The chase to find Violet had begun. Which newspaper would be the first to discover what had really happened to Violet Charlesworth? Now, in addition to the story being an entertaining mystery, it had become a circulation war.

Meanwhile, the outwardly stoic Charlesworth family, who appeared to be unwilling to leave Boderw, had battened down the hatches as they endeavoured to deny anyone entry at the home. Cassie Hughes, the family's cook, was kept a virtual prisoner inside the house for seven days, despite requesting to leave. Her enforced incarceration implies that provisions were plentiful inside Boderw – perhaps the Charlesworths had anticipated such a siege of their property?

In the interim, in an impatient attempt to move the story forward, the *Morning Leader* newspaper offered a £50 reward (now £7,500) for information leading to the discovery of Violet's whereabouts:

£50 REWARD

Miss Violet Gordon Charlesworth of 'Boderw', St Asaph (Flintshire), 'The Hall', Calne (Wilts), and Flowerburn House, Fortrose, has disappeared mysteriously. It has been given out that she dashed over the cliff at Penmaenbach Point, near Llandudno, following a motor-car accident there on the night of Saturday, Jan. 2. The body has not yet been found. Her return is anxiously awaited by her relatives and friends and by business firms in various parts of the country who have had dealings with her.

Unsurprisingly, public attention now reached fever pitch. Readers of Britain's many newspapers began to report possible sightings of Violet across the length and breadth of the country. First, it was rumoured that she had escaped to America, no doubt fuelled by the emerging news that she had been witnessed boarding a ferry to Ireland. Next came the startling news, revealed in an anonymous letter from someone at St Asaph to the *North Wales Chronicle*, that Violet had in fact been hidden away inside Boderw on the night of the car accident, and had remained there ever since:

I have good authority for stating that the family of Miss Violet Charlesworth are aware of the whereabouts of "the demure young lady" who was stated to have lost her life in that peculiar motor accident which is supposed to have taken place near here. She is not many miles from me at the time I am sending you this message, and I confidently predict that before many days have passed this will be an admitted fact. The house of mystery, as Boderw, the family residence here, is now called, is guarded day and night. The blinds are still drawn, but behind them hovers, I have reason to believe, the central figure of the amazing tragedy, which has turned to farce in such an extraordinary way. Entrance to the house is naturally very difficult to obtain, and many people who have tried have found dogs sufficiently fierce to prevent any desire to gain a closer acquaintanceship.

While the gathering swarm outside Boderw swelled on a daily basis, Violet remained blissfully unaware as she boarded the morning mail boat, the *Lochinvar*, for Craignure on the Isle of Mull. Her journey was undisturbed. Although the wind was cold, the weather was fine and settled, and the boat was quiet; it was January and the tourist season still many months away. There was no pier at Craignure at that time so Violet had to wait offshore for the small launch, *Lochaline*, to pull up alongside *Lochinvar* to ferry passengers and provisions into the harbour. She did not seem to mind, despite the chilling breeze. It was now Wednesday 6 January. Violet was almost 400 miles from the scene of the accident, and as far as she was aware no one had noticed her or recognised her. Perhaps the Isle of Mull would be a safe place for her to hide until the storm of speculation had passed. She knew no one on the island, but thanks to a summer visit there in 1907 she was familiar with its geography.

Crowd invades Miss Charlesworth's garden at St Asaph

Violet arranged transportation to the only town on Mull, Tobermory, situated on the northern edge of the island at the entrance to the Sound of Mull. On arrival in the town's Main Street, she quickly located a pleasant four-storey hotel, the Mishnish, which offered views across the harbour. Her appearance surprised the hotel keeper, who rarely let rooms in January when demand was usually so low. Nevertheless, Violet was quickly offered a comfortable room and signed the visitors' book under the name 'Miss Margaret MacLeod'. She explained that she was visiting Mull to find some long-term rural accommodation, perhaps on a farm, where she would be allowed to kennel her dogs. The hotel keeper suggested one or two potential names and places, for which Violet expressed

'Officials cannot enter Charlesworths' home'

her gratitude. She then took refuge in her bedroom, after four gruelling days of travelling. Sleepily gazing out at the fishing boats in the harbour through the draughty sash window, Violet tried hard to concentrate, as she contemplated her next move.

At least she could now rest safely in the quiet backwater of Tobermory, following her exhausting journey. She slowly closed her heavy eyelids …

Meanwhile in North Wales, the true extent of the Charlesworth family's debts began to materialise. The following advertisement appeared in the *Welsh Coast Pioneer*:

> St Asaph: – Boderw to be Let, a charming Country Residence, close to St Asaph, three reception and eight bedrooms, kitchen, etc; good stabling and motorhouse, also large garden. Good railway service to Liverpool, Manchester, etc. Apply St Asaph Telephone 10.'

In the meantime, sightings of Violet continued unabated. A huge crowd gathered at Worthing railway station in Sussex after a woman wearing a red coat was seen arriving on a train. The press immediately made enquiries, and to their delight discovered that a Lady Frances Charlesworth lived in the town. Assuming a family relationship, a large crowd assembled outside her residence, forcing her to issue a statement denying that she was Violet Charlesworth, or in any way related to her.

A Mr Hubert Charlesworth of Whitford, Holywell, was compelled to insist that several Welsh newspapers publish the following:

> DISCLAIMER. Mr Hubert Charlesworth, Wern, Whitford, Holywell, North Wales, has asked us to express, through our columns, his thanks for kind enquiries with regard to the late accident near Penmaenmawr, but wishes us to announce that the parties affected are in no way connected with himself or family.

Cartoon of the Day.

"I lay and pay 3 to 1 nobody finds the lady."

Next, a mysterious postcard was received by the police in Newcastle:

> Newcastle-on-Tyne, Jan 1909. – I have come here, and am going to commit suicide. My body will be found in the River Tyne – Violet Gordon Charlesworth. Please inform my relations.

Cartoon of the Day.

The postcard was unstamped and bore a Newcastle postmark. Although it may have been another clever distraction technique by Violet, the police considered it to be nothing more than a hoax.

In Ipswich, the story of a young woman looking to rent an apartment caused another press stir. The mysterious lady had placed a 10-shilling deposit on a flat but had never returned. Several locals swore that the lady matched Violet's description; however, she was never traced.

THE MISSING LADY FOUND BY 'Erasmic' Soap

"The Dainty Soap for Dainty Folk."

On Friday 8 January, with no confirmed sightings of Violet yet reported, two local merchants in North Wales managed to obtain a *sine die* adjournment (a

The Missing Imp, a popular cartoon of the time, detailing the search the Violet

Violet, a newspaper ink drawing used in the search for the missing woman

postponement with no specified end date), for a county court appearance that Violet had been ordered to make regarding her many unpaid accounts. In that area at least, most people seemed convinced that Violet was very much alive and still due to receive her huge inheritance – and was therefore still obliged to pay her outstanding debts.

On Saturday 8 January matters took a more sinister turn when the Welsh newspapers reported that a body of a young woman had been discovered in the River Dee. The revelations prompted a flurry of reporters' telephone calls to Boderw. After numerous attempts, a correspondent from the *Daily Mail* was finally rewarded for his persistence. Joseph Gratton, again acting as the Charlesworths' spokesman, appeared strangely uninterested by the news, especially considering that the family still claimed to believe that Violet had vanished into the Irish Sea a week earlier:

'Mr Gratton, have you or the family heard that the body of a young lady has been recovered from the River Dee?'

'The family have not heard of it,' he replied.

'Mr Gratton, may we call on you at Boderw to discuss it further?'

'It is no use you coming to see me here unless you can produce authoritative evidence that the body of Miss Violet Charlesworth has been found.'

The reporter probed a little further: 'Will you tell me why you keep Boderw locked and will not see anyone?'

Only silence followed, as the exchange operator informed the reporter, 'I'm sorry, Sir, no 10 St Asaph has rung off.'

As the days passed, further sightings of Violet were reported across the country. An attractive lady in a red coat was seen viewing a property for rent in London, and another lady, similarly attired, caused a commotion when she boarded the Rosslare to Fishguard ferry, then a London-bound express. This information was speedily wired to the capital and, in anticipation that the lady was indeed Violet, a sizeable number of curious reporters gathered at Paddington station in the hope of meeting the mysterious runaway. They were understandably disappointed to discover a much older, and somewhat bemused, lady. In fact, so many sightings of ladies in long red coats were reported that the phenomenon caused a seismic change in female fashions. In a quirky and unexpected subplot, red motor cloaks (until then considered a must for fashionable Edwardian ladies) saw a huge slump in demand. Instead, across the cities of England department stores reported a boom in the sale of darker cloaks and coats, as discerning ladies quickly tired of the suspicious looks and accusing glances which their red coats had so suddenly attracted.

On 10 January, after reading Violet's description in the morning papers, a hotel manager in Kingstown, Ireland, recalled noticing a lady with a red coat and large travelling chest departing by the Holyhead-bound ferry in the early evening of Sunday 3 January. He said that he was certain the woman was Violet.

On the morning of the Sunday 11 January the skipper of the Irish fishing vessel *Jenny* discovered Violet's message in a bottle just off the coast at Rosslare. The bottle, still tightly sealed, was passed to the Wexford police, who on opening it dismissed the incident as another hoax, even though the writing on the note was identified as being that of a woman – and later was discovered to be very similar in style to Violet's. In this era of assumed male intellectual superiority, little credence was given in a woman's ability to create such a subtle and well-thought-out distraction tactic.

A contemporary advertisement for Vinolia soap cashed in on Violet's disappearance

Another possibility which could explain Violet's sudden impulse to place that message in a bottle may have originated from the other woman dressed in a red coat (who ultimately boarded the Rosslare–Fishguard ferry and was mistaken for Violet). Perhaps Violet noticed her on the station platform, or even shared a railway carriage with her, and noticed the label on her luggage. There is even a possibility that Violet did not leave the bottle on the shoreline in Wexford at all, but instead confided in the mysterious other lady and asked her to throw it over the side as the ferry passed the Tuskar Lighthouse. It is intriguing to speculate on the meticulous and cunning nature of Violet's mind.

However, the opinion of those in authority in the Edwardian era seldom credited the 'fairer sex' with such a cool-headed and thorough attention to detail. Instead, the establishment was routinely horrified and distracted by the behaviour of those women involved in the suffragette movement. In fact, it would be no exaggeration to state that the male establishment's opinion of the female sex had sunk to its lowest ebb. On the same day that Violet's message in a bottle was discovered, many newspapers also reported the story of Lord Avebury's speech to the House of Lords with as much contempt as they reported the Violet Charlesworth story,

> These women are viragos who disturb public meetings, and who brawl in the House of Commons, bite stewards, and kick policeman, have no claim to represent, nor are they entitled to speak in the name of the women of England. I am not satisfied that the majority of Englishwomen even wish for the franchise.

A week had now passed since Violet's disappearance. There had been many claimed sightings, but none that could be confirmed by the authorities.

Meanwhile, the saga in St Asaph had been continuing apace. The family's behaviour had been odd, to say the least. The many creditors gathered outside Boderw presented a united, and concerned, front. Many of them had realised that their outstanding bills, cheques, and IOUs had been signed by Violet alone. If she had been killed or had vanished without a trace and they wished to receive any sort of financial redress, they would need to prove two things. First, that the whole family had benefited from Violet's activities, and secondly that the entire family had been complicit in the affair.

The newspapers had little more to add to the story other than the convenient connection between the date of the accident and Violet's 25th birthday and her much-trumpeted inheritance – now just a couple of days away. Surely the two were connected, the press conjectured; the coincidence seemed just too great. Meanwhile the ever-vocal crowd of creditors remained outside Boderw peering through the iron gates and, together with a clutch of newspaper reporters, waiting impatiently for a glimpse of the family or the slightest sign of movement.

In Birmingham, news of Violet's supposed accident and disappearance (together with a description of the missing lady) had been widely reported in the city's newspapers. The station clerk at New Street railway station contacted the city police after the description of Violet, reported in the *Birmingham Daily Mail*, tallied with his recollection of the lady calling herself Mrs Miller, who had called at the left luggage office a week earlier, enquiring about a large box in that name. He declared that the encounter had lodged in his memory, as the lady had left empty-handed after being unable to provide any identification in that name. Only following her hasty retreat had he noticed that she had scribbled out that name from the receipt book. He had thought the incident odd at the time.

Two officers from the city police arrived at the station and forced open the box. Inside it the officers found a cabinet portrait photograph of Violet Charlesworth, several photographs of Boderw, a book with the name V. Gordon Charlesworth inscribed inside, a number of picture postcards of Flowerburn House (Violet's home in Scotland) – and a collection of expensive furs. The samples of handwriting within the box seemed to match that obtained from the lady calling herself Mrs Miller. The police officers soon managed to locate the two larger boxes that Violet had despatched from Scotland, which were now in storage at the offices of the Midland Railway Company. These were prised open by a detective superintendent from the Birmingham City Police and Superintendent Rees from Conwy Police, summoned especially to Birmingham for the occasion.

These boxes, according to a contemporary police report, weighed

> nearly three-quarters of a hundredweight and were found to contain jewellery, stationery and writing materials, photographs of Miss Charlesworth, a valuable set of Copeland China, carefully wrapped in a leopard skin rug, silver, an elaborately embroidered cushion bearing the word "chummy", several more valuable animal skins, a number of letters addressed to "Violet" and a fine bear skin rug.

The contents of the three trunks clearly indicated a carefully thought-out plan, orchestrated by a person desperate to conceal their most important valuables in the face of mounting debt. Rees, having seen the contents of the boxes and heard the railway clerk's description of the lady, conceded to a waiting reporter that

> I have no doubt, from what I hear, that Miss Charlesworth was in Birmingham last week. The description which I have

received of the lady who called at New Street station for one of the boxes exactly tallies with her. Where she is, at the present time, however, I have not the least idea.

Now the public demanded answers from the occupants of Boderw. A constant chant of 'Where is Violet?' echoed day and night from the crowd outside the gates. Inside, with the blinds drawn and the lamps lit, the family plotted their next move.

Finally, it seemed the proper time for the family to make their response an official one. On Saturday 9 January a persistent reporter from the *Daily Chronicle* was granted access to Boderw for the purposes of interviewing Albert alongside the entire Charlesworth family. Despite the police finally admitting that they now considered Violet to still be alive, the interview clearly demonstrates the Charlesworth family's determination to continue with their previously agreed version of the story. As later events will show, this interview also seems to imply that the entire family were complicit in the cover-up surrounding Violet's disappearance.

First, Albert gave a detailed description of the accident: 'Shortly after we had re-started from Bangor,' he stated, 'Miss Violet asked to take the wheel. "I have not driven lately," she said to me, "and I think I will drive tonight."

'I tried to induce her not to do so, but she persisted, and she wanted to drive. We therefore changed places, Miss Lillian being in the seat behind. Miss Violet had driven about two miles when the accident happened. It seemed as if the wheel had been snatched from her hands, and the car took a swift turn into the wall. I gave Miss Violet a pull, and the next moment I was thrown out of the car, and fell some distance down the cliffs. When I was recovering a boy passed me, apparently on his way down the road. Then I climbed up to the roadway, and Miss Violet had disappeared. I think she had gone over the cliffs. My belief still is that she fell down as I fell down.'

'Now, Watts', queried the reporter, 'let me be plain with you. Let me tell you what a good many people think about this accident. The suggestion is that Miss Violet was not in the car at the time of the accident; that you were driving, with Miss Lillian as the only other occupant; that you purposely chose a portion of the road where there was a gap in the wall, that you got off at the foot of the incline, put on the switch, and let the car run gently into the gap. It is said that the injuries to the car are quite consistent with that theory. What do you say?'

'I say that that is untrue,' returned Albert. 'What you have described to me did not happen. I have told you the truth.'

'Did it not occur to you then, Watts, when you came to yourself, that you ought to go down the cliff and look for your mistress?'

'I do not remember half that happened,' came the chauffeur's reply, 'I heard the people shouting to each other that it was dangerous for anyone to go down there.'

The pressman did not give up, but continued to probe Albert for satisfactory answers: 'How came it that the glass screen was broken?'

'I don't know. I cannot account for that. If I did say that Miss Violet was thrown through the screen I could not contradict that. I could not be certain whether she was or was not.'

Albert was then questioned regarding his own, somewhat ambiguous, position in the Charlesworth household: 'It is suggested,' the reporter said, 'that you were on terms of friendship with Miss Violet?'

'So I was,' Albert quickly replied, 'but I never transacted business for her.'

The reporter continued, 'At Chiswick, for example, you and Miss Violet had tea together at your landlady's home?

'Yes, but that only occurred once.'

'Was your position any other than that of a servant to Miss Violet?'

'Certainly *not*!' Watt answered emphatically.

'And no inferences can be drawn from her having tea with you as stated?'

'No. I was chauffeur, and she was my employer. That is all.'

'Who paid you your wages, Mr Watts?'

'Miss Violet.'

'And are you remaining on here at the house?' the reporter enquired.

'There is nothing to remain for. But I cannot go until this matter is cleared up.'

'Were you told when you came here what the financial position of the family was?'

'No,' replied Albert. 'I knew a lot of money was spent – just for motors and the like.'

'Did it ever strike you to ask if the family had plenty of money?'

'Well' – Albert hesitated somewhat in his answer – 'I always understood there was plenty.'

The reporter then pushed him further regarding Violet's well-known motoring escapades, 'I know all about the night motor rides on which you went with Miss Violet.'

'The explanation is simple enough,' Albert said. 'Miss Violet was extremely fond of fast motoring, and she preferred to journey at night because the roads are clear then. That is all.'

'Finally, Watts, is it still your belief that your mistress went off the cliff?'

'I am sorry to say that it is.'

Miss Lillian Charlesworth was next to be questioned. The family by this juncture may well have regretted granting permission for her to be interviewed; however the reporter did not stop for breath: 'The suggestion is, Miss Charlesworth, that your sister was so financially embarrassed that she invented this accident to escape from her liabilities.'

'That is simply not true. It is cruel, and it is a libel.'

'Did you not know she has very heavy liabilities?' asked the reporter.

'I know so now, but I had no knowledge of them until after the motor-car accident. I only knew of one or two small creditors who were threatening her.'

'And you do not think these were so much that they drove Miss Charlesworth to suicide?'

'Oh dear, no,' Lillian replied.

'Will you tell me where she was supposed to get her money from?'

'I cannot say much about that. I must not,' Lillian replied, appearing to be reluctant to answer, before eventually continuing, on the assurance that the newspaper would not publish the name, 'she was engaged for seven or eight years to a gentleman named _____.'

The *Daily Chronicle*, honouring its end of the bargain, did not publish the gentleman's name, although from Lillian's story it is clear that she was referring to Violet's fictitious benefactor as against her fiancé, Dr Hughes Jones.

'He came of a rich family,' she continued, 'he was a gentleman ranker[15] and he died. He had very wealthy connections, and it was through him that she came by her money. There were several wills by which she benefited. Assignments were made in her favour. Certain conditions attached to each will. I cannot tell you all of them, but one of them was that the trustees could withhold the money from my sister for any length of time they so wished. The newspapers have been full of false statements. I do not believe that Violet owed anything like the amount stated.'

Feeling that he had somehow managed to persuade Lillian to reveal the truth, the reporter pressed her again, 'It is suggested, Miss Charlesworth, that your sister was secretly married to another well-known gentleman?'

However, this was quickly rebuffed by Lillian: 'Nothing of the sort. The story she always told us, and our friends, was that the money was obtained under a will.'

'Miss Lillian, can you give me the name of anybody under whose will she benefited, in addition to the gentleman whose identity you desire to keep quiet?'

'I know there were wills, but I am not at liberty to give you the names. We think that she has been the dupe of someone in connection with her speculations. I am sure she has been a victim. Someone has been robbing her. They have induced her to do these things, and she has been led away. Some of this will come out. You must not believe all the reports of her owing

---

15 A 'gentleman' soldier in the ranks, rather than an officer.

money all over the country.'

'But there is simple evidence.'

'Yes, there is evidence, I suppose, of some debts.'

'Was your sister insured?'

'No, she was not. It has been said that we insured her, and that we were going to somehow benefit by her death. Please contradict this; it is cruel.'

The reporter changed the subject: 'Will you swear that you have not heard from your sister since the second of January?'

'Certainly.'

'What have you to say about her boxes being found at Birmingham?'

Lillian and her father

'I cannot say anything,' Lillian replied.

'There can be no question that they were her boxes?'

'I am told so; I cannot explain it, but we are bound to think now that she sent them there some weeks ago, perhaps with the object of raising money on the contents.'

'Why were they addressed to a Mrs Miller, then?'

Lillian's response was defiant: 'I cannot possibly say.'

'You say that the newspaper statements claiming that the accident was "a fake" are untrue?'

'Most decidedly.'

'It was not planned, then, in order that Violet might gain an opportunity of escaping her creditors?'

'Oh dear, no.'

'Tell me why you and your sister obtained a Bradshaw at Bangor.'

'We were both going up to London on the Monday to see the solicitors, and we wanted to find out the trains. That is all.'

'You have told me that you do not think your sister committed suicide?'

'I am sure she did not. Why, before we started out for that ride she was more than usually bright. I remember that we had the gramophone on for some time, and she was greatly amused. We had a lot of funny tunes playing. She was always so cheerful that it is quite absurd to think of suicide. Indeed, hers was a rather lively disposition.'

Next, the *Daily Chronicle* hoped to interview Violet's mother, Miriam. The family claimed she was too ill to face scrutiny, however, following much protest she eventually appeared from her sickbed.

Would the obviously distressed Miriam finally reveal the truth?

14: The Game

As Miriam prepared to face the inquisitive presshound, the family's concern was only too clear to all those present.

To those present, she seemed to be both anxious and unwell. In addition, her version of Violet's complicated love life appeared to be a very different one: 'My daughter had engaged herself to be married to a North Wales doctor, and had kept it dark for a considerable time. She was worried by the demands made upon her financial resources, and was greatly affected by the breaking off of her engagement with the doctor. As to the accident, of course, I knew nothing, except that Violet seemed happier than usual on the afternoon when she and the others started out. She came into the room to me, and said, "Good-bye, mother, we are going. We won't be long. We shall be back soon," and that was the last I ever saw of her.'

At this point Mrs Charlesworth broke down, and the interview was suspended while she attempted to recover her composure. After a moment, with tears in her eyes, she blurted out, 'I had no opportunity of laying her dear body to rest, or even of knowing where she lies.'

After regaining her composure Miriam continued, 'When it came to ten o'clock that night I began to feel anxious. I went downstairs to a friend who was staying with me and expressed my anxiety. The friend, a medical man, tried to console me.'

Presumably this 'medical man' was Dr Miller, who had been attending to Miriam at that time, and who had most probably provided Violet's inspiration for the name on the luggage label she had attached to the deposited luggage at New Street station.

'Go on, Mrs Charlesworth,' the reporter urged.

'Then, by and by, I went and lay down on the sofa, but I could not rest, so returned to my bed. When it came to two o'clock in the morning I went downstairs again. I could see something had happened, but they would not tell me at first, only saying that there had been an accident. But at last they told me — cruellest of all – that one was reported dead, and two others seriously injured, and until late morning we did not even know which one it was.'

Barely taking a breath, the reporter continued his robust questioning of Violet's mother: 'Taking first your statement, Mrs. Charlesworth, that your daughter was passionately fond of you, and the fact that she knew that in a few days there must be an exposure that would cause you the utmost grief, do you not think it possible that to avoid exposure and to shield you she may have left and sought death, or determined to avoid her troubles by a pretended fatal accident?'

'She would not do that,' came Miriam's forthright reply. 'She had too much spirit for that. She would face the trouble, whatever it was, and would fight to the very last.'

Next to be questioned was Violet's brother Frederick, who seemed slightly more sceptical regarding his sister's antics: 'To my mind, my sister's existence was not an altogether satisfactory one. She intimated to me that she would become possessed of considerable means at the age of 25, and that in the meantime she would receive an annual income. She did not tell me any details as to the sources of the income, except that the capital was controlled by trustees. She somewhat resented my inquiries, and I did not pursue them beyond a certain point. It seemed to us all that a few days after each quarter day[16] she had funds.'

'Are you still convinced, Mr Charlesworth, by the report of your sister's accident, in spite of having her boxes at Birmingham?'

He replied, 'I am entirely convinced. The view of the family is that we firmly believe she is dead; but, of course, we shall be thankful if, after all that, it would turn out that she is alive.'

'You don't think she may have gone away, concealing her identity in the hope of avoiding the distress that the exposure of legal proceedings would involve?'

'I can quite believe she would do anything for her mother, but I cannot disbelieve the statements of my sister Lillian and the chauffeur. Besides, she appears to have been quite happy around the time of the accident, and she would know what a blow her death under such circumstances would be to us all. She would also know that the public attention attracted by her reported death would almost certainly lead to revelations which she would wish to keep from being made. A good deal has been said about her having the house at Calne, but as my mother told you, she wanted it for kennel purposes. It was not far distant from where I was living, and was within easy motoring from London.'

'Then I may take it that it is the view of the whole family that Miss Violet is dead?'

'Yes, we firmly believe she is dead, but, of course, we shall be thankful if, after all, it should turn out that she is alive. It has also been stated that my

---

16 Quarter Day, on 25 March, June, September and December, marked the end of each quarter-year – spring, summer, autumn and winter – and was traditionally a day on which rent, bills and outstanding credit accounts became due.

sister Violet is concealed in this house. You have already seen my mother's bedroom, my own, and other rooms. If you care to do so you are entirely at liberty to examine every other apartment.'

Unsurprisingly, the *Daily Chronicle* seized upon the open invitation and searched the house from top from bottom; however their labours revealed no trace of the missing lady.

Finally, Violet's father, David, was emphatic in his defence of his daughter: 'She has been made the agent of cleverer and more unscrupulous people than herself. I have not an atom of doubt,' he declared, 'that some gambler has got hold of her or made her his dupe, using her for his own financial gain. She never learned anything about bills or stocks and shares here, and someone must have taught her. She didn't meet them here, for we have never had a stockbroker or anybody of that kind here. No, I am certain she has been victimised by some gambler or other. I was astonished when I heard of it all. And so was every member of the family. We knew of her motoring, and that she dressed nicely and had jewellery. But we know nothing about bills and things of that sort. She did not talk about things like that much, but used to go up to London on business, and I suppose she carried it on there. I always understood she had inherited ample amounts under those wills she spoke of.'

Following the *Daily Chronicle*'s interview, the family decided to add some legal weight to their statements regarding the events of 2 January. Early on the morning of Monday 11 January a taxicab arrived at Boderw. In the gloom of a cold and misty sunrise, three occupants from the house left by the back gates and were whisked away in the direction of the railway station.

The three elopers from Boderw had fully intended to keep a low profile. Nevertheless, their plans were easily exposed by a ravenous media. On leaving Boderw, Lillian, accompanied by Albert and Joseph Gratton (seemingly ever-present at the family's side), had made their way to Rhyl and boarded the early train to Chester. At the cathedral city they quickly transferred to the 9.40 am service bound for London Euston. However, an eagle-eyed reporter at Rhyl railway station had witnessed the trio arriving and made enquiries at the ticket office as to their final destination. On discovering that the group were due at Euston station around midday, he hastily wired his London office. Within a matter of hours, unknown to the three escapees, a sizeable welcoming committee had been arranged for them. On their arrival at Euston, they were stunned to greeted by a retinue of reporters, photographers, and curious members of the public. Shocked by the attention, and clearly shaken, Joseph addressed the amassed journalists and announced, 'It will soon be over now.'

The events that followed that day were comprehensively reported in no less than 56 regional and national newspapers. In fact, throughout 1909 Violet received a greater degree of coverage than that afforded to either the prime minister or King Edward VII.

> The party arrived at Euston about two o'clock, and a large number of pressmen were in waiting for them. Declining to answer any inquiries, Miss Charlesworth and Mr Gratton left the station on foot. They turned out of the Euston Road into Upper Woburn Place, passing the Hotel Gwalia, where Miss Violet Charlesworth had previously stayed, and going on through Russell Square. Opposite the Hotel Russell they called a cab, and drove off through Southampton Row. They were followed by a number of pressmen in cabs down Kingsway and into Fleet Street. At No. 18, the office of Messrs Amery-Parkes and Co., solicitors, both visitors alighted, and had an interview with a representative of the firm. The chauffeur, it is said, reached the office by another route. When the news spread that Miss Lillian Charlesworth was at the offices of Messrs Amery-Parkes, Macklin and Co., a great crowd gathered outside, curiosity being accentuated by the fact that about a dozen taxicabs containing journalists, intent upon tracking Miss Charlesworth and her companions, stood on the opposite side of the road. Ultimately the footway became so blocked that a number of policemen had to undertake the task of keeping the footway clear. At dusk the crowd was so great that the doors of the solicitors' office had to be closed, and then it was discovered that a party of photographers had secreted themselves on one of the landings inside with the object of securing flashlight snapshots of the party. Members of the firm exercised their wits to devise some means of getting rid of the intruders, but the fact that there was only one staircase baulked their efforts. At about seven o'clock a taxicab drew up at the door, in readiness to convey the party to Euston for the return journey to St. Asaph by the 7.30 pm train. Waiting behind were about a score of other taxicabs containing more reporters ready to follow Miss Charlesworth and her friends. The police had some difficulty in keeping clear a passage from the door to the taxicab, so great was the crush.

Following the party's chaotic return to Euston station, the solicitors issued an official statement on behalf of the family,

> From Messrs Amery-Parkes, Macklin and Co., Solicitors, of

Fleet Street, London, on Monday 11 January 1909 – A member of our firm has conducted an exhaustive examination, lasting four hours, of Miss Lillian Charlesworth, Mr Gratton, and Watts, the chauffeur. We see no reason to doubt that the accident as described to us by the chauffeur and Miss Lillian Charlesworth did in fact happen, and the statements made are not inconsistent with the allegation that Miss Violet Gordon Charlesworth met her death as a result of the accident.

However, if the Charlesworth family assumed that an officially worded statement given in the presence of a solicitor would miraculously make their story suddenly appear more credible, they were to be sadly disappointed. The amassed ranks of newshounds scented a cover-up. Macklin, their solicitor, was forced to summit to an interrogation from the eager reporters on the steps of the office, as he left. Reading from his shorthand notes, which he had hastily gathered during the interviews, he addressed the press:

I interviewed all three, Miss Lillian Charlesworth, Watts, and Mr Gratton, separately, and subjected them to examination. It was a pretty rigorous one, too, I assure you, and I could find nothing at all inconsistent with the death of Miss Charlesworth as the result of the accident. I had Watts in here and discussed the whole affair with him, and he satisfied me that he was telling the truth. To obtain corroboration he was then seen by my partner, Mr Amery-Parkes, and he entirely agreed with me that the man was speaking the truth. Watts told me that he was thrown 30 or 40 feet. He was not rendered unconscious. He says he does not remember ever being unconscious in his life. But he was dazed and could not remember clearly what happened. He admitted that he had made contradictory statements. I think that is all quite consistent with a man going through a motor-car accident. He seems to be a highly nervous man. The only thing that puzzled me was the discovery of the boxes at Birmingham railway station. I believe that these were left by someone else, who probably knows a good deal about the question. The shorthand notes taken at the interviews will take about seven hours to transcribe fully. These will be submitted to the police and others who have a right to see them. I only agreed to see the visitors on condition that I could issue a public statement if I saw fit. They have consented to the shorthand notes being shown to the authorities.

Following their escape from the large crowd outside the solicitor's office, the party of three hurried back to Euston station. Again, their demeanour caught the attention of the gathered newspaper reporters, who noted,

> Miss Lillian Charlesworth was accompanied by the number of photographers usually only attached to the most exalted persons. The attentions thus displayed to her were not appreciated, and Miss Charlesworth not only declined to be interviewed, but persistently covered her face with the cover of a very handsome brown fur cloak so that she could not be photographed. She was not in mourning, her attire instead consisting of a green felt hat trimmed with brown fur, and a three-quarter length grey coat.
>
> At Euston station the object of this extraordinary public interest jumped out of her cab, and with her fur collar covering most of her face, ran at top speed to catch the 7.30 pm express for Holyhead. The lady was only just in time, and she, accordingly, jumped into a second-class compartment. A ticket collector, unaware of the lady's identity, bounded after her for the tickets. "We want thirds," said Miss Charlesworth. And that was the lady's only public utterance.

While events took their course in London, it was far from quiet at Boderw in North Wales. Mr T.S. Adams, an auctioneer and magistrate from Mold, along with the local under-sheriff, visited the house in an attempt to seize goods and effects. However, David Charlesworth refused to open the door. The rear door to the property was also barred and Mr Adams left empty-handed. The jeering crowd at the gates baited him to batter down the door. Instead, he returned in the late afternoon as darkness fell and removed one of Violet's much-loved pedigree dogs, and took it away to be auctioned; the Borzoi, which had been chained up in the yard barking hungrily, was clearly extremely grateful to be released.

When the express train finally arrived at Rhyl around midnight, it was not to be the end for Lillian, Joseph, and Albert. As they alighted from their carriage, they were met by a reporter from the *Daily News*, together with a large group of inquisitive onlookers. Lillian asked the reporter to escort them to the police station, that they might elude the worst of the unwelcome attention. Once at Rhyl Police

Sherriff's Officers still unable to enter Boderw

Station the trio left unnoticed by a rear door and vanished. It would be the last time any of the three would appear in public for many months.

Once the onlookers outside the police station realised that the objects of their interest had disappeared, it was assumed by everybody that the trio must have somehow returned to Boderw on foot. However, a clutch of reporters stationed outside the house confirmed that no one had entered or left Boderw that day, with the exception of the footman, Campbell. The windows had been barred and the blinds drawn, and all endeavours to gain access had been futile.

Sheriff's Officer at the Charlesworths

A search party, led by Inspector Pearson from the Rhyl Police, scoured the nearby country lanes and villages without success. The trio seemed to have disappeared. Boderw appeared empty and silent, save for Violet's barking dogs, still tied up in the yard.

The following afternoon Adams the sheriff's officer, visited Boderw again, this time holding execution writs amounting to several thousand pounds. These writs empowered him to enter the premises regardless of the occupants' consent, and seize any goods or articles. On arrival, he found the front gates unbarred. He approached the front door. The bell had been disconnected, so knocking was the only way in which he felt he could make himself heard. But despite continuous knocking, the house remained silent, with only the sound of the dogs breaking the eerie silence.

Meanwhile, In contrast to the deathly silence at Boderw, many of Violet's creditors received the following letter from her solicitors:

> Dear Sirs,
>
> In accordance with our instructions we have filed notice of intention to defend this action on behalf of the defence, but we expect that you are already aware that Miss Violet Gordon Charlesworth met with a fatal accident on Saturday last? We shall be glad to hear that under the circumstances your clients do not propose to press the action relating to her outstanding account for the time being.
>
> Yours,
>
> Messrs Amery-Parkes, Macklin & Co.,
> 18 Fleet Street, London.

The strange inertia at Boderw continued into the following day. Reporters continued to knock at the front door, slip notes through the letterbox, and telephone the house. Their requests usually went unanswered, or were met with a curt 'Who are you?' or 'I know nothing of a note!' – and finally from Violet's father, David: 'You may take it officially from me that Miss Violet Charlesworth is not here. We have heard nothing of her; we believe that she is dead. That is all I can say.'

By Wednesday 13 January there had still been no confirmed sightings of Violet. Rumours abounded. One theory speculated that she was a on a ship steaming towards New York, the next that she had been seen hiding inside Boderw; another that she had been spotted taking lonely night-time walks in the countryside a few miles outside St Asaph. There was no truth in any of these rumours. The newspapers, desperate to keep the story alive after eleven days, maintained a presence outside the gates to the house; however, there seemed to be little news to report. Meanwhile the number of anxious creditors willing to publicly declare themselves mushroomed on a daily basis. Many arrived at Boderw personally, all hoping to see for themselves if Violet was really there. Most were thwarted by the burly, moustached security guard the Charlesworths had now seen fit to employ.

At 2 pm on that Wednesday afternoon there was a buzz of excitement outside the house. Noting that there was no policeman on duty at Boderw, a local gamekeeper (who was among the many owed money by the family) scaled the gate at the back entrance to the property. Ignoring the 'Beware of the Dog' sign, he forced open the bar that fastened the back gate from the inside, and threw open the gates. Within minutes, 20 or so onlookers, together with a handful of photographers, flooded onto the premises. One creditor took a writ from his waistcoat pocket and pinned it to the front door. Others jeered and chanted outside the windows, while several more dogs barked from inside the kennels. Much to the crowd's disappointment, however, thick blinds obscured the windows to the house. But then, a sudden cheer erupted when one protester noticed a ladder at the side of the building and an open upstairs window. He quickly mounted the ladder, but was too late, as the blind was hastily pulled down before he could peek inside the bedroom. Suddenly, there was a shout from downstairs as three members of the gathered crowd noticed that a larder window on the ground floor at the side of the house was without a blind. They did not require the use of a ladder and were able to observe through the window. Inside the room, David Charlesworth was seen stooping with a lighted taper in his hand, apparently searching for something among the provisions in the well-stocked larder. However, before the gathered reporters could attract the attention of the others, he placed a large piece of brown paper over the window pane.

Meanwhile, at the front porch a group of young ladies attempted to peer inside the house when a sudden loud bang from inside the property, as if a gun had been discharged, caused them to scream. In a state of panic, they quickly fled the premises to the comparative safety of the road outside the gates. The remainder of the crowd waited inside the grounds, but were soon dispersed by Sergeant Connah and two burly police constables, who had been summoned by Joseph Gratton. Before the gathered creditors were escorted away from the grounds, they managed to glance through the ground floor windows of the property, each of them noticing, with increasing despair, that the pickings left inside would be slim indeed. Violet's collection of motor cars was gone. There appeared to be little in the way of furniture remaining inside the house, and the majority of the fixtures and fittings at Boderw belonged to its owners (a family from Berkshire who had let the property to Violet), and therefore could not be removed to recover Violet's debts. The house had been placed on the market three weeks before Violet's disappearance, in response to her overdue rent. It would later transpire that her lease agreement was due to expire on Lady Day, 25 March 1909, and that it would not have been renewed by the owners due to her failure to maintain regular payments.

Following the arrival of the police, the crowd slowly melted away. The occupants of Boderw, breathing a sigh of relief, appeared at the windows once more. Several witnesses claimed to have seen Lillian and Albert walking around inside the building, and occasionally peering through the windows. It was also noted by these witnesses that neither Lillian nor Albert appeared to be 'too ill to speak to anyone' (the message given to any callers choosing to knock at the door). The only person to leave the house during this period was the young footman George Campbell, who was occasionally sent out to purchase supplies. As he came and went, the reporters outside repeatedly plied him with questions, but they were always given the same answer: 'I know nothing.'

Meanwhile, in the vacuum of new information, several rumours began to circulate. Several newspapers reported that Superintendent Rees had received scores of letters offering solutions to Violet's disappearance. One letter suggested employing the services of Sherlock Holmes (it was genuinely believed by many members of the public that the detective was in fact a real person, who would be able to locate the missing lady). Another letter put forward the rumour that Violet had kept a secret locked room at Foryd Lodge (the Charlesworths' previous home) to which only she had access.

Perhaps, most bizarrely, was the suggestion that the police employ the services of a local clairvoyant and palmist from Rhyl, Madame Sheringham. Bizarrely, it transpired that she already possessed a track record in predicting Violet's behaviour. In early 1908, a local jeweller, Mr Benjamin Glass, had been persuaded by Violet to supply to her goods to the value of £500: 'I have always paid you before, haven't I?', implored Violet, 'and this is such a small sum compared with what my fortune will be.'

However, Mrs Glass (unlike her husband) was less than impressed with Violet and promptly consulted Madame Sheringham on the matter. The reply from the clairvoyant was sadly predictable,

'Your husband is about to enter into a very important business transaction. He will be unfortunate and have great difficulty in getting his money. He will get some back, but not all.'

Madame Sheringham's prediction would prove to be surprisingly accurate. Mr Glass chose not to follow the sage advice of either his wife or the spiritualist, and in the end he would only ever receive £200 of the £500 he was owed by Violet. The remaining £300 due (now £46,000), created much financial hardship for the Glass family, from which they never recovered.

In the meantime, there appeared to be little else that the press could report. Violet had seemingly vanished without a trace. All the alleged sightings of her had proved to be red herrings. From the rumours of her escape to America to the use of a clairvoyant, it seemed that the story had finally run its course. While creditors continued to lodge their claims for repayment with the Rhyl County Court (with varying degrees of optimism), the public's interest finally seemed to subside. The crowds of onlookers outside Boderw gradually dwindled, and the newspaper hacks turned their attention to other stories, particularly the terrible murder of ten-year-old Mary Donnelly in County Durham, and the mobilisation of the Austro-Hungarian forces in Europe.

Perhaps the Charlesworth family could now breathe a little more easily. Had Violet escaped her debt once and for all? With her conspicuous red motor cloak still at Pullar's in Glasgow being dyed dark blue, surely nothing could give her away now?

However, not even Madame Sheringham could have foreseen the next twist in the tale.

15: The Reveal

Despite a comprehensive search by the police and local fisherman from Conwy, Violet's body had yet, of course, to be recovered. The body of the young woman found drowned in the River Dee was confirmed to be someone else. Following the discovery of Violet's luggage at New Street railway station in Birmingham, Superintendent Rees was now forced to reinterview Albert and Lillian. Perhaps under the threat of being charged with wasting police time, the pair revised their original statements (given on the day after the accident). With some coaching from the family's solicitor, Albert now presented this version of events,

> I am now of the opinion that she (Violet) did not go down the rocks. Although I did say that night that she went through the glass and got thrown over the rocks into the sea, I am now of the opinion that she did not. I was stunned and did not know what I was doing. I am convinced that I have now got over the shock and am convinced that she was not thrown from the car at all, but remained in a heap in the front of the seat until she walked away in the direction of Conwy.

Lillian confirmed Albert's amended version of events, adding:

> we were driving on the right side of the road. I felt a terrible jerk and heard my sister scream. I got out, feeling stunned, and when I came to myself I was lying on the ground ... I was very much upset and do not remember anything else.

The statements had an air of rehearsal and contrivance about them. Interestingly, just as the pair had both used the word 'catapulted' on the night of the accident, on this occasion they both opted for the word 'stunned'. Yet, despite the complete reversal in their evidence, there was little clamour to charge the pair with wasting police time.

Although a string of further county court judgements for unpaid debts were filed against Violet at Rhyl, and daily revelations of her extravagant lifestyle continued to fill the newspapers, the search for answers had mostly ground to a halt by 17 January.

While the public's Alamo-like siege continued outside the locked and darkened Boderw, members of Fleet Street's press legion slowly drifted away, distracted by the scent of another story. Meanwhile, we can return to a snowy Tobermory on the Isle of Mull. In 1909, with restricted channels of communication available to Violet on the island, she was forced to rely on the limited number of newspapers delivered to the Mishnish Hotel. Her quest for information on the search for her missing body and any possible police conclusions was a delayed and a frustrating one. While she waited, Violet seemed intent on establishing a more permanent hiding place on Mull; the Mishnish was not a suitable long-term haven for her. To keep her presence on the island a secret, she swiftly grasped the urgent necessity to locate somewhere quieter and more isolated than Tobermory, the only real population centre on the island.

Soon after her arrival on Mull she had enquired about other, more suitable, accommodation. As during that cold, dark and wintry January there were virtually no visitors to the island, a well-dressed and fashionable young lady such as Violet wandering along Tobermory's Main Street would certainly have been conspicuous in the extreme. Her wardrobe was one of statement, not of camouflage. Gossip was sure to follow. A blossoming tree cannot hide in a street; it needs a forest.

Mishnish Hotel, Tobermory

Following a recommendation from the hotel keeper at the Mishnish, Violet visited a quiet farm located at Baliscate, on the gently sloping hills outside Tobermory. Baliscate had been the site of one of the first settlements on the island, prior to the establishment of the town of Tobermory. She hoped that the farmstead would offer her quiet and anonymous accommodation, together with sufficient space for her St Bernards. She clearly intended to make Baliscate Farm her secret hideaway for a considerable amount of time. Violet enquired at the farm about the possibility of space to kennel her dogs, and even discussed the possibility of having a purpose-built structure erected in the farmyard. She agreed to take the lodgings, signing a three-month lease with an option to renew. Violet told the owner that she would move in on Saturday. She then returned to the hotel in Tobermory to settle her affairs there.

Meanwhile in Tobermory, a chance encounter was about to signal the beginning of the end for Violet. However, it was not to be her eye-catching outfits that proved to be her downfall, but her sweet tooth.

On Monday 11 January, the western parts of Scotland were still enduring icy blizzards, mirroring the conditions being experienced at that very moment by Ernest Shackleton's *Nimrod* expedition, which had been forced to turn back after advancing to within 112 miles of the South Pole. Violet decided she could tolerate the claustrophobic surroundings of her hotel room no longer and, braving the wintry weather, decided to indulge her weakness for cakes. She visited the Tobermory Bakery, to which she had called into two years earlier on her previous visit to the island, and treated herself to her favourite treat, a Bath bun. She recalled the shop's special recipe, in which they baked an extra lump of sugar inside the bun to complement the sugar sprinkled on the top. Bizarrely, it was this sweet and simple pleasure – as against her indulgence in furs, jewellery, motor cars, and country estates – that proved to be the catalyst that would eventually bring about her demise.[17]

Mr Neil Mactaggart, the owner, thought Violet looked strangely familiar, and he was strongly reminded of the beautiful and fashionable young lady who had caused such a stir on the island in the summer of 1907. Mactaggart swore that the lady he was now serving was the same lady, although he did not know her name. Just as Violet had never forgotten the taste of the Bath buns, Mactaggart had remembered her visit 18 months earlier. Nevertheless, at that moment he had no reason to connect the news of a missing female motorist in North Wales with the attractive lady now standing at the counter. However, later that evening, he happened to see a description of Violet in the *Oban Times*, under the headline 'The Welsh Cliff Tragedy'.

He became instantly convinced that the customer in his shop was in fact the missing Welsh motorist, and contacted Police Constable Malcolm Mackay in Tobermory. Coincidentally, PC Mackay – like most of the country's newspaper readership – had been avidly following the story of the Welsh Cliff Tragedy. He, too, had become suspicious of the fashionable female stranger newly arrived in town.

Mackay in turn contacted the owner of the Mishnish, who had also privately questioned this strange and enigmatic visitor from the mainland, who seemed to have no discernible purpose for being on the island in a cold and unwelcoming January. The hotel owner's misgivings increased when, on the afternoon of Tuesday 12 January, Violet announced, 'I intend to visit Oban on the mainland tomorrow, on business for a few days. I will be back on Saturday. I shall settle my bill then, and I will leave some of my luggage here at the hotel in the meantime, so you know I will be back. I have engaged

---

17 In an unexpected subplot to Violet's story, following newspaper revelations that her fondness for a Bath bun had indirectly led to her exposure, sales of Bath buns rocketed across the nation. The *Daily Mirror* even published a photograph of the Tobermory Baker's speciality.

rooms at the farmhouse at Baliscate, which you kindly recommended, where I shall take possession this week. I have written to the farm and informed them I will be taking up residence on Saturday.'

Following Violet's departure for Oban on 13 January (without settling her bill) the Mishnish staff decided to undertake some Sherlock Holmes-esque detective work of their own. First, they checked the hotel's visitors' book. They could distinctly remember Violet signing the book on her arrival as 'Miss Margaret MacLeod'. Mysteriously, that page had somehow been carefully removed without the hotel keeper's knowledge. Violet was clearly covering her tracks. Yet despite that rather strange occurrence, a torn page from a visitors' book was hardly sufficient evidence to prove a crime had been committed. Nonetheless the hotel keeper sought guidance from PC Mackay. Acting on the constable's instructions, the hotel staff then searched Violet's room. Assuming that she would not be returning until Saturday, the hotel keeper turned the key and entered the room. Just as Violet had promised, two small cases had indeed been left in the room, although on examination they proved to contain little of value. In fact, they appeared to have been left purely as a decoy, since the contents consisted mainly of a pile of old newspapers from the mainland. Crucially though, the cases held nothing that could positively identify them as belonging to the fugitive Violet Charlesworth (nor to anyone else).

Their next discovery was more intriguing, however. On the dressing table in the bedroom stood a small medicine bottle. The owner of the bottle had clearly attempted to score out the handwritten label and date, using a knife. Nevertheless, some of the lettering still remained legible: '_ _ ol_t' and 'C_ _ _les_ _rt_'.

On its own it was not enough. In frustration they continued their search. Finally, they unearthed a vital clue. There, at the bottom of the wastepaper basket, lay a small ripped-up piece of paper. The staff removed it carefully and, flattening out the torn segments on the table, attempted to rearrange the words. Finally, it was the evidence that the police and the rest of the country had been searching for – substantive proof that Violet Charlesworth had not been thrown from her motor car and perished in the sea, but was still very much alive.

The hotel keeper immediately contacted Mackay, who in turn wrote to Superintendent J. Ivor Davies, the Deputy Chief Constable for Flintshire, in North Wales,

From: – Malcolm Mackay, constable in Tobermory, Argyllshire

Date:- January 14, 1909

Sir,

I beg to inform you that a young lady arrived here on the 6th inst. She put up at one of the hotels.

After reading about the motor smash in Wales I got suspicious, and told the hotel keeper to watch her correspondence.

On the 13th inst. this hotel keeper called me, and produced scraps of a telegram found in this young lady's bedroom. After putting the pieces together, the telegram read as follows:-

"Handed in at Coleman Street

Reply paid.

To Miss Violet Charlesworth, Boderw, St Asaph.

Why no letter as promised? Necessary to commence

– Ovated" [18]

A St Asaph postmark was also visible on the telegram, Sir.

She engaged rooms at a farmhouse near this town, and was to have taken possession of the same this week. While engaging these rooms she asked the farmer's wife if she would be allowed to keep a St Bernard dog.

She left here yesterday for Oban without paying her bill, saying she would be back on Saturday. The hotel keeper has kept some of her luggage. When she first arrived at the hotel she signed her name in the visitor's book as Margaret MacLeod. After she left yesterday the page was found to have been cut out.

From the description of this lady and the finding of the telegram in her bedroom I am fully convinced this is the missing lady motorist.

P.C. M. Mackay, Tobermory

---

18 Ovated was a telegraphic address abbreviation similar to our modern-day URLs or postcodes. As a telegram sender was charged by the number of the words used on each telegram sent, it was common to use an abbreviated form which could be referenced by the telegraph office personnel from a directory of names, then directed to the recipient's nearest post office. Interestingly, even today there are still several organisations known by their original abbreviated telegram address, Oxfam, Interpol, and Interflora being the best-known examples.

The Deputy Chief Constable of Flintshire at first suspected that the sighting was yet another case of mistaken identity. As there had already been many sightings of ladies in red coats which had all emerged as red herrings, he wanted to check the authenticity of the torn-up telegram. Ovated turned out to be the shortened address for the London firm of stockbrokers Fenton, Dale & Co. – Violet's stockbrokers, and her single largest creditor. The deputy chief constable then contacted Fenton at the stockbrokers, who responded:

> The telegram was undoubtedly sent by this firm to Miss Charlesworth about a month ago. In fact, I wrote the wire myself. Our letter work is in the hands of solicitors who are acting for us against Miss Charlesworth, but as far as I remember the full text of the wire was as follows:- "Why no letter as promised yet present? – Ovated"
>
> It refers to a cheque which we held from Miss Charlesworth and which was due to be presented. Our telegram was addressed to Miss Violet Charlesworth, at St Asaph. We previously addressed her by a different name, but since discovering her true identity, we have always addressed her as Violet Charlesworth, by instruction of our solicitor. Recently she had been unable to give us a permanent address, and had asked us to send her letters to the Chancery Lane safe deposit building.

The safe deposit centre, which had opened in 1885, was located in a secure basement vault under Chancery House, in Chancery Lane. It had swiftly built a reputation as the most secure place in London in which a wealthy person might store their jewellery, money, or documents well away from prying eyes. Tantalisingly, Violet did not even disclose the presence of her secret strongbox at the vault to any of her family and friends. Its contents have never been disclosed, nor was anyone contacted during the research for this book even aware of its existence. In fact, I conclude that her amassed creditors (with the exception of Fenton, Dale & Co., who were under the impression that Violet used her safe deposit box only for the safekeeping of legal documents) were completely unaware of its existence. Had her creditors been aware of it, we might now have a much greater knowledge of the true number of victims to fall under Violet's spell, not to mention another explanation for her frequent visits to London.

Despite the untold fortunes undoubtedly contained inside the Chancery Lane Safe Deposit Centre, no attempt to break into its vaults was ever successful. Indeed, in 1943 the vaults, with their steel-reinforced walls almost 4 feet thick, emerged intact when a German bomb completely obliterated the building above it during an air raid. Chancery House was rebuilt a decade later, and now the London Silver Vaults – a large subterranean market containing antique dealers and jewellers – operates on the site once occupied by Violet's mysterious safety deposit box.

Returning to the statement given by Mr Fenton to the Deputy Chief Constable of Flintshire, regarding the telegram found in Violet's bedroom:

> Although Miss Charlesworth's correspondence was normally sent to the Chancery Lane safe deposit, this matter was urgent, and we sent it direct to her home at St Asaph. It was handed in by our clerk at Coleman Street telegraph office in London, to be wired on to Miss Charlesworth.

After Fenton was given a description of the young lady seen on the Isle of Mull, he added:

> I see that the lady seen at Tobermory was described as wearing a dark coat. She wore a coat like that on several occasions when visiting me, although it was red in colour. It was a long coat, trimmed with squirrel fur, and reaching nearly to her feet.

Yet despite this corroborating evidence, the Flintshire police still sought confirmation of the telegram referred to them by PC Mackay in Tobermory. Deputy Chief Constable J. Ivor Davies telegraphed the constable in Tobermory once more: 'MacKay, is your letter authentic?'

He received the following reply: 'To J.I. Davies, Superintendent of Police, Mold. Perfectly genuine – Malcolm Mackay, constable.'

Davies then wired an urgent telegram to Superintendent Rees in Conwy, 'The lady referred to in Mull has now been identified as Miss Violet Charlesworth. Wire instructions.'

Rees then telephoned the Charlesworth family at Boderw. Lillian answered the call, and responded to the superintendent's news in a seemingly unsurprised manner: 'Thank you, Superintendent, the family are extremely thankful my sister had been found. I will proceed to Oban by the earliest possible train.'

Meanwhile Violet, who had now arrived back on the Scottish mainland at Oban, checked into the MacPherson's Palace Temperance Hotel in George Street, under the name of Miss Margaret Cameron MacLeod.

The following statement (given a few days later to the police by the hotel's proprietor, Mrs MacPherson), seems to indicate that Violet had grown wary, believing she had been recognised on the Isle of Mull. This helps to explain her sudden departure from Tobermory after she had gone to the trouble of securing lodgings at Baliscate Farm.

OBAN POLICE STATION, ALBANY ST

STATEMENT By Mrs MacPherson, Palace Temperance Hotel –

Miss Cameron MacLeod arrived on Wednesday last. The young lady had exquisite jewellery, including a striking waistbelt of beautiful workmanship, a beautiful diamond ring, and a pearl ring.

In the evening I had a chat with her. She told me she had come from Tobermory, and left there because she had been followed about by people who were under the mistaken idea that she was Miss Charlesworth. She told me, "Of course, that's all nonsense. I have met Miss Charlesworth, and she's a nice young lady. I saw her, and was introduced to her, last year at the Highland Gathering in Inverness."

I said to her, "She was very popular there, wasn't she? I think she gave a silver cup to be competed for at the gathering?"

"Really, I don't know," replied Miss MacLeod. "I was merely introduced to Miss Charlesworth. But it is a funny thing. I know Tobermory quite well. I was there a year ago with my sister and a gentlemen. We had a very pleasant time together."

"You didn't meet Miss Charlesworth there?" I asked.

"Oh, no," she replied.

"I have just received some London newspapers, full of the affair," I told her.

"Let me see them," replied the young lady, with a laugh; so she took them and read extracts from them, laughing all the time at the newspaper portrayal of this most extraordinary Charlesworth girl.

"What a dreadful person she must be!" I said.

"Dreadful!" replied Miss MacLeod.

END OF STATEMENT

However, despite perhaps detecting the landlady's suspicions, Violet had little choice but to spend a quiet evening in the hotel and celebrate her 25th birthday in solitude – that being, ironically, of course, the day on which she had told so many people that she would inherit a fortune.

It was a fate, some might say, she deserved.

This verse, adapted into an Irish melody, appeared in several newspapers during January 1909:

THE LOST REGAINED
(An Irish Melody in Motor-cloak Guise).

The missing maid to the North has gone,
'Mid Scotia's hills you'll find her;
The well-known cloak she has girded on,
And disguise is left behind her!
"Violet, sweet," says the Irish Bard.
"While hordes of Pressmen claim thee;
One pen thy devious ways shall guard,
And once more rightly name thee!"
The bolt soon fell, but the Pressmen's chain
Could not keep her proud soul under;
Through the luggage-lift she escaped again,
And burst their plans asunder!
She said, "No scouts shall capture me –
I am the soul of red-clad bravery."
And Violet evermore is free
From Pressmen's galling slavery!

Oban c.1909

16: The Counter-Bluff

Meanwhile, back at Boderw, news of Violet's discovery in Scotland had reached the people, albeit now comparatively few, who still maintained a day-and-night vigil outside the house, stamping their feet in an attempt to fight the cold, and listening to the sound of a piano from within the Charlesworths' home drifting through the icy night air.

The news of Violet's discovery galvanised the family into action. Under cover of darkness, at 10 pm on the night of Saturday 16 January, Lillian, together with Joseph (described in the newspapers as 'the gentleman farmer, family friend, spokesman and lodger at Boderw') left the grounds by the back gate.

Attempting to remain as silent as possible, the pair pushed their bicycles for a few hundred yards along the dark lane, before hurriedly mounting them and cycling off in the direction of Rhyl. Even though few people there had ventured outside to brave the bitter temperatures and icy streets, the pair's efforts to remain unnoticed were soon thwarted. Two particularly resilient and devoted pressmen happened to be smoking a cigarette on the corner of The Row, and were alerted by a barking dog. They instinctively looked up and noticed the light from two bicycle lamps piercing the gloom. They set off in hot pursuit.

The reporters quickly guessed the cyclists' destination and, despite having to find a taxi, arrived at Rhyl railway station before Joseph and Lillian. The journalists watched, unseen, as the pair arrived, left their bicycles at the station, and boarded the overnight mail train to Crewe. They appeared to be making a conscious effort not to be seen together, in that Joseph entered a third-class carriage alone, and Lillian, wearing a dark motor cloak, climbed into a separate one. They both pulled down the blinds of their individual compartments and remained out of sight. The two reporters also boarded the train, and all four travelled to Crewe, arriving in the small hours.

Early the next day, Sunday, after an uncomfortable and cold two-hour wait at Crewe station, Lillian and Joseph boarded the morning express as it sat idling at the platform. They waited impatiently for its departure north to Scotland, but unfortunately for them their efforts to remain incognito had been unsuccessful; news of their journey had been wired by the two eager reporters to fellow correspondents all over the country. So despite the early hour, a crowd had gathered at Crewe station to witness the spectacle. Joseph and Lillian, having raised the blinds in their carriages to see what the commotion was, and clearly ruffled by their reception, refused to answer any questions and quickly pulled the blinds down again. However, the unwelcome attention from the press and public was not the only thing which would make the journey an uncomfortable one. Scotland was in the middle of a tremendous snowstorm, the worst experienced for a generation.

Over the previous 24 hours a severe blizzard had raged across the west of Scotland. Snow had fallen unabated for an entire day and night, leaving the ground blanketed. Drifts of up to 15 feet in depth covered the roads, and the towns and villages were cut off. The West Highland railway line was blocked in several places, and its passengers were forced to spend hours on stranded trains. At high points across Rannoch Moor, between Glasgow and Fort William, drifts reached 20 feet in height. While snowploughs struggled to force their way through, some fortunate passengers on one train kept their spirits up by eating and drinking their way through the contents of the goods van, including whisky, cakes, and a consignment of sausages and haggis being transported in preparation for Burns Night on 25 January; the guard cooked the food for them on his portable stove. In addition, they were entertained by a piper who had been travelling on the train, and by the sight of violent lightning, culminating in a stinging hailstorm.

It was along this difficult route that Joseph and Lillian would need to make the final leg of their rail journey. Meanwhile, Violet, perhaps believing that she had temporarily evaded the press again, had even found time to wire Pullar's in Glasgow and arrange to have her now blue motor cloak forwarded to Oban Post Office, and then to take a return trip to Dunblane on Friday 15 January, fortunately before the worst of the snowstorm arrived. Seemingly oblivious to the fact that her description, together with an ink drawing, had been prominently featured in newspapers and displayed outside police stations and post offices across the country, she proceeded to visit Dunblane Cathedral and the Hydro, and to wire several telegrams from Dunblane Post Office – in full view of her own picture on the wall.

However, on her return to MacPherson's Hotel in Oban, Violet was to receive a nasty shock. Once inside the hotel she ordered afternoon tea in the drawing room and warmed herself in front of the roaring fire. While Violet waited for her refreshment, she passed the time by flicking absentmindedly through the pages of the local Oban Free Church's prayer book left on the side table for the enrichment of the hotel's guests, and failed to notice a smartly dressed man, 34 years of age, who had entered behind her. His name was Frank Dilnot. He looked around the room, then walked purposefully towards Violet.

Without attracting her attention or waiting for her to glance upwards, he gleefully announced, 'At last! I have the pleasure of addressing Miss

Violet Charlesworth.' Dilnot had been tracking her whereabouts since the first day of her disappearance, rushing across the country, following up any reported sighting of the mystery heiress. Still a young reporter at this stage, Dilnot would later become editor of *The Globe* and the *Daily Chronicle*, write the definitive biography of Lloyd George, and become president of the Association of Foreign Correspondents in America.

Violet closed the prayer book with a snap but otherwise seemed unruffled. 'I am not,' she replied firmly.

Taking a small notebook and pencil from his pocket, Dilnot did not wait to be invited, but sat down beside her. 'You are Miss Charlesworth.' His remark was very much a statement rather than a question. He continued, 'I am the Oban correspondent for the *Morning Leader* and *Daily Mail*, and I would like to speak to you.'

Violet flushed with well-rehearsed *faux* anger. 'I shall be very glad to answer all your questions, but you must admit I have a big grievance against certain members of your profession, and I can only say I shall have resource to legal proceedings if I am any further annoyed.'

The reporter, perhaps softened by her seemingly delicate nature and attractive appearance, instantly regretted his initial accusation, and his next question was far more contrite in nature, 'You're not Miss Charlesworth? Really and truly?'

'Really and truly, upon my word of honour.'

'Yet you are the very image of her photo,' Dilnot insisted.

'I have never seen any photo of her, except in a Scottish halfpenny newspaper,' Violet replied.

'Then who are you?'

'Miss Margaret Cameron MacLeod of Inverness.'

'Then who were your parents?' the reporter asked bluntly (he had naturally assumed from Violet's polished appearance and air that her family must have been well-connected).

She flushed with anger, 'That's no business of yours! I have no parents; I am an orphan.'

'And who were they when they were alive?'

'I refuse to answer; but you surely may take my word for it.'

The reporter persevered in his line of questioning, 'But, surely, you don't mind telling me. If all the world swears you are Violet Charlesworth, and you swear you are not, what harm is there in giving me your pedigree to prove it?'

'I shan't', Violet snapped. 'So there!'

Still, he persisted, 'Will you tell me then, why you are here at this wild season of the year, all by yourself, and shutting yourself up in dark rooms, and all that?'

'I love this place; I always loved it. I love it for the sake of old associations. That is the sole reason.'

Dilnot changed tack: 'Are you going to be here long?'

'Oh yes; for some time, I expect. But why I should be worried about my likeness to Miss Charlesworth is past all comprehension. It's the newspapers, I expect. Something was published yesterday about my being in Tobermory. I tell you, I am not Miss Charlesworth. I have never seen her in my life.'

In making this point, Violet failed to remember mentioning to the hotel's proprietor, Mrs MacPherson, that she had previously met Violet Charlesworth in Inverness. It was a slip that a wily reporter like Frank Dilnot could easily check. Violet continued, unaware of her mistake, 'I see you don't believe me, by your eyes. Now, will you accept my word of honour as a lady that I am Margaret Cameron MacLeod, and not Violet Charlesworth?'

'Perhaps I ought to,' the reporter said, 'but it is impossible for the eye to see or the mind to conceive two Violet Charlesworths in this world, as there seem to be at this moment.'

Violet stamped her foot in frustration and blurted out, 'What more can I say? It's too bad, it's too bad! I am insulted right and left!'

'I am very sorry. I hope you didn't think that I—'

'Oh, not you,' said Violet, interrupting him, 'but you have presumed upon a defenceless girl away on her holiday, and I must ask you to terminate this interview at once.' With that, she stood up, gathered her long skirts in her left hand and swept out of the drawing room and upstairs to her bedroom. It was enough for Frank Dilnot. Soon after, his report of the encounter appeared in the *Morning Leader, Scotsman, Glasgow Herald,* and *Daily Mail.*

THE GREAT MOTOR MYSTERY SOLVED. VIOLET CHARLESWORTH FOUND!

There she was, the absolute picture of the photographs I had seen – a slim, well-proportioned young lady, with soft wavy-brown hair, complexion slightly tinged with brown, brown spots here and there, and wonderful brown eyes of the most amazing eloquence, beneath fine sweet brown eyebrows. The curious form of her mouth – just a fine twist to it, behind which white teeth shone – clinched the matter, and made identification certain. Miss Charlesworth was wearing a soft greyish blouse, a big brooch of pearls in a true lover's knot, and a long chain swinging from neck to waist. Here, the neat blouse was snugly zoned by a gold belt, and at the belt hung a heavy gold pencil-case, four or five inches long, by a small gold chain.

I opened the door for her. She swept like a young queen out of the drawing-room and disappeared upstairs in a whirl of angry draperies. As she passed by I noticed a very quaint ring she was wearing. It was a circle of gold, nearly as large in circumference as a shilling, and around it were small pearls. This is the ring you may see in the newspaper photographs of Miss Charlesworth. She told the landlady here that her fiancé gave it to her. I asked the landlady, Mrs MacPherson, for her impression of the young lady, to which she replied, "You should see her in her bridal white! She wears that of an evening. Then she's got a beautiful gown of soft grey, a big white hat, and furs – good Lord, but they are bonny!"

Even if she desires to get away from Oban by rail she cannot now, for a big landslide occurred on the railway line soon after I arrived here. No trains have come through since my arrival. Oban stands, a thing of beauty, apart from all the rest of the world, with Violet prisoner here, and no getting away, except to Mull – which is not likely. The landslide will probably delay the arrival of Mr Gratton and Miss Lillian Charlesworth very considerably. They are due here at nine o'clock on Monday morning, all being well.

And so Violet, to all intents and purposes trapped in Oban, had little choice but to await the arrival of her sister and Joseph on Monday. Jolted by Dilnot's sudden appearance at her hotel, Violet took pen to paper and wrote to the *Glasgow Herald* (which immediately published her letter),

Macpherson Palace Hotel, Oban, Saturday, 16th January.
Dear Sir,

I shall feel greatly obliged if you will at once contradict the rumour which has appeared in the daily London and Scottish Press to the effect that it is believed that the missing Miss Violet Charlesworth has been for about eight days staying in Tobermory, and that the lady crossed from Tobermory to Oban a few days ago, saying that she would return about Friday. The rumour is also to the effect that the lady's luggage was left at the Mishnish Hotel, Tobermory. May I inform you that the lady in question was not Miss Charlesworth, and is not the owner of the luggage at the Mishnish Hotel. I am the lady who crossed from Oban to Tobermory in the mail steamer Lochinvar, having travelled previously from Aberdeenshire, my native shire, and put up for a time at the hotel I have named. I afterwards made inquiries for respectable rooms in the locality, with the idea of staying some few weeks in the interval, by way of improving my knowledge of my mother tongue, Gaelic. On Wednesday last I came to Oban, and both on the boat and since have been made the recipient of a great amount of annoyance through the absurd idea gaining ground that I was Miss Violet Charlesworth. At first, I was inclined to treat the whole thing as a joke, but after seeing mention of it in the columns of the Press, unless same is accordingly contradicted by the Press in general, and done at once, I shall instruct my legal representatives to take whatever steps they consider advisable in my interests against the Press for libel. It appears me that someone, in the absence of real facts about the lady, are very much overstepping the boundary when such statements are made. I have been the innocent object of them.

Believe me, yours truly,
(Miss) MARGARET CAMERON MACLEOD.

The impact of the letter's publication in the *Glasgow Herald* and other newspapers was rather overtaken by several other particularly grim and poignant stories dominating the news at that time. From the story of a murdered English lady whose throat was slashed on a French ocean liner, the tragic loss of a Leith fishing vessel, the *Fidra*, with all hands, to the continuing aftershocks of the Italian earthquake, and a terrible railroad crash in Colorado in which 68 people were killed, Miss MacLeod/Violet's tirade seemed far too selfish and self-indulgent to be taken seriously.

It turned out, however – perhaps as a contrast from this other depressing news coupled with the relentless winter weather – that the public saw the exposure of Violet as a welcome distraction and even as enjoyable entertainment. Fuelled by the nation's presses keen on increasing their circulation, the public eagerly awaited developments.

Meanwhile, following a protracted delay in which their train was forced to wait while a huge snowdrift was cleared from the line, Lillian and Joseph finally reached Oban and hastily made their way from the railway station to MacPherson's Hotel in George Street. Violet had deliberately picked this quiet and unassuming establishment, hoping it would not attract too much attention. Its modest ground-level doorway, next to the Royal Bank of Scotland, meant there was no grand public entrance. And if she was being pursued by the press, they might well assume she had booked into larger accommodation, such as the Royal Hotel. But despite her reasoning, Violet's plan had failed to work.

A small group of pressmen had followed Lillian from the railway station. Dilnot had already engaged rooms at the hotel for the travellers, and was waiting in the hotel's small reception area for their arrival. At noon precisely, Joseph and Lillian walked confidently into MacPherson's Hotel. The reporter would later infer that the pair were familiar with the hotel, as they did not ask for directions and seemed to be aware of the hotel's layout, 'as if they knew it before'.

The new arrivals spoke briefly to Mrs MacPherson, then Joseph went into the drawing room. Lillian hastened upstairs, followed by the reporter, and walked straight into Violet's room without knocking or announcing herself; Dilnot thought this action inconsistent with the lady in the room having claimed to be Miss MacLeod, a complete stranger to the Charlesworths. Lillian left the door to Violet's room ajar (seemingly for the benefit of the listening reporter) and spoke to her sister, who was lying on the bed.

'I am not Miss Violet Charlesworth,' responded Violet.

'I have come all the way from Wales to see you,' replied Lillian.

'Then you may go back,' answered Violet, 'I am too ill with worry, and as soon as I have recovered I am going to take action for libel against all the newspapers.'

The door to the bedroom was then closed abruptly from the inside, and Dilnot, despite pressing his ear to the door, was unable to hear the remainder of their conversation.

Five minutes later Lillian emerged, looking pale and harassed. She went downstairs and joined Joseph who was warming himself in front of the drawing-room fire.

Dilnot, who had followed Lillian downstairs, approached her and enquired, 'Is the lady upstairs your sister?'

'The lady upstairs is not my sister', Lillian replied, her hands visibly trembling. 'She is not Violet Charlesworth. I have come all the way to Oban for this!'

'Is she like her at all?' the reporter asked.

'I couldn't say.'

Dilnot then produced a photograph of Violet, taken in 1907 at the McIsaac and Riddle Photographic Studio in Oban, during her visit there: 'Is that a photograph of your sister Violet?'

'Yes.'

'Then that is the lady upstairs.'

'How do you know?' snapped Lillian.

'Because I was with her yesterday face to face for ten minutes,' he answered, 'and observed every feature most closely.'

Lillian glanced again at the picture and, this time a little more hedged in her answer, replied, 'That is not a very good photograph.'

'Yes, it is!' Dilnot exclaimed, becoming ever more incredulous, 'And you swear that the lady upstairs is not she?'

'It is not she!' cried out Lillian. 'And I must ask you to terminate this interview at once.'

The reporter persisted, 'Now, confess that you are not telling the truth, and that you are doing nothing but trying a great game of bluff on me, and on the police, and everyone else.'

Lillian became outraged, her cool exterior cracking, 'How dare you, a gentleman, treat a lady in this manner? Leave the room instantly.'

'Denials are useless,' responded the pressman. 'You had better make a clean breast of it.'

'I have nothing to make a clean breast of,' retorted Lillian, 'and I shan't say another word.'

The reporter turned to Joseph, who had maintained an embarrassed silence throughout the interview, and said, 'Come, Sir, put an end to all this fooling.'

He shook his head wearily and answered, 'I haven't seen her. You must take this lady's word for it. I can say nothing.'

At this point, a police officer knocked the door and entered the drawing room, his large frame filling the doorway. He announced – rather nervously for a man with such a large presence, 'Inspector MacKenzie, from Oban Police Station. Are you Miss Lillian Charlesworth? I would very much like to speak to your sister.'

By this time, a number of other reporters had taken up residence in the hotel's lobby. Rather enjoying the dramatic scenes, Mrs MacPherson directed them into the hotel's coffee room. Lillian requested that they be asked to leave immediately.

Meanwhile, scores of telegrams addressed to Miss Violet Charlesworth were delivered to the hotel by a harassed Post Office cable boy. All of them had been wired from various newspaper editors across the country.

This rather blatant attempt to trick Violet into accepting a message did not work. Violet simply refused to acknowledge them, claiming, 'I am Miss MacLeod, not Miss Charlesworth.'

Lillian once again denied that she was the sister of the lady in the room upstairs and, after the questioning was temporarily stopped for lunch, she retired upstairs to the room of the alleged Miss Margaret Cameron MacLeod, where she remained for the next two hours.

The absurdity of the fact that on the one hand Lillian and 'Miss MacLeod' claimed to be strangers who had never met before, yet on the other were now closeted in a room together, was not lost on either Frank Dilnot or Inspector MacKenzie. Dilnot then urged the inspector to seek a visual confirmation : 'Here is my photo of Violet. Fill your eye with her image and then raid her bedroom and for goodness' sake see for yourself!'

MacKenzie, emboldened by the challenge, went upstairs. He returned a few minutes later with a perplexed expression upon his face, 'I have seen her, and it is right enough. A baby couldn't mistake her. But she says over and over again "I'm Margaret Cameron MacLeod." That is all I can get out of her.'

MacKenzie then sent off a wire to Conwy Police Station: 'Miss Lillian Charlesworth failed to identify the lady here as her sister Violet. Letter follows.'

And so the stalemate continued. The two sisters, together with Joseph, remained hidden behind a locked bedroom door. The inspector returned to Oban Police Station, after asking to be kept abreast of any developments; and Dilnot drifted off to sleep on a drawing-room armchair, having barely slept for three days in pursuit of his quarry. Like a game of poker, bluff played counter-bluff.

17: The Upper Hand

Two hours later, Dilnot was woken abruptly by Mrs MacPherson, who shook his arm furiously, 'Wake up! I will have her here no longer. I am losing my wits. It is a dreadful business, and I may tell you that all three of them – Mr Gratton, Miss Lillian, and Miss MacLeod – are going south by the forenoon train. I knew she was no lady! No real lady would leave her boots so close to the fire to dry.'

Mrs MacPherson sent her boots boy with the news to the police station in Albany Street, and Inspector MacKenzie, then joining the reporter, announced to him, 'They say they want to get out of this place, which is rapidly becoming a hotbed of newspaper men. They are going to Perth, or Glasgow, to get out of the way, and once there Miss MacLeod will leave them.'

To Dilnot's complete surprise he was then joined in the drawing room by Violet, who had silently entered the room and stood like a man might, with her back to the roaring fire. He later described her appearance as, 'Like a tragedy queen, who tried to quell me with her flashing brown eyes. Miss MacLeod (as she calls herself) is a lady of medium height, pale faced and slightly freckled. She wore a light grey skirt and cream-coloured blouse.'

Lillian also entered the room, slightly behind Violet.

Violet angrily blurted out, 'You are the pressman I spoke to yesterday, aren't you?'

Frank Dilnot nodded his head in confirmation, then spoke, 'May I take it that the written contradiction to the newspapers that you are Miss Violet Charlesworth still holds good?'

'Yes, I emphatically deny that I am that lady. Now, please show me that that photograph of m—, of Miss Charlesworth', she demanded imperiously.

Dilnot handed her the image.

Violet gazed at it, 'Me! Pah! That is not me.'

She turned to her sister, 'Do you see any likeness?'

Lillian answered, 'There is none whatsoever, my sister has a different colour of eyes from Miss MacLeod who, as you can see, has brown eyes.'

'But most amazingly like you', Dilnot replied.

Violet narrowed her eyes and, looking at the photograph again, answered, 'Something like, I suppose.'

'Wonderfully like you. Did you ever have a twin sister?'

'Never, I told you yesterday, I am an orphan, Margaret Cameron Macleod, that was born in Inverness, and that my parents are dead. I won't tell you another word. Now go, please go, and let you and me never meet again.'

With that, Violet twirled dramatically and began to walk out. The reporter called after her, 'Miss Charlesworth!'

'What?'

"May I have the photograph back, please?'

Violet's face flushed, and she sheepishly handed back the image before announcing, 'I am leaving. Please ask the landlady to send in my bill.'

Before she could exit Dilnot asked, 'Have you visited Tobermory before?'

Violet nodded in agreement.

Seizing on the opportunity, he leapt in, 'What about that torn telegram found in the wastepaper basket at the Mishnish Hotel, and the missing page from the visitors' book, and also the medicine bottle?'

'I know nothing of these things. I can give no explanation for it,' Violet answered. 'I may say that it is my intention to proceed to Glasgow, then I shall go to Aberdeenshire, my native county, for a few days. First, I am going back to Tobermory to get my luggage and settle my account.'

Lillian added defiantly, 'Yes, Glasgow will be our headquarters for the night. If we are to be shadowed as we have been in the past, we shall seek police protection. We have been followed even from Wales.'

Dilnot made a mental note that Violet, or Miss MacLeod as she continued to call herself, had not a trace of a Aberdonian accent, nor any Scottish accent at all. In fact, both Violet and her sister (although, of course, they still maintained that they were not acquainted) sounded almost identical in their accents, with something of a Midlands or Northern English burr to their voices.

The three travellers made the short journey to Oban railway station. Dilnot hastily grabbed his few possessions, notebook, and coat, and hurried after them. If the trio had hoped for a quiet departure, they must have been sorely disappointed, as a large crowd of onlookers had gathered at the station and surged onto the platform. News of the exact location of the trio's first-class compartment had already been divulged to the waiting masses, and the carriage was besieged by those anxious to witness Violet for themselves. Steam and smoke from the locomotive billowed into the cold afternoon air as the party quickly made their way to the platform for the Glasgow-bound train. Members of the crowd – women booing and men cheering – tried vainly to thrust copies of folded newspapers at Violet, perhaps hoping that she might sign their copy, or maybe simply hoping to detect a whisper of recognition on her face as she was confronted with the banner headlines bearing her name.

THE MISSING MOTORIST FOUND!
VIOLET IS ALIVE AND WELL
THE CLIFF TOP MYSTERY SOLVED!

The three were ushered onto the train by the guard and into their compartment, in which they instantly drew the blinds. While several reporters remained on the platform, others, including Dilnot, also boarded the train. As the guard waved the train away, he was inundated with questions from the eager pressmen. Probably for the only time in his life he was asked to make a press statement.

He did so, gleefully: 'Mon, 'tis the day of ma life. The news that Miss Violet is in the train has spread all along the line, and crowds have assembled at most stations t' gaze and admire the wee lady.'

En route to Glasgow the train made several stops. And indeed, at each station a sizeable line of onlookers had gathered along the platforms in the hope of being afforded a fleeting glance of the famous missing motorist. It seems that the Scottish public needed no convincing that Miss MacLeod was indeed Violet Charlesworth. But despite braving the cold and the snow they were not to be rewarded; the trio kept the carriage blinds tightly closed throughout the journey. At Taynuilt, one of the quieter stations along the route, Joseph hopped off the train and quickly wired a telegram of instruction forward to Crianlarich station, requesting that three hot drinks and refreshments might be brought aboard the train there. It seems that they had no intention of leaving their carriage until their arrival in Glasgow.

The train finally steamed into Buchanan Street station, Platform 3, at exactly 9.30 pm. Any hope of a quiet arrival was cruelly dashed as the three picked up their luggage and waited for the guard to open the carriage door onto the platform. A significant number of onlookers had already gathered inside the station, and began to cheer and jostle as the travellers alighted the train. A large group surged around Lillian and Violet, impeding their progress along the platform. Joseph quickly hailed a porter and entrusted him with two oblong dressing cases and two brown leather bags while he hurried outside to engage a taxicab. Meanwhile, Lillian, slightly panicked by the large swaying crowd, attempted to usher and hurry Violet out of the station concourse and into the taxicab. Violet however, rather unexpectedly, seemed oddly at ease. She walked serenely and leisurely, even enjoying the attention of the crowd and the admiring glances as the gathering parted enough to allow them access to the four-wheeler cab. Joseph and Lillian pulled Violet into it, and the cab sped off down West Nile Street, then along Gordon Street, finally pulling up at the junction with Hope Street outside the impressive curved entrance to the seven-storey Central Station Hotel, not far from the spot at which Violet had arrived in Glasgow two weeks earlier.

Joseph paid the driver, then accompanied the two ladies inside, where they booked rooms for the night (Violet and Lillian under the name MacDonald, and Joseph under the name R. Cameron), before dining in the restaurant. Dilnot, who had followed Violet to the Central

Glasgow Central Station Hotel

Station Hotel, hastily arranged a room for himself. On seeing Violet entering the restaurant, he spoke to her again and warned her of the huge number of journalists and photographers now targeting the hotel. Many had already engaged rooms, and many more were outside. Each one had been tasked by their editor with attempting at all costs to obtain an all-important exclusive interview with the fugitive. Although Violet remained calm and collected, she was now visibly fatigued and was overheard remarking to the chambermaid that she was 'nervous and exhausted'.

Violet realised that she could not escape the ever-increasing mass of reporters without revealing her true identity or obtaining some outside assistance. But the fact that Joseph and Lillian had travelled alongside her, and booked hotel rooms with a supposedly complete stranger – the purported Miss Margaret Cameron MacLeod – was, of course, already enough evidence for the eager pressmen. Violet, meanwhile, still clung to the forlorn hope of maintaining her charade.

The following morning, Tuesday 19 January, Joseph breakfasted alone, then paid the hotel bill for himself and the two sisters. Meanwhile, upstairs a reporter accosted Lillian in the corridor: 'I put it to you that the lady who is sharing rooms with you is none other than your resurrected sister.'

Lillian responded, 'Well, I am not at liberty to say at present. We have not decided where we are going to go. I will not fail to let you know if we reach such a conclusion.'

She, of course, had no intention of warning the press of their departure, and had every intention of slipping away unnoticed. Lillian returned to her sister's bedroom and said, 'I don't know how we shall get rid of them, but we must find a way of escaping them.'

Violet agreed, and replied, 'I will speak to the pressman, Mr Dilnot.' Another bold plan was swiftly forming in her mind.

Following the discussion with Lillian, Violet decided to engage Frank Dilnot's help; Now, the former foe, who had been chasing her for several days, might prove a useful ally. She approached him with her idea, and he agreed immediately.

Full details of the riotous events that followed were thought to have been lost to the mists of time. However, during my research for this book I was lucky enough to uncover a forgotten series of articles written by Frank Dilnot three years later, under the banner '*The Adventures of a Newspaper Man*'. Out of print for more than a century, Dilnot's personal account details precisely what happened during the following 48 hours:

> Miss Charlesworth placed herself in my hands in order to escape the little army of my colleagues who were besetting her. She indicated that she might have something of interest to tell me if I could get her away to Edinburgh, and I accordingly made plans to help her and her sister to get out of the hotel. Fortunately, I had with me a colleague from London and with his help I set to work.
>
> First of all, in order to put the other pressmen on the wrong track, we went and bought four first class tickets on the 11.30 Caledonian train to Edinburgh, a fact which became quickly known and caused journalistic pickets to be established on the station's departure platforms, and then I secured a motor-car and had it taken round to the back entrance of the hotel, where the public never went. With the motor-car in waiting, my friend and I mounted the stairs to the room of the ladies, whom we found ready garbed for departure. With them, we emerged into the corridor, and some of our competitors who were on guard there immediately made ahead of us, descending the stairs to the hall of the hotel in order to get the rest in readiness. But the ladies and ourselves, instead of going downstairs, went upstairs to the floor above, and passed along to the extreme end of the corridor, where, as I had previously ascertained, there was a whitewashed stairway used by the servants, descending through the various floors to the basement.
>
> Down this stairway we hurried, trusting to good fortune that our motor-car had not been discovered. We were in luck's way; the car had been undetected, and we packed ourselves in it, and away we went for Edinburgh.
>
> Once there, by all that was unfortunate, a London journalist, who happened to be in the city, spied me as we passed the post office. I pretended not to see him, and hoped that he would not recognise me, a false hope, as I subsequently discovered.

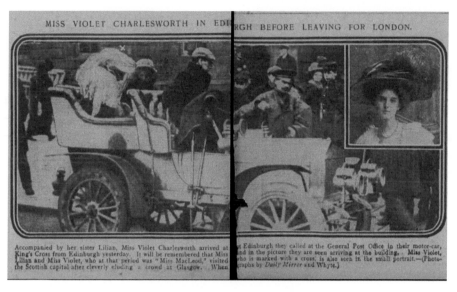

MISS VIOLET CHARLESWORTH IN EDINBURGH BEFORE LEAVING FOR LONDON.

Accompanied by her sister Lilian, Miss Violet Charlesworth arrived at King's Cross from Edinburgh yesterday. It will be remembered that Miss Lilian and Miss Violet, who at that period was "Miss MacLeod," visited the Scottish capital after cleverly eluding a crowd at Glasgow. When at Edinburgh they called at the General Post Office in their motor-car, and in the picture they are seen arriving at the building. Miss Violet, who is marked with a cross, is also seen in the small portrait.—(Photographs by *Daily Mirror* and Whyte.)

Violet Charlesworth in Edinburgh

Unfortunately for the sisters, the motor car in question was large, yellow, and conspicuous in the extreme, and they were spotted by two London press photographers who had recognised Violet from her image in the newspapers; they even managed to take photographs. They would later state that it seemed from the manner of the group's journeying about the country that 'every step is being stage-managed according to some preconceived arrangement.'

Conceivably Violet, after previously shying away from publicity, was beginning to see the value of it. If her days as a fraudster were about to come to an end, perhaps she hoped to become a sort of Edwardian influencer, earning money purely from her fame. For most of 1909 she would become the most talked-about lady in the land, temporarily deflecting the bile of the male establishment away from the suffragette movement.

Returning to the memoirs of Frank Dilnot,

> I took the ladies to the Carlton Hotel, secured a suite of rooms
> for them, and was preening myself in the happy confidence that
> I had eluded the journalists in Glasgow. Foolish optimist was I.
> By some means or other, they had secured the scent, and once
> in Edinburgh suspicion was turned into certainty by the man
> having already seen me in the motor-car outside the post office.
> It was a heavy task from this time onward through the evening
> and till late in the night to keep them at bay, and, indeed, one
> of them managed to get through and secure an audience of

the ladies. It was eight o'clock that night when Miss Violet Charlesworth, hitherto known to me as Margaret MacLeod, said that she was, in fact, the missing Violet. A statement from her explaining her disappearance appeared in my paper next morning.

"Yes, it is no use denying it any longer – I am Miss Violet Charlesworth. I fled to Scotland on a sudden impulse, and finally went to Oban."

She was to go to London with her sister in order to elaborate her statement to her solicitor, and it was my part to escort her thither. When we left Edinburgh by train, about ten o'clock on Wednesday 20th January, there was a considerable crowd on the platform, and, of course, it was soon spread abroad by most of the evening papers, that Violet Charlesworth and her sister were on the way to London. This accounts for the fact that, although I had a reserved first-class compartment, and kept the blinds down whenever we were in a station, we had a group on the platform at every stoppage, sometimes a considerable crowd, all anxious to see the girl in my charge. I remember dashing out at York station to get some papers at a bookstall, and in the course of my sprint had two halts, one caused by a local reporter, who desired to get something for his evening paper, and to whom I gave a twenty seconds' interview, and the other was an unexpected encounter with Mr Arthur Henderson, M.P.,[19] who stopped me with a chaffing word.

Back again into my compartment, I began a consultant [sic] as to what our course of action should be on arrival at King's Cross, where it was now certain there would be a crowd waiting to meet us. Several things had to be guarded against. One was the zeal of rival newspaper men, who would not flinch from a friendly and temporary kidnapping of Miss Charlesworth from under my eyes, and the other was the public attention which might lead to demonstrations, embarrassing, if not otherwise unpleasant.

I arranged with my two charges the course of procedure. Violet was to take my arm on alighting from the carriage at King's Cross, and was to maintain her hold on me under any pressure, and was at the same time to say no single word of any kind in response to questions which would no doubt be

---

19 Arthur Henderson was a firebrand Scottish trade unionist, and in 1909 leader of the Labour party – a party which Dilnot would later join.

forthcoming. Her sister, Lillian, was to follow the same course with my colleague. Once on the platform, we should exit in order to find the motor-car which would be waiting for us.

We arrived at 6.15. The crowd at King's Cross was even bigger and more excited than I had expected, and as the train slowed up the people surged round the carriage. I realised that it would be almost impossible for us to descend, and that if we succeeded in doing so, we should be in midst of trouble at once. So, I decided to keep the blinds down in the compartment and to remain there for a minute or two, in the hope that the public would scatter, and that my friends with the car would come and help to deliver me from my unenviable position. A minute or so passed, and the crowd showed no signs of diminishing. The girls were on tiptoe to leave, and I stood ready to take advantage of any slackening of the throng on the platform.

Suddenly the door on the line side opened, and one of the two men standing there exclaimed, "This way; come along, quick! Come down here and over to the other platform."

The girls made a move forward. With a momentary suspicion that the men might in some way be enemies, I pulled the girls back, because I felt that they were under my protection – at any rate, for the time being.

"It's all right," said one of the men. "Don't you see, I'm the stationmaster?" and I caught a glimpse of the braid on his coat and silk hat, and realised that his help was genuine.

We assisted the girls down onto the line, and then onto the platform opposite, and, with Violet's arm linked in mine, and her sister's linked in that of my colleague, we made a dash for the gates.

Our manoeuvring had become known by this time, and a great part of the crowd was pushing pell-mell round to meet us. We met the stream of people at the gates, and were suddenly encircled by a clamouring throng, in the middle of which were reporters who were quite determined to get some kind of announcement from Violet, or, alternatively, a statement from me. I realised for the first time, the insistence and forcefulness of the modern newspaper man.

Vainly did I try to keep them at bay. One or two of them, I am quite sure, would have been prepared to wrest Violet from my arm, but she clung close to me, thoroughly frightened – I think not merely by the eagerness of the Pressmen, but by the excitement of the surging crowd which assailed us on all sides and prevented us from making progress in any direction. It was difficult to know what to do because, in the midst of the gathering, and with night upon us, I had no means of picking out our motor-car, nor any immediate place of shelter.

Meanwhile, the crowd eddied us against the door of a four-wheeler. Here was refuge for a moment, at any rate. I thrust my charge inside, and my colleague did the same for her sister, and then, shouting to the man to drive on anywhere, I got in myself.

As good luck would have it, I no sooner shut the door than two of my friends with the waiting motor-car appeared nearby, and I indicated to them that they should follow us, so that we might change vehicles as soon as we were well away from the excitement. We started off in our four-wheeler, followed by a string of taxicabs and hansom cabs chartered by other journalists, but we were all right now. Some three or four hundred yards away the motor-car pulled up, and I had the four-wheeler stopped just behind it, and rapidly got the girls from one conveyance to the other.

After that, we soon left all our followers behind.

The strain on the girls had been heavy, and I may be permitted to relate that Violet Charlesworth, who was the subject of so much adverse criticism and wonderment that day, tried to hide the tears rolling down her cheeks.

That was my encounter with Violet Charlesworth.

Now, stranded in London, Violet faced ravenous reporters, vengeful creditors, and an insatiable public. Financially, she was in ruins. Her supposed death in the motor-car accident had been exposed and her fake identity as Miss MacLeod uncovered. Her property, vehicles, and assets were being repossessed, and her fiancé, Dr Hughes Jones, had disowned her.

However, the story of her fake inheritance had yet to be disproved, nor at this stage even questioned (at least officially). Violet knew that she would need to find some way of attempting to repay her debts, but could she simultaneously maintain her reputation and avoid being exposed as a fraud? All she would require was brazen faith in her invented back story and the knowledge that the authorities would find it difficult to disprove. After all, as Edward H. Smith would state in his 1923 book *Confessions of a Confidence Man: A Handbook for Suckers,* 'the difference between a trick and a confidence trick is merely confidence'.

Nothing For Something

This ditty was published in *The World* magazine, following Violet's motor-car accident of 2 January 1909:

THE CLIFF COMEDY

We heard that she had left the scene,
Projected through a motor screen;
The tragedy made England start,
And deeply touched the public heart.
But now the cold police declare
The missing lady wasn't there,
And sympathy is changed to curses,
She deeply touched so many purses.

18: The Pay-Off

On Monday 18 January 1909 three stories dominated the nation's newspaper headlines: the discovery of a lady purporting to be Miss Margaret MacLeod on the Isle of Mull, Lillian's farcical and theatrical claims that 'the lady is not my resurrected sister', and the heart-wrenching story of Ernest Shackleton's battle to return safely from the South Pole. Indeed, you might be forgiven for assuming that the pantomime still playing out at Boderw would have taken second stage. In fact, the drama in North Wales was turning out to be every bit as newsworthy as those three stories.

Described by the newspapers as 'The Siege of Boderw', events came to a dramatic head after sundown on that Monday evening. After being denied admission on several previous occasions, Sergeant Connah and PC Hughes were waiting outside the property, armed with a commitment warrant from Staffordshire police, which they intended to execute. The authorities had been waiting patiently for a legitimate reason to enter the property, and the serving of the warrant at last gave them a justifiable one.

Their previous attempts had been unsuccessful; the Charlesworths had simply denied them entry. Now, with Lillian, Violet, and Joseph away, the police felt an easier opportunity to gain access had finally presented itself. The sheriff's officers were also in wait outside the property, hoping to gain access. Then at 7 pm word came that Frederick, Violet's brother, and Heywood, Lillian's chauffeur, had been seen leaving the property via the back gate and walking north, in the direction of Rhuddlan. The police calculated that only David and Miriam now remained inside, along with Albert. Sergeant Connah did not anticipate any resistance.

Under instruction from Superintendent Davies, PC Hughes and Sergeant Connah scaled the wall surrounding the property, closely followed by Adams and Kelly, the burly sheriff's officers, who had been watching the proceedings from the rooftop of a nearby outbuilding. Sergeant Connah knocked sharply on the front door of Boderw. He heard movement inside, but no one came to answer the door.

The Charlesworths employed a security guard at Boderw during the 'seige'

The sergeant knocked again and shouted out abruptly, 'I have a warrant from the Staffordshire police here, against the chauffeur Albert Watts for a breach of County Council bye-laws, relating to the lighting of motor-cars. There is a fine of 19 shillings and 6 pence which you have failed to pay. Please open the door immediately.'

Finally, George Campbell opened the door an inch or so, and peering around the gap asked cautiously, 'Who is it?'

'I am Police Sergeant Connah, and I wish to see Watts.'

George opened the door fully. To the complete surprise of the two policemen on the doorstep, the two sheriff's officers stormed past them and through the open doorway into the dimly lit hall. Wild confusion ensued. Sergeant Connah shouted at the sheriff's men to leave immediately. David Charlesworth bawled at the policemen, 'You have no right to enter after sunset!' (Warrants supposedly could not be served after sunset – that day, around 4.30 pm – without special permission from a magistrate.)

Albert rushed from the adjoining room into the hallway, and called out to the massive St Bernard, which was barking incessantly – and which was rather confusingly also called Sergeant! – 'Sergeant, at 'em!'

Seeing the dog bounding towards him, Kelly pulled a menacing wooden truncheon from the folds of his long overcoat. Known as a life preserver, the weapon was a leatherbound wooden club of around a foot in length, with weighted ends and a rope wrist loop, and capable of inflicting untold damage. As Kelly raised the weapon, intent on clubbing the snarling dog, Miriam Charlesworth leapt forward and, grabbing its collar, attempted to pull it aside. In the commotion she was thrown to the ground and promptly fainted. PC Hughes was immediately sent out for a stimulant to revive her.

Soon after that Frederick returned. Stunned to see the commotion, he remonstrated angrily with the officers: 'Our solicitor has advised us that you should be kept out at all costs. I thought an entrance to this house was impossible!'

He immediately telephoned the family's local solicitor, Mr Radcliffe from Rhyl, who arrived shortly afterwards, in hope of restoring peace.

Under Radcliffe's watchful eye, Sergeant Connah explained the original object of his visit to Albert: 'You will have to spend the night in the St Asaph police station unless you pay the fine.'

'I have no money,' Albert replied.

As the sergeant prepared to escort Albert to the police station, David, stepping in, announced, 'I will pay the fine.'

Next, Kelly and Adams, the sheriff's officers, accompanied by Frederick, began systematically combing each luxuriously furnished room, creating an inventory of the goods contained therein. Kelly warned Frederick, 'Each item belonging to Miss Violet Charlesworth will be requisitioned for auction and used to repay her creditors.'

Frederick replied, 'The only things belonging to Violet are a sewing machine, a large iron safe, and a few other small articles. The two pianos, skin rugs, art, and other "*objets de vertu*" belong to Mr Gratton, Lillian and my mother, Mrs Miriam Charlesworth.'

The officers sealed the safe for future examination, and by 10 pm calm seems to have been restored to Boderw; David had paid the outstanding fine on behalf of Albert, the sheriff's officers had left (perhaps with less than they had hoped for), and the police had retreated from the grounds.

However, while the Charlesworths were distracted by these chaotic events, the family's cook, young Cassie Hughes from Pontblyddyn, was elsewhere, meeting with stunned members of the press as she gave details of her escape from Boderw on the previous evening:

> I have been engaged as cook at Boderw for a little more than twelve months, and I am glad now to be out of the house. I had not been outside for three weeks until last night, when, against the wishes of those in the house, I escaped last night with my brother's help and went to chapel.
>
> The family all along have wished to detain me inside the house, and insisted that I should say nothing to anyone in the outside world. I have had terrible letters from my brother this week, trying to persuade me to come home, and the Charlesworth family have refused to allow me to come out.
>
> Violet Charlesworth, I believed, was at the bottom of the sea. I now believe she may be in Scotland. They all lived well, and the house at Boderw is full of beautiful furniture, worth thousands of pounds. Their midnight drives, which were very frequent, I could never understand. Sometimes Miss Violet went alone with Watts, and sometimes with Miss Lillian and her father.
>
> They told me that they did this because the road was clear. They never had any neighbours visiting the house. The only visitors were Dr Miller and Dr Hughes Jones.
>
> I cannot say how the family got their living. I was always given to understand that Miss Violet was coming into a fortune on the 13th of this month. She had lots of beautiful clothes and jewellery, and has told me that her young man left her a thousand pounds' worth of jewellery. I used to sit with her for hours in her bedroom, and the whole of the conversation was about motor-cars and dogs. She was passionately fond of these.
>
> She told me she had been engaged to a young man whose

Christian name was Vincent. I don't remember the other name. She was always fond of soldiers. He, however, died at sea, she told me, on a voyage home, and she had been broken down in health since.

She said she always got his money monthly from trustees, and I always believed her, because money with her seemed so plentiful. She was always buying dresses.

Since the supposed accident I have been perfectly miserable, and the family have been miserable too. We have had lots of letters and postcards from people who gave no names or addresses. The letters always arrived in a private postbag.

Miss Charlesworth told me that people were painting them blacker than they were.

On the day of the accident Miss Violet and Miss Lillian were out with Watts in the motor-car. Both the ladies said to me that they were only going for a short drive, and were coming back for tea at half-past four. We waited up till one o'clock in the morning, and then Sergeant Connah and another policeman came and told the chauffeur, Heywood, and the page, and Mr Gratton to prepare for the worst, as one of the Miss Charlesworths was killed, and the other two seriously injured.

Mr Gratton and Heywood borrowed the neighbour, Mr Buxton's, car and went to Penmaenmawr. They landed at our place about half-past four. I did not see Miss Lillian that night, and not till Sunday evening. She sobbed when she saw me. She said she was a little better.

I said, "It is very sad about poor Miss Violet."

"It is," she replied.

Since Miss Violet left the house on that Saturday she has never been back here to my knowledge.

I don't know very much about the family. When they first moved to Boderw, Miss Violet and Miss Lillian came to my house at Pontblyddyn in their motor-car, with two chauffeurs and Mr Gratton. I have always been paid my wages regularly every month, and only today Mrs Miriam Charlesworth paid me my monthly wages.

The gathered journalists, keen to uncover the dramatic details of Cassie Hughes' escape from Boderw, interviewed her brother, who stood protectively at her side while explaining the details of the previous night's adventures:

I motored down early in the morning, intending that my sister, who has been shut up in Boderw against her will, should leave the house at once. I went down to the house about half-past three in the morning, tried the front gate, and found it locked. Then I went round to the side door, which bears the legend "Beware of the Dog".

I had heard of this, and so carried a stout stick. I climbed over the high gates, which were locked and barred. I then knocked quietly at the door, but obtained no reply. I shouted "Cassie" three times up to her window, but there was no answer. Then the page boy came to the door and asked me what I wanted.

I said, "I want to see my sister."

She came to the window, and then an old man wearing long grey whiskers also came to the window. He told me to, "Stop a minute". He then came downstairs and, opening the door slightly, said, "Is there anyone else with you?"

"No," I replied, and he admitted me, then locked the door behind me.

Despite the early hour I was taken into the morning-room, and a large St Bernard dog leapt at me, and licked my face. The dog knew me. I had seen it before.

Mrs Charlesworth, a lady with dark hair but fairly advanced in age, came into the room, and said, "Take a seat, please. Why do you want Cassie away so sudden? Is it because of this mystery, or on account of family illness?"

"My aunt is ill," I replied, "Cassie's leaving has nothing whatever to do with the mystery."

Mr Charlesworth, in a very excited manner, then repeated his wife's question, and added, "Tell the truth!"

They then sent for Watts, who was upstairs asleep in his room, and instructed him to see if anybody else was outside. They asked me, "Are you on your own? Is anybody around?"

I replied, "I don't think so; nobody saw me come in here."

My sister had by this time come downstairs, and on seeing me burst into tears. On seeing this I said to her, "You have got to come home tonight. I am not going from this place without you."

I was prepared for trouble and blocked the way while my sister hastily packed some of her luggage. After throwing on her hat and heavy coat we went to the back entrance, Mr Charlesworth and Watts following. I dragged her out of the door whilst they tried to prevent us. Her luggage was first thrown over the wall. I sprang up on the gate, got hold of my sister's arm, and pulled her up. Watts was pulling her back down with one foot and old Mr Charlesworth with the other. I called out for help, and men waiting on the outside seized her arms and eventually managed to land her safely in the road. We sprang into the waiting motor-car and drove away.

I am delighted that she was got away safely, because we were very anxious about her.

After presenting their remarkable stories to the press, both Cassie Hughes and her brother gave the St Asaph police a sworn statement of the circumstances surrounding their dramatic escape. Nevertheless, it appears that no charges of unlawful detainment were made against the Charlesworths, nor was any action ever taken.

Meanwhile in London Violet's tribulations continued. Events, it seems, were moving apace. After narrowly escaping the hounding press at King's Cross she made her way across the capital to Fleet Street, and the offices of Messrs Amery-Parkes, Macklin & Co.

Four hours later, Violet emerged from their offices to be faced by a surging mass of reporters and approximately 400 onlookers, who were restrained by a line of police constables. Violet's ghostly pale face was only matched that day by a newspaper story, declaring that a thousand human skulls were to be openly displayed in the crypt of Hythe Parish Church in Kent. It seems the Edwardian public's thirst for a sensational story knew no bounds.

Messrs Amery-Parkes, Macklin & Co. swiftly released copies of their agreement with Violet to the Press Association, outlining that an urgent meeting of her creditors was to be held:

23rd January, 1909
Madam,

In reference to your request that we should continue to act for you, we write to say that, as you have expressed your willingness to comply with any suggestions which we may make for the benefit of your creditors, we are prepared to act on your behalf, but only to the extent of endeavouring to assist your creditors to obtain payment of the amounts due them from you. We will do this upon the condition that you will bind yourself to disclose fully the whole of your assets, including jewellery, and; to transfer the whole, together with any money, which is now payable to you, or which is to become payable to from prospective engagements, employment or otherwise, or so much as your creditors think proper, to a trustee for the benefit of your creditors until they are discharged in full, or until they have received such a composition as they may at a meeting have expressed their willingness to accept.

On these conditions, and these conditions only, we will agree temporarily to act in the manner we have stated, and will proceed to call a meeting with your creditors.

We think you should be present at this meeting in case your creditors desire to question you.

Yours truly,
(Signed) AMERY-PARKES, MACKLIN AND CO.
and Miss V.M.G. Charlesworth.'

Violet's reply – as was her wish – was also widely published in the newspapers,

In reference to your letter of today's date, I write to say that if you will agree to continue to act for me in the manner which you suggest, I am prepared to carry out the conditions which you have laid down, and to attend any meeting of my creditors which you may call. I shall be obliged if you would give publicity to this correspondence.

(Signed) V. Gordon Charlesworth

By now, Violet clearly appreciated the importance of public attention – not just as an attempt to gain universal sympathy and support, but as a means of generating enough income to repay her creditors. Had she lived today, it is almost certain that she would have become a social media star, appeared on tawdry TV reality shows, and written a sensational exposé. However, although the options available to Violet in 1909 were very different, she was not slow to grab any opportunity which presented itself.

Her urgent need to repay (or, at least, be publicly seen to be attempting to repay) her debts was made ever more apparent as the series of repossessions, creditors' claims, and bankruptcy hearings snowballed. First, Mr F.J. Gamlin, a Rhyl solicitor, acting on behalf of the owner of Boderw, served the Charlesworth family with a Notice of Claim for outstanding rent, amounting to £74 (now £10,000).

Secondly, even more public scorn was heaped on Violet when, after being formally summoned, she failed to appear during a farcical hearing at Rhyl County Court in the case of Messrs J. Price and Co., St. Asaph, v. Miss Violet Gordon Charlesworth. Mr Joseph Lloyd, solicitor, appeared for the plaintiffs. However, neither Violet nor her lawyers, Messrs Amery-Parkes, Macklin & Co., attended. Mr Lloyd, with a theatrical flourish, then produced a letter from Violet's solicitors, dated 5 January, two weeks earlier, when the world beyond Boderw had still believed that Violet was dead. The packed public gallery (who had all attended in the hope of an appearance by Violet) jeered and roared with laughter as Lloyd read the letter out loud:

> In accordance with our instructions, we have filed notice of intention to defend this action on behalf of the defendant, but we expect that you are aware that Miss Charlesworth met with a fatal accident on Saturday last. Under the circumstances we shall be glad to learn that your clients do not propose to press the action for the time being.

Mr Lloyd now asked for judgment to be granted in favour of his client, as a result of Violet's discovery in Scotland. The registrar clerk, Mr J. Fenna, instructed the usher to call the defendant outside the court. The usher farcically bellowed 'Call Miss Violet Gordon Charlesworth!' three times to an empty hallway outside the courtroom. There was, of course, only deafening silence. After a short interval the registrar remarked, to jeers from the crowd, that he had since received a second letter from Violet's solicitor withdrawing the original letter and asking for an adjournment of the case. The registrar suggested that 14 days would be suitable.

Mr Lloyd replied, 'This will be no good for my client. At present there are goods at the house which they could seize belonging to Miss Charlesworth, but in 14 days goodness knows where those goods will be.'

The registrar clerk remarked that an attempt to seize goods immediately might not be effective, as the sheriff's officers had already been unsuccessful on several occasions.

Mr Lloyd replied, 'My client wants the order carried out immediately. It is quite clear that the sheriff's officer does not know the ropes!'

Amid peals of laughter, the red-faced registrar granted an immediate order in favour of Messrs J. Price & Co.

While this theatrical legal farce continued, Violet had been offered an unexpected – and every bit as flamboyant – chance to present her side of the story to the public. It is safe to say that the opportunity did not go as expected.

Almost as soon as Violet's discovery in Scotland had been announced she was contacted by several theatrical agents who wished to sign her for a series of music hall appearances. As she was offered a series of deals ranging from £100 to £400 per week, Violet saw a relatively easy opportunity to recoup some of the money she had lost – and gain some public adoration into the bargain. She promptly agreed to a contract with Mapleson and Co. Ltd, a leading London opera and concert agent, to appear three times nightly on the capital's music hall circuit for a fee of £400 (now over £60,000) per week, with the proviso that three quarters of her earnings would be passed on to her creditors, and the remainder (less a tiny amount for her living costs) being used to pay her ever-increasing legal costs. The vast sum of money that Mapleson and Co. were able to offer a first-time performer like Violet is a measure of music hall's popularity at that time.

Before the advent of cinema, radio, and television, music hall was the largest, most lucrative, and most popular form of entertainment available to the British public. A huge number of cavernous venues were constructed across the country – including 375 in the greater London area alone – many of them able to hold over 1,000 people. Performances ran on a thrice daily, seven-day-a-week, conveyor belt. The public flocked to see stars such as Marie Lloyd with her trademark parasol, or Dan Leno – 'The Funniest Man on Earth'. As music hall's popularity grew, new turns were needed to bolster the entertainment on show. Agents reached out to find more working-class talent. They kept a keen eye open for acts capable of conveying contemporary newsworthy events to the audiences. Nevertheless, as a caveat to would-be performers, while the audiences, lubricated with cheap beer, were happy to cheer and sing along to such songs as 'Champagne Charlie', or laugh with performers such as Alfred Vance, they were merciless to any artist whose performance was thought to be lacklustre. Sadly, many of these great auditoriums no longer survive, but even the few that do, such as Wilton's in East London, give a faint idea of the intimidating atmosphere into which Violet was forced to step.

Initially, Violet suggested that she might perform songs of her own composition in a short sketch show which could headline a night of variety entertainment. However, the eventual 14-minute sketch, entitled 'A Clever Woman', in which she was persuaded to appear was anything but that. The demeaning, humiliating, routine involved Violet simply walking on stage in a replica of the infamous crimson motor cloak and re-enacting a rather stilted portrayal of her adventures, whilst a narrator gave a vocal rendition of the events. Before each performance the narrator would announce that Violet was far too nervous to sing, a comment intended to gain the audience's sympathy. Alas for Violet, this tactic had quite the reverse effect.

Predictably, the raucous London music hall audiences were neither patient nor supportive towards her performance, and they openly hissed, booed, and jeered. One lady in the audience shouted out, 'You're a wicked woman!' Unsurprisingly, under such morale-sapping verbal attacks, Violet's theatrical career lasted for only a few performances. As these contemporary reviews amply illustrate, a consummately gifted fraudster Violet may have been, but a theatrical star she was not.

Bristol Times, Saturday 6 February 1909:

MISS CHARLESWORTH AS A "VARIETY STAR" – MIXED RECEPTIONS

Miss Violet Charlesworth made her first public appearance as a variety "star" at the Islington Hippodrome last week.

There was a packed audience, and Miss Charlesworth was announced on the programme as "Miss Violet Gordon Charlesworth, acclaimed by the entire press of the universe as the missing lady, who will make her initial appearance on any stage."

She was introduced onto the stage by a gentleman of the name of MacLeod, who made a preliminary speech lasting about a quarter of an hour, descriptive of the motor accident in Wales.

The audience did not view Mr MacLeod's utterances with any degree of unanimity. When he described how the motor-car ran into the gap in the wall, the gallery became vociferous, and there were rude cries of "Rats", "Come off it", etc.

Miss Charlesworth herself was obviously nervous. She stood in the middle of the stage, while the audience cheered, shouted, laughed, and hissed.

She took off her coat and stood revealed in the plaid of her clan – every bit of her appeared terrified. She whispered to Mr MacLeod, who then informed the audience that Miss Charlesworth wished to thank them from her heart for their very generous reception.

In the evening Miss Charlesworth appeared at the Canterbury Music Hall, after an explanatory statement by her manager. She was, he said, no adventuress (laughter and cries of "oh, oh!"). She was "simply a little girl (laughter) endeavouring to entertain her audiences by singing some of the songs she had herself composed"."

Miss Charlesworth, attired in her red motor coat lined with fur, then walked on to the stage, and was received with applause, intermingled with "boos", and some hissing. She was deathly pale and apparently extremely nervous and incapable of smiling.

Her manager asked the indulgence of the audience as, acting under doctor's orders, Miss Charlesworth was unable to sing. He requested, however, to express her appreciation of the cordial reception the audience had extended to her.

Miss Charlesworth then advanced a few steps nearer to the footlights, and in a tremulous voice said, "Ladies and gentlemen, I thank you from the bottom of my heart for the manner in which you have received me."

She bowed, and the curtain was rung down amid applause, laughter, and some hissing.

Canterbury Theatre, London. Courtesy of arthurlloyd.co.uk

London Evening Standard 6 February 1909:

THE LADY OF THE CLIFF.
MISS CHARLESWORTH
ON THE MUSIC HALL STAGE.

Miss Violet Charlesworth faced the music on Monday in more than one sense of the word. Advertised as "The Lady of the Cliff Mystery", she appeared in two matinées and three evening bills at Collins's Music Hall, Islington, the Canterbury, Westminster Bridge Road, and the Paragon, at Mile End. At each performance there was a house full to overcrowding, and it was evident that the young lady would not get an altogether favourable reception. Solemn music was played before the turn, and when the curtain went up the public were somewhat irritated by a gentleman – who concealed an obvious nervousness under a strenuous smile. He entered into a long history of the events which had led up to the appearance of Miss Charlesworth, and denied the statement that she owed a firm of solicitors £10,000; and taking the audience into his confidence, assured them that the lady was "not a dashing adventuress", but a nervous little girl who was doing her best to pay her creditors. This statement, which was over-elaborate, was continually interrupted by derisive cries, shrill and ear-splitting whistles, loud laughter, and that peculiar style of repartee which distinguishes the galleries of the Paragon, Mile End, and the Canterbury Music Hall. The bland gentleman, still trying to be cheerful, then said, "I have much pleasure in introducing Miss Violet Charlesworth."

At the back of the stage the curtains parted. and there stepped out a slim girl in a Scottish cap and a long red motor-coat, trimmed with fur. She faltered towards the footlights and bowed low, while her "interpreter" explained that this was indeed the missing lady motorist who had been found in the famous red cloak. On his amiable suggestion she slipped off the cloak and stood revealed in a kilt and jacket of the Gordon tartan.

At each music-hall there was the same rather pitiable performance. The gentleman accompanying her begged for the indulgence of the audience because, owing to Miss Charlesworth's shattered nerves, "the doctor had forbidden her to sing her two songs, "Good-bye, Mavourneen" and "Good-bye, Girlie". Miss Charlesworth was white to the lips, as she stared forward at the great audience in the dim light, and heard their laughter, the repeated shouts of scorn, the prolonged hooting, the sharp volleys of clapping of those who sympathised with her, the steady hissing of those who were determined to show their disapproval. She was obviously terrified.

Her worst ordeal was the Canterbury. The audience there would not even listen to the smiling gentleman with his "explanation", and all parts of the great audience capped his remarks by very scornful and very pointed rejoinders.

Miss Charlesworth looked as if she were on the verge of fainting. She swayed slightly, and kept moistening her lips, and once or twice smiled in a piteous way. This time she was not asked to take off her red cloak, but her manager hurried her off the stage instead, to the sound of a final burst of laughter.

If her fleeting career on the halls was not to be demeaning enough, the daily newspapers carried a constant stream of humiliating stories which threw Violet's life into a darker and darker corner. Her grand homes at Fortrose and Calne had now been repossessed. While she was rehearsing for her brief career as performer, her creditors at The Hall had held a public auction of her few remaining possessions at the Corn Exchange in Calne.

The furniture and curios sale was packed with curious members of the public, many of them keen to secure a souvenir. The sale raised £153 for Violet's creditors, including one St Bernard dog sold for 11 guineas, and 22 shillings for Violet's collie. The auction, far from being a dignified event, proved to be another boisterous affair, as the local newspaper noted, 'A great deal of amusement was apparently displaced by the crowd, who seemed to treat the sale as a huge joke.' Herbert Parry, the auctioneer, in a sarcastic reference to Violet told the prospective bidders, 'All items must be paid for, *before* being taken away!'

Following the humiliation of the auction and her failed music hall appearances, Violet returned to Boderw, her one remaining home – for the time being, at least.

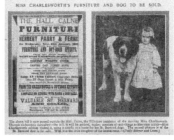

The sale of Violet's furniture and dogs at The Hall in Calne
attracted huge public interest

19: The Money Box

Still crushed by the harsh reviews of her stage performances, Violet was then to endure further humiliation when an auction sale of her much-loved possessions from Flowerburn House was held at the Music Hall in Inverness. The public again attended in droves, anxious to own a trinket belonging to the star of 'A Clever Woman'. The articles sold included several valuable pieces of furniture and some rare ornaments. A full-sized oil portrait of Violet with a St Bernard dog fetched £7, and a stuffed tiger shot in India £12. Some beautiful oil paintings, a collection of valuable silver and plate, several bronzes, and Violet's dog kennels all fetched high prices.

There was to be no respite for Violet, as the humiliation continued. A meeting was held at Boderw at the end of January, attended by a representative from each of her creditors. It was made clear to Violet that her family would be evicted from Boderw by no later than the end of her lease term on Lady Day (25 March). The family would soon be homeless.

Mr Radcliffe, the Rhyl solicitor, explained that Miss Violet Charlesworth had executed a deed of assignment transferring her interests to another party, which would be legally registered after that meeting. Objections were, however, raised to Joseph Gratton acting as trustee, as Violet's deed had proposed. Eventually it was agreed that after the deed had been registered Joseph should transfer his trusteeship to a person to be appointed by the creditors. Radcliffe added, 'Miss Charlesworth's debts amounted to £1,500 [now £250,000], the largest creditors being Mr Gratton who was owed £583, Mrs Martha Smith from Derby for more than £400, and Dr Edward Hughes Jones, Rhyl, for £238. The last two amounts were stated to be due in respect of a guarantee given by Mrs Miriam Charlesworth to Miss Violet Charlesworth, by which the mother had not benefited. There was also a claim for £76 rent. It was stated that Miss Violet Charlesworth hoped to be able to pay her debts in full.'

Several creditors' meetings were held in both Edinburgh and London. An agreement was reached for all Violet's assets to be assigned to Mr Charles J. Munro of Edinburgh, who would now act as her trustee and judicial factor. He was to collect 'any salaries which Miss Charlesworth may be entitled to until the creditors are paid in full'. Following the initial creditors' meeting, Violet certainly (publicly, at least) gave the impression of appearing fully transparent and cooperative with the proceedings.

Charles Munro endorsed this arrangement when reporting to the second meeting of Violet's creditors on Tuesday 9 February: 'The creditors in London have agreed to fall in with the proceedings in Scotland. Miss Charlesworth's assets are calculated to be £7,393. It was impossible to give accurate statement of her liabilities, but at present, the claims amount to £20,000 [now £3 million]. Considerable expense and delay have been saved by Miss Charlesworth's concurrence in the award of sequestration, and I have received three-fourths of her first week's salary in connection with her music-hall performances.'

Violet continued her attempt to repair her reputation and reimburse her creditors by agreeing to an – ill-advised, as it turned out – newspaper interview with the *Daily Mail*. The interview, whose tagline promised 'Miss Violet Charlesworth to tell the true story of the motor-car accident and her escape to Scotland', did little to achieve either. The *Daily Mail* agreed to pay Violet £200 (now £28,000), of which £60 went on her solicitor's costs. As agreed, the balance, less a small amount for Violet's subsistence, was returned to Mr Munro, her trustee for distribution to her creditors. It appears, however, that the *Daily Mail*, which syndicated the transcript of the interview to more than 100 newspapers worldwide, profited much more from the arrangement than did her beleaguered creditors.

Sadly for Violet, the interview not only did little to assist her rehabilitation but also was widely derided. Whilst it contained certain truthful elements such as her description of the journey to Scotland, it also contained several convenient omissions, including her detour to Ireland and the complicity of her family. She continued to peddle the myth of her inheritance, and generally sought sympathy for her plight rather than show the required amount of contrition. The press and public dismissed out of hand her claim to have run all the way from the scene of the accident to Conwy railway station (a distance of more than 2 miles) and generally deplored her blatant attempts to garner public sympathy. Unfortunately for Violet, the interview was badly timed, clashed with the horrific story of the 'Tottenham Outrage', an armed robbery and brutal murder of a 10-year-old boy and a police constable in London by Latvian anarchists. The shocked British public were in no mood for the selfish attempts at self-pity from a young lady who had tricked her fiancé and defrauded a trusting widow. In the public eye, Violet descended from Cinderella to pantomime villain in a matter of days.

She was to be humiliated even further over the coming weeks and months.

The full transcript of Violet's disastrous *Daily Mail* interview, not seen in print for over a century, is reproduced in Appendix B.

By February and March of 1909 Violet's fragility must have been obvious to those around her. She spent almost all her time 'convalescing from her weak constitution' at Boderw, peppered with occasional visits by train to her solicitors in London.

Now a figure of public derision, she passed the long hours not on exhilarating motor-car journeys or at expensive restaurants, but in her bedroom at Boderw with the windows heavily veiled. Tensions within the family must have been running high at this juncture. Frederick, tired of having to publicly defend the family, returned to Bath to seek employment. Her mother's health also seems to have deteriorated under the strain of the investigation and the constant glare of publicity (there were still as many as 100 onlookers regularly massed outside the gates to the house). Dr Miller visited the house several times during the winter and spring of 1909 as Miriam complained of chest pains and dizziness.

Violet's public attempts to appear penitent and cooperative towards her appointed trustee and creditors do not, from our perspective, seem to tally with the actions of the family. First, she never disclosed the existence of her strongbox (secured in the vaults of the Chancery Lane safe deposit in London) at any creditors' meeting, nor is it mentioned in any list of her assets. It appears that its secrets and treasures were something Violet did not wish to disclose at any price. Feasibly, the revelation that such a safety deposit box even existed, and the disclosure of its contents, might have dragged other potential creditors unwillingly from the woodwork, possibly even well-known and respected public figures. Perhaps Violet held further aces up her hand-embroidered sleeves. It is entirely probable that given the extraordinary level of her expenditure during the previous five years (which her list of known creditors does not adequately explain), there were as many as a dozen or more men who did not wish to come forward at the expense of their marriage or their reputation, or both.

In addition, Violet's offer to assist her appointed trustee in every way possible and to declare her assets in their entirety does not tally with a visit her father, David, to Snow Hill railway station in Birmingham on Thursday 11 February. This was the day prior to the official bankruptcy sale of the items found in Violet's luggage (which she had despatched to Birmingham prior to her disappearance), and that evening he made several attempts to gain access to the office at the railway station, presumably in an effort to retrieve those possessions. When access was denied him, David became both abusive and aggressive. He was subsequently arrested, and following a night in the cells he appeared at Birmingham Police Court in the morning. Yet more embarrassment was heaped upon the family, when both local and national press were tipped off, in advance of his court appearance,

Western Gazette, 19 February 1909:

CHARLESWORTH CASE. MISS VIOLET'S FATHER REPORTED IN TROUBLE

At the Birmingham Police-court on Friday morning an elderly man named David Charlesworth, whose age was given on the charge-sheet as 64, and his address as Boderw, St. Asaph, and who was said in court to be the father of Miss Violet Gordon Charlesworth, was charged with being drunk and disorderly at Snow Hill Station, and refusing to leave when requested.

Mr Evers, who prosecuted on behalf of the railway company, said the prisoner came from Boderw, St. Asaph, a place which was rather well known at the present time. At half-past five the previous night he was very drunk, and had to be removed several times. Asked what he had to say, prisoner repeated that he was not drunk; only excited. The Stipendiary Magistrate stated: "You will have to pay fine of 5 shillings." The money was paid, and Charlesworth left the Court. Asked as he was leaving the building whether he was the father of Miss Violet Charlesworth, he walked away without making any reply.

David's none-too-subtle attempt at retrieving Violet's belongings had heaped yet more embarrassment upon the beleaguered family.

After the mortification of her music hall appearances, Violet was unceremoniously dropped by her theatrical agent, Mapleson & Co. It was officially announced to the press that Violet had been forced to cancel what would have been her final stage appearances at the Shoreditch and Clapham theatres on Monday 15 February, her agent issuing the statement: 'The strain of the excitement has considerably affected her and she is unable to appear on Monday night.'

Nonetheless, for a brief period after the motor-car accident Violet was undoubtedly what would now be called 'box office'. Postcards of the crash site at the Devil's Thumb sold for three times the price of pictures of music hall stars such as Phyllis Dare. A Flintshire photographer and artist attempted to cash in on Violet's notoriety by lodging a copyright application for all known photographs and portraits of her. He did not succeed.

Walter Bentley, Violet's theatrical agent (1880)

As the weather improved, opportunist tour coach operators, taking full advantage of the event, offered curious members of the public charabanc tours of Boderw, together with a view of the crash site at Penmaenbach Point, and a dramatic running commentary.

Despite her own music hall career stalling, the two songs Violet had composed in 1907 were performed on stage by other artists. A sensational melodrama, entitled 'The Motor Chase', was staged at the London Hippodrome. The playlet featured a real car hurtling down a specially constructed ramp from the ceiling of the theatre into a tank of water on the stage. The audience cheered and gasped as the motor car crashed into the water, and those in the front row were frequently soaked!

The *Weekly Dispatch* serialised her life story in three instalments, and Violet was even asked to write a number of fictional love stories for publication in women's magazines. It has always been assumed that none of Violet's short stories had survived; however, during the research for this book I was able to unearth one, which had languished for more than a century in Australia. For those wishing to wonder at Violet's fertile and romantic imagination, 'A Heart of Gold' is reproduced in its entirety in Appendix E.

Violet was clearly undeterred by her music-hall failure. She was approached by another – and far more influential – theatrical agent, Mr Walter Bentley. A former Shakespearean actor and protégé of Henry Irving, Bentley was much respected and would go on to establish the Australian Actors' Association in 1910 and Walter Bentley's College of Elocution and Dramatic Art in Sydney. Aged 59 at the time of their first meeting, he was impressed with Violet's slim figure and beauty, and believed he could turn her into a star of that exciting new medium – the silent movie.

He foresaw a career for Violet as a 'serial queen', a title being given to the new starlets of serial one-reel movies being produced in America. Soon, actresses such as Pearl White and Helen Holmes would be become household names as melodramatic heroines in such films. Bentley sincerely hoped to transform Violet in a British version. Ruffell's Imperial Bioscope Pictures Ltd and the Rosie Film Company intended to produce a 20-minute one-reel film entitled 'The Welsh Cliff Mystery', telling the full story of the Violet's dramatic motor-car accident and her subsequent escape. In the days prior to the construction of purpose-built cinemas, Bioscope shows travelled the country, creating a fairground-style attraction at which short films were shown using the latest Bioscope projectors. Interspersed with dancing girls and musical accompaniment. These events (complemented by a weekly magazine, *The Bioscope*) entertained thousands of people at nightly shows from 1898 until the Great War.

And so it was that on Saturday 13 February 1909 Violet's brief film career began. The Welsh press eagerly reported the excitement that surrounded the filming of 'The Welsh Cliff Mystery'.

North Wales Weekly News, 19 February 1909:

CINEMATOGRAPHING A MEMORABLE FLIGHT

> Two motor-cars drawing up in front of the Castle Hotel, Bangor, about half past two on Saturday afternoon attracted some attention, which was increased when a lady in a red motor cloak stepped out of one of the cars, and, followed by her companions, entered the hotel, which, it will be remembered, was the scene of Miss Violet Charlesworth's consultation of a railway guide on the night of her sensational disappearance in January last. After partaking of light refreshments, the party emerged from the hotel, and, being photographed, returned the way they came.
>
> It transpired that the party consisted of Miss Violet Charlesworth and her sister, a couple of London actresses, and Miss Charlesworth's London manager (Mr Walter Bentley), and that the purpose of the trip was to obtain a cinematographic view of the whole of the journey made on the 2nd of January, with cinematographic pictures of the principal points of interest.

The film was completed at lightning speed – unlike the production times associated with motion pictures today – by director J. Rosenthal, and was shown at Bioscope tents, town halls, and early picture palaces around the country during March and April of 1909. Under various titles, including 'The Welsh Cliff Mystery', 'The Violet Charlesworth Cliff Mystery', and simply, 'Miss Violet Charlesworth', the film enjoyed moderate success, proving popular with audiences.

During the research for this book, I contacted both the British Film Institute and the Library of Congress Silent Film Archives in the US, in a vain attempt to track down the original film canisters containing the reels. Sadly, however, the film does not appear to have survived. The Library of Congress estimates that between 75 and 90 per cent of all the silent films ever produced have been lost forever. Most of this rich historical legacy – and our only opportunity to witness moving footage of Violet – was destroyed by the movie studios, who saw little future value in storing canisters of film once their theatrical runs had ended. The volatile and flammable nature of early nitrate film stock coupled with the expense and vault space required for storage, made it not economically viable to keep the majority of movies. Occasionally, dusty canisters of old film stock are discovered in the dark recesses of abandoned picture palaces. Perhaps, one day, 'The Welsh Cliff Mystery' will dramatically resurface, just as Violet did.

In the interim, between March and May 1909, Violet's creditors continued jockeying for position in the race to obtain their share from the paltry amounts available. As mentioned previously, it had been agreed between her English and Scottish creditors that three quarters of her earnings (from the music hall performances, articles, and any other income) should be divided among them, and that one quarter should be retained by Violet 'to defray her expenses until her creditors were paid in full'. Even the 'small' proportion allocated to Violet raised eyebrows among the public and her aggrieved creditors. In an era when the average working man would consider himself lucky to earn £50 a year, Violet claimed £10 in living expenses for Week One of her bankruptcy. This figure – now £1,500 – was *not* seen by the public as an attempt by her to live frugally.

Meanwhile, in Paris the elaborately and solidly constructed Eiffel Tower celebrated its twentieth anniversary. Unfortunately, unlike that testament to French design, Violet's intricately assembled façade was crumbling all around her. Miriam publicly denied any knowledge of her daughter's inheritance, claiming that she, like everyone else, had believed the story of Violet's £150,000 legacy. The family, given notice to quit Boderw, began the desperate search for other accommodation – this time on a much reduced budget, of course. Frederick, having returned to Wiltshire to continue his career as an engineer, was presumably happy to distance himself from the scandal surrounding his family. There also seems to have been some friction between David and Miriam, who both cited poor health as an excuse to avoid public appearances. However, it seems highly probable that their escalating money difficulties, Miriam's manipulative nature, and the embarrassment of David's appearance at Birmingham Police Court would have added to their woes.

In strict contrast to the preparations currently under way around the country for Self-Denial Week – organised by the Salvation Army and the suffragette movement to raise funds for the poor, and for the campaign for universal suffrage – Violet was increasingly being seen by the public as pampered, unsympathetic, and self-indulgent. At her next scheduled creditors' meeting in London, she claimed to be too ill to attend. The members of the public, who had turned up en masse in the hope of glimpsing the 'mysterious lady motorist', resorted to hoots of derision when the chairman announced to the bankruptcy hearing: 'I have received a medical certificate to the effect that Miss Charlesworth's health has broken down, but it is hoped that she will recover if not disturbed for a few days.'

When the extent of Violet's expenses were declared to the hearing, the news was met with open hostility from the gallery. One newspaper reported the proceedings as a 'mockery of justice for those left penniless', and as 'the great disappearance comedy'.

All told, Violet received a total of £405 in earnings from her various music hall appearances – a sizeable sum, equating to over £60,000 today. From that sum she claimed living expenses amounting to £112 (now £17,000). This was *not* seen by the public as an earnest attempt by her to live frugally in an effort to repay her creditors. After her solicitors' fees had also been deducted, there were barely any crumbs left on the table from which Violet's hungry creditors could feed. The meeting was adjourned.

Perhaps the most damaging allegations against Violet's reputation and public image were caused by the appearances at her next bankruptcy hearing of her three most aggrieved creditors: Dr Hughes Jones, her ex-fiancé; Mrs Smith, the widow from whom Violet had defrauded her entire life savings; and Gamages, the prestigious London shop from whom Violet had purchased an exorbitant amount of furniture.

Violet duly presented herself at the proceedings, appearing sombre and dressed in all black. She was instantly labelled 'The Merry Widow' in the press, as she continued to persist with her story of a supposed inheritance, as this snippet from the hearing of 21 May 1909 details:

> Miss Violet May Gordon Charlesworth was subjected to an hour's examination. The case, at the instance of Messrs Gamages & Co., of London, was against Miss Charlesworth, of Flowerburn House, Ross-shire, and Charles John Munro, trustee of her sequestrated estate. Henry John Denniss, assistant counting-house manager at Gamage's, gave evidence to the effect that Miss Charlesworth visited their establishment, and that, as a result of an interview in the Inns of Court Hotel, certain rugs were in due course delivered to Flowerburn House. These consisted of tiger, polar bear, and leopard skins. Miss Charlesworth's proposal, it was said, was that at the delivery of the goods she would forward a cheque for half the amount, the balance to be paid at the end of September last year, when she expected to receive a large sum. Mr Hampton, also from Gamage's, gave corroborative evidence. Miss Charlesworth said she was twenty-five years of age, and that in July last year she had purchased goods from Gamage's. On the day after her visit Mr Denniss and Mr Hampton appeared at the Inns of Court Hotel, where there was some conversation as to payment. Miss Charlesworth claimed that she made no statement to Denniss and Hampton about being entitled to a large sum of money.
>
> Question: "What were your expectations?"
>
> Answer: "I was engaged to be married to a doctor in North Wales, and from time to time I had received money from him,

and was expecting to receive more from him in September. I was engaged to the doctor, and I quarrelled with him in December last, the engagement then being broken off."

Q: "The doctor has now made a claim for above £5,000."

A: "The doctor led me to understand he was wealthy, and he offered me two motor-cars. When I ordered the goods, I believed all that I had to do was to get money from him when I required it."

In cross-examination, Miss Charlesworth stated, "The doctor's name was Edward Hughes Jones, and we were to be married in January last. I was engaged to him eighteen months, and I was due to receive £2,800 from him when I attained the age of twenty-five. I also expected to receive a large sum of money from an old friend, Mr Alexander MacDonald,[20] of Melbourne, Australia. He asked me to marry him, but I refused. He was to give me £155,000."

Q: "Why was the promise not fulfilled?"

A: "I do not know why the promise was not fulfilled."

Q: "Why did you disappear in January if you expected this money?"

A: "Through fright after the motor-car accident, on account of what the Press had said."

The case was adjourned.

It was also announced that some items of jewellery belonging to Violet were to be sold at auction. According to the auctioneer's statement the items were 'lately the property of Miss Violet Charlesworth, being placed for sale to cover an advance made to her'.

Violet appeared to be in delicate health, and shortly after the hearing left for the south by the afternoon train.

In May 1909 there was a rather mysterious development. Following the family's eviction from Boderw, Violet seems to have taken up temporary residence at 19 Brompton Square, an exclusive address in Knightsbridge, one of London's most prestigious districts, which should have been well beyond Violet's apparently reduced budget. She was given lodging there by the owner, Stewart Forster, an extremely wealthy well-connected man of private means. It can only be assumed that he was another of Violet's

---

20 Fortunately for Violet, this basic error in her evidence – testifying that Mr Alexander MacDonald was to give her £155,000, when in fact in 1904 Violet and her mother had first created the story of the fictitious Mr MacDonald being swept overboard during a violent storm in the Bay of Biscay – appears to have gone unnoticed.

gentleman friends, and had been a perfect target for her inheritance scam. Although his name does not appear in any public list of her creditors, it is probable that he did not wish his name to be mentioned in the bankruptcy courts. In addition, like many others at this stage in the saga, he had no reason to disbelieve Violet's convincing inheritance yarn.

Brompton Square

It seems that they may have first met through a mutual love of motor cars – and speeding. Forster, a renowned motoring enthusiast had in 1907 been fined £5 plus costs for 'driving a motor-car to the danger of the public, at speeds of 30 mph, through Dunstable on market day'. On the very same day, Violet too had appeared before the Dunstable magistrates on a similar charge. In his defence Forster had claimed: 'The population of Bedfordshire do not like motorists.'

While staying in the comfort of Brompton Square, Violet failed to attend two further bankruptcy hearings at St Asaph and a garage sale of items from Boderw designed to help raise a further contribution towards her debts.

She excused herself from both proceedings by sending telegrams to the St Asaph County Court. The first, wired from Mayfair Post Office in London, read: 'Have today satisfied English Bankruptcy Court too ill to undergo examination. Too ill to come to St Asaph.' The second, telegraphed from Worthing in Sussex (where presumably Violet was enjoying some restorative sea air) simply stated, 'Not well enough to attend.'

Nevertheless, Violet had no need to fret unduly. Her mother Miriam appeared on Violet's behalf, claiming that many of the items destined for the sale at Boderw did not belong to her daughter but to her. As a result Violet's various creditors seemed to have found it extremely difficult to prove ownership of many of the lots listed at the sale that day. So the auction only raised a further £46.13s. towards Violet's estimated debts of £27,000. However, on 11 May Messrs Debenham, Storr & Sons held an auction of some of Violet's jewellery at their salerooms in King St, Covent Garden, on behalf of the creditors. Mysteriously, many of the more valuable pieces in Violet's collection do not seem to have been present, and the proceeds from the sale did little to dent the huge outstanding debt. Violet appears, at this stage at least, to have successfully kept the majority of her diamond jewellery collection concealed from the authorities.

Meanwhile, the full details – described in Chapter 21 – of Violet's shameful defrauding of the elderly and vulnerable Mrs Smith, also turned Violet's few remaining public sympathisers against her.

This was followed by more public disquiet and an official reprimand when Violet failed to attend her next scheduled bankruptcy hearing at the London Bankruptcy Court on 29 May 1909. It was widely perceived that she was disrespecting both her situation and those she had swindled. The rather acidic *Weekly Dispatch* (which only two months previously had reputedly paid Violet £400 for her exclusive series of articles) stated,

SWELLED NECK

Miss Charlesworth's Latest Excuse for Not Attending Bankruptcy Examinations:

On the day fixed for the examination, Miss Charlesworth did not appear, and a medical certificate was handed in declaring that she was suffering from a swelling in the neck, a rapid pulse, palpitations, giddiness, and sleeplessness. Mr Mellor (speaking for the creditors) supposed that Miss Charlesworth was simply trifling with the court, as she had done ever since the proceedings started. She was now trying to obtain more money from the court for what she called expenses; but none of it has been used for the purpose for which it had been meant.

Nevertheless, a further adjournment was reluctantly agreed to. This decision did not meet with public approval, particularly when one newspaper claimed to have witnessed Violet sampling Britain's first soda drinking fountain while attending the Women's Exhibition at the Prince's Skating Rink in Knightsbridge. The exhibition, held between 13 and 26 May 1909, had been organised by the WSPU, with the proceeds going towards the suffrage campaign fund.

Throughout that summer and into the autumn of 1909, Violet persisted with the story of an inheritance which, she claimed, 'by rights, I should have received at the beginning of the year'. She even began to portray herself as the wronged person in the drama – sadly let down by a broken lover's promise. Viewed through our 21st-century lens, it seems incredible that she

Women's Exhibition, 1909

was neither challenged nor questioned further by the police. No charges of wasting police time were brought over the motor-car accident, her escape to Scotland, or her subsequent claim to be Miss Margaret MacLeod. Perhaps, though, in the jaundiced male view of females in that era, that type of behaviour was simply to be expected, in which case no attention would be paid to it.

The warm summer of 1909 passed without incident for Violet. After appearing in *The Times* newspaper alone 31 times in a space of just three weeks, she temporarily disappeared from the public gaze after successfully lobbying for yet another adjournment of her next scheduled bankruptcy hearing. On this occasion, her London physician, Dr Walter Rigden, presented himself at the London Bankruptcy Court on Violet's behalf. He provided a sworn statement, claiming:

> I have seen Violet this morning; but she now appears so ill, it would not be possible to positively identify her from the photograph you have produced here. She is now suffering from neurasthenia and a weak heart, and is very ill indeed. She was anxious to attend, however, but I considered that it would be too dangerous for her health for her to do so.

It is not clear exactly what Violet hoped to achieve by seeking constant postponements to her bankruptcy examination. The authorities and creditors were hardly likely to give up, roll over, and simply forget their grievances. Maybe she hoped that gaining time would somehow enable her to find a way out, or maybe she hoped that at the very least the public would simply lose interest in her case, and that the resulting daily invasion of her privacy would cease. Her tactic was, at least in part, successful. In St Asaph, Boderw had been boarded up and a sign exclaiming 'WARNING: TRESPASSERS STAY OUT!' had been nailed to the gate by the land agents, J.M. Porter & Elcock. Meanwhile, the public's attention had been temporarily diverted by the opening of the Victoria and Albert Museum in London, the first monoplane flight across the English Channel by Louis Blériot (winning a *Daily Mail* prize of £1,000 in the process) and, more disturbingly, the force-feeding of suffragettes on hunger strike at Birmingham's Winson Green Prison.

Finally, after a welcome lull for Violet, she was thrust back into the limelight of public scrutiny in October 1909. Unable to feign illness any longer, and with the patience of the authorities exhausted, her long-delayed final insolvency examination was held at the London Bankruptcy Court. It would be one of the last times Violet was ever to be seen in public.

Tuesday 12 October 1909 saw a huge gathering of both public and press in Carey Street. Those that arrived early enough managed to squeeze inside the courtroom; those not so fortunate gathered in a huge crowd outside. The *Daily Mail* set the scene:

> A young woman with a pale but clear complexion made an appearance. Regular features, dark eyes, small mouth, and a dimpled chin, a dress of grey-striped flannel, with a white feather boa, and a black hat with white feathers. She was Miss Violet May Gordon Charlesworth. She seemed incapable of speaking above a whisper, and says she has been ill.

Nevertheless, the official receivers, represented by a Mr Hough, appeared to be in no mood to make allowances for her delicate appearance or sex.

He started out with a direct attack: 'Miss Charlesworth, you have alleged to your creditors that you were entitled to a fortune, currently lying in the hands of trustees, variously estimated at from £75,000 to £250,000, which was to be yours on your coming of age, and was to come from a person in Melbourne, Australia, who had promised you £155,000. There is no confirmatory evidence, and the promise has not been fulfilled, and is not likely to be fulfilled.'

Violet did not answer other than to confirm to the court: 'My name is May Charlesworth.'

'Yet you have two other names – Violet and Gordon?'

'Yes,' Violet replied, in a barely audible whisper. 'I have always used them.'

'When you were in Derby, Miss Charlesworth, your family were in pecuniary difficulties?'

'I do not know.'

'But you know that before you went to Rhyl your mother had been forced to borrow money?'

'I do not know.'

'You know a Mrs Martha Smith?'

'Yes,' Violet answered.

'Did you meet her in Wolverhampton and express your gratitude for her generosity in loaning you money?'

'I am sorry, I do not remember meeting her in Wolverhampton and thanking her for the loan of money.'

Mr Hough warned Violet that he would return to the subject of Mrs Smith later in the proceedings.

Next to be addressed was the thorny issue of Violet's memoirs for the *Weekly Dispatch*, published in late January and early February. Nine months had now lapsed since their publication, and her story of a spectacular inheritance seemed more fantastical with each passing day. Violet's public pledge to 'do anything in my power' to pay off the outstanding creditors now seemed an empty promise.

Not surprisingly, with the *Weekly Dispatch* articles now seeming to expose Violet as little more than a brazen liar, she attempted two new diversionary tactics, both to distance herself from the stories and question their authenticity.

'You wrote the story published in the *Weekly Dispatch*, Miss Charlesworth?'

'No.'

'But you dictated it, or at least supplied the materials?'

'No; I did not see the newspaper's representative for more than a quarter of an hour.'

'But you must have seen the proofs? You were paid £400 for the interview, were you not, Miss Charlesworth?'

'Yes; that was at Edinburgh,' Violet answered.

Surely it must have been a long interview, then?'

'Not very long.'

'Is the published story correct, then, Miss Charlesworth?'

'Yes, but not entirely correct.'

'I think the amount of £200 was paid to your solicitors towards their costs in this case? Is that correct, Miss Charlesworth?'

'Yes.'

'Has an account been rendered for the remaining amount?'

'I do not know. Not to me, anyhow,' Violet replied, rather sheepishly.

'I put it to you, Miss Charlesworth, that your failure is due to extravagant living, and also due to gambling on the Stock Exchange?'

Violet acknowledged she had spent excessively on motor cars, furniture, and dogs.

Hough next returned to the claims of Mrs Martha Smith, and those of Dr Hughes Jones: 'Did you tell Dr Hughes Jones that you were entitled to a fortune on attaining twenty-five years of age?'

'No.'

'Then you and he are at issue on that?'

'Did he say so?' Violet interjected. 'Then he is wrong.'

Hough then returned to the subject of Mrs Smith. At the mention of her name, Violet shifted uncomfortably in her seat; 'Is it a fact that you told Mrs Smith that by the action of a kind friend you would become entitled to a fortune of £150,000 when you were twenty-one?'

'No.'

'And when you passed twenty-one and the fortune failed to materialise, you changed the story to twenty-five?'

'No.'

'Who was to give you this fortune, Miss Charlesworth?'

'Mr Alexander MacDonald. He mentioned £155,000.'

'Was it to be had in land or houses, or securities?'

'He did not say.'

'What was Mr Alexander MacDonald to you?'

'Nothing more than a friend.'

'Was he a young man?'

'Yes, a young Scotch colonial. He was about thirty-seven or thirty-eight. I met him when I was seventeen, and knew him till I was twenty.'

'Why did he promise this £155,000?'

'He was very fond of me. It was a surprise. I met him first at a party in the Caledonian Hotel, Edinburgh. I was staying there.'

'Without a chaperone?'

'Yes,' Violet replied.

At this admission a noticeable murmur of disapproval was audible in the court – perhaps Edwardian morals saw this as a graver offence than that of cheating a widow and a doctor out of their life savings.

'Is there anyone who can confirm your story, Miss Charlesworth?'

'I do not know of anyone. The fortune was to be placed in the hands of trustees. He did not give me the names of the trustees or of the solicitors.'

'Can you give me the name of any person who knows the address of Mr Alexander MacDonald?'

'No.'

'And can any person verify the amount of money promised to you is anything more than a myth?'

'I do not know,' Violet replied. 'Neither my father, nor my mother, nor my sister knew him.'

'Has Mr Alexander MacDonald any representative?'

'He was represented by Colonel Williamson and Mr Francis Williamson; they are his trustees,' answered Violet.

'Can you give me the name of anyone who has ever met Mr MacDonald or the trustees?'

'No.'

'It seems to me that Mr MacDonald may be a myth as far as corroborating any of your evidence is concerned,' Hough commented.

Next, in an unfair, underhand, and cynical attempt to paint Violet as a sexually as well as financially devious individual, he asked a probing – indeed, rather leading – question which brought a murmur of disapproval from the gallery: 'Think carefully before giving your answer. Did you give Mr MacDonald any personal reason or favour for making his promise?

'No. He was very fond of me.'

His obvious attempt to portray Violet as a woman who might have seduced a gentleman in return for financial favours was typical of the hypocrisy of the Edwardian era. Whilst the love affairs of King Edward VII with his mistress Alice Keppel, and that of Kier Hardie, the founder of the Labour party, with Sylvia Pankhurst, were open secrets, any such innuendo hinting at promiscuity on the part of Violet, a *female*, would have seen her publicly derided.

With Violet's personal reputation now openly questioned, the final blows were landed as Mr Hough continued his assault: 'Do you remember saying to Dr Hughes Jones that your promised fortune was £250,000, or that you told Mrs Martha Smith that your young man had left you £75,000?'

'No,' replied Violet.

With a dramatic flourish, Hough produced a letter from his pocket. 'I have here a letter which you wrote to Dr Hughes Jones: My dearest Edward, It cuts me to the heart to ask you for money; I, who will one day have £7,000 a year and an estate.'

Like a chess grand master Hough had trapped Violet. It was near checkmate. He remorselessly continued, 'As to your dealing with Fenton, Dale & Company, stockbrokers, you do not remember if you told them that you would receive £250,000?'

'No, I do not remember that,' Violet answered.

'I want to point out, Miss Charlesworth, the enormity of making these statements to the stockbrokers, if untrue. Again, are you serious when you say you did not make them?'

'Yes. I did not make them.'

'You never had an allowance under trustees?'

'No.'

'Then why did you write a letter to Dr Hughes Jones and your stockbroker in which you speak of your trustees making you an annual allowance? Furthermore, in these letters, you use the name of Mr Gordon as that of your trustee. I am now going to show he was a myth.'

At this stage in the examination, Violet broke down and openly wept, resulting in a protracted delay to the hearing.

After the recommencement of proceedings Violet admitted claiming to be in receipt of a yearly allowance amounting to £1,000. Sensing that she was now weakened and vulnerable, Hough pressed her further: 'Many of the statements you made to the stockbrokers were incorrect. You wrote a letter about The Hall, at Calne, saying that you had "two vanloads of valuable foreign curios and furniture". You had no such collection of furniture or curios. It was all fiction, claiming that your imaginary trustees were to furnish the hall at a cost of £2,500. Let me ask you, beyond the loans you were obtaining, you had nothing with which to pay your debts?'

'There was the money from Mr MacDonald.'

'Oh, this MacDonald fortune!' exclaimed Hough sarcastically, amid an outburst of laughter from the court.

With that outburst, any shred of dignity that Violet might have still retained evaporated. After further questioning from Hough, in which he highlighted her profligacy by mentioning her extravagant expenditure on motor cars, jewellery, and houses, the proceedings drew to a close.

The official receiver had thus demonstrated publicly that Violet was a liar, a fraud, a manipulator, and a callous con artist. She left the hearing to a fanfare of loud jeering from the gallery and from the crowd outside. Surely, with Violet's fraud now seemingly proven, the story of her fabled inheritance openly mocked in court, and the public clamouring for her arrest, the police would at last be forced to act.

But Violet had managed to disappear once before. Could she do so more successfully a second time? Or would the long arm of the law finally bring her to justice? Violet, it would transpire, had one more trick up her immaculately tailored sleeve.

20: The Hurrah

Autumn faded into winter, as 1909 reached its conclusion. The first British branch of Woolworths opened in Liverpool, and the House of Lords rejected Lloyd George's 'People's Budget', thereby triggering a general election. The death was announced of William Powell Frith, the respected painter, and the public worried about the king's worsening health.

Violet's appearance at her last bankruptcy proceedings had been a public relations disaster for her. Her fraud seemed strikingly obvious to everyone in the public gallery, and to those who read the following day's newspapers. She could produce no evidence of her benefactor – the elusive Mr MacDonald – nor provide details of her supposed trustees. Nor was she able to contribute another farthing towards her outstanding liabilities. Worse still, the solicitors acting on behalf of Dr Hughes Jones and Mrs Smith were pressing for criminal proceedings against Violet on a charge of obtaining money by false pretences. Her reputation was in tatters and her finances in ruins. With the authorities assuming she was comfortably ensconced in the elegant surroundings of 19 Brompton Square in Knightsbridge, she did not plan on waiting too long for the inevitable knock on the highly polished Georgian front door.

Even before her bankruptcy hearings had concluded, and despite having assured the official receivers that Brompton Square was her place of residence, she had in fact already moved out of the property, thereby ending whatever arrangement she had in place with the owner, Stewart Forster.

Following her final appearance on the penultimate day of her bankruptcy examination in October, Violet hastily packed her remaining possessions and boarded a train north to Scotland. She journeyed to Moffat, a small and secluded spa town nestled in the Scottish borders county of Dumfriesshire. There, by arrangement, she joined her mother, father, and sister at Windsor Cottage on Selkirk Road, on the outskirts of the town. Following their eviction from Boderw, the family had rented the small villa in late September on a six-month lease (with favourable terms, and requiring no deposit) from a Mr David Denholm. The Charlesworths were now in a dire financial situation. Whatever the tensions within the family, they would need to muster alongside Violet under a unifying flag, to enable the truth about Violet's sham inheritance to remain a secret. Miriam was now, without doubt, seriously ill. Lillian appeared tired and drawn, later referring to their situation at this time as 'one of extreme poverty'.

The parents had rented Windsor Cottage under the name of Cameron, with Lillian taking the name Miss Gordon. David and Lillian occasionally left the house to buy provisions. Violet, on the other hand, was seldom seen out of doors, and then only after dark, when she was accompanied by a large St Bernard. It seems that she had become a virtual recluse.

The family would later claim that they had taken the step of changing their names and removing themselves from the limelight purely to avoid any publicity. This was not entirely the case. Violet, despite insisting that she had informed the authorities of her new address, had, during her bankruptcy hearing in October, confirmed her place of residence as 19 Brompton Square.

In addition, the Charlesworths' new arrangement raises one further question: why had David Denholm agreed to rent Windsor Cottage to a family now infamous for their unpaid bills and spiralling debts – and without even asking for the security of a deposit?

The answer is a surprising one, not reported or indeed known at the time. It seems there was a family connection. In fact, Denholm was related to Miriam Charlesworth on her mother's side. It would also emerge that Denholm, in addition to being in dire financial straits himself, may even have provided part of the inspiration behind Miriam's original fraud scheme in 1903. He had once served as a respected magistrate and as the commissioner of police in Moffat. Unfortunately, it appears that his expensive taste for fine living (in similar vein to Violet), led to his eventual downfall.

After losing his well-respected position as a magistrate in 1890, he had only been able to secure employment first as a labourer, then as an agent for Garland & Rogers, a Leith firm of builders. While employed there, one of Denholm's responsibilities was the collection of outstanding accounts from the firm's customers. However, he fabricated a series of letters and telegrams purporting to be from Garland & Rogers, thanking customers for the receipt of their payments and confirming that all their accounts were up to date, while pocketing the money for himself. By means of this fraud, he embezzled more than £200 (now £34,000) until his arrest in 1893 and subsequent incarceration in Maxwelltown Prison, Dumfries. It thus turned out that for Violet, who had spent her adult life adorned in Gordon tartan and claiming to be of noble Scottish ancestry, her actual Scottish pedigree was a much less glamorous – indeed, tarnished – affair.

By 1909 Denholm, a middle-aged man and both financially and personally disgraced, might perhaps have rather sympathised with his relations' predicament, hence his offer of the Cottage.

Meanwhile, south of the border the police were now investigating the case against Violet and Miriam, using the evidence supplied by Mrs Smith and Dr Hughes Jones. Violet's fabled inheritance now appeared to be merely a work of fiction. But how could the authorities prove this point? After all, the majority of Violet's creditors still believed her tale, and many others still refused to come forward and testify, their pride more damaged than their ample bank accounts. Indeed, their strange reluctance can be summed up in a phrase often attributed to the writer Mark Twain, 'It is easier to fool a man than to convince him he has been fooled.'

A new tactic would be needed: rather than spotlighting the victims, it was time to follow the money.

Detective Inspector Harry Allbutt of the Derby police force contacted the surviving family of General Gordon of Khartoum. Violet, claiming on many occasions to be a goddaughter of the general, had stated that he had bequeathed her a sum of £75,000 to be conferred on her 25th birthday. She had even taken to calling herself Violet Gordon Charlesworth to add some credibility to the story. On making enquiries, it was confirmed that on his death in 1885 General Gordon had in fact left only £2,300 in his will, mostly comprising property, which had been bequeathed to his sister. There was no mention of any other sums of money, or of Violet. In fact, it was established that none of Gordon's descendants had ever heard of either Violet or the Charlesworth family. This comes as no surprise, since, at the time of Gordon's death in January 1885 Violet (then still known as May) had just reached her first birthday in the family's modest house in Lovatt Street.

Next the Derby City Police wired an international telegram to the Melbourne Police in Australia, in an attempt to establish the existence of the mysterious Alexander MacDonald, whom Violet claimed had gifted £150,000 in trust to her. At her last bankruptcy hearing, Violet had stated that he was a resident at the Menzies Hotel in Melbourne and that he had written to her from there.

Both the Melbourne police and the Menzies Hotel confirmed there was not, nor had there ever been, a person of that name and description resident there.

From these two pieces of information, the police, it seemed at last, had the evidence they needed.

So why did it then take them so long to instigate a criminal investigation into the lady variously described by the newspapers as 'the best advertised woman in England' or 'the siren in the scarlet cloak'?

There are three reasons. First, Violet was very, very plausible and utterly convincing. Her inheritance scam was so well polished and so often repeated, and had been delivered with such apparent veracity, that it seemed completely impossible to comprehend that her story was anything other than the truth. This effect, known to psychologists as 'the illusion of reality', fooled almost everyone who encountered Violet – from Mrs Smith, the lonely and trusting widow, to highly qualified and wealthy professionals such as her solicitor, her stockbroker, and her doctor. After all, how else could she have *possibly* afforded three country houses, motor cars, furs, and fabulous jewellery?

Secondly, in a similar manner to the story created by Madame Thérèse Humbert and discussed in the appendices to this book, Violet's fictional inheritance was harder to disprove than prove. Many people simply accepted her story. To question it, without evidence, would have been seen as most improper in a society where the word of a lady was beyond question.

And lastly, Violet was a master at disguise, delay, and disappearance. Her expensive and immaculate dress sense hinted at breeding and trustworthiness in the class-deferent Edwardian society. Her delaying tactics had successfully stalled both her discovery and eventual bankruptcy examination for a year or more. Even following the motor-car accident, her status as the most talked-about person in the country, and her final bankruptcy hearing, Violet had already managed to evade discovery for several weeks by secreting herself in Moffat, well away from the glare of the public and the media.

And so Christmas 1909 passed without incident in Moffat, and as 1910 dawned the Charlesworths welcomed a chilly New Year. The anniversary of the supposed motor car accident passed (which was not mentioned in the newspapers), and Violet celebrated her 26th birthday quietly and without friends.

On 15 January 1910 the Liberal Party won a narrow victory in the general election, and on the 31st of that month Dr Crippen murdered his wife and buried her body beneath the cellar of their London home (although the truth would not be discovered for several weeks). Conceivably, when the story later emerged that Marconi's telegraph system had been used to warn the American authorities of Crippen's escape across the Atlantic, Violet may have ruefully remembered how a year earlier reporters had used the wire service to give their colleagues advance warning of her journeys.

By the beginning of February 1910 Violet was perhaps beginning to believe that the skeletons in her cupboard would lie undiscovered. After all, she reasoned, it had been almost four months since the bankruptcy hearing.

This was, however, to change dramatically on the morning of Sunday 6 February, when the family were rudely awakened by a sharp knock on the door of Windsor Cottage. Outside their front door stood Inspector Carruthers from Lockerbie Police Station, clutching a photograph of Violet in one hand and a warrant for her arrest in the other. He was accompanied by Sergeant Morrison from the Moffat Police.

Inspector Carruthers announced himself formally: 'Miss Violet Charlesworth? Mrs Miriam Charlesworth? We are acting on a warrant issued on behalf of the Derby City Police. Under the conditions of the Debtors Act 1869 you, Miss Violet Charlesworth, and you, Mrs Miriam Charlesworth, are charged with obtaining £401 by fraud and false pretences from Mrs. Martha Smith, a widow, of Derby, in 1908, and with conspiring on the 12th November 1908, and on other divers days thereafter, to obtain unlawfully, fraudulently, and by false pretences from said Mrs. Smith and Mr Edward Hughes Jones, certain large sums of money, and to cheat and defraud them thereof.'

Violet and her mother, their faces transfixed in horror, did not answer the charge.

It seems that several residents of the small spa town had finally managed to reconcile the description and photographs of Violet in the newspapers with the young, well-dressed young lady seen walking a large St Bernard after dark through the town.

After Violet had recovered from the shock of the police officers' arrival, she freely admitted her identity and explained that she was not attempting to flee justice, merely to hide away from the intrusive gaze of the media.

The arrest of Violet Charlesworth

Violet and her mother accompanied Inspector Carruthers to Moffat Police Station, where they spent the night in the station cell as they awaited the arrival of Detective Inspector Albutt from Derby. During their overnight incarceration, Violet was (according to a statement issued by the police) 'very communicative, narrating various episodes of her career. She also seemed to be very grateful for any consideration shown to her while in custody.'

Interestingly, during the original application for the arrest warrant in Derby on 3 February a special dispensation had been granted for its execution to be carried out in Scotland. Although under the original terms of the 1869 Debtors Act the territorial extent of English arrest warrants did not normally include Scotland or Ireland, it was felt that due to the staggering sums of money involved and the huge public interest in the hunt for Violet, justice should be allowed to take its course.

Detective Inspector Allbutt arrived in Moffat around at 8 pm on Monday

7 February, to escort Violet and her mother back to Derby on the following morning's train. Unusually, the 50-year-old detective inspector's fearsome wife, Elizabeth, was accompanying her husband on the journey. It appears that she had expressed severe reservations about the idea of her husband being alone for any period of time in a railway carriage with the woman who, according to the *Daily Express* newspaper was the 'beautiful, young scheming seductress in the red cloak who had seduced the middle-aged Dr Hughes Jones'.

By Monday morning the news of Violet's arrest had become public knowledge among the townsfolk of Moffat. Unaccustomed to excitement in their quiet backwater, and keen to gain even a fleeting glance of the 'Mysterious Lady Motorist', as *The Times* had labelled Violet, a large crowd had gathered outside Moffat railway station to watch Violet and Miriam Charlesworth's departure by the 11.33 am southbound train. The pair, having been placed in a taxicab, were driven from the police cells to the station. Meanwhile, on the platform Inspector Albutt awaited their arrival, along with his wife Elizabeth, and Lillian. Violet's father remained in Moffat. Several newspaper reporters were also present, and a description of the events was telephoned and wired to their various news desks in time for the evening editions,

> Miss Violet, who was pale and tired-looking, appeared to feel her position keenly. She wore a navy-blue costume, with a bright green coat, a white feather stole, and a black hat with black ostrich plumes, and she carried a travelling rug. Her mother, who followed, was sobbing, and had to be helped to the compartment in the train.

Violet, despite appearing 'pale and tired-looking', obviously still maintained her keen fashion sense.

At Beattock Junction the travelling party joined the Liverpool and Manchester express, where a first-class compartment had been reserved for them – the detective inspector's wife, no doubt, insisting on occupying the seat between Violet and her husband!

Although the Derby police had endeavoured to keep the arrest secret, the story had spread quickly across the country. The group was due to arrive in Derby at 6.10 pm, by which time the early evening newspapers had already published details of the arrest. So, fearing a demonstration at the station, the police made an extraordinary arrangement with the Midland Railway Company, to disrupt the usual schedule by having the express train stopped at the previous station – Nottingham Road – in order that the group could alight there unseen. According to railway regulations, this concession was only permitted under very special or extreme circumstances, usually reserved for royalty or in times of war.

When the express steamed into Nottingham Road station for its unscheduled stop, the platform was empty, barring a few railway employees and the Chief Constable of Derby Police Force, Captain Henry Mansfield Haywood. The two women were then quickly bundled into a waiting taxicab and taken to Derby Police Station, where they would spend their second night in custody. An arraignment hearing had already been scheduled for the following morning at the Derby Borough Police Court.

Violet and Miriam both appeared tired and pale as they were escorted into the police court on the morning of Tuesday 8 February. They were described to the magistrate as, 'Miriam Charlesworth (married), and May (otherwise known as Violet) Charlesworth, of Windsor Cottage, Moffat, where they have been living under the name of Cameron.'

Mr William Durnford, a solicitor from the Council Chambers Temple in London, appeared for the defence, while Mr Pearce, the public prosecutor, together with the chief constable himself, Captain Haywood, appeared for the Crown.

Captain Haywood informed the court: 'These proceedings have been taken by the Director of Public Prosecutions on the information of Martha Smith, of 57, Victoria Terrace, Macklin Street, Derby. The first charge is laid under the Debtors Act. The other charge is laid as a result of statements made in the proceedings of Bankruptcy against the defendant, to which the Public Prosecutor has declared, "these facts disclose the obtaining of large sums of money from Jones, a medical man at Rhyl. There was no truth in the statements by the defendants, and we submit that the mother and daughter have acted in collusion, and should be committed to trial. The statements made are sufficient to allege a charge of conspiracy against the defendants."

'We wish to apply for a remand in this case. It was impossible to bring all the evidence before the court today as the prisoners were only arrested on Sunday morning, on the warrant granted by the court on February 3rd. It is hoped that our case might be completed by Tuesday next in order that it might be taken at the forthcoming Assizes, which, I believe, commence on February 24th.'

At this point Durnford, speaking on Violet's behalf, interjected: 'We earnestly hope that the remand will be for at least a week to enable the defendants to prepare the case for their defence. I suppose that there must be a remand in this case, and I have been instructed by my clients to apply for bail. As to the amount of bail, I hope it will be fixed at a moderate amount, otherwise it would prove be absolutely prohibitive for my clients. It is well known that the defendants are in extremely distressed circumstances at the present time. The bankruptcy proceedings have stripped the younger defendant of every shilling of her means. Both defendants are now in a position of extreme poverty, and there is no possibility of their attempting to get away from the jurisdiction of the court.'

Haywood stated he had no objection to bail in principle, but reminded the court of the large sums of money involved in the case.

The bench, led by the Mayor of Derby, Dr Henry H. Arnold Bemrose, retired to reflect, and on returning to court announced that the prisoners would be permitted bail provided they could each provide a surety of £200, or if either of the prisoners could produce one of £400 (now £55,000). Clearly, that payment was now well beyond Violet's newly humbled circumstances.

Violet and Miriam were led, distraught, from the police court, and remanded in custody at Derby Jail for a period of 16 days while the case against them was prepared.

The lack of public sympathy now commanded by Violet can be easily gauged from the report of the police court proceedings that appeared in the *Nottingham Post* the following day,

CHARLESWORTH CASE

Accused Women Brought Up at Derby and Remanded

ALLEGED CONSPIRACY

Violet and her Mother Looking ill and Apprehensive

HEAVY BAIL DEMANDED

The notorious Violet Charlesworth to-day experienced a new sensation – that of the prisoner in the dock; and judging by her appearance she by no means found it the most pleasurable episode of her momentous and extraordinary career. She entered the Derby Police Court with her mother by a door to the rear of the magistrates' bench, again cheating the little crowd which had gathered in the precincts of the court in the hope of getting a glimpse of the famous prisoner; and if ever there appeared on a woman's face the expression of fearful apprehension it was in the face of Miss Violet Charlesworth at that moment. Her face is thin almost to haggardness, the cheek bones showing prominently; her complexion, pale to absolute sickliness, giving greater prominence to the startled eyes which roved furtively about the court with the fear of the hunted.

The two women (who were accompanied by Inspector Allbutt, the officer who fetched them from Scotland the previous day) came hesitatingly into the court, and, guided by the inspector, passed round and into the dock, where they stood to hear the charges against them with heads bowed as though in a vain endeavour to hide their faces from the 40 or 50 people in the well of the court, whose eyes were fixed upon them. They murmured "Good morning" to their solicitor, who sat in the front of the dock, but that was the only occasion on which either of them spoke during the whole of the proceedings. They were not asked to plead.

In the dock the mother, Mrs Charlesworth, appeared the more distressed of the two, and each moment seemed as though she was about to burst into tears – but no tears came. Mrs Charlesworth is apparently very ill. She is suffering from heart disease, and several times during the proceedings was in an almost fainting condition. By her side sat the police matron, who occasionally administered smelling salts.

Dry-eyed also, the younger woman maintained her self-control sufficiently to enable her to bow with some degree of dignity when her name was called; and a distinct frown crossed her face when the clerk referred to her as "May" instead of her adopted name of Violet. Afterwards she showed little interest in the proceedings, though the frequent moistening of her bloodless lips and the wearied manner in which she occasionally pressed back her hair from her forehead were indication of the uneasiness of her spirit.

The wheels of justice must have seemed slow and grinding, for both Violet and Miriam, as they endured their long, tedious, and uncomfortable confinement in the cells at Derby Prison. Finally, their boredom was abruptly interrupted early on the morning of Wednesday 23 February 1910, when the pair were woken and told to prepare to be escorted to the Derby Assizes at the Guildhall for the beginning of their fraud trial.

Had Violet and Miriam's day of reckoning finally arrived?

21: The Short Count

The *Derby Daily Telegraph* takes up the story,

VIOLET IN TEARS – PRISONERS GHASTLY PALE
The Charlesworths on Trial at Derbyshire Assizes

Every inch of seating accommodation was occupied at the Derby Assize Court this morning when the hearing of the four charges against May (otherwise Violet) Charlesworth and her mother, Miriam, was taken by Mr. Justice Charles Darling. The court is an extremely small one, and only a fraction of the general public who wished to see the prisoners were able to find accommodation. It was not surprising that the majority of those who were spectators, were members of the fair sex – ladies of a fairly good social standing, judging by appearances – and their smart apparel lent a dash of brightness to the otherwise sombre interior of the court.

The two prisoners were at once placed in the dock, the hum of whispered conversation which had prevailed prior to their appearance being immediately hushed. They were accompanied by a female warder. Mrs. Miriam Charlesworth was the more affected of the two prisoners, appearing very weak and much dazed by the circumstances in which she found herself. Violet, on the other hand, was quite cool and collected, but both prisoners looked ghastly pale. Violet sat quietly in the dock and followed with evident interest the counsel for the Crown's opening statement. Mr. Ryland Atkins, K.C., M.P., and Mr. Moresby White were appearing for the prosecution, and Mr Henry Maddock and Mr. Leon Freedman defended. The Office of the Official Receiver was represented by Mr. Seward Pearce.

Lord Justice Darling

The judge, Mr Justice Darling, took his seat at 10.30 am and the two defendants were escorted to the dock, where they were granted permission to sit rather than being forced to stand. Miriam Charlesworth 'breathed heavily and was in a half-fainting state'. After the charges were read formally to the court, both women pleaded Not Guilty.

In his opening statement for the prosecution, Mr Ryland Atkins, outlined the accusations against the defendants:

> May, otherwise Violet, Charlesworth and your mother, Miriam Charlesworth, face charges of conspiracy, fraud, and false pretences. The allegation is that by these means the accused obtained £401 from Mrs Martha Smith, a widow, of Derby, and large sums of money from Dr Edward Hughes Jones, of Rhyl. The jury should, all through the proceedings, bear in mind that the offences apply to each of them, for while I will submit at the end of the case that there are ample grounds for convicting both the prisoners, it is open to find one guilty and not another. The facts of the case, although not complicated in the sense that they are not in any way confusing, are somewhat numerous, and I ask for your careful attention while I relate in narrative form what will be proved by the evidence.

The charges were something of a disappointment to the gathered masses from Fleet Street. No mention was made of Violet's £10,000 debt to her stockbroker, her numerous overdue accounts to tradesmen and hotels across the country, her flight from justice, or the rumours of love affairs with MPs and other notable public figures. It was also announced that her father, brother, and sister would not be called as witnesses.

Nevertheless, there were still many questions on the lips of the anxious reporters, eagerly gathered with pencils and notebooks in hand. First, how could a jury from Derby retain their independence after hearing details about the Charlesworths' treatment of one of their own citizens?

And secondly, would Mr Justice Darling, renowned for his strict sentencing and acid wit, be influenced when confronted with two pale and drawn female defendants? 'If Mr Justice Darling's reputation is anything to go by,' the *Daily Mirror* speculated, 'the mother and daughter may find themselves in penal servitude for seven years.'

Mr Ryland Atkins explained the background to the case and described how in 1900 Miriam had first told Dr Barrett, also of Derby, that her daughter Violet was to inherit a fortune.

He then turned and addressed the jurors directly: 'Members of the jury, the Charlesworth family had moved to Wolverhampton, but in 1903 returned to Derby, which is when the first sum of money was obtained from Mrs Martha Smith, again using the story that Violet was coming into a fortune of £75,000. The money, Mrs Smith was told, was left to Violet by a man to whom she was engaged, but who died on his way home from India, his body being buried in the Bay of Biscay. Violet, the story went, was looking forward to dropping a wreath as near the spot as possible to where the body of her lover was buried. For two or three years, further sums of money were obtained from Mrs Smith by Mrs Charlesworth and her daughter. A good deal of correspondence passed between the Charlesworths and Mrs Smith, the three common characteristics in these letters being expressions of faith in God and references to Divine guidance; of references, obscure references, to litigation (which Violet claimed had caused a delay in the receipt of the inheritance); and expressions of regret that they had not paid Mrs Smith, and generally wishing her every kind of happiness.'

Atkins then related an incident concerning Dr Hughes Jones at Boderw, 'In 1907 Violet was suffering from some illness, and Dr Hughes Jones was called in to attend her. Soon afterwards he received a letter from a London firm of solicitors, Messrs James and James, thanking him for the care he had taken of Miss Charlesworth, and he also later received two scarf-pins, apparently from a Mr Robert Gordon, through the firm of solicitors, one for himself and one for his brother, who was in partnership with him. These, it was inferred, were chosen by Miss Charlesworth herself.

'In May 1907 Dr Hughes Jones became engaged to be married to Violet, who told him the story of her coming into a fortune of £150,000 when she was 23. Next, a letter was received by Dr Hughes Jones enclosing £30 from Violet's trustees, also purporting to come from Mr Robert Gordon.

'The following events, however, are very different. A few days after the engagement Violet's new fiancé lent her £100, by way of a cheque. The letters from Mr Robert Gordon were written from Derby, but were, in fact, in handwriting which will be deponed to be that of Miss Violet Charlesworth.'

Mr Atkins then produced evidence for the court to prove that the £100 given to Violet by Dr Hughes Jones was cashed in Derby by a person who signed herself V.M.G. Charlesworth.

The counsel for the prosecution continued in unrelenting fashion: 'In the course of eighteen months Dr Hughes Jones advanced Violet a sum of not less than £5,000, and during their correspondence the fortune she claimed to be inheriting seems to have risen from £150,000 to £250,000.

'It was after receiving these sums of money that Violet launched out into all sorts of expenses. She took a house in Wiltshire at a rental of £189; and used it for her St Bernard dogs; and a few weeks afterwards she took a house in Scotland at a rental of £250. In January 1909, the "month of the happy birthday", Miss Charlesworth and her sister motored in North Wales, and Violet disappeared over the parapet of the road. It was supposed that she was killed, but she was afterwards discovered by an enterprising pressman at Oban. Then followed proceedings in bankruptcy. Remember, her wildly extravagant life was begun only when these large sums of money had been obtained, and not before.

'No one has seen the strange, benevolent young man who, after an introduction at a Highland ball, had supposedly left Violet £150,000 or £250,000, whichever version of her story you choose to believe. In fact, I submit that the whole story of the fortune was an entirely false statement.'

Evidence of Violet's bankruptcy proceedings followed, showing that her liabilities were £12,719 and her assets £2,232. Following the deduction of the winding-up expenses in the legal case, there would be very little left indeed for the creditors.

In addition, Violet's Stock Exchange liabilities now totalled £12,700; however, these debts were not included in this litigation. Violet had now defrauded Mrs Smith, Dr Hughes Jones, and her London stockbrokers of more than £25,000 (now £3.75 million). This sum includes only a small fraction of the money she owed to the various tradesmen, house agents, retailers, car manufacturers, and hotels she had swindled. It includes neither the jewellers nor those private individuals who wished not to be named. Violet Charlesworth was undoubtedly one of the most prolific con artists in history. Her total score can only be imagined.

Returning to the trial, Mrs Smith was called to the witness box by the Crown. In front of her hometown jury, Mrs Smith made a sympathetic witness,

'The largest single sum I advanced them was £80,' she began. 'In October 1905 I travelled up to Rhyl when I heard that Miss Violet was giving silver cups away in connection with rifle competitions. I said to myself, "if she could do that then she could pay me some money." I took with me the I.O.U.s which Mrs Miriam Charlesworth had given me on behalf of her daughter, who was a minor at that time, so Violet could make out a new one in her own name as she was now 21. I stayed two or three nights with the Charlesworths. Violet destroyed the small I.O.U.s and instead wrote out a large one for the amount of £380, 7 shillings.'

'Mrs Smith,' Mr Atkins enquired, 'was anything else said on the subject of the fortune?'

'Yes, but it was just general talk. Although I became rather uneasy about the money and went over to Rhyl again to enquire, Violet went out in the afternoon with the dogs, and when she returned she told me she had seen her lawyer and that the money would be all right.'

'Did you advance any further sums?'

'Yes, the Charlesworths often came to Derby. In fact, I drew all I had out of the bank, and that closed the account.'

There was a collective gasp of breath in the packed courtroom.

'And, Mrs Smith, did you think Mrs Charlesworth spoke the truth when she told you of her daughter's inheritance?'

'Yes, I believed Mrs Charlesworth was speaking the truth when she spoke about her daughter's fortune.'

Mr Atkins then read aloud a passage from one of Violet's letters to Mrs Smith:

> My trustees are resigning, and I shall be made a ward of the Crown until I am twenty-five – Your loving friend, Violet.

Mr Justice Darling interrupted the prosecution at this point to clarify a point with the witness: 'Mrs Smith, are you able to tell when people are telling the truth?'

'It did not prove so in this case,' Mrs Smith answered sadly, producing a sympathetic murmur from the public gallery.

Darling replied, 'If you do know how, then I wish you would tell me.' While this generated a burst of laughter among those present, it did nothing to soften the attitude towards Violet and her mother.

When the merriment had subsided, Mrs Smith was asked to relay to the court the story of Violet's final demand for money, in November 1908. She responded: 'Miss Charlesworth called on me and asked for a loan of £200. She said she had had that sum stolen from her motor-car, and she did not want her trustees to know. I gave her a sovereign, that I had by me, and said that all I could do was to let her have the last £20 that I had in the Co-operative Society. She said she only required the loan of money for a fortnight.'

'Was that all the money you had, Mrs Smith?'

'Yes, and they knew it. They knew perfectly well how I was situated, and that I was anxious about my own child. They told me that if anything happened to me before my own girl could maintain herself, they would never see her want. It was all religion with them, and I trusted them thoroughly.'

Mrs Smith was then asked what she did after hearing reports of the accident at Penmaenbach Point.

'I read a report in the newspaper about the motor accident and I at once wrote and asked Mrs Charlesworth which of her daughters had gone over the cliff, as no Christian name was mentioned in the report.'

Miriam's hastily written reply to Mrs Smith's enquiry was then read out loud for the benefit of the jury,

> My sufferings have been very great. Cannot say much, but leave it in God's hands. Her body has not yet been found. The house is full of people now. Later on, come.
>
> With love, affectionately,
>
> Miriam Charlesworth

It was a shameful moment for Violet and her mother – and all twelve members of the God-fearing all-male jury[21] looked disapprovingly in their direction.

Next, Dr Hughes Jones gave evidence. He related the story of Violet's fortune and of the couple's engagement. The doctor explained Violet's deception, how she had convinced him that her trustees had objected strongly to their engagement, and the upset it had caused him. The prosecution then produced their next exhibit, a letter from Violet to Dr Hughes Jones, which he had received in 1908, and which included the following passage,

> Colonel Williamson [one of Violet's fictional trustees] is determined to win me yet. I shall not get a penny from Colonel Williamson unless I break the engagement. All my fortune would have been yours.

Violet's letter also made yet another request for an additional loan from the doctor, and she expressed her deep regret in having to break their engagement:

> I who will one day have £7,000 a year and an estate. It is cruel, bitterly cruel, laddie.

There were many terms of endearment in Violet's letters, and when Mr Atkins read them out loud, Violet broke down and openly sobbed. There was a brief halt to the proceedings while she was attended to by a female warder.

Atkins turned to the jury, still brandishing Violet's letter in his hand for dramatic effect, 'Careful inquiries have been made, members of the jury, but no single person has ever heard of the trustees mentioned in this letter, and no corroboration has been obtained of Miss Charlesworth's story, or of the existence of these imagined trustees.'

After a short recess to allow Violet to compose herself, the questioning of Dr Hughes Jones continued: 'Doctor, did Miss Charlesworth give you any reason why she said her fortune had risen to £250,000 instead of £150,000?'

'She said she did not like to boast.'

---

21 Female jurors were not permitted until the Sex Disqualification (Removal) Act of 1919 had been passed.

A further letter from Violet to the doctor was also read to the court. During this communication, Violet spoke up, explaining that, 'The trustees are purchasing for me a house in Devonshire, worth £18,000 [now £2.6 million], as a coming-of-age present, and when I was last in London all my future jewellery was brought out from the bank for me to see.'

(Interestingly, Violet's reference to jewellery in this letter was not seized upon by her creditors, so it seems to have been taken, like the mention of a fictional house purchase in Devon, as another of her fabrications.)

Under cross-examination by the Counsel for the Defence, Mr Henry Maddox, Dr Hughes Jones was asked: 'Exactly how much did you see of Miss Charlesworth during that time?'

'I saw Violet a good deal during 1906 and 1908.'

'At that time had you any reason to doubt her truthfulness?'

'*No.*'

'On the intimate footing between you both, and from your knowledge of men and women, you believed her be a truthful girl?'

'Yes, I did.'

'Would you have advanced the money if she had been a poor girl?'

'No. The money had taken years and years of my life to save.'

'You saw these motor-cars being used by her, five or six of them?'

'She had several.'

'Doctor, did everyone in the village think she was an heiress?'

'Yes, they did.'

Following the adjournment, Mr. W.C. Holloway, the managing director of the Minerva Motor Company, spoke to confirm that Violet 'had ordered various motor-cars from the firm'.

Next followed a discussion regarding the trustees' letters, in the name of Gordon and MacDonald, posted from 13 Olivier Street, Derby, and forwarded to Violet in Wales. The handwriting on the letters was agreed to be identical – or at the very least similar – to Violet's.

Despite the stockbroker's debt not being included in the original charges against Violet and her mother, evidence of Violet's transactions with Messrs Fenton, Dale & Co. was presented by Percival, the stockbroker's representative: 'On differences,'[22] he explained, 'she owed the firm £10,000, and on money lent £700.'

'She had a winning and truthful way with her, then?' Mr Atkins asked.

'Yes.'

'You trusted her to the extent of £10,000?'

---

22 Losses. British stock market terminology was – and can still be – obscure. For example, 'consideration' means 'payment'.

'We did not trust her. Miss Charlesworth mostly gave orders to sell, but she did not deliver.'

Mr Justice Darling again intervened, 'Then she was selling what she had not got? How came you to trust her to that extent?'

'It was inevitable,' replied Percival, much to the amusement of the court. 'It is the way business is done.'

'But you would not do it for everyone?'

'She said she would make up the differences.'

'What did she tell you then?' Darling enquired.

'She told me of her fortune.'

'Have you often been taken in like that?'

'No, Your Honour.'

At which point those gathered in the courtroom once again burst into laughter. The crowd packed into the public sections of the Guildhall were evidently enjoying the drama of the proceedings and, following the half-hour luncheon interval, quickly retook their seats for the afternoon's events, which began with the case for the defence. Already the majority of those in attendance believed Violet to be guilty. The complicity of Violet's mother still seemed undecided. However, the afternoon's proceedings would show that Miriam had absolutely no intention of going to prison.

The Counsel for the Defence, Mr Henry Maddox then called Miriam Charlesworth to the stand.

'In 1902,' Miriam testified, 'after the return of my daughter from Brighton, she told me that she had met a young gentleman in the south of England by the name of MacDonald, who had promised to give her £155,000. She told me to cheer up, as things would be different when she reached the age of 25. He was a young man who thought a lot of her, and she urged me not to have any fear.'

'At that time were you in poor circumstances?' Maddox enquired.

'Yes. When I first met Mrs Smith and she learned I was in straitened circumstances she offered, quite voluntarily, to lend me £5. Other sums were offered too, and these I accepted. After borrowing the first £5, Mrs Smith remarked to me "Never mind if I am not repaid in this world, I shall be in the next." '

Atkins cross-examined for the prosecution: 'Did you not think it rather odd that a young man should suddenly want to give Violet £155,000?'

'I thought it was very kind.'

Miriam's answer caused a murmur of laughter in the courtroom.

'Did you ask if she was engaged to him?'

'No,' Miriam replied emphatically.

'Did you ever see Mr MacDonald?'

'No,' Miriam responded, before adding in a rather feeble tone, 'I am as innocent as a child in this.'

'Do you still believe all this story today?' Atkins enquired.

'Objection!' interjected Maddox for the defence, 'surely it is unfair to ask the mother such a question, so that the answer might be used against her daughter?'

Mr Justice Darling overruled the objection: 'The question is perfectly fair. Please answer it, Mrs Charlesworth.'

'Your Honour, I cannot really believe it now, because when Violet became 25 years of age, I questioned her about it and she began to cry, asking me not to say any more.'

Maddox continued the case for the defence, 'So, practically, Mrs Charlesworth, your family lived by what Violet provided?'

'Yes. Violet is now writing a book to pay back her creditors.'

Maddox finished the case for the defence with his summation to the jury: 'The reason why Violet was not put into the box was because when she underwent her examination in the Bankruptcy Court, she emphatically stated that the story of her meeting a man named MacDonald was true. There is no evidence to substantiate this', the defence counsel confessed, 'but she did not withdraw the statement. She persisted in it, and all her actions and sayings have been consistent with the tale she told her mother.

Violet outside the court

'Many of the things she did were doubtless to give an air of truth to what she believed to be true. What Mrs Charlesworth did, on the other hand, was done under the impression that her daughter's story was true. This credulous, simple woman believed, just as all the other people had believed, in Violet's story.

'If the daughter was clever enough to carry out a scheme of this kind, was she not clever enough to deceive her own mother? You have been asked to extend your sympathy to the creditors in this case, but to convict the others.'

Dr Hughes Jones outside the court

He pointed at the two defendants in the dock, 'In finishing, may I state that this story, which began in romance, ended in the tragedy of the motor accident and Violet's disappearance. A woman who could do that could surely deceive her mother?'

At 5 pm, following another adjournment, Mr Justice Darling began his summation to the jury. He commended the defence on their efforts and declared that Violet's writing of the letters, 'purporting to come from Mr Gordon, the fictional trustee, was extraordinarily ingenious.'

After a lengthy review of all the evidence, Darling pointed out to the jury, 'Even if you do not believe such an incredible story, it does not necessarily follow that someone else might not have chosen to believe it.'

With his final point, Darling directed the jury to what he believed to be the strongest single piece of evidence to contradict Mrs Charlesworth's defence: the evidence given by Dr Barrett of Derby regarding his conversation with her a decade earlier, in 1900.

At 7.25 pm the jury were instructed to retire and consider their verdict.

22: The Tell

Twenty-five minutes later the jury returned to a hushed courtroom.

'Have you reached a verdict in this case?'

'We have, Your Honour.'

'How do you find Miss Violet Charlesworth?'

'Guilty in respect of all charges in the indictment.'

'And how do you find Mrs Miriam Charlesworth?'

'Guilty in respect of all charges in the indictment.'

Both women, looking worn and fatigued, were asked to stand as Mr Justice Darling spoke. He directed his comments first to Violet, 'You are an exceedingly clever and ingenious woman. You have not scrupled to compromise yourself in marriage in order to get money, but to write letters over and over to Dr Hughes Jones saying how you loved him. You took from him, as he told this court, practically the earnings of his life. Your story of fortune was so improbable that its very improbability alone induced people to believe it. Who could invent such a story?'

Turning to Miriam Charlesworth, Mr Justice Darling resumed his preamble to the sentencing, 'For some time I was not certain whether you had not also been deceived, but the evidence of Dr Barrett made it plain that when Violet was a young girl, it was you who had the plot in your mind. You certainly did not derive the idea from your daughter; but Violet, being indoctrinated by you, developed it most ingeniously by fraud upon fraud.'

Returning his wrath to Violet, he continued, 'Violet Charlesworth, you are a woman who, if well directed, might have been successful and possibly had a distinguished future. I trace the instigation of this crime to your mother.

'I therefore pass a sentence of five years' penal servitude on both defendants.'

Violet, whose demeanour throughout the trial had been remarkably composed, received the sentence with external calmness. However, Miriam, who had been revived by smelling salts several times during the day, collapsed and had to be assisted from the courtroom.

Violet remained outwardly calm and shook hands with her solicitor before speaking to several onlookers. Only, as she descended the steps away from the public gaze, did the faint smile on her drawn face begin to evaporate.

Special permission was granted for Lillian to see her sister and mother before they were taken away to await transfer to their allotted place of incarceration.

In the coming days there were two surprising developments to follow, and the press, still aware of the public attention the case had generated, reported enthusiastically on these 'remarkable sequels to events in the Charlesworth case'.

First, and somewhat surprisingly given the weight of evidence, Violet's solicitor launched an immediate appeal against the verdict.

Secondly, two days after the trial, in a highly unusual and surprising development, Mr Justice Darling sent special instructions for Violet and her mother to be recalled to the Assizes at Derby where, they were informed, he intended to address them. The matter received widespread newspaper coverage:

THE CHARLESWORTH CASE

Sentences Reduced to Three Years' Penal Servitude

At Derby Assizes to-day, Mr Justice Darling reduced the sentence of five years' penal servitude passed on Violet Charlesworth and her mother to three years' penal servitude. Mr Justice Darling gave instructions for Violet Charlesworth and her mother to be brought from prison and placed in the dock, but the latter was too ill to leave gaol. Addressing Violet, who looked extremely haggard, he said that when he passed sentence of five years' penal servitude on the prisoners, he gave directions that it should not be recorded. He had since considered the matter carefully. He had refrained from passing sentence on the conspiracy element of the indictment. Violet had not added to the enormity of the crime by going into the box at the trial and committing wilful perjury, which was often done, though he could argue that he had taken this into consideration. As he had given her the maximum sentence, he now felt justified in reducing the sentence to three years' penal servitude. The same reductions would also apply in the mother's case; he understood that she was very ill and would need to spend a good deal of time in the prison infirmary.

To our modern eye, this may appear a slightly unusual and irrational ruling, however it is probable that Mr Justice Darling was motivated by a feeling of pity towards the apparent ill health of Violet and her mother, combined with the generally prevailing attitude of sympathy towards the 'gentler sex' at that time. Nevertheless, he made it perfectly clear that

Nothing For Something

Miriam should not be treated any more leniently because of her heart condition, although he did add that she 'should be entitled to expect to receive a similar level of healthcare in prison'.

Another interesting fact, neither known nor reported at the time, involved a negotiation between Violet, her barrister, and the judge – a negotiation which had occurred prior to the trial. Only later was it disclosed that Violet had offered to plead guilty in return for the charges against her mother being dropped. Her offer had, however, been refused, as the Crown firmly believed their case against the pair was strong enough to secure both convictions without difficulty.

Considering Violet's track record and her mother's attempt in court to blatantly divert the blame entirely onto her own daughter, it was undoubtedly the least ignoble and least selfish act of Violet's narcissistic life.

Nevertheless, an important question remains unanswered. Did Violet and Miriam receive a fair trial? The matter can only really be answered by fully considering the attitudes prevalent in 1910. It could certainly be argued that Violet's polished appearance and aloof manner did little to assist her case, and probably turned the jury against her. But neither did her mother's ill health help soften the Derby jury, who, like any jury, would always likely to look negatively on someone who had defrauded one of their own, the elderly Mrs Smith.

It must also be considered that in 1909 and 1910 the Women's Suffrage Movement had evoked a surprisingly brutal reaction from the country's male-dominated authority. Although Violet could not be described as a suffragette, she had made several prominent men appear extremely foolish, and she had, into the bargain, been accused of 'impersonating a lady not of her class' – both of these being offences not likely to be easily forgiven by the egos of the jurymen.

Nonetheless, there was a glimpse of light for Violet and Miriam. In addition to Darling voluntarily reducing their sentences, mother and daughter were also given permission to appeal the fairness of their convictions at the Criminal Court of Appeal.

Their appeal was held on Thursday 17 March 1910 and brought with it considerable public interest. Despite some concern now being voiced in the press about the prospect of two 'obviously ill, fraught, and burdened women being confined to jail among the hysterical suffragettes', the appeal judges on the bench made their hostility plain from the start, informing the defence counsel that he would be wise not to press for a reduction in the sentence, hinting that the original term of five years might well be reimposed, should he choose to persist.

Yorkshire Post, 18 March 1910

THE CHARLESWORTH CASE – APPEALS OF MOTHER AND DAUGHTER DISMISSED

In the Court of Criminal appeal yesterday, before Justices Lawrence, Jelf, and Bray, Miriam and Violet Charlesworth, who were found guilty of conspiracy and false pretences at Derby Assizes recently, and sentenced by Mr Justice Darling to three years' penal servitude, appealed against their conviction and sentence.

Mr Roskill, K.C., for Miriam Charlesworth, in stating the grounds for appeal, said that there were separate counts against either of the prisoners. A great number of false representations were made by the daughter in the absence of the mother. No distinction was drawn between the parties in the summing up, and the jury were never told to be careful to distinguish statements made by the daughter when the mother was absent. Mr Roskill then raised the question of the length of the sentence, and on this point Mr Justice Lawrence said: 'Are you sure you are quite wise? There is an alternative course.'

Mr Roskill: 'I know your Lordship's powers, and I will say nothing more.'

Mr Maddox said he was instructed on behalf of Violet Charlesworth to appeal against the severity of her sentence.

Mr Justice Lawrence: 'Are you not in an even more dangerous position?' (There was laughter.)

Mr Maddox: 'I respectfully submit——

Mr Justice Jelf interrupted him: 'A wicked conspiracy, extending over years?'

Maddox decided not to press the matter further. Mr Justice Bray stated that Mr Justice Darling had put the case clearly before the jury, and the Court of Appeal saw no reason to interfere. The appeal would be dismissed.

So there was to be no reprieve for Violet and her mother. They were transported from their temporary holding at Derby Jail to begin their sentences at Aylesbury Prison in Buckinghamshire. The Victorian jail had been converted to a women's prison in 1890, and had already garnered a reputation for housing some of Britain's worst female offenders, including Kitty Byron, who had murdered her lover Arthur Reginald Baker in 1902, and Edith Carew, who had poisoned her husband Walter in 1897. During Violet and Miriam's term inside, the government also began to incarcerate the increasing number of militant suffragette activists. In 1912 the prison was infamously used to force-feed suffragette campaigner Violet Bland during the Aylesbury Prison hunger strike. Bland would later write about her harsh experiences in the suffragette magazine *Votes for Women*,

> During the strike the wardresses were transformed into inhuman brutes and fiends ... It is said some of the wardresses are nurses. I say it is a parody on nursing, and the places where such nurses are produced should be instantly closed ... they twisted my neck, jerked my head back, closing my throat, held all the time as in a vice. I gasped for breath, and suffered tortures mentally lest the food which they were trying to pour down my throat should go into my lungs. They do not expect, or intend, one to swallow the food, but pour it into one's stomach as through an open water-pipe ... there was really no possibility of the victim doing much in the way of protesting, excepting verbally, to express one's horror of it.

It was into this intimidating environment that Violet and a clearly ailing Miriam Charlesworth were transported on Thursday 17 March 1910.

Meanwhile, away from the austere walls of Aylesbury Prison, King Edward VII was suffering from a severe attack of bronchitis, and the country feared the worst. And in Derby, the *Derbyshire Telegraph* organised a relief collection to raise funds for the impoverished Mrs Smith.

Aylesbury Prison

As Violet and her mother were escorted under the imposing brick and stone arch, and through the grim gates, the reality of their new existence was made abundantly clear to them. Gone were the expensive furs, silks, and jewellery, the country houses, and the midnight motoring jaunts. For the next three years their lives would change in every conceivable way. The effect prison life would have on each of them would be a profound one.

Any respect that Violet had managed to garner for herself on the outside was stripped away in a flash. Each of the 285 inmates were to be treated, dressed, and disciplined in an identical fashion. The Aylesbury Prison officers were familiar with housing what we would now call celebrity prisoners, and made every effort to ensure they did not receive any special concessions. The majority of Aylesbury's inmates had been placed there to serve sentences of penal servitude, meaning they were required to undertake hard manual labour and to earn their keep. Any indiscretions would mean a loss of the few privileges which existed.

Immediately upon arrival, Violet and Miriam were locked in a reception cell and instructed to be silent (talking by inmates was not permitted, unless addressed first by a wardress). After an examination by the prison doctor, followed by a humiliating body search to ensure they were not concealing any contraband, their own clothes were taken away and placed in storage, and their personal details were recorded in the prison ledger. Details of their respective entries still survive:

> Miriam Charlesworth, 58, married, no occupation, tried before Mr Justice Darling 23rd and 25th Feb, 1910. Guilty of false pretences, 3 years P.S. [*penal servitude*]. Born Newport, Salop, 1851. 5' 3 ¼" complexion pale, hair – black turning grey, eyes – brown, marks – nil, date when final servitude expires – 8th March 1913. Number 191015. Can prisoner sew? – yes.
>
> May Charlesworth (otherwise known as Violet), 26, single, no occupation, tried before Mr Justice Darling 23rd and 25th Feb, 1910. Guilty of false pretences, 3 years P.S. Born Stafford 1884. 5' 3 ½", complexion pale, hair – dark brown, eyes – brown, marks – nil, date when final servitude expires – 8th March 1913. Number 191016. Can prisoner sew? – no.

From that moment onwards both prisoners were only to be referred to by their prison numbers. They were then asked if they could read and write. On nodding that they could, they were handed a document which they were instructed to read and confirm that they understood fully:

GENERAL ROUTINE OF
H.M. FEMALE CONVICT PRISON
AND STATE REFORMATORY, AYLESBURY

Prisoners shall rise at five o'clock a.m. and go to bed at ten o'clock p.m. The lights in all cells shall be put out at the hours prescribed for going to bed.

Prisoners shall be required to place their clothes outside the doors of their cells at night.

The following routine of labour and duty amongst all classes of Prisoners in Gaol shall, as far as practicable, be carried out, viz:-

At 5 o'clock	Waking-up bell, Rise.
From 5 to 6	Wash and clean cells (scrub floor & door, fold bedclothes, clean utensils).
From 6 to 8	Bakehouse, Kitchen Duty and cleaning corridors.
8 to 9	Chapel.
9 to 10	Breakfast, Cleaning.
10 to 12	Kitchen Duty, Laundry, Twine making, Sewing room, Gardening.
12 to 1	Dinner and oakum-picking.
1 to 4	Prison Exercise (in silence).
4 to 6	Bakehouse, Kitchen, Sewing room, Twine making.
6 to 7	Supper, clean dining area and common areas.
7 to 9	Instruction, Reading.
10 o'clock	Bed (Electric Lights turned off).

A visit to the prison library is permitted twice-weekly.

After confirming their understanding of the prison routine, Violet and Miriam were sent to the bathhouse for their once-weekly ablutions. The baths were arranged in rows, and a modicum of privacy was afforded by a series of partitions. However, a low door at each cubicle entrance enabled the wardresses to observe each bather and to chase away the mice and rats that scurried under the partitions.

Violet and Miriam were then supplied with their official prison uniform (to be worn at all times), consisting of an extremely unflattering long grey dress, with loose-fitting skirts, made from a coarse, thick, and uncomfortable material. The dress was to be belted tightly and worn with a long white apron. Prison undergarments were supplied, which were ill-fitting and rash-inducing. Prison issue stockings (without suspenders or garters) were provided; these were thick, black, and shapeless, and each inmate was forced to improvise in an effort to prevent them from constantly slipping down. Heavy prison shoes were also issued to each prisoner, along with an identification disc bearing their prisoner and cell numbers.

Next, prisoners' hair was cut to a standard length, tied up tightly in a bun, then secured with a white bonnet fastened under the chin. Prisoners were expected to wear their hair and bonnet in this fashion at all times – with the exception of sleeping – when confined in the infirmary, or while taking their weekly bath.

After their initiation, Violet and Miriam were assigned a prison cell each. The prison was composed entirely of single cells located on each level of the three-storey hallways. Those on the upper levels were accessed via a narrow gangway. Below, suspended across the hallway, a protective netting or screening acted as a deterrent to those attempting suicide.

Each cell, approximately 5½ feet in width and 8 feet in length, contained a narrow single bed, a small table, a three-tier corner shelf (on which inmates were permitted to keep a small number of approved books, family photographs, a toothbrush, if one was requested by the prisoner, a tin or enamel mug, and a tiny mirror). A small stool and a floormat were provided for prayers. As Violet and Miriam entered their cells, in Block B3, they were presented with one roll of dark brown lavatory paper (to last a week), a Bible, common prayer and hymn books, together with a booklet on hygiene and feminine cleanliness, and a leaflet entitled 'The Narrow Way', containing the following passage from the Bible, which all inmates were ordered to memorise:

Aylesbury Women's Prison

Nothing For Something

Because strait is the gate, and narrow is the way which leadeth unto life, and few there that find it.

Matthew, 7:14

Following the allocation of their accommodation, a tearful Violet and her distraught mother were given a whispered warning from a neighbouring cellmate regarding the wardresses. These guards were to be feared and respected in equal measure. They paraded the corridors dressed in their uniform of long black skirt and black blouse, adorned with a white collar, black bonnet and a thin belt, from which hung a long chain and a jangling set of keys. Fraternisation between the wardresses and detainees was generally not encouraged, and conversations usually consisted only of appeals from the inmates, usually requesting a visit to the infirmary or other such excuse to avoid the monotony of daily work. The requests were generally dealt with impatiently and with little sympathy. In fact, if a wardress began swinging her keychain in an irritated fashion, the inmate would quickly desist, realising the futility of her request.

Violet and her mother were ordered into the office of a stern-looking senior wardress, who informed them exactly what their penal servitude would entail.

Employment within the prison was allocated based on the prisoner's experience in the outside world. As the majority of the inmates at Aylesbury were working-class women, used to long hours and hard work, Violet and Miriam would find this transformation particularly daunting. Most of the 285 prisoners had in normal life been housemaids, cooks, seamstresses, barmaids, cotton-spinners, nurses, or laundry maids, and had been allocated their prison employment accordingly. If any quantum of hierarchy did exist within prison life, it could be found in the allocation of work. Nurses could expect to find employment in the prison infirmary, cooks in the bakehouse or kitchen, seamstresses in the sewing room and so on. For Violet and Miriam, who had been physically idle, having led a pampered life, and had few such skills, their experience in prison was to be a particularly difficult one. Work in the prison garden involved back-breaking shifts with heavy wheelbarrows, or hours spent bent over a hoe or spade, weeding and planting. When the weather was colder, a prisoner on those menial duties might be thankful to be rostered on an indoor shift, perhaps to scrub the stairways, clean the lavatory block, or chase the rats away from the kitchens. An unlucky prisoner might curse their luck (and their aching back) after hours spent leaning over the bread troughs in the prison bakehouse, kneading the dough, or nursing blistered and red-raw fingers after a shift in the twine-making factory. Worse still were the painful burns and scalds picked up in the oppressively hot prison laundry or during a lengthy shift in the kitchens, where the principal cook handed out the most laborious and uncomfortable tasks to the newest inmates, or those to whom she had taken a dislike.

Those convicts who had been imprisoned – by the male-dominated legal system – for murdering their lovers, husbands, or newly born babies were regarded with a strange respect and sympathy by their fellow inmates. Those who had been declared legally insane and recently transferred from lunatic asylums were regarded with apprehension and mistrust, this in a world where mental illness was seen as a stigma, still treated as though it were an infectious disease. Many of these women had committed a crime which, had it been perpetrated by a man, would have certainly been interpreted, and treated, very differently.

All the inmates at Aylesbury Women's Prison were forced to dress identically (with the exception of those brought up in the Roman Catholic faith, who were allowed to wear a cross and keep their rosaries close by). Violet, who had previously sought to make an impression wherever she went in life, was now forced to become an anonymous figure, to be routinely ignored, despised by other prisoners, and chastised for her lack of application or hard work by the senior wardress during her weekly inspections.

During the first four weeks of their incarceration Violet and Miriam spent the majority of their non-working time confined to their cells. As this occurred in March and April, the cells were cold and damp. However, as summer approached they were permitted to spend more time in the communal areas, although all inmates were still prohibited from speaking. Nevertheless, this 'association' time still offered some light relief from the stuffy, airless cells. Occasionally during these times extra chores were handed out, generally to those not well enough for more active work, including knitting men's socks, embroidering nightgowns, and dressing children's dolls. These tasks, which helped the prison finances, were mandatory, especially for Miriam, frequently considered too unwell for stints in the prison garden, dough-making, or long shifts in the prison laundry room.

Exercise, taken daily between 1 and 4 pm, involved a circular walk around the prison compound. Inmates were forced to walk 6 feet apart, and talking was not permitted. However, after a prisoner had served the first nine months of their sentence, she would be allowed to walk and talk in a group of two or three. This must have offered Violet and Miriam a chance to communicate, and perhaps even make new acquaintances among the new influx of middle and upper-class suffragette prisoners who swelled the ranks of Aylesbury Prison in late 1910 and 1911.

Exercise was taken regardless of the weather, and no overcoats were issued in the winter, although during the summer months a wider-brimmed bonnet was introduced.

With the arrival of the generally better educated and socially more mobile suffragette prisoners, the government introduced additional strict regulation at the prison to ensure that these new arrivals could make no attempt to differentiate their style of dress. The Home Secretary's new guidelines were designed, 'to ensure uniformity in respect of the wearing of prison clothing, bathing, hair-curling, cleaning of cells, employment, exercise, books, and otherwise.'

There was, however, some relaxation in the new rules, permitting friends and relatives to send in extra food parcels from the outside. But there is no evidence that Violet's family did so. In fact, following Violet and Miriam's imprisonment, Lillian and David moved away from Moffat, to rent rooms at 56 Coltart Road, Toxteth, Liverpool. Frederick also relocated again; first to Wolverhampton, then to the West Country to seek employment as a motor engineer, no doubt wishing to distance himself from the rest of the family. Indeed, there is no surviving record of a visit being made to the prison by any family member. Presumably in an attempt to avoid public scrutiny and disgrace, David and Lillian also changed their surname from Charlesworth to Coulson (that of Lillian's estranged husband). They even registered themselves under that name in the 1911 census.

And so the dreariness of prison life dragged on for Violet and her mother during 1910 and 1911. News from the outside world was controlled and limited. The prisoners were informed of the death of King Edward VII and the ascent of his son, George V, to the throne. A special memorial service was held in the prison chapel.

Prisoners, unless informed by visitors, were not made aware of the arrest, trial and execution of Dr Crippen, or the launch of the SS *Titanic* in Belfast, or even the introduction of the first saucy seaside postcards. Neither were they told the outcome of the general election (in which, of course, they were not allowed to participate). Violet and Miriam were officially recorded on the 1911 census as 'Inmates of Aylesbury Prison', despite not agreeing to their names being registered as prisoners. Had they known it at the time, Violet, Miriam, and the rest of the female prisoners at Aylesbury would have taken some delight from the news that the prominent suffragette campaigner Emily Davison had hidden herself inside a cupboard buried in a basement underneath Westminster to be avoid being registered in the census.

Nothing highlights the mundanity of Violet and Miriam's daily existence more sharply than the daily diet served to the prisoners:

Breakfast	Bread and a pint of sweet tea.
Dinner	Bread, meat, potatoes, and cabbage.
Tea	Bread and a pint of cocoa.

Although bread was baked daily in the prison bakehouse, the prisoners were only allocated bread at least 24 hours old; the freshly baked bread was reserved for the wardresses.

Following breakfast, as the prisoners returned to their cells to prepare for morning work, they were also handed two ounces of butter (the daily ration). Their evening cocoa was topped with a thick layer of grease to help ward off the night-time cold, although this was universally despised by the inmates.

There was to be no outside saviour for Violet and Miriam, nor some dramatic Houdini-like escape. Instead, the days slowly transformed into weeks, and the weeks into months. Miriam's health became steadily worse due to her heart condition. Violet, too, became drawn, paler, and noticeably thinner (she was already slim, even on entry to prison). Yet the pair gradually grew accustomed to the life of a detainee. It seems they were model prisoners during their confinement, attending to the tasks allotted to them, and generally causing little trouble to the wardresses. It is tempting to imagine Violet behaving in a similar manner to some of the early upper-class suffragette prisoners (who had expected their beds to be made for them), but there is no record of this. Instead, Violet, after having earned the privilege of being allowed slates, boards, pencils, and paper, wrote several short stories, from which she hoped to earn some much-needed income following her release. Until recently it was commonly believed that these stories had been lost forever. Fortunately, during the research for this book I uncovered one of these missing tales, and it is reproduced in Appendix E at the end of the book.

The summer of 1911 was a hot and uncomfortable one for the inmates at Aylesbury Prison. Cells became like ovens and there was little relief to be had, indoors or out. The unbearable heatwave, during which time the highest temperature ever measured in the UK at that time was recorded at Raunds in Northamptonshire – less than 50 miles away from the prison – made life almost unbearable for Violet and Miriam.[23] The only crumb of comfort was the privilege granted to well-behaved first-timers of a Star

---

23 On 9 August 1911 a temperature of 36.7°C (98.1°F) was recorded at Raunds in Northampton. This record stood for almost 80 years, until it was finally broken during the heatwave of 1990.

Class – slightly lighter – summer uniform.

Early in 1912 the atmosphere at the prison changed dramatically as the force-feeding and disciplining of suffragette prisoners on hunger strike began in earnest at Aylesbury. Violet, Miriam, and many other inmates must have cried themselves to sleep in their cells as they listened to the sound of hunger strikers being dragged from their cells and frog-marched to a punishment cell. Frog-marching (a phrase many of us have heard, but never questioned its origins) involved seizing the prisoner by their arms and forcing them to march forward. For the suffragette prisoners, however, a further gruesome twist was added. The unlucky inmate's arms and legs were grabbed from either side by a two wardresses, who then turned the prisoner upside down. The poor detainee was then carrying upside down, with the wardresses making sure to bump the prisoner's head on each step during the painful journey to the punishment cell.

The agonising screams, humiliation, and suffering of the suffragette hunger strikers doubtless lived long in the memory of every female prisoner unfortunate enough to have been incarcerated in Aylesbury Prison during that era. The discomforts caused by denying the body food – such as cramps, sore and bleeding gums, vomiting, and loose flesh – were superseded by the brutal indignity of the tactics, almost akin to rape, employed to force-feed the hunger strikers. After the painful bruising of the shoulders and back caused by the many unsuccessful attempts to force a tube into the victim's throat, the doctor would often rachet open the prisoner's mouth with an iron vice-like tool and insert the food, then force the victim to swallow. If this failed, a longer tube would be pushed down the throat, or sometimes through the nostril, into the stomach. If this failed, the prisoner might even be subjected to overwhelming physical force to subdue them, after which they were force-fed by a tube inserted in their rectum or vagina. It was later revealed that new tubes were not always readily available, and that dirty tubes, previously used on diseased or mentally ill inmates, were often utilised.

In November 1911, under this increasingly dark and intimidating atmosphere, Mr Durnford, the solicitor who had originally represented the Charlesworths at their appeal hearing, wrote to Winston Churchill, then Home Secretary, with regard to Miriam's failing health. Churchill agreed to an inquiry into Miriam's health; however, on receipt of the report he wrote back, stating: 'The opinion of the medical officer did not justify Mrs Charlesworth's release – Winston Churchill.'

Violet's sister Lillian was then granted permission to visit the prisoners, and she again appealed for mercy in the case, claiming that both her sister's and mother's health were 'seriously impaired'.

Finally, in January 1912, and after yet another Christmas spent behind bars, Violet and Miriam received the news they had longed for. They were to be released early, after serving two years of their three-year sentences. Their release, on licence, had mainly been granted due to their growing ill health. However, Violet's good behaviour, discipline, and stoicism during her incarceration, was also taken into account. It was perhaps the only time in her life that she had been forced to work for her existence, or exhibited any degree of self-discipline.

And so, on Monday 5 February 1912 (after 1 year, 10 months, and 18 days of incarceration) Miriam and Violet walked out through the prison gates, blinking in the bright winter sunshine.

During the years of their imprisonment the world had changed considerably. The new king was sitting on the throne, tensions across Europe had risen, and in Britain a national coal strike was being threatened. Shortly after their release Captain Robert Falcon Scott CVO would reach the South Pole – albeit for his expedition to fail in the greatest British heroic style.

How had prison affected the two women? Miriam's health had certainly, and irreversibly, worsened. Violet, too, seemed a mere shadow of the immaculately attired lady who had entered those austere gates in March 1910. Had her spirit been trampled, and had her desire for a lavish lifestyle been forever diminished? Maybe Violet had learned a new steely resolve and grim determination to never return to the prison environment. Or perhaps, just perhaps, she intended to play one last trick on a gloating establishment?

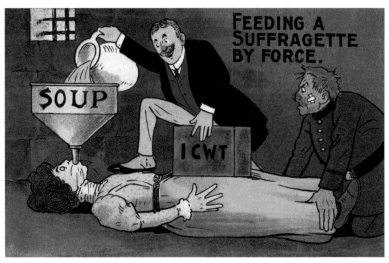

The force-feeding of suffragettes at
Aylesbury Prison

23: The Getaway

As Abraham Lincoln reportedly declared in 1858:

> **You can fool all the people some of the time,
> and some of the people all of the time,
> but you can't fool all the people all the time.**

As we shall see, Violet Charlesworth might just have been the exception to that rule.

In these final two chapters I will attempt to unravel perhaps the most intriguing mystery in the affair of 'the vanishing beauty in the red cloak' (as she was described by the *Daily Telegraph* in 1912). The possible answers are tantalisingly manifold. The art of the truly great con trick is to leave your mark so bewildered and so unsure of what really happened that long after you have disappeared into the sunset they are still asking questions. If that is the benchmark of a great con artist, then Violet Charlesworth may well have been the twentieth century's greatest, and probably its most stylish. More of that later.

Violet Charlesworth
released

First, however, we must deal with the aftermath of her release from Aylesbury on 5 February 1912.

There was an initial flurry of press interest. Almost immediately after the news of her release had been cabled to the Press Association (in a statement which did not reveal Violet's intended destination), reporters from several newspapers began the quest to locate her new home. It would only take the first newshound a matter of days to pick up the Charlesworths' scent and make some hasty travel arrangements for the journey north, back to Moffat.

On their release, Violet and Miriam returned to Windsor Cottage, David Denholm's house in Dumfriesshire, the small villa where they had originally fled to avoid arrest in September 1909. Put simply, Violet and Miriam had nowhere else to go. They were penniless (publicly, at least) ex-convicts, who now wished to remain incognito while they recuperated from their imprisonment. Lillian had returned to Windsor Cottage to welcome her sister and mother home, although David does not seem to have been living there at the time.

In similar fashion to their arrival at the address in September 1909, Violet and Miriam had no intention of revealing themselves to either the press or the local townsfolk.

Their first shock came from a newspaper in which Violet discovered that the well-known and respected racehorse owner Mr Cecil Leveson-Gower had named his new racehorse Violet Charlesworth. In a conversation with friends, in which they were discussing possible names for the steeplechase mare, he had apparently declared, 'What better than "Violet Charlesworth"? If this horse of mine can run as fast as she did, I'm going to win a lot of races!'

The horse proved to be popular with the punters, winning several races between 1910 and 1913 – including at Lingfield on the weekend of Violet's release. The horse added considerably to Leveson-Gower's wealth and kudos in those pre-war years. He later served during the Great War as a captain, and in 1919 was awarded an MBE. Violet herself did not benefit from her famous namesake, and certainly would have baulked at the sporting pages' description of the horse as 'one of the gamest little fillies that ever looked through a bridle'. Perhaps some of Violet's victims might even have attempted to recoup their losses with a wager on the horse named after the woman who had fleeced them.

If this constant reminder of her infamy was not sufficient to infuriate Violet, we can only imagine her upset and anger when just five days after her release the family heard an unexpected knock on the door of Windsor Cottage. An enterprising reporter from the *Dundee Courier* had become the first journalist to track her down. With the intention of obtaining an exclusive interview, he travelled to Moffat, arriving at the cottage on the evening of Saturday 10 February. David Denholm answered the door and 'flew into a violent passion on hearing the intention of my visit', according to the newshound's notes. The reporter's own words best describe the events,

> I called late on that Saturday evening, to be met by Mr Denholm who answered the door. My visit was brought to an abrupt end by Mr Denholm who flew into a violent passion on hearing the intention of my visit. However, this was not before I was blessed with a peep of Miss Violet Charlesworth, who appeared in the window next to the door. I can best describe her as having a look of mental strain depicted on her countenance, although still retaining much of her characteristic charm and manner.
>
> Returning again to my endeavour on Sunday morning, I paid another visit to the cottage, which showed definite signs of occupancy, smoke issuing from the chimneys of several rooms which have not recently been occupied. Voices, evidently those of females, were quite audible even from outside on the Selkirk

> Road. I was, however, chagrined in that my entrance this time was effectually barred, the gate having been securely fastened overnight by means of a heavy chain and padlock. I was able to climb over without difficulty, however, Mr Denholm, on witnessing me, declared that I had been hoaxed into supposing that Miss Charlesworth lived there, and ordered me to leave. I advised Mr Denholm to keep cool and not get excited, it was not good for so old a man. He conveyed me to the gate, shouting that he would not have pressmen coming about the house. Entrance barred!

This seemingly insignificant incident, during which the reporter had witnessed Violet through the window of Windsor Cottage, was in fact the last confirmed sighting of Violet Charlesworth ever recorded. With the exception of the short story[24] which she sold to the *Northern Weekly Gazette* to be published in October 1912, from that moment on Violet Charlesworth seems to have quite simply vanished from the face of the earth.

What happened to Violet and her family is a question which has for many years puzzled those who have become obsessed with her story. Many have laboured to solve the mystery; most have given up. From time to time a possible solution is offered, but none has proved to be satisfactory.

There are several possibilities, but before we explore them, we should first mention the bit-part players in Violet's melodrama.

Mr Justice Darling

Charles John Darling was a lawyer, former Unionist and Conservative MP, and high court judge. His surprisingly lenient sentencing of Violet and Miriam Charlesworth – and particularly his unprecedented decision to return to court just two days after the trial, to reduce their prison terms from five to three years – went somewhat against his fearsome reputation.

This may partly be explained by his poor health, which had blighted him throughout his life, although he may have felt some compassion for Violet and Miriam, who both appeared distressed and unwell in court. Aged 61 at the time of the trial, he belonged to the Victorian generation who still considered women to be the fairer and gentler sex. Violet, it seems, possessed a natural gift for winning the sympathy of middle-aged and older men.

Following his death in 1936 at the age of 85, long obituaries in the newspapers contained details of the more sensational cases in which he had been involved, including those of Dr Crippen, Roger Casement – and, of course, Violet Charlesworth.

---

24 Mentioned earlier, and reproduced in Appendix E

Mr Henry Maddox

Violet's defence barrister during her trial would later become Sir Henry Maddox and an MP in Stanley Baldwin's Conservative government. He earned considerable praise as a barrister for offering his services under the Poor Person Rules (similar to legal aid today) to women such as Violet, who could not afford legal representation. Lord Justice McCardie declared: 'The Bar of England is the stronger for his example.'

Mrs Martha Smith

The Derby widow who Violet so cruelly defrauded of her entire life savings lived a long life despite the humiliation of the 1910 court case. Although at the time of Violet's trial Mrs Smith was already 59 years of age, she lived for another 33 years, eventually passing away in 1943 at the age of 92. Her financial difficulties caused by Violet were offset in 1910 by a generous collection organised by the *Derbyshire Telegraph*; however she never quite escaped the embarrassment of the questions levelled at her in court, nor her failure to see through Violet's inheritance fable: 'They had all the money I had saved, to the last £20,' she later said. 'I trusted them thoroughly. I was simply and solely taken in by them. I should have loaned the money through a lawyer.'

Dr Edward Hughes Jones

The respected Welsh doctor never fully recovered from the personal, emotional, and financial damage inflicted on him by Violet. Born in 1865, and having settled in Rhyl in 1893, by the time he met Violet in late 1906 he and his brothers had established one of the leading practices in North Wales. Dr Hughes Jones was a deeply religious man who read the Bible every day, so following the humiliation of his treatment by Violet, and her emptying of his bank account, his faith must have been sorely tested. Aged 44 at the time of Violet's trial, he continued working for a further 38 years, partly because of the resulting financial necessity, and partly due to his abiding sense of duty. In addition to serving on the Rhyl Urban District Council he became senior surgeon to the Royal Alexander Hospital and senior medical officer at the Rhyl War Memorial Hospital before eventually retiring, in his early eighties, in 1948.

He also pushed for the building of a new maternity home in Rhyl and he campaigned zealously on behalf of a young lady from Rhyl who had been fined for showing a light during the threat of a Zeppelin air raid in 1916.

Although he survived two world wars and the death of his father, mother, brother, and sister, coupled with the trauma of many difficult medical cases, Dr Hughes Jones never truly recovered from his love for Violet. In a recently discovered letter written in 1983 by an elderly man, Mr J.E. Roberts, who recalled meeting Dr Hughes Jones after the news of Violet's deception had emerged:

> As a young coach builder in Rhyl I cut my hand rather badly, and was treated by Dr Hughes Jones. It was generally known in the town that she had fleeced him of a large sum of money. When he treated me, he looked as if he were in a trance and just tore the bandages off. The healed incision on my left hand does remind me of those days.

Edward Hughes Jones died in December 1949 at the age of 84, at home in Rhyl. His obituary was published in the *British Medical Journal* on the anniversary of Violet's birthday.

Albert Watts

The young chauffeur who helped fraudulently stage the motor-car accident remained at Boderw in the immediate aftermath and through the resulting media furore. Following Violet's exposure in Scotland and the eviction of the family from Boderw, he returned to London to work in the motor trade. We know that as a younger man Albert had earned a living at Downing College in Cambridge as a shoeblack and by repairing bicycles for students. It was there that he had developed his love for all things mechanical, and he eventually migrated to London to seek employment in the motor trade.

Albert, despite his involvement in the staged motor accident, seems to have avoided being on the receiving end of any criminal charge. In 1909 he visited his old landlady in Cambridge, proudly displaying a gold watch which he claimed had been given to him by Violet. Just before Christmas 1910 he posted a Christmas card to the same landlady, bearing a London postmark and signed by him and his fiancée. Little is known of his later life, although he was still working as a chauffeur in 1933 when, ironically, he was obliged to give evidence following a genuine motor-car accident – this time as a witness.

There were many rumours of a love affair or strong connection between Albert and Violet, even of a secret marriage, although there is no evidence to support this theory other than his claim to have received £3 a week in salary from Violet – more than twice the average working man's stipend.

The name Albert Watts will, however, appear once more in the Violet Charlesworth story.

Mr Joseph Gratton

The mysterious Joseph Llewelyn Gratton is a rather enigmatic cast member in the drama of Violet's life. Originally the Charlesworths' landlord at Foryd Lodge, upon the death of his wife he became their lodger at Boderw.

Joseph seems to have been either completely duped by the Charlesworth family or totally complicit in their fraud; either way, he was obviously heavily under their influence. There are several interesting factors to mention. First, at Violet's bankruptcy hearing he was listed as a major creditor (having loaned her over £500), yet he seems to have been happy to drive to Penmaenmawr on the night of the accident and, despite police instructions to the contrary, collect Lillian. In addition, he appears to have been content to act as an official spokesman during the Siege of Boderw, then to accompany Violet's sister on the journey to Scotland at the request of the police. Alongside Lillian, he then became complicit in the ongoing deception by also claiming to the police 'that the woman staying at the hotel is not Miss Violet Charlesworth'. Yet he too seems to have escaped any criminal charges for his part in the deceit.

Perhaps Joseph merely lodged at Boderw rent free in lieu of monies due to him, or conceivably he was yet another middle-aged man besotted with Violet. He was 40 years of age at the time of Violet's staged motor-car accident.

Following the Charlesworths' eviction from Boderw, Joseph moved to his brother's farm, Fron Haul at Rhuddlan, where he lived the quiet life of a sheep farmer, occasionally competing at the Royal Welsh Show. Following his brother's death, Joseph managed the farm until passing away in 1954 at the age of 84.

Joseph, although living a quiet and isolated existence, will also appear on one further occasion in the Violet Charlesworth mystery.

Mr Frederick Charlesworth

Violet's brother seems to be the only member of the family not to have become swamped by the scandal surrounding the motor-car accident and the uncovering of her fraud.

He appears to have initially trusted Violet and her inheritance story, although he may have been somewhat naïve in believing it so readily. At the time of Violet's supposed accident Fred (as he was known) was living in Bath, working for the Prudential Insurance Company. After being told of his sister's apparent death he returned to Boderw to support his mother and father.

When the press interviewed Fred in the week following Violet's disappearance he spoke honestly:

> My father is naturally very much upset at the affair, and has declined to be interviewed, but I will give you my impressions of the mystery. I am firmly resigned, and expect to hear that the worst has happened to my sister. I believe that she has gone over the cliff. My sister had always been most reticent in regard to her business affairs. I was aware that she had trustees and an estate left to her, and a Mr Gordon, from whom she obtained money. But I had no idea that she was apparently in any financial difficulties.
>
> I last saw her at Calne for about two hours in the early part of November. I had cycled to Calne and just as I was entering the town I saw her driving in a motor-car. It was here that I first learned that she had creditors.
>
> So far as I know she had no love affair. Our mother is an invalid.

Once the dust had settled following Violet's bankruptcy, Frederick seems to have limited his contact with the rest of the family. Around 1910 he moved to 86 Newbridge Street, in Wolverhampton, with his wife Ann and their three children, then to Bloomfield Road in Coventry, where he worked as a motor engineer. Aged 42 at the outbreak of the Great War, he was not called up to fight, and in the 1920s he became a car salesman in the Midlands. Unfortunately, it seems that his wife died at a comparatively young age, after which he became the manager of a timber merchants in Warwickshire. In later life he lodged for many years with the Goodall family at their home, Nailcote Cottage in the village of Balsall Common. This arrangement seems to have suited Frederick, who at this stage had been a widower of many years, and may possibly have had some financial difficulties of his own (he had filed for bankruptcy in 1954).

Frederick appears to have outlived the rest of his family and the other characters in this story, eventually passing away at Nailcote Cottage in 1967, at the grand old age of 94.

There is no surviving record of him visiting Violet in prison, nor of any further communication between the siblings, nor of anyone remembering Frederick ever divulging Violet's location.

Mrs David Charlesworth, Miriam

Violet's mother's health was irreversibly affected by the period spent in Aylesbury Prison. She appears to have suffered from a heart condition throughout her life. No doubt the family's conspiracy surrounding Violet's motor-car accident and the resulting publicity placed a huge strain upon her, and exacerbated her condition.

Miriam appears to have been a difficult and calculating woman. Was her decision to plead Not Guilty at her trial and then deny any knowledge of Violet's crimes a cynical attempt to avoid prison for herself? Or perhaps a calculated plan previously agreed with Violet? We simply do not know. It does seem that, like Violet, her illness was used conveniently whenever a situation became difficult.

Following her release from prison Miriam returned to Windsor Cottage in Moffat, to lodge with her relative David Denholm. Her husband did not return to Windsor Cottage with her. Following Denholm's death, Miriam moved to Chorley in Lancashire, where she passed away in December 1920 at the age of 69 from her heart condition.

Mr David Charlesworth and Miss Lillian Charlesworth

After Violet and Miriam had been imprisoned and the family evicted from Boderw, David and Lillian moved to Coltart Road in Toxteth, Liverpool. As mentioned earlier, they adopted the surname Coulson, that of Lillian's estranged husband, Walter, although Walter appears to have remained in Birmingham during that period. On his death in 1924 he left his estate of £1,380 to Lillian. It is possible that she lived into her nineties in Manchester, but there is no concrete proof of this.

We know very little about the movements of David and Lillian from the 1920s onwards. However, there is every chance that their destiny was inexorably tied up with the riddle of Violet's disappearance. The answer to the fate of all three is probably either a very simple and sadly tragic one, or perhaps one of the most effective frauds ever perpetrated.

In the vernacular of the confidence trickster, it will soon be time to play Find the Lady.

Miss May Charlesworth

Also known as Violet May Gordon Charlesworth, Violet Gordon, Violet Talbot, Violet Mackenzie, Margaret MacLeod, Miss Mackay, Violet Cameron, Violet MacDonald, Mrs Miller (and, as you will discover, probably several other names too) …

As mentioned earlier, Violet and her mother relocated to Windsor Cottage in Moffat following their early release from prison. The comparative ease of their discovery by members of press no doubt infuriated Violet. Coupled with the continual newspaper reminders of her notoriety generated by her namesake on the steeplechase course, she naturally craved anonymity. It is almost certain that she then did something she had done on many occasions before – changed her name.

In 1912, prior to the introduction of passports and other officially printed documentation, it was a relatively easy task for a person to change their identity. Most formal introductions, requests for bank accounts, etc, were achieved through letters of introduction or by handwritten application forms. As mentioned earlier, passports were not introduced until after the Great War, and the early driving licences were also filled in by hand from information supplied by the applicant, and did not contain a photograph. Although records of births, deaths, and marriages were technically a legal requirement, many people forgot, or chose not to register them.

Even today, it is still not a legal necessity to register a change of surname, although if a person were to require legal documentation in that new name a deed poll would probably be required. A century ago the process was a far easier one, and many people chose to take on a new identity. Some did so to escape an abusive husband, a criminal past, or a weighty debt. Many did so purely for the sake of fashion.

The mystery of Violet's vanishing trick following her prison release almost certainly involved a successful change of name. But how did she achieve it?

In the introduction to this book, I mentioned that Violet had perpetrated three frauds during her lifetime. The first fraud, her inheritance scam, was highly effective and has been copied on many occasions since (most recently in the case of Anna Delvey, which featured in the Netflix TV series 'Inventing Anna'). Unfortunately, the obvious flaw in Violet's scheme – her 25th birthday being its endpoint – meant that the deception was destined to unravel and expose her. Her second con trick, the staged accident and her subsequent disappearance, was rushed, panicked, and ill-executed. However, it seems that her final deception (or, at least, the final trick of which we have any definitive proof) was so well executed that Violet, together with her father and sister, appear to have simply evaporated into thin air.

From the publication of her short story in October 1912, the name Violet Charlesworth is noticeably absent from all official registers, documentation, and newspapers. There is no recorded proof or photograph that conclusively links the Violet Charlesworth of our story with any confirmed marriage, death certification, or official notification of any kind. Nor is there any completely verifiable record connected with her father or sister.

However, before I begin to discuss the various possibilities surrounding Violet's disappearance, it is worthwhile mentioning the events that occurred immediately after her release on 5 February 1912. Shortly afterwards, sea trials of the *Titanic* began. Then on 15 April 1912 the ship sank after striking an iceberg, with the loss of 1,512 lives. The story of the investigation, resulting lawsuits, and personal anguish would effectively wipe every other story from the pages of the nation's newspapers for many months. Violet was clearly no longer considered newsworthy. And from then until the advent of the Great War in September 1914, the news prominently featured the outrage caused by the firebombing of post boxes by the suffragette movement, the 1912 Olympics, a summer of floods, and the discovery of the Piltdown Man. As a consequence the name Violet Charlesworth slipped from the nation's consciousness. Then came the terrible devastation caused by the war, combined with the nation being distracted for several years by the 'Spanish' Flu pandemic. This multitude of catastrophic events, following hot on one another's heels, provided ample distraction from Violet's shenanigans.

So how *did* Violet disappear so effectively, and what happened to her?

The first possibility is a very simple and sad one. That she died very soon after being released from prison, having changed her name. The fact that she suffered from an apparently undiagnosed medical condition almost from birth is irrefutable. There are many descriptions of Violet that mention her wearing a veil to hide her 'sallow appearance and tired expression' or 'muddy complexion'. The more unchivalrous descriptions also referred to the 'brown spots on her face and brown eyes of a curious reddish tinge'. There is a distinct possibility that she suffered from Addison's disease, a hormone deficiency of the adrenal glands, which a century ago would often result in death at an early age. (Jane Austen, too, suffered from this affliction.) Now treatable with hormone replacement therapy, the disease may have been responsible for Violet's physical appearance and her lethargy.

If this was indeed the case, it is probable that her incarceration in Aylesbury Prison would have exacerbated the condition. Perhaps Violet lived the lifestyle she did, recklessly cramming so much into her first 25 years, knowing that she would not be expected to live for long. Selfish, perhaps, but understandable.

There is one death certificate archived in the National Records Office for a lady named Violet Charlesworth, who died in 1922. However, the middle name, date of birth, place of birth, and family record do not match. It does not appear to be the same person. This leaves us with an intriguing riddle. if Violet did not pass away at a young age, exactly how did she manage to vanish quite so effectively?

24: Find The Lady

Since the early 1920s many journalists and researchers have sought a morsel of proof that might solve the riddle of her disappearance. No one has yet been able to do so. Perhaps this is a measure of just how successfully Violet managed to fool us all.

I have spent almost three years of my life travelling the country, painstakingly gathering together every scrap of information I could find, in a quest for the same. In doing so, I have become absorbed and consumed in the answer to this mystery, desperately hoping that Violet might have made some small mistake that would eventually lead me to a definitive answer. It seems, however, that perhaps Violet might have proved too clever for us all.

All is not entirely lost, nonetheless. We are left with several intriguing possibilities and a handful of enticing clues that just might provide the answer that has eluded everyone for more than a century.

First, there is the romantic (and admittedly unlikely) proposition that Dr Edward Hughes Jones forgave Violet. During her trial he admitted that he had loved her before he ever knew she was an heiress to a fortune. Perhaps he took this opportunity to display his true feelings for her.

Whilst this version of events would make a happy ending, it is extremely unlikely, and there is no evidence to support this theory. It is also hard to imagine that Violet could have returned to Rhyl without being recognised and remarked upon.

Conceivably, and infinitely more likely, Violet found another wealthy man and married quietly, and under a different name – perhaps without her future husband even knowing her true identity. After all, she was rumoured to have met many older men, including MPs and lords, in both Scotland and London. If she did so, then she would have successfully managed to achieve the resulting lifestyle and anonymity she desired, without leaving any clue as to her previous identity.

Another alternative is that Violet, using a new name, moved to a different part of the country and re-invented her fake inheritance story all over again. Perhaps, after several years of relative poverty and hardship, she found the draw of easy money too hard to ignore. The newspapers in 1915 regularly featured the story of Lady Ida Sitwell, who had received a mere three-month prison sentence for a stocks and bonds fraud. Perhaps Violet thought the potential rewards outweighed the possible risks.

However, exactly how is it possible to prove that Violet did indeed attempt to carry out her fake inheritance fraud all over again? It is almost impossible to establish with any degree of certainty, of course. Nevertheless, undaunted by the task, I attempted to solve the puzzle by approaching it from a different angle.

My train of thought was as follows: assuming at the outset that Violet had managed to successfully change her name without raising suspicion, then any official records regarding a similar fraud case could not be linked to the name Violet Charlesworth. Instead, they would only mention her new name. So I checked for similar crimes of fraud under aliases that Violet had previously used (MacDonald, Talbot, Miller, Gordon, MacLeod, and Cameron, to name but a few); however I was unable to locate any. No luck so far.

Undeterred, I changed tack. On reflection I reasoned that if Violet had invented another pseudonym it is unlikely that she would have re-used a name that might be recognised or associated with her. Therefore, this time I began to scour official records for similar frauds under new and different names. This time I cross-referenced my search by establishing whether the names of these other female fraudsters had any traceable past or recorded ancestry. Did they have a matching birth certificate, baptism record, census return, etc? In other words, had these women existed on paper prior to the dates of their crimes?

After weeks of fruitless searching, I had gradually begun to lose faith in this line of investigation ... until at last I unearthed two intriguing possibilities.

First, the case of Mary Brady, which bears so many of Violet's hallmarks that it is simply too coincidental to ignore.

Mary Brady appeared at the Manchester Assizes in November 1919 accused of 'larceny, fraudulent conversion of sums of money, and making false entries in a cash book belonging to her employers, Messrs Thoresen, Shipbrokers, of Manchester, London and Christiania,[25] resulting in the theft of £22,000' (now £1.5 million).

Sir Edward Marshall Hall

The case, in a similar manner to Violet's court appearance, aroused an intense degree of public interest, and the press even remarked on the similarity of the case to that of Violet's. Mr Langdon K.C. and Mr Gilbert Jordan appeared on behalf of the Crown, and Mary was defended by

---

25 Now Oslo.

Nothing For Something

Sir Edward Marshall Hall K.C., Britain's most famous barrister. Mary– like Violet – clearly had deep pockets.

The accused was described by reporters present in the court as

> an attractive woman, aged about 30, fashionably attired, with brown hair and eyes, who was attended in the dock by a prison wardress. The lady claimed to be feeling unwell and, on his Lord Justice McCardle's directions, was allowed to be seated after the pleas had been entered.

Mary had taken employment with the shipping firm four years previously and had systematically used her position during that period to embezzle large sums of money to finance her affluent lifestyle. She was unable to provide any personal history or documentation, and accounted for these gaps in her background by explaining to the court that (despite not having an Irish accent) she was the daughter of an Inspector in the Royal Irish Constabulary. She claimed that:

> my father died when I was 14, at which time I chose to enter a Franciscan Convent as a novice. I later came out to engage in a business career, and I am a woman of proven business capacity.

There was widespread derision in the courtroom at Mary's preposterous claims, and the astute Sir Edward wisely advised his client to change her plea to one of guilty of all charges.

He then constructed his defence plea in an attempt to engender some sympathy from the judge:

> When arrested, my client openly stated, "I cannot lie; I have the money." She gave the company's secretary every assistance in locating the remaining money, and she is a woman of exceptional business capacity.

When asked by Lord Justice McCardle where the money had gone, Mary replied,

> On dresses, furs, jewellery, furniture, and a house. I paid a sum of £2,000 in cash for one of my purchases. I was also concerned in two businesses, one of which made a loss, for which I needed to borrow £1,000 from a money lender. I lived in one of the principal hotels in the city for a time, and I lost heavily at cards.

Sir Edward added,

> In the whole of my professional experience I have not met a case such as this. If the facts had been stated in a novel they would have been looked upon as improbable and ridiculous.

She conceived the idea because large sums of petty cash passed through her hands, sometimes as much as £50,000, and one of her mistakes was to take larger and larger sums to cover up smaller ones previously misappropriated.

Her sister was married to a man of means, and my client's defence is being provided by money supplied by her sister's family. My client informs me that she is engaged to be married to an Army officer, and at such time she will receive a handsome allowance. Notwithstanding any sentence his Lordship might pass, that gentleman is prepared to make her his wife so that she might be given another chance.

At this stage in the proceedings, Lord Justice McCardle seemed to noticeably soften towards the young woman in the dock, who appeared close to fainting. In his closing statement before sentencing he stated,

I sympathise with a woman in the prisoner's position – a person of great charm of manner and of exceptional business ability – but she has brought degradation and dishonour upon her family. The prisoner's course of prolonged dishonesty called for a substantial punishment. You will be sentenced to twelve months' imprisonment.

Many present in the court that day had expected Mary to receive a far harsher sentence. In a similar vein to Violet, had this frail defendant also managed to garner the sympathy of the judge? The case seems to bear a remarkable similarity to Violet's – so much so that in my opinion Mary Brady warranted further investigation. Interestingly, despite some extensive background checks, I was unable to locate a birth certificate for someone using that name, nor was I able to track down any corresponding records of her existence prior to her trial in 1919. Notwithstanding the similar descriptions and lifestyles, at the time of the offence Mary was also employed within a few miles of Violet's mother's address in Chorley.

Coincidentally, when Mary was first incarcerated, her entry in the prison ledger recorded her details as '5' 3 ½", complexion pale, hair – brown, eyes – brown'. Identical in every way to Violet's entry log in the Aylesbury Prison register of 1910.

There is no record of Mary following her release from prison. She, too, seems to have vanished into thin air.

Remarkably, however, the saga of Mary Brady is not the only tale to bear a striking similarity to that of Violet Charlesworth.

Two decades later, in July 1941, Britain had entered the darkest days of the Second World War; the Luftwaffe were pounding the cities of Britain while the German navy were disrupting its Atlantic supply chains. The newspapers, tasked with offering their readership any modicum of light relief, gleefully reported the bizarre, almost comical, story of Wynne Mariette Stuart-Campbell, the remarkable tale temporarily distracting their readers from the horrors of war.

Lady Campbell, as she insisted on being addressed, claimed Scottish heritage like Violet, and declared herself to be the widow of Sir John Campbell, a Scottish Royal Marine officer who had been killed in a Moroccan air crash four years earlier.

Wynne Mariette Stuart-Campbell

In 1941, Wynne Mariette Stuart-Campbell was arrested and charged with 'posing as a Surgeon-Commander in the Women's Royal Navy Service [the WRENS] and subsequently using this position to gain access to Royal Naval facilities', including the luxurious officers' mess and the various hotels and restaurants reserved for high-ranking officials. She claimed to be the daughter of the late Lord George Crichton Stuart, the brother of the late Marquess of Bute. But all these relations had now passed away and for obvious reasons were unable to confirm her story. Nor was she able to prove her marriage, claiming that she had married Sir John Campbell in Paris and due to the war was unable to request a copy of her marriage certificate.

In researching Wynne's claim regarding her late husband's plane crash, I contacted the archives of the Bureau of Aircraft Accidents (BAAA) in Geneva, which since its creation in 1990 has been carefully cataloguing all recorded historic aircraft accidents. There were just two plane crashes in Morocco during 1937: the Air France airmail cargo plane, *Antares*, flying from Dakar to Casablanca, which crashed with the loss of six crew (all French); and a private single-engine light aircraft that crashed at Meknès, killing its two female passengers and the pilot. The name John Campbell does not feature in either accident report.

In addition to her dubious claims of marriage to Sir John Campbell, Wynne's claim to be a surgeon-commander was also false. In fact, she was merely a driver employed by the WRENS to transport senior officers speedily between naval bases and top-secret meetings. Employed due to her exceptional driving abilities, she had then grossly misused her naval base security access pass.

During the trial she gave her age as 45 (Violet would have been 56 at this time). However, it was noted that 'she had the appearance of being somewhat older'. She even claimed to be unwell during the proceedings, requesting a seat instead of standing, as expected. 'Lady Campbell' was sentenced to three months' imprisonment, though this was overturned on appeal and reduced to a suspended sentence. This judge, as in Violet's case, was sympathetic to Wynne's claims of poor health; her suspended sentence seems an extraordinarily light punishment, especially given the wartime conditions. However, this was by no means the end of the matter.

Wynne's regular visits to various naval installations in the UK resulted in her meeting a married officer, Commander Bowerman. In October 1941 she was arrested and charged again, this time with registering under a false name at a Liverpool hotel, an offence under Britain's wartime regulations. Wynne had signed the hotel's register 'Mrs W. Bowerman', and argued that she had not realised this was a crime. Again, Wynne claimed to be feeling unwell, both at the time of signing the hotel's register and while appearing in court. On this occasion she was fined £10, with an additional £4 10s 6d in costs.

Commander Bowerman divorced his wife, and married Wynne in 1942. During the remainder of the war, while her husband was away on active service, he granted Wynne a generous monthly allowance of £40 (now £3,000). This seems to have satisfied her expensive tastes, at least for the duration of their marriage. However, following the couple's separation in 1949 her allowance ceased, and it would not be long before Wynne returned to her previous lifestyle.

By the end of 1949 Lady Wynne Mariette Stuart-Bowerman (as she now preferred to be called), had befriended a businessman in Yeovil, Mr Bruce Moon, and his wife, Pearl. For some time, Mr Moon had been seeking some new outside investment in his substantial garage and taxicab company. At an afternoon tea party at a Yeovil hotel Mr and Mrs Moon were introduced to Lady Wynne, who they later described as 'dignified, fascinating, and beautifully dressed in a crimson-red corduroy suit. She boasted of a friendship with the Duchess of Kent and referred to the Queen as "Betty".'

The exact nature of that conversation was later explained by Pearl Moon:

> Lady Wynne informed us that she would love to invest in our business, however, although she received an income of £5,000 a year from trustees, she had one small snag. Lawyers were holding up the settlement of her vast inheritance and settlement until the following January. However, she told us that her father was the late Lord George Crichton Stuart, the brother of the late Marquis of Bute, and that she was due to inherit £167,000 [now £6 million]. We listened spellbound to stories of her childhood at Glamis – and how she used to play with the Queen.
>
> She casually mentioned her castle in Scotland and her shooting lodge in Leicestershire. She then came round to the

tiresome topic of money, explaining to us that, while her lawyer sorted out her estate, she would need to borrow money to meet her expenses. She promised to pay it all back with 100% interest, and she would then put as much capital back into our business as we could use.

Wynne borrowed substantial sums from the Moons, and several of their friends, over an 18-month period, spending that money on accommodation at the Ritz Hotel in London, a large home in Aston Tirrold in Berkshire (at which she threw lavish entertainments), and on two racehorses. Her tactics seem to have been uncannily like those of Violet's, including writing post-dated cheques, buying Pearl Moon a pair of jade earrings (as a gift from her fictional trustees), and sending handwritten letters in which she pleaded for a longer period of time to repay the money she owed,

> 16 December 1949
> Dearest Pearl,
>   I have just had a request from my trustees for £925 11s 6d, for income tax to be paid before Christmas Day. I just feel I can't bear it any more and pray for the end of January, when this strain will be lifted from us all.

And then

> 19 December 1950
> Dearest Bruce,
>   I know that you, Bruce, have done all you can as guarantor, and Pearl, in a lovely trusting way, has done her part valiantly. But I am paying everything back double in January. So keep a firm hold on your confidence and don't let any tiny doubt mar our Christmas time.

Gradually, as the date of her supposed inheritance loomed, and then lapsed, Wynne asked for more and more money, 'for legal expenses and stamp duty', adding, 'if you help me now, this will prove your friendship.' She even promised Pearl Moon 'a set of black pearls given to me by the Shar [sic] of Persia.'

Predictably, the Moons never saw a penny and were thrown into bankruptcy, at which point the story came to light. Wynne Mariette Stuart-Bowerman was subsequently charged and at the Old Bailey in October 1951 was sentenced to two and a half years in prison.

As part of the preparations leading to her trial, Wynne was investigated by both MI5 and Scotland Yard. Despite the high-level nature of this inquiry, the officials were unsuccessful in uncovering any information about the mysterious Wynne Mariette Stuart-Campbell prior to 1940 – when she had first appeared before Bow Street magistrates on a charge of 'Three accounts of obtaining money by false pretences.' The authorities were unable to locate a birth certificate in her name, nor under any other name variation she had used, or indeed any other details. Wynne claimed to have lived in the small town of Stapleford in Nottinghamshire during the 1920s and 1930s; however no such records could be traced.

Wynne was released from prison on 11 October 1954, and there is little record of her following that date, with the exception of an entry in the official records recording her death in January 1973 and giving her age as 78.

Was Wynne Mariette Stuart-Bowerman really Violet Charlesworth? We shall never know for sure. But the parallels are certainly remarkable. From her immaculate wardrobe to her fascination with jewellery and her claimed Scottish ancestry. Her penchant for the colour red, her dark hair (which she occasionally dyed blonde, as was the fashion at the time) and brown eyes, the use of a gift from fictional trustees to sweeten her victims, and the pleading letters. There are certainly many striking similarities. It does not end there, however. Two further coincidences are also worthy of mention.

While attempting to trace Violet's whereabouts, I uncovered details of a lady using the name Violet Charlesworth living with her sister in Nottinghamshire during the early 1930s. Frustratingly, however, the trail quickly ran cold. But coincidentally, at the exact moment that the name Violet Charlesworth disappears from the Nottinghamshire records, the name Wynne Mariette Stuart begins to appear in the town of Stapleford. Perhaps it is just that – a coincidence – until you consider the fact that the Nottinghamshire Violet Charlesworth, also resided in the same town, Stapleford. A twist of fate perhaps? But certainly an unlikely one.

Secondly, the name Wynne Mariette is an uncommon one. If Wynne was in fact Violet, then where on the earth did the inspiration for her new alias arise?

Earlier in the book, I mentioned the possibility that Violet's inspiration for her plans and schemes may well have arisen from the many books and stories she had devoured. Violet was, after all, an avid reader. Interestingly, a serialised story entitled 'The Marrying of Mariette' by the author May Wynne was first published in July 1933. Did this provide Violet with the inspiration for a new identity. It is certainly an interesting coincidence.

Perhaps Violet/Wynne really did return to her old ways under another name. If she did so, then she certainly managed to keep her past life completely hidden from her new family until her death in 1973, at which point her guilty secret died with her.

Yet the search for the vanishing 'heiress' is still not over. There are still more possibilities in the quest for Violet Charlesworth.

Another strong possibility is that she moved abroad. Just prior to the staged motor-car accident she had already informed a close friend of her intention to escape overseas. And it also seems highly probable that a Cunard steamer to America was her reason for travelling to Ireland on the night of the crash. Of course, assuming Violet did venture abroad, it would be virtually impossible to locate her without knowing under which name she chose to travel. The task has been likened to looking for a needle in ten thousand haystacks. In addition, shipping records are notoriously incomplete, many having been lost over time. To compound matters further, once a person had reached their intended destination there was nothing to stop them changing their name yet again.

Undaunted nevertheless, I began to trawl through shipping manifests and passenger records, looking for anyone who might conceivably be our missing lady. Two entries piqued my interest. First, in July 1912, shortly after Violet's release from prison, a Margaret Cameron MacLeod (the name Violet had used when hiding in Oban) journeyed from Scotland to Nova Scotia in Canada, and then on to America. Sadly, there is little information available, other than her age, given as 23.

Secondly, and perhaps of more interest, a Miss May Charlesworth was listed as a passenger on board the Orient Line's SS *Orsova,* which sailed from London to Melbourne, Australia, in July 1920. She listed Melbourne as her intended place of residence – also the supposed residence of Violet's imaginary lover, Mr Alex MacDonald. Perhaps he really did exist after all?

In addition, Miss May Charlesworth's date of birth on the shipping manifest is given as January 1884, identical to that of Violet.

Many years later, in 1954, these coincidences even prompted an Australian journalist to search for the mysterious May Charlesworth. There had been a renewal of interest in the case at that time, following a series of British newspaper articles prompted by the unearthing of Violet's sheet music in a London second-hand shop. No doubt the journalist's editor hoped to land a newsworthy scoop. The reporter in question successfully managed to locate May Charlesworth in Australia, who was by that time a lady of 70. Although there was a strong resemblance to the 44-year-old photograph of Violet in the journalist's possession, the elderly May vehemently denied being Violet, and with little else to go on the story ground to a halt. The lady in question died a few years later, effectively ending that line of enquiry.

Undaunted, I did not give up in my quest to unearth what really became of Violet Charlesworth. Applying the same lateral thinking that I had utilised earlier, in asking myself if other frauds had been committed under different names, I pondered another question. Although Violet had clearly been extremely careful and methodical in both changing her surname and hiding her location, making her almost impossible to trace – what if those around her had not been so thorough?

At this point, Albert Watts and Joseph Gratton return to the story.

As I noted earlier, following the family's eviction from Boderw, Joseph moved to his brother's farm, Fron Haul at Rhuddlan, where he lived out the remainder of his life as a sheep farmer. An additional fact, which I did not mention earlier, is that in 1915 Joseph married a Margaret Williams; at the time of their marriage Joseph was 46 years of age and his new bride 31.

Perhaps, on the face of it, this may not seem relevant. Nonetheless, it is interesting to note that I was unable to trace any record of Margaret Williams prior to 1915, and that she gave her date of birth as January 1884 – the same as Violet.

Finally, Albert, the chauffeur, with whom Violet was rumoured to be having an affair, moved back to London following Violet's trial, and returned to work in the motor trade. I was unable to trace any further details regarding him, apart from an entry in the General Records Office listing a marriage at Kensington Registry Office in 1924 between one Albert C. Watts and Violet May Palin. Violet Palin was also listed as having a sister named Lillian. However, admittedly, this seems more likely to be a coincidence.

All of these possible solutions to the riddle of Violet's disappearance are plausible. We shall probably never know for certain what really became of Violet Charlesworth. Just like those who were seduced by Violet's fantastic inheritance story, we find it impossible to know for certain just what to believe.

It is also interesting to note that following Violet's release from prison, there seems to be little record of Lillian or her father, David. This also seems to be highly suggestive, and unlikely to be merely a coincidence.

The fact that Violet's safe deposit box was not mentioned in either her bankruptcy hearing or trial, and that its existence seems to have escaped scrutiny, strongly suggests that following her release from prison she was able to swiftly plunder it and finance a successful disappearance. As the Chancery Lane Safe Deposit Centre is now long gone, along with any records of ownership or provenance, any secrets Violet may have kept there have long since vanished with her.

Chancery Lane Safe Deposit

As with all great confidence tricks, the real art is to leave your victim uncertain as to whether they have been defrauded at all. Violet certainly managed to achieve this for several years, until she was finally forced to admit otherwise at her trial. Indeed, many people – including Martha Smith and several newspaper journalists – were still vainly searching for proof of her inheritance for many months following her alleged car crash.

Violet's avarice and weakness for the finer things in life was succinctly summed up by her friend Margaret:

> Violet never soiled her hands with work, and always appeared to me to be rather tired. Her mania at first was for soldiers. Then she went in for everything Scottish, and finally motoring. I think that was her downfall financially.

Yet despite her obvious flaws and humiliating exposure in court, perhaps Violet managed to succeed in executing the greatest con trick of all – to successfully disappear without a trace, carrying a clutch of valuable diamonds, whilst simultaneously leaving everyone believing that she was penniless, having already paid her dues to society.

The romantic and the writer inside me is tempted to believe that Violet completely fooled everyone. Perhaps she was never actually as sick as she pretended. After all, her convenient bouts of illness seemed to occur only when they might garner her some additional sympathy – particularly in court – and they certainly didn't affect her ability to live life to the full.

Violet, like a predatory black cat nonchalantly strolling away from its prey, will now be remembered not for the business and personal reputations she ruined, nor for the poor victims whose lives she destroyed, but for the flair, style, and consummate ease with which she fooled the male establishment, whose efforts had been temporarily diverted by their vicious persecution of the suffragette movement.

To paraphrase the late Terry Pratchett's astute observation: 'Style. That's all anybody remembers in the end.'

It is just possible that Violet fooled the entire establishment in 1910, and continued to do so for many years afterwards. After her aggrieved creditors received only a pittance in return for their generosity to Violet, and after she had served the relatively light sentence of two years (especially considering the vast sums involved), I rather like to imagine that she withdrew the contents of her secret safe deposit box at Chancery Lane (which she held under yet another alias), changed her name once more, then vanished abroad, without leaving a trace, to live a well-funded retirement. Perhaps she ended her days driving into the sunset at the wheel of an expensive motor car – one she had yet to pay for – clad in a beautiful crimson motor coat.

In the dullest moments of our safe and comparatively mundane lives, I suspect there are many of us who would begrudgingly rather admire her for it.

Postscript

Whatever eventually became of Violet, her spirit lives on in an ever-increasing number of inheritance scams now being reported around the globe. From well-known frauds – such as that perpetrated in the 2010s by Anna Delvey in New York to the case of Kim Older in Sussex, England, who in November 2024 was convicted of committing a carbon copy of Violet's scheme on a number of victims – it seems that thanks to the growth in online dating websites, social media, and computer technology, the potential number of easily reachable victims grows ever larger.

In November 2024 Chicago Police successfully prosecuted a gang running a sophisticated inheritance scam worth over $20 million. With criminals now leveraging AI to create even more convincing schemes, it is no surprise that Security, the leading American journal and thinktank, estimates that 15 per cent of all adults worldwide have been targeted by inheritance scams.

I wonder how many of today's shadowy fraudsters operating their cold-hearted scams realise they are walking in the footsteps of a trailblazing 25-year-old lady with a weakness for fast motorcars and fine clothes?

**'Who is going to believe a con artist?
Everyone, if she is good.'**

Andy Griffith

Appendices

Appendix A: Violet's known creditors

These creditors were listed at her 1909 London bankruptcy hearing

Petitioners	Amount	2025 Equivalent	Details
Fenton, Dale & Co.	£12,700	£1.9 million	Stock market losses
Dr Edward Hughes Jones	£5,430	£810,000	Loans, never repaid
Mrs Martha Smith	£401 7s	£60,000	Loans, never repaid
J.W. Benson & Co.	£500	£76,000	Jewellery
Benjamin Glass Antiques	£300	£45,000	Jewellery and antiques
Minerva Motor Co.	£1,200	£180,000	Unpaid car payments
Dingwall Outfitters	£60	£9,000	Bagpipes, tartan, etc
Calne Carpenters	£230	£35,000	Construction of kennels
Gamages Furniture	£238	£36,000	Rugs, silver, furniture
Gamages Department Store	£75 5s 4d	£11,500	Unpaid store account
Inns of Court Hotel	£50	£7,500	Unpaid hotel bills
Gwalia Hotel, Holborn	£25	£3,750	Unpaid hotel bills

Continued - Petitioners	Amount	2025 Equivalent	Details
Gardener, The Hall, Calne	£20	£3,000	Unpaid account
Kennelman, Calne	£30	£4,500	Unpaid wages
Wilkinson & Co., Decorators	£80	£12,000	Brasswork and lacquering
Suttons, builders, Calne	£40	£6,000	Building work at The Hall
Calne Ironmongers	£50	£7,500	Gates and railings
Hills of Calne	£203	£31,000	Ornamentation of front gates with gold leaf paint, wallpapering, plastering
Kastner & Co., London	£105	£16,000	Piano, Gramophone
Whiteley's Garage	£640	£96,000	Unpaid car payments, etc
White City Embroiderers	£46	£7,000	Unpaid bill, silk, linen, etc
Charles Harris, Calne	£94	£14,100	Unpaid rent, The Hall
Various dog breeders	£231	£34,700	Unpaid dog breeding fees
Various other stockbrokers	£2,014	£301,000	Unpaid market losses
J.E. Price & Co., St Asaph	£28	£4,200	Unpaid grocery account
Joseph Gratton	£538	£80,800	Loans, never repaid

Continued - Petitioners	Amount	2025 Equivalent	Details
Foryd Lodge, Rhyl, Mr Gratton	£76	£11,500	Unpaid rent
A. Fraser & Co, Inverness	£800	£120,000	Furniture, silks, silver
Daimler Motor Co. London	£600 (est)	£90,000	Unpaid car payments
Baileys Garage Stafford	£127	£19,200	Unpaid garage account
North Western Hotel	£5	£750	Unpaid bill
St Asaph Gas Co.	£8	£1,200	Unpaid gas supply bill
Mishnish Hotel, Tobermory	£2	£300	Unpaid bill
Shaftesbury Ave Motor Co.	£40	£6,000	Unpaid garage bill
Total: £26,986 12s 4d		**2025 Equivalent Total: £4,040,500**	

Appendix B: Violet's *Daily Mail* interview

Taken from two interviews given by Violet to a special correspondent, and published in the *Daily Mail* and *Manchester Courier* on Friday 22 January 1909:

> Miss Violet Gordon Charlesworth, the missing lady motorist from Boderw, has tonight authorised me to give through the *Daily Mail* the story of the adventure with the motor car at Penmaenbach Point, together with some details of her remarkable life.
>
> She stayed at the Central Station Hotel in Glasgow. A score of reporters were early this morning in the hall of the hotel waiting to see her. Some of them even waited upstairs in the corridor outside the bedroom door. But the demure, frail little lady outwitted them all. Some were still looking for her when she had already reached Edinburgh, having travelled down with her sister and two gentlemen [*Frank Dilnot and Joseph Gratton*] by motor-car.
>
> Miss Charlesworth answered my questions instantly, without sign of faltering. Her manner was quiet, her words low, but she always looked one square in the face, and was never at a loss for a reply.
>
> "Yes, I am Violet Charlesworth," she said; "Violet May Gordon Charlesworth. I was baptised May Charlesworth, but that was by a mistake, and from just after baptism I have been known as Violet May Gordon."
>
> It is a delicate question to put to a lady, but what is your age, Miss Charlesworth? -
>
> "Twenty-five. I was born on January 13th, 1884."
>
> Where was that?
>
> "In a town in the Midlands, the name of which I should prefer not to make public at present."
>
> And your parents, what were they?
>
> "My father was an engineer at Messrs Donnah's engineering works. He left there when I was about three, so I cannot tell you much about that, can I?" said Miss Charlesworth, smiling.
>
> Where did you go from there?
>
> "To Stone, a place eight or nine miles distant. We were there three or four years. I can recall that because we went there about the Jubilee year." [*1887*]
>
> Was your father still in the engineering works?

"No, he was employed by the Prudential Assurance Company. We left Stone in 1889 or 1890, or something like that."

Where was your next home?

"At Chesterfield; on the outskirts of the town."

Did your father continue in the same occupation?

"Yes, but he was in a better position. We were only in Chesterfield eighteen months, and then my father went to America."

Was that because of another change in his profession?

"No, he simply went abroad on a holiday – sightseeing. He went to America alone, purely for pleasure. He had come into possession of means by then. My father's brother had died in Canada and left him money. I might incidentally say that my father was of good family, who were of independent means, and he was brought up as a gentleman."

Do you know the amount of the bequest to him?

"No, I don't at all; but on receiving it, or at any rate about that time, my father left the Prudential Assurance Company."

Is it correct that your mother, Mrs Charlesworth, conducted dancing classes in Derby?

"No, that is a pure falsehood. My mother has never danced at all."

In those days you would be going to school, I suppose?

"That another thing I want to contradict. It has been stated that I went to a board school. That is untrue. I was educated at home by private governesses, because I was always very delicate, and the only school I ever attended was Miss Wilson's private school, and that was for only one quarter."

Had you a private income of your own?

"Yes, I had."

Have you benefited under the will of anyone?

"No, but I had expectations through assignments. My income was from an allowance."

What happened next?

"When we left Derby we went to Stafford and stayed with friends for five or six months. Then we went to Wolverhampton for a season, while the exhibition was on. From Wolverhampton we went to Foryd Lodge, close to Rhyl. That was about four years ago, because I had my twenty-first birthday party there, I remember. We went there on the advice of a doctor because it was near the sandhills, and on account of my health. I used to suffer from asthma. The house was let to us by the late Mrs Gratton, who held Foryd Farm, about 400 yards away."

Can you explain how you first made friends with Mr Joseph Gratton?

"Certainly. It was when we commenced proceedings in connection with the breaking up of an old cruiser in the harbour close to our house. My mother asked for an injunction because of the dangerous way the pieces of iron fell about. Mr Joseph Gratton had himself been struck."

Is it true you that while you were at Foryd Lodge you used to have the blinds drawn during the day, and go out on night excursions in motor-cars?

"It is quite untrue. We lived just as ordinary people. It is also untrue that whenever I went about, I was heavily veiled."

How long were you at Foryd Lodge?

"Nearly three years; until September 1907. We then thought of taking a place in Kent, but Mother found Boderw, and as that was convenient, we went there."

Boderw is a much more imposing place that Foryd Lodge. Was there an improvement in your circumstances?

"No, I cannot say so. My parents were never short of money."

You had a motor-car of your own?

"Yes. I had a motor-car about fifteen months ago. I had it as a present from a very dear friend. It was a 24-horsepower Minerva. I sold that car and hired another Minerva of greater horsepower. This was the car I was driving at the time of the accident. Driving is a passion of mine."

Is it true you were in financial difficulties?

"Yes, it was quite true. Although it is not true that I owed a stockbroker £10,000."

You owed money in various parts, then?

"Yes, for furniture at Flowerburn, in Scotland, and various things."

Were you in a financial position to take Flowerburn?

"Yes; I had a lot of money at the time, and expectations. I also took The Hall in Calne, for the season, I wanted it for a place for my St Bernard kennels."

Was there any preconcerted plan on the part of yourself and your family to disappear after the accident?

"I emphatically deny it!"

Can you tell us the story of the accident?

"The greater part of the morning I spent in romping with

one of my St Bernard dogs. Then after luncheon I made up my mind to go for a motor run. It was about 3:30 before we were ready to leave. My chauffeur Watts was driving. I was alongside him and my sister was inside the landaulette. It was a most enjoyable run, so we went on to Bangor for tea at the Castle Hotel. I asked for a timetable, my object being to look out for a train to run to London on Sunday, so that I could keep an appointment with my solicitor.

"It was on the St Asaph side of Bangor that the car was not pulling nicely, and the chauffeur got out to see to it. After passing through Penmaenmawr I took the wheel. "He did not wish me to do so, and though I had not driven for some time, I am used to driving and I am considered a good driver. Not long after I had taken the wheel we went up the steep hill towards the place known as Penmaenbach Point.

"How the accident occurred, I do not exactly know any more than this – that I felt the wheel sort, of tremble under my hand. What I think is that a stone, or something, caught the wheel. It requires so little to turn a car. I was driving on the right side of the road. The car suddenly swerved into the wall overhanging the sea. At the time I did not see there was a gap in the wall, and I completely lost my presence of mind. I was not able at the moment either to apply the brake or put on the clutch. I remember giving a fearful scream, and I remember hearing my sister also scream. I attempted to rise in my seat. The car came to a standstill on the edge of the cliff, and my idea was to get clear of the car, as I saw the water beneath me. My chauffeur caught hold of my arm and dragged me towards him. Just at that moment my chauffeur was either flung or jumped from the car. After that I seemed to get a wee bit stunned. When I came to myself, I simply saw the car on the brink of a precipice, and my sister and my driver had disappeared. I gave one wild look round, and then impulse came into my head to get away from the horrible associations of the place. I had lost my hat, which was a grey motor cap, and I ran, just as I was, in my crimson motor cloak, bareheaded, down the road into Conway [sic]. I thought my obstinacy in persisting in driving the car had been the means of causing the deaths of my sister and Watts. I kept in the shadow of the rocks, so that though I met a woman and one or two youths I was not noticed. I did not stop running till I reached Conway station. A dread of something – I do not know what – seemed to follow me."

And what did you do next, Miss Charlesworth?

"I caught the 9:25 train at Conway Station for Crewe. I had no ticket. I paid my fare at Crewe. I had still only the silk mackintosh hood of my motor cloak to cover my head. At Crewe I felt an impulse to go back, but had not the courage. I asked a porter at Crewe when the Scots train ran, and I booked a third for Glasgow, on the four minutes past one train. I got into an empty carriage, and passed the night as best I could. Some people entered the carriage at Wigan. It was between seven and eight when I arrived at Glasgow. I took some refreshment at the North British Hotel, but before that I picked up some luggage – one box, which had been in Glasgow a long time, the box which was later sent to Tobermory. I had left it at the station because I was frequently running between England and Scotland.

"The greater part of Sunday I spent in my own room lying down. On Monday morning I saw in the daily papers the account of the accident, and you can imagine how thankful I was to know that my sister and Watts were safe. Still, I was too frightened to let anyone know my whereabouts, though I was acquainted with people living in and near Glasgow. It dawned on me that I might possibly be found owing to my crimson coat, which always attracted a good deal of attention. In meantime I had not entered the hotel wearing the coat, but had carried it on my arm in Glasgow. I took the crimson coat to Pullar's the dyers, and asked them to dye it blue. I gave them the name of Mackay, and asked them to communicate with me at Oban Post Office. I left Glasgow by the two o'clock train from Buchanan Street Station for Oban, but I missed my connection and stayed the night at Stirling, which I left on Tuesday morning by the 5:20 train.

"It arrived at Oban somewhere about nine. At Oban I caught the mail steamer to Tobermory. I went to the Mishnish Hotel. As to the torn telegram, I know nothing about it."

Did you read anything further about the accident after the first day?

"Yes, I read the papers every day."

What did you think when you read of the hue and cry there was for you?

"I can hardly say, but frankly I had not the courage when I saw how much trouble it was causing, and the more the papers said the less courage I had to own up."

Was it your intention to continue in concealment for an indefinite time?

"No. As soon as I had seen or heard that steps were being taken by my solicitors or relatives to prove my death, as they had every reason too, thinking that I was dead, I should not have allowed them to remain in ignorance any longer."

Appendix C: Pleading with her stockbroker

Some of Violet's correspondence to Fenton, Dale & Co.

The following letters, written by Violet, are perfect examples of her craft. Who among us could have resisted her?

Boderw, St. Asaph, N. Wales. 2-4-08

Dear Sirs,

Thanks for yours. I am sorry you do not see your way to arranging the matter I mentioned to you, on terms before stated. It is so secure and yet so simple, I fail to see why you should not entertain it, because the bills would only be a security for a time. In the event of stock going against me, my loss would be covered to you by the bills, January next. If stock did not go against me, then when I had made so much from the bargain I would deal on margin and take back the bills from you. You will see my way is both straight and honourable in every way.

If you will do this for me at once I will sign a bill to the amount of £200 to you, as a gift on account of your letting me use the value of another bill for £1,200 (one thousand two hundred) in stocks and shares, the bill to you (and for you) for £200 to be payable on September 30, 1908. I feel sure you will do this favour for me, and I have got the bills ready to sign, and upon receiving a wire from you at Westminster Hotel, Chester, on Monday, before 1 p.m., I will post them to you signed on Monday. Unless you will do this at once I shall trouble you no more, but get the same thing done elsewhere, because my position is quite sound.

Kindly wire me at Chester, Monday, without fail.

You will see that the interest for such a service, £200 for the use of a bill for a short, most likely for £1,200, is very high, because you would be secure in any case,

Yours,

V. G. Charlesworth

P.S. – My own place will be "Woodlands," Calne, Wilts, which is at present being decorated for me. I have a shooting box my trustees have taken for me fourteen miles from Inverness.

Bod Erw. St. Asaph, N. Wales. 2-4-08

Dear Sirs,

I thank you for yours received and I enclose Bills (in the value of one hundred each bill) altogether to the value of £1,400 (one thousand four hundred), £1,200 for the following purpose, namely as security against loss on your side in the event of the stock which I buy with the value of the bills going against me, and same bills to be held by you until January 15th, 1908, and to be presented then at my Bankers or to be redeemed by me at different times or altogether before that date. The same amount in Bills to be entirely at my disposal in the buying of stock as I choose at any time.

Also upon the understanding that profit made by me (if any) on bargains shall be sent to me in cash upon request. Or placed to my credit at my Bankers, and no profit to be held be you as security against the bills, which latter will be paid when they fall due. Also that I may draw the profits (if any) as I desire, and the bills will be held as margin. This is perfectly above board and quite straight and perfectly fair to you and to me.

I have not a £50 bill, so have sent two signed bills of one hundred each (£200) and a cheque for £75. I cannot get a here without a little comment, so if you will get me and send to me, to sign you for £75, as interest due on July 2nd, 1908. I will do so, and you can then return my cheque (just dated) you will see are due on October 1st, 1908.

I hope you will find things right. I think you will. If this matter goes straight you will find in me next year one of your best clients. Please sign acknowledgement stating with conditions as I have mentioned, and also open up for me first price to-morrow morning Bear account in 375 Unions, 3 per cent margin. Please wire the price you open at, but don't supply any information besides, you understand what I mean, and put address please.

Yours,

V. Charlesworth

P.S. – I trust you will find everything right. If you will kindly wire price opened at I shall be glad.

Nothing For Something

The Dreadnought Hotel, Callander, April 11, 1908

Dear Sirs,

I received your wire at Inverness, but too late to write you that night, as I did not return until late with one of my trustees from near Fortrose, where they have, on my behalf, leased a shooting estate for me, so, although I am at present at Callander, having just come down from Inverness, I leave for Wales on Monday, so please let me have a reply to my home address per return – favourably, I trust.

It is namely this – will you allow me to make the sum of £500 on the strength of the bills before starting to redeem all the first bills? Let me know by return of post if you will do so. I will then wire you the amount of stock that I wish you to open up for me at once. Although you refused the £2,000, you will not surely refuse the £500?

Yours,

V.M.G. Charlesworth

Flowerburn House, Fortrose, Ross-shire

Dear Sirs,

I enclose bills, but I have advanced the date three months. I dare not, as soon as I come into my money, pay too much out ...

I have a shooting party, and have so little time.

Will you do me a further favour of sending me £500 on a bill of my own, backed up by a responsible gentleman in the medical profession of splendid position ...

I have so many expenses now that the shooting season is on, and my allowance is not enough. I rely upon you.

I shall be in Inverness all day to-morrow. You will be quite safe with it backed up specially.

Yours truly,

V.G. Charlesworth

Flowerburn House, Fortrose, Ross-shire. Tuesday Morning

Dear Sirs,

I am writing to ask you if you will grant me the further favour of lending me the sum of £950 (nine hundred and fifty), that is including the £225 which you have arranged for me already, as soon as you see the jewels to the value of £400 and agreement, note, etc. My idea is this – jewels up to the value of £1,150 (one thousand one hundred and fifty pounds) are to be the security, with promissory note and agreement and interest, you to retain possession of £600 (six hundred pounds) worth of jewels, and myself to hold the rest, so as to wear them.

Have you been able to close last Unions No. 2 account? Say in wire.

Yours truly,

V. Gordon Charlesworth

P.S. – Will bring jewels then on Saturday.

Boderw, St Asaph, N. Wales. 12-5-08

Dear Sirs,

Re my letters to you some few weeks ago asking you to advance me or rather pay me £400 of profit I have made, you in reply wished me to give you my Trustees' address, for them to, in a way, secure the settlement of the Bills when falling due.

If you will kindly remember I told you once before with regard to them, that they had made me understand not to refer any stockbrokers to them for information.

I told you I would not at any price have them know again, but that your money was quite secure.

It was quite understood I think between us that my Trustees have nothing to do with these private affairs between us, it would only make trouble all round. Which need not be, the Bills would be met one the very day on which they matured.

But afterwards you asked me to allow profits to go towards redeeming the bills which were just given. I am quite willing that this should be, although you know quite well that the bills were promised to stand over until they matured. I have up to now I think made over £500 profit which is thanks to you in a certain measure. Will you now pay me the £400 cash. I am sorry to ask you under the circumstances, and if it were only close upon the 30th June I would not ask you again after what has been passed, until the Bills I just gave had been redeemed. I require £400 of it because I do not have my allowance until June 30th (quarterly). If I have not paid back or redeemed bills by this date, I will pay you the £400 out of my allowance. In short, please send me Bill made out for £400. I will sign and return same to you, to be payable June 30th 1908. This will quite secure you in sending me the £400 now, out of what I have made as profit. You will admit that this is quite fair and generous and I want the money in bank notes for Friday morning. Please don't fail me. I am acting generously with you and quite fair. It seems to me strange that you should have any doubt in my position.

If what I have told you was not true, do you think that I would have on a long lease and furnish in the best possible style, The Hall, at Caine?

Certainly my trustees have given the order, with my permission, for The Hall to be splendidly furnished, throughout, and not to exceed the sum of £2,500 to the furnishers. And the goods will go down as soon as the decorations finish this month.

But The Hall is leased by me, and the gardeners are paid by me, and have been for a few weeks.

So you see you are quite safe. If you ever dreamed you would not be.

So please send me bill to sign by express delivery. I will then send same back, and you can send me by return registered notes for £400. The bill for end of June will quite secure you.

I trust you will not write me again troubling me for information. I have promised my trustees not to give [this] to any in your profession while under their control.

I am quite fair, more than many would be. Later on, you will find out for yourselves that my position is better than you have ever been led to believe by me. Please wire me to-morrow morning as follows:-

"Letters received, will accept, sending tonight as stated in your letter."

Don't wire anything else. I do not wish the small post office at St. Asaph to know my affairs.

I rely upon you this time, and you will be glad ere long that you have granted my wishes. Yours very truly.

V. Charlesworth

Boderw, St. Asaph, N. Wales. 20-6-08.

Dear Sirs,

l enclose bills for £2,500 for the following:- £2,250 as security for last outstanding balance and extra to invest now in small amounts, while the present account is still open, or until I can close same, and the remaining £250 for you to hold as interest or brokerage, and to get the bills discounted at a broker's as soon as you can.

What I would ask you is this, will you kindly allow me to use £500 of that remaining above the balance owing, to make small investments now, and to draw same as soon as it reaches about £150.

I trust you will do this, and shall be glad to receive your wire to that effect tomorrow morning as early as possible to Poste Restante, Chester.

Yours truly,

V. M. Gordon Charlesworth

Bod Erw, St. Asaph, N. Wales

Dear Sirs,

Please send me agreement to sign and have witnessed re furniture, plate, furs, etc. (I have over £100 worth of furs alone and hundreds of pounds of furniture, all my own, besides diamonds valued at over £1,500, motors, etc.).

Do not fail to grant me this, and to arrange it at once, because I want it by Thursday morning in notes.

I shall be due to-morrow, I expect, because two van loads of my valuable collection of foreign curios, some furniture I have had for years, and all sorts of things are going from my childhood home to my residence in Scotland. Don't fail me, please.

Yours truly,

V.G. Charlesworth

Appendix D: Violet the songwriter

Alongside her talents as a fraudster, Violet also wrote several songs, one of which was published by W. Morley & Co., Music Publishers of Great Portland Street. In 1906 she wrote to the well-known children's author and poet Clifton Bingham, requesting his help in crafting her song 'Good-Bye, Girlie, I Must Go!' The song was then set to music by Edward St Quentin, a pen-name of Alfred Rawlings. Like Violet, he too had an Australian connection.

Good-Bye, Girlie, I Must Go!

Sweetheart, see, the morn is breaking,
List and hear the bugle's call,
Soldier lads away are marching,
Some to conquer, some to fall.
Gallant hearts and true are beating,
While the colours wave on high.
And the bugles sound the summons,
Girlie, I must say good-bye.
Girlie, on the field there's raging.
Now, the fight for victory,
Bravely every heart is striving
For their dear ones over sea.
Where the battle fray is raging
Gallant lads go forth to die –
Dear, unto their aid they call me,
Girlie, I must say goodbye.

Chorus:
Good-bye, Girlie, I must go,
I must march, must march away,
For the call to arms is sounding
Through the land today;
Sigh not, sigh not, little Girlie,
Though your tears may flow,
The bugle tells me I am wanted -
Good-bye, Girlie, I must go!
Hark and hear the brave boys cheering,
Over is the hard-won fight,
I can see the colours waving,
in the camp-fire's flick'ring light.
Don't you hear them cheer me, Girlie.
Cheer your hero lover true,
As to martial music sounding,
He comes safely home to you!

Appendix E: Violet's short story, 'A Heart of Gold'

Following Violet's release from prison, and prior to her disappearance, she made one final attempt to earn a living from her artistic pretensions, by submitting a short story to the *Northern Weekly Dispatch*, a periodical which regularly published stories under the banner 'Tales of Love and Tragedy.'

Violet's story was published on 19th October 1912. We do not know how much she was paid for its publication, but no doubt she took a huge pride in its inclusion. Typical of the type of romantic fiction which readers devoured at that time, the story gives us a valuable insight into Violet's imagination and innermost thoughts and perhaps some glimpses of the life she had led (or wished she had led!).

A Heart of Gold
by Violet Gordon Charlesworth

Part I

"Alistair, you can trust me to be true to you. Even unto Life's end. Even unto life's end, my darling."

Lieutenant Alistair Gordon. leaning up against the broad mantelpiece in the spacious drawing-room at Douglas House, repeated the words grimly as he looked tenderly down at the pale face pillowed against his breast.

"But it is hard that I may not hear from you, or even write to you," he added "Was ever love tried like ours? Marie, my little love," he continued, passionately, as he strained her to his breast, "if I were to lose you I think I should go mad. I can hardly realise that this is the last time we shall ever see each other, for Marie, I dare not think for how long. Perhaps years. You here in Auld Reekie, and I in a foreign land thinking all the time of my little Marie, and longing for a glimpse of her dear face."

The fair arms of Marie Douglas stole upwards and clasped themselves round her lover's neck.

"Yes, it is hard, dear," she whispered, softly, "but when you have got your step you will come home, and then perhaps father will give in."

"But, Marie, what if I never get my step? What if I never come home?" Alistair cried, hoarsely.

"But you will," she cried, smiling up into his grave, set face, her eyes full of tears; "you must. It would break my heart if you never came back."

The young soldier's clasp tightened; he bent his heed and pressed kiss after kiss upon the little tremulous mouth, the soft, wavy hair, the delicately rounded cheeks.

"God helping me, dearest, I will come back," he cried.

Heart to heart the lovers stood, each thinking of and dreading the parting which must shortly come. Alistair was the first to break the long silence.

"Sweetheart," he whispered, "may I not ask your father to relent? If he would only allow us to write to other, once in every six months even, it would be something to look forward to.

"He would never consent." Marie replied, sadly. "Oh, Alistair, let us wait, all will come right; I feel it, will."

"Your father will marry you to some other fellow when I am out of the way. Sir Richard, for instance."

"Never, Alistair, never." The girl's soft voice rang clear as a bell through the long room. "I like Sir Richard, but I could never love him. You have won my heart, dear, and," - her eyes shining with the great depth of her love – "you are just all the world to me. I will wait for you, and love you till the end. Nothing shall part us, dear love, but death. And." she added, "we will not say goodbye here. I will see you tomorrow, in the dear old castle. 'Twas where we met, 'tis there we will part. Go now, dear one, while I have strength, and before my father comes."

"But, darling, he knows I was corning today to say goodbye."

"Yes," she cried. "I know, I know. But, oh, Alistair, he will ask me sorts of questions, and I cannot them just now, dear. When you are gone, dearest, then I will try to be brave, for your dear sake."

Was it by chance, or had some kindly hand placed among the flowers in John Douglas's, drawing-room ivy, beautiful, bright-green ivy? At any rate, it was there, and in the breast of Alistair Gordon it awoke memories of a happy past, echoes of Bonnie Strath Gordon, around whose walls and towers it clustered,

"See, darling," he said, taking a spray of the green leaves from the table, "this is the badge of the Gordons. Its motto is steadfast, and you and I are going to prove it. We two are going to keep each a spray, and should either of us prove false we will return the ivy, and that shall be the sign. The sign, sweetheart, that will never come," and he laughed boyishly as he slipped the emblem of faith within his tunic.

And Marie, her soft eyes shining, unfastened the brooch nestling against the gleaming white of her throat, and, slipping the ivy between, said, bravely:

"And when you receive back this ivy and brooch, Alistair, then, and only then, will you know I have ceased to love you."

It was a simple ornament, and had been one of Alistair's gifts to the girl of his heart. It spelled the one word "Bydand." It was the motto of the Gordon's, and, translated, meant "Watchful," and now, as he watched her replace the brooch, he thought of the day when, among the sweet-scented heather, he had given it to her, and her words - "Bydand - Alistair, our love shall prove it. And in all we undertake our watchword shall be in all truth Bydand.' "

He was bending to kiss her upturned face and whisper good-bye until the morrow, when a slight sound behind warned them they were not alone. Simultaneously they both turned and beheld the wrathful face of John Douglas. Not a word of the lovers' parting had escaped him.

"A pretty enough scene, I warrant you," he cried furiously, striding across the room and fixing a pair of fierce eyes upon Alistair, "If I allowed you lo come here for five minutes I did not give you leave to act the part of lover towards my daughter."

Alistair started.

"Since Marie and I love each other, Mr Douglas, he returned, quietly, "I have every right to act a lover's part towards her."

"Indeed. You forget Miss Douglas is yet under age, sir."

I forget nothing," Alistair replied. "But in a few months Marie will be of age, and have a right to choose who and where she will. Her love is mine, and only mine. Nothing you may say or do can alter that fact, Mr Douglas."

"Before then, Mr Gordon," was the stinging reply, "Marie will be a bride."

Alistair's pale face went a shade paler, and his eyes blazed.

"Is your daughter's happiness nothing to you, Mr Douglas?" he asked, sternly.

"Marie will marry Sir Richard Geary, my business partner, in less them three months," returned the squire. "Marry you? No, a thousand times no. I would rather see her dead than the wife of a poverty-stricken lieutenant."

The officer's face flamed at the taunt, but, standing his ground manfully, he retorted hotly –

"I may be poor, sir, but that does riot alter Marie's love for me. And a Gordon of Strath Gordon is the equal in birth of a Douglas of Kelvin brae."

"Equal or not you shall never marry her, not though you begged for her on your knees."

In a torrent the proud blood of the Gordons rushed through Alistair's veins until face and neck were dyed in one crimson flood. He squared his shoulders and lifted his dark, proud head, and the gaze of John Douglas for a second sought and traced the pattern of the rich Turkish carpet, rather than meet the fiery glance of this imperious young soldier, who, in the glory of northern dress, looked like some young chieftain of old as his voice, clear and ringing, echoed through the room.

"I am not likely to do that, sir; but, by clan and dirk, and all that a Gordon holds dear, I vow that Marie shall be my wife, and none other's. A Gordon's word is his bond; I have vowed to win Marie, and I will do so, unless she herself breaks that vow."

The girl's tearful eyes were lifted to her father's face, hard and unrelenting.

"Oh, father, father, how can you be so cruel?" she said, brokenly. "I love Alistair, and I will never marry anyone but him. Alistair, dear Alistair; I will see you to-morrow before you go, and in life and death remember I am yours." And with one long look into each other's eyes she turned and went slowly from. the room.

"Now, sir," Squire Douglas said, turning to Alistair, "have you anything further to say? If not, go - and never set foot in my house again," touching the bell as he spoke. Then, to the footman who answered the summons, he ordered "Show this soldier out, John."

The words stung Alistair to the quick, and his passion-strained face quivered under the fresh taunt. But he had himself well in hand, and with proud, distinguished bearing, as a Gordon of Bonnie Strath Gordon, he passed out into the bright sunlight, little guessing under what circumstances he would cross the threshold of Douglas House again.

* * *

Part II

There was a dull, grey sky overhead when the immortal Black Watch marched out of Edinburgh Castle next morning.

With tartans fluttering in the light breeze, headed by the pipe-major, the pipers came four abreast, playing the stirring strains of *"Scotland Yet."*

Outside the castle gates were little knots of people who had braved the early morning hour to speed the brave Highlanders, who during their sojourn the castle had strengthened the ties of good feeling which were universally expressed towards the gallant corps.

A Scottish cheer, full and deep, rose and fell, echoing far over the Calton Hill, and breaking on the silver waters of the Firth of Forth. The pipe tune changed to *"Hielan' Laddie"*, and here and there above the pipers' skirl can from Scottish throats, "Will ye no come back again?" as relatives and friends clasped hands with their dear ones as the Black Watch men, their bonneted heads held high, their white-gaitered feet keeping time to the pipers' skirl, marched out through the barrack gate. Kilts swung side by side in rhyme, and the proud array of brooches gleamed fitfully on the shoulder plaids of the Scottish laddies, as they marched down the Princes Street en route for the station.

* * *

Among those who had seen the departing troops. within the castle was Marie Douglas.

"My bonnie darling." cried Alistair fondly, "I did not expect to see you, really, on account of the earliness of the hour."

"I had to come, Alistair. I promised, you know, and I persuaded Aunt Annie to accompany me."

Alistair Gordon took the elderly lady's hand in a warm clasp, as he cried: "Mrs Maitland, how can I thank you?

"Don't try, laddie." she returned, gaily. "It isn't likely I'd let you go myself, without bidding you good-bye.

"It's awfully good of you, though," he said, a strange wistfulness creeping into his voice; then, added, in a lower tone, "Mrs Maitland, cannot you give me a gleam of hope?"

"Trust in Providence, and bide a wee, laddie. All will come right presently."

"I wish I could think so," he said moodily.

"You're not going to tell you're a Gordon and a Black Watch man, and cannae trust and wait?" laughed Mrs Maitland. "No, no; I've known you since you were a wee laddie, and I ken you're made of different stuff than that. You'll be coming back with a more gold lace on your coat in no time. Though it's bonnie enough you look now, I'm thinking, in all your warpaint."

"There's many an aching heart under the auld tartan to-day, for all the glamour and glory. Mine for one," he responded. with a dreary laugh.

"You're wanted in the square. sir." It was Alistair's orderly who spoke, standing stiffly to salute. "Very well Macphall, I'll come."

The man retreated, and Alistair knew that the greatest of all moments had arrived for him, the moment which meant parting from the one who was all in all to him, and whom he might never see again.

Marie, her soft cheek pressed against the rich folds of his plaid, strove bravely to stifle her sobbing, and to whisper instead words of encouragement which she knew were sorely needed by the one who, at the call of the pibroch, must sally forth, and away ayont the borders of his native land.

"Be brave, little girl," he whispered, gently raising the tear-stained face and taking toll of the sweet lips. "Good-bye, my darling, my little Marie, my loved one. God watch between me and thee when we are absent one from the other."

One swift embrace from hearts too full for speech, one last passionate kiss, to Alistair the seal of their love troth, to Marie an eternal farewell, and Alistair Gordon hurried out on the square as the last company of soldiers fell into line.

One of the finest sights in the world is to see a kilted regiment on the march, and so thought Mrs Maitland as, with Marie by her side, she looked down from the castle battlements at the bonnie lads assembled below.

"Quick march!"

Nothing For Something

The colonel's voice rose clear commanding above the tumult, and in response the battalion moved forward as one man. The tramp of feed sounded farther and farther away. The skirl of the pipes became fainter and fainter on the morning air. They had gone, the gallant Highlanders, and with them Alistair Gordon, for whom already in Marie's heart a cry was awakening.

* * *

"Lieutenant Gordon."

"Sir Richard Geary."

Such was the greeting between the two men as Alistair stepped briskly on to the platform with his company.

"Can I have a few moments alone with you, Mr Gordon?"

"I'm afraid not; what you have to say must be said here. It is, as you must admit, hardly a time for private conversation," was the cold reply.

The baronet was piqued. but when he spoke again his voice was as cheery as ever.

"I have come purposely to see you, Mr Gordon. As man to man, will you answer me one or two questions?"

The young officer's lips curled ever so slightly under his well-trimmed moustache. His voice carrying a note of intensity with it, sounded strange in the ears of Sir Richard, who, in his heart of hearts, had a very kindly feeling towards the popular lieutenant.

"That, Sir Richard, depends on the subject."

Sir Richard hesitated, the entraining was rapidly being pushed forward, and soon Lieutenant Gordon, with no knowledge of what was in Sir Richard's heart, would be whirling away southwards.

"You love Miss Douglas, and the dearest wish of your heart is to make her your wife?" Sir Richard asked, with British bluntness.

Alistair flushed, and his bonneted head, if possible, went a shade higher, as he answered with a careless smile –

"Since you have so accurately guessed the state of my feelings towards Hiss Douglas, there is no need for us to discuss the matter further. It might only lead to unpleasant complications."

Sir Richard winced. To be taken by this cool, youthful Scotsman was a little gailing. To be treated with such utter disregard was new to him, but to pursue the subject further would most likely not improve matters. And, in point of fact, Alistair's words had declared it at an end as far as he was concerned.

"Under the circumstances, then, I will say goodbye and God speed," he said, stretching out his hand as he spoke.

The two rivals clasped hands, the single word good-bye falling hard and metallic from Alistair's set lips. The baronet raised his hat and moved away; the soldier returned the courtesy with his gold-mounted hat by way of a salute done with military precision. Then, with his face white and set, he slipped swiftly into the compartment.

* * *

Marie sat in her blue and white boudoir at Douglas House, looking listlessly at the flashing gems lying on her lap. Diamonds and sapphires, rubies and pearls all lay in one brilliant mass as she had emptied them carelessly from their cases. Suddenly she gathered them up in the skirt of her dress, and crossing over to the window, drew up the blind with a jerk. Then, sitting down before the casement, her beautiful eyes stravaiged restlessly to the outlines of the fine old castle lifted like some weird monster against the heavens, which look almost blue in the intenseness of the moonlight. Once again, she was within its grey walls, once agaln she was pressed against a manly breast, and an eager voice whispered undying love. It was but a dream now, a beautiful dream which had lost its reality in a cruel silence which had followed it.

"Twelve months," Marie said to herself, softly, "twelve months to-day since Alistair went away. Only a year, yet to me it has been an eternity. Oh, Alistair my love, your cruelty has broken my heart. I thought you loved me but it was only a foolish dream, and in three days I shall be a bride. I shall vow before God's altar to love, honour, and obey - all the time knowing I have no love to give. For it is yours, my beloved, and will be until I die."

With the air of one who has tasted the cup of happiness, and then seen it dashed ruthlessly from the lips, Marie gathered up the sparkling gems, which had fallen unheeded to the floor, making no sound as they fell on the thick velvet pile carpet, and, walking to the inlaid secretaire, she laid them upon it, then, taking a key, unlocked one of the drawers and drew out a slip of paper and a small box. With trembling fingers she raised the lid and gazed at the contents - only a spray of ivy clasped within a brooch bearing the solitary word "Bydand." and by its side a companion spray, which told of Gordon's broken vow.

Twelve months before it had been a thing of treasure lying pressed over a soldier's heart- Six months later it was sent to Marie from a far-off foreign station, and with it a few scrawled, unsigned lines, telling how the writer had regretted the vow so thoughtlessly made before leaving the far-off northern city, and with a heartbroken cry Marie had laid them - the emblems of her love troth and Alistair Gordon's - side by side and locked them away. They were but the relics of days unmarred by mistrust in human faith.

Marie touched the bell which was answered by her maid.

"I shall not come down to-night, Annie," she said. "Tell my father I have a bad headache, and I think I shall go to bed."

The maid started at deadly pallor of her young mistress 's face. "Are you ill, Miss Marie?" she inquired, anxiously.

"No, Annie, I am not ill, only very, very miserable," the tears welling up into her eyes as she spoke. "You can go now." she added. "I wish to be alone. and you need not come in again to-night; I can manage quite well myself."

The maid withdrew quietly. On the corridor she met Sir Richard Geary.

"Where is Miss Douglas?" he asked, kindly. "Is she not coming down?"

"Miss Marie is in her room, sir. She wished me to tell the master she had a headache, end would not come down to-night.

Sir Richard thanked her, and passed on, pausing as he reached Marie's door.

"Marie, my child., you shall he happy yet." he breathed softly. "You shall marry the one you love. God helping me darling, you shall."

A vision of a stalwart figure, a pair of dark eyes which the love-light glittered, a broad shoulder with a Gordon plaid thrown carelessly across, and a young dark-haired, with lone lashes veiling a pair of soulful eyes, looking up into the earnest face of her lover, rose before his mental gaze.

The vision was the plighting of the love troth between Alistair Gordon and Marie Douglas at Kelvinbrae, where Sir Richard and the gay young Highlander had been her father's guests many months before. Sir Richard had been an unseen spectator of the little affair and now it rose up in strong force before him. His heart told him, with a pang of anguish, that such love as he read between them then would live and live for ever. He dragged himself wearily down the great staircase into hall, startling the footman with his ghastly face. But Sir Richard's resolve was made, and, without a word he passed out into the night.

John Douglas, coming suddenly from the dining room, caught a glimpse of a dazed agonised face, and a strange foreboding of coming evil flashed before him as he retraced his steps to make the most feasible suggestion for the unwanted absence of Sir Richard Geary, the prospective bridegroom.

* * *

Part III

As the hall door closed with a heavy clang behind him, Sir Richard Geary drew a deep breath, which, half a sigh and half a laugh as it was, sounded, even in his own ears, strange and unreal.

Neither knowing nor caring where he went, he stumbled on and on, oblivious of all save one thing - John Douglas, his friend, on whose honour he could have staked his life, had bitterly, cruelly deceived him. It was close on midnight when he returned to the house.

"Anyone up, John?" he said to the servant who opened the door.

"No, sir, I think not. Mr Douglas was the last to retire, I believe."

The baronet crossed the polished entered the library. A man-servant brought him a daintily laid tray, but he waved it aside, and as the door closed, rose, and, crossing to the window, threw open the casement, letting in the still chilly air, which acted like a charm on his overwrought nerves. How long he stood there he knew not, but the dawn was breaking before he pulled himself together with a great effort, and made his way upstairs; not to sleep - there was no thought of sleep in Sir Richard's mind - but to prepare for the bitter ordeal which lay before him.

The morning broke gloriously fair, not a cloud dimmed the deep blue of the sky; the tweet-tweet of the birds, as they warbled out praises from the sylvan shades of the elms, sounded divine as they floated in on the flower-scented air through the half-open windows, and found an answering echo in Marie's heart.

Surely - she questioned - God would not let such a marriage take place as hers would be, a loveless marriage? He would find a way. She would trust him, trust Him to the end. She would plead once more with Sir Richard - would tell him she could not love him as a wife should love her husband. But no, it was not likely that he who had always waved her pleadings aside would listen now. It was too late. She must marry him, though her heart be breaking. It was her father's wish too; he had given her the choice of marrying Sir Richard and leaving her home for ever - and she had chosen Sir Richard. He did at least love her, which Alistair never had done, or how could he have sent such a heartless little note? And yet she loved him; she should love him, and only him, always.

* * *

Sir Richard knew that she had not deceived him, but he had only patted her cheek and smiled, telling her she would soon forget when she his wife, and that time was the great healer.

How little he knew Marie, or the depth of love. She had loved once, and would never love again.

Her face looked white and pinched. and there were dark rings under her sad eyes, which looked wistfully on while the maid laid out a couple of dresses.

"Which will you wear, Miss Marie - your blue frock, or the pink one?"

"Neither, Annie: I will wear white, all white. White means truth and purity, doesn't it? And I shall never wear it after I am married. It would only double the falsehood I shall be acting."

"Oh. Miss Marie, dear Miss Marie," cried the girl; "won't you tell the master? Tell him you f!annet marry Sir Richard. And perhaps_"

"No Annie; I shall never do that again,"' Marie interrupted, "I have told him so many times, but he refuses to listen."

The while she had been speaking, Annie had robed her in a pure white gown. with a mass of soft white lace nestling against the full throat.

A servant tapped lightly at the door.

"Sir Richard Geary," the girl said, "would be pleased if Miss Douglas would come to him in library soon as possible."

And five minutes later, cool and collected, with her queenly form drawn to its full height, Marie entered the handsome apartment. which was one of the chief features at Douglas House.

Sir Richard was standing before one of the French windows, looking absently across the fine sweep in the lawn. when Marie's voice broke in.

"Good morning, you wished to see me I believe?" she said, coldly.

Sir Richard turned, and the girl noticed with a slight start how aged he had grown since yesterday.

"Good morning, Marie," he said, gravely. "Yes, I wished to see you," pulling a chair forward as he spoke, and leading her to it. "Are you better – is the headache quiet gone?" he added, gently.

"Quite, thank you," she replied. There was an uncomfortable silence. It was quite evident that Sir Richard was labouring under some great emotion, and Marie, as the watched him, felt the resentment surging within her breast give place to infinite pity.

"Marie, child," he said at last, - and she thought his voice had never seemed so full of gentleness as now – " I am going to put some questions to you. Nay, not out of idle curiosity," as he saw her start, "no , dear, not that. I want to make you happy if I can, little Marie."

"What is it you wish to ask me?" she faltered, without raising her eyes

"Do you still love Alistair Gordon? Do not be afraid to tell me, dear; I can bear it."

"Yes, Richard, I do love him, and always shall."

It was the first time she had ever used his Christian name, and a glad light leapt into the baronet's blue-grey eyes as it fell from her trembling lips.

"If you found that he still loved you, would you marry him, Marie?"

Her eyes, bright with unshed tears were raised to his. Sir Richard did not need to hear her low "Yes" to know what his answer was to be. The lovely eyes spoke volumes.

He turned to the window for a second, striving to gain the upper hand of himself. He paced the length of the room, once, twice, then, coming to a full stop in front of her, said quietly –

"From now, dear, I wish you to understand are perfectly free as far as I am concerned."

"I - I don't understand you," she said, wonderingly. "Free? You mean our wedding will not take place?"

"That is what I do mean, Marie," he said, smiling. "You are free to marry the man you love, and who loves you as much to-day, perhaps more, than he did a year ago. Yes, yes, I know what you would say; but it – there - there has been a - a mistake, little girl."

To know that Alistair, whom she had thought false, still loved her, and that now she was free to marry him, was too much for Marie, and, laying her head on Sir Richard's breast, she burst into tears.

He soothed her as a father would have done, and presently, when she was calmer, put her gently back in the easy chair, and, kneeling beside her. took her little hands in his and told her all. How he had been deceived into thinking she would learn to care for him in time. And how he had wrung the truth from her father. whose purpose was to see his only child become Lady Geary, instead of the wife of a plain lieutenant.

"We have both been cruelly deceived, dear," he went on, stroking the quivering hand he held; "you in the thought that Alistair Gordon had been false to you - and, child, I believed it, too; but now I know he never sent the ivy spray to you. Marie. Your father, in some way not unconnected with money, persuaded one of the men in your lover's regiment to send the letter and the spray of ivy you received. The plan worked admirably, but, thank God. I was able to find it out in time.

"Last night," he continued, hoarsely, "I chanced to be under the balcony, when I heard your heartbroken words. They cut me like a knife, Marie. I think I was almost mad for a time. Then I heard a whisper that your laddie was coming home on leave; it seems it was right. For, as luck would have it, he arrived in Edinburgh last night. He knew nothing about your impending marriage, Marie, until he reached home. And I – well, I am proud to know him, that's all, proud to think I was the first on his arrival to congratulate him on his good fortune. He is not Lieutenant Gordon anymore, but Captain Sir Alistair Gordon of Strath Gordon.

Almost as soon as he got his commission, his uncle, the laird, died, leaving his nephew something like five thousand a year rent-roll and the bonniest place in the country."

"And Alastair," Marie whispered, with downcast eyes.

"Alistair is longing to see you, dear. He has already seen your father and forgiven him for was so nearly the ruin of three lives. Your father now, Marie, is quite willing for you to marry Alistair instead of me on the day already appointed. In fact, he cannot help himself, for Gordon and I are determined there shall be no more delay." Sir Richard Geary laughed - laughed though his heart was breaking. He loved Maire, and for her sweet sake would stand by and see her wed another, and in that act prove has his heart's best gold.

"Marie, dear," he said, "your father is sorry for the part he played. You will forgive him, will you not?"

"I will try." she whispered.

Richard pressed little hand in his, then quietly slipped from the room as someone else entered.

"Marie, my darling!"

"Alistair, my Alistair!"

A girl's glad cry blended with a man's deep voice. They had entered the gates of Eden at last.

Appendix F: Smoke and mirrors: Violet in her own words

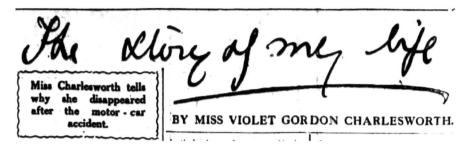

Miss Charlesworth tells why she disappeared after the motor - car accident.

BY MISS VIOLET GORDON CHARLESWORTH.

Not seen in their entirety for more than a century, the following are the transcribed, handwritten notes prepared by Violet for a series of three articles which were published in the *Weekly Despatch* from Sunday 24 February – 7th March 1909.

At the time Violet's articles were printed, she still hoped to convince the world that the motor car accident had been entirely that – an accident – and that she had only then disappeared from fear and panic, rather than from any attempt to deceive. It must also be remembered that, at this stage, the story of her mythical inheritance was still largely believed by the public. She was seen by the public as a foolishly extravagant young lady; and not the fraud she would later be exposed as.

The Story Of My Life
By Miss Violet Gordon Charlesworth

'It is not easy for a girl of twenty-five to pick up a pen and write that she is the person for whom all of the country has been searching for a fortnight.

I am the girl who has been compared with Becky Sharp (*the cynical seducer and social climber from William Thackeray's 1848 novel Vanity Fair*), who has had adventures that are without number, who is at once, romantic, daring, and demure. Scattered debts have been said to be vast sums, motor-car rides have been turned into midnight raids for dark and unknown purposes. That because, horror- stricken with the awful shock of an accident, I fled unthinkingly from a place where I believed I had accidently caused the death of my sister, I have been accused of some extraordinary plot and far-reaching design. As a matter of fact, I do not think I am such a thoughtless, unfeeling person as has been suggested. I believe I have very similar feelings to other girls of my age and circumstances.

Having said this, I can acknowledge that my experiences have been extraordinary, for now fate has thrust strange adventures on to me. At twenty-five, I find the eyes of the country on me, and I find the feeling very uncomfortable indeed, and I wish I could escape all the publicity. I intend to tell, plainly and simply, my version. I shall relate the circumstances of the incident of Penmaenbach Point and my adventures afterwards. They say I am a remarkable girl. I can only state that I have had to pay heavily for anything my adventures have led me into.

My Early Life

I will start at the beginning. I was born on January 13th, 1884, at a town in the Midlands. My father was a man of good family, who worked for a firm of engineers. My mother was a lady of Scottish extraction. When I turn my mind back, the first memory I recall is Queen Victoria's Golden Jubilee when I was three years old. My mother and my father gave me a doll, from which I developed a passion for dolls which I kept until I was seven years old, when I became tired with the whole lot of them and developed a love of books. Not children's books, which I detested on account of their tales of history particularly, preferring instead tales and stories of a solemn nature. I remember distinctly how fond I became of reading. As I write this, a story came to me about cutting my hair, which hung in the hallway for people to observe! For one day, as a little girl, I took a pair of scissors and cut off as many of my curls from my head as possible.

We went to live at Chesterfield, after a great event in my family occurred. My father's brother died in Canada, and my father determined to go on a sight-seeing expedition to the Americas shortly afterwards. I remember how he left one day. I was awakened in the night as he said 'good-bye', and I remember being upset at the thought of him being so far across the water. After he had been in America a few weeks, he wrote to us saying how he appreciated living there, and how he would like my mother to go out there. My mother preferred to stay in England, she could not bear the thought.

At School

I was not very old when I had my first illness, and I was a delicate child. My mother, in her anxiety, took me with her from place to place. We had a good many friends with whom we often stayed. Besides, I often went on numerous visits to relatives, and I have been fortunate indeed in having a good many friends, with whom I often stayed.

I have the first demonstration of their kindness during that period, about the time my father came home. I had been sent away for some weeks, but it had been determined that I would return before the day my father came home so he would not come into the house and I would be away.

After a period of less than a year my father came home from Canada and America, and it was, of course, a joyous occasion. My sister Lillian, the family, and some friends went to Liverpool to meet him. He brought back with him a heap of presents, including a stuffed pug dog, which I kept for years, and which I used to show to friends when they came to visit.

It was not long after my fathers' return that we moved to Derby, where my father resumed his engagement with an insurance company. We were a very happy family, my father, mother Miriam, sisters, brother, and myself. My sisters, though they were considerably older than me, were almost my only companions. If you had known our family circle, you would have thought it very excellent training for an adventuress, as I have been called within the last few weeks. I have always been a slim, delicate girls, very fond of my home, very fond of books. There has been a good deal of reference in some of the papers to my education. And it has been stated over and over again that I went to Board school. It is not, perhaps, of very great importance, but I never attended a Board school or any elementary school of that kind for a single day (*Board schools were the first state run elementary establishments, established in Britain following the Education Act in 1870. The intention of Board schools was to make education available for all children. Funds were raised via a local rate and the fees of poorer children were paid from this fund. They were administered by School boards until being replaced by Local Education Authorities, following the Education Act of 1902. Clearly Violet thought this an important enough issue to highlight*).

For one quarter I went to a private ladies' school, but my health was so delicate that my mother did not like to send me to any kind of school for longer that period, and I was educated at home by a private governess.

We all went to stay some months at Stafford with friends, and I remember the shock when my father had a stroke there, an occurrence which laid the foundation of broken health from that time onwards.

I was growing up now and was getting the first taste of a woman's enjoyments. We always had a good many friends, and there was no lack of amusement for us. When I was between fifteen and sixteen I learned to ride a horse, much to my delight, and an old friend of my father's used to bring round a led horse with his own in the mornings, and I used to go off with him riding and have delightful times. I was sixteen when there occurred one of the events of my life – my first motor-car ride. Some friends called at our house, with a motor-car, and I went off with them for a spin. Can I ever describe the delights of that ride! The swiftness, the power, the ease, the sense of command woke in me feelings which it is almost impossible for me to explain. The motor-car was to me a thing of life. It grunted with satisfaction, responded to a touch, sprang fiercely to the spur, and finally was obedient and silent, a thing motionless and dead, but to be awakened to life with five seconds' effort. I think the poetry of the machine affected me. From that time onwards I had a passion for motoring, and I have it still. Perhaps it has played some part in bringing about the unfortunate position in which I have stood of late. I had frequent opportunities for motoring, and I eagerly seized them.

I went out with friends often. Before I was seventeen I was doing not only short journeys but hundreds of miles into the country with friends. There would be parties of us for, of course, I never went alone. Motoring was a new element in my life. I was now beginning to get a taste for luxuries – a taste which, stupidly indulged, has brought me much difficulty and much sorrow.

Seventeen opened to me new vistas of life in many ways. Existence became a great thing for me. I had no idea there were good things in life. It was while I was seventeen that I met the man for whom I had a great love. He was a gentleman of private means, who had returned to this country after serving as a Volunteer in the South African war. He was twenty-three years of age. Four or five months after I met him, I became engaged to him and I was very happy. There are some things too precious to be dealt with in public, and this is one of them. It is quite impossible for me to put into words all I felt. When I say that the gentleman to whom I was engaged died when I was twenty, I am saying that which cannot possibly convey much to the reader, but which for me meant a sudden black world of misery. Everyone who has lost a friend will know how hard it is to realise the loss. I could not believe what had happened was real, for a time. I was just stunned. When I did realise it; I think my heart just broke in two. There was nothing left for me. The world was quite empty.

It was about this time that my parents departed from the Midlands and went to live in North Wales. We took the Foryd Lodge, a house just outside of Rhyl, which belonged to Mrs Gratton, who held the Foryd farm. She and her sons lived but a quarter of a mile from us.

Mr Gratton

Seriously ill for months as the result of the shock from my friend's death, I had little interest in the outside world. Even when I was getting better I stayed indoors and would not go out all. Gradually I recovered from my physical illness, though the effect of my great loss remained with me for a long time.

There has been frequent mention throughout the week of Mr Joseph Gratton, a gentleman who has lived with us at Boderw in St Asaph. His association with us is easily explained. Mrs Gratton, his mother, Mr Joseph Gratton, and his brothers were our near neighbours at Foryd Lodge, and we all became acquainted and friendly. As time went on the friendship increased, and Mr Joseph Gratton, who now lives at Boderw, was much liked by my mother, and was frequently at our place. Eventually, when his mother, Mrs Gratton died, the family separated, and Mr Joseph Gratton, having no home of his own, came and made his home with us. That is all there is to be said about that matter.

While we were at Foryd Lodge I did a lot of motoring, going out with friends frequently, on journeys long and short, and always enjoying the runs. My passion for motoring never left me. A lot of nonsense has been written about my midnight rides and my heavy veil. I went out, like other people, in the daytime, and wore a veil on occasions just the same as other ladies who are motoring. I had no dark secrets to conceal.

Here I had better state quite frankly that I was acquiring expensive habits and planting the seeds of the extravagance which was afterwards to bear such bitter fruit. I was thoughtless and unheeding, and I did not look ahead. I had none of the strong ambitions which an adventuress ought to possess. I had no thought of being associated with rich people, with very clever people, nor did I desire to shine in any public way. Probably it will seem laughable to those who are bitter against me when I tell them what the ambition was that I cherished privately. Strange as it may seem, in the midst of all my pursuits I clung to an old, deep-rooted desire, and that was to become a nurse. But possibly critics will cynically say that is inconsistent with what happened later. I merely mention it in passing as a simple fact.

My Financial Affairs

We were at Foryd Lodge three years, and then shifted to Boderw, down at St Asaph. That was in 1907. We are now approaching the fateful period of my life, the period during which my great trouble has arisen, with the culminating disasters of the accident and all that followed it. Let me make it quite clear that two years ago I had not lived beyond my means, that I kept within my allowance, and had no difficulty about finances. My parents were always comfortably off. I had better explain, too, another matter, that relating to my dealing in stocks and shares. Some few years ago, when I was twenty, I used to get a lot of circulars - I don't know how people obtained my address -, and in these circulars were particulars as to financial operations. I learned some of the technical terms and their meanings in this way, and as an inquisitive girl, made a very small venture. I forget exactly what I touched – some kind of American speculation, I think. It was, however, in the smallest way. In the course of four of five weeks I made two pounds profit. I did not touch anything else in this line for a period of eighteen months or more. The remarkable fact to the public, I suppose, is that a country girl of twenty should dabble in these things at all. Well, I did so, and that's all there is to say about it.

But let me say here that among the scores of misstatements that have been made, none is more incorrect than the one which suggests that I owe £10,000 on account of my operations. It is perfect nonsense.

January 2

But to come back to this last two years, with its heavy burdens, its foolishness, and its dire results. I was, as I have said, acquiring expensive habits.

Then, fifteen months ago, came my first motor-car, and though that could not be considered extravagance, since it was given to me by a dear friend, it set me further on the track of enjoyment, and took me on in directions which I have travelled since. One car led to another. I motored almost continuously and made journeys by night and day. In the course of a year I made journeys totalling over sixty thousand miles. Other expenses came. I took Flowerburn House, in Ross-shire, as a shooting estate, so that I might invite my friends to stay with me from time to time in Scotland. Much of the money I owe went in furnishing and equipping Flowerburn. True, I has expectations, but I took steps such as I had never taken before. I engaged the place at Calne, in Wiltshire, because I wanted headquarters for my St Bernard kennels.

And, so, we come on into January, when people were pressing me and I was in financial difficulties. My birthday was on the thirteenth, and I was expecting that then I should come into a very large amount of money. With what feelings that day was looked forward to may be imagined. Before the great day was reached, there intervened the occurrence of January 2nd, with the accident to the car and all its results. Fate has played strange pranks in my life. Never has there been a more dramatic interposition than on that Saturday, when, with business troubles pressing me, my motor crashed into the sea wall at Penmaenbach Point, and set hundreds of thousands of people searching ruthlessly for a frightened country girl. What happened on that fateful day I will know set forth.

Before I go on to tell what happened on the fateful Saturday, however, I had better explain that it was my normal condition to be comparatively happy, and to be unruffled by any fear for what might happen in the future. I was feeling very seriously harassed that day though, although I was in good spirits.

I got up rather late that morning; but I do not remember the exact time. But I do remember when I came down there was, for me, a communication by post waiting for me, namely a New Year's card. There were several domestic issues to attend to; and then later in the morning I went out into the garden to see my St Bernard, and had a good time stomping about together. I have told how fond I was of dogs, and if I could spend time with them, I used to go for a run in the car with some of them nearly every day.

The Momentous Motorcar Drive

The weather on this Saturday was fine, and I understood that the roads were in excellent condition. This reminded me that I wanted to go to London to see my solicitors on Monday, and, always preferring to journey by motor rather than by train, it was in my mind that I might run up in the motor, so I sent for my chauffeur, Watts.

"Will the tyres of landaulette stand a run to London and back?" I asked.

Watts replied, "I do not think they will."

We went to the garage and had a look at the tyres together. I knew they were in a bad condition, as I had ordered another set from the Minerva Motor Company.

After Watts had examined the tyres he had decided in his opinion that they would not stand a run to town, and he was even in doubt if it would be advisable to go out with them on even quite a short journey. I go into this matter in detail because it quite possible that the condition of the tyres may have had something to do with what happened afterwards, and I do not wish to pass any little points which may help to make clear subsequent occurrences. There was then this little discussion about the tyres and, in the course of it, I expressed surprise that the new tyres, which I understood had been despatched from London, had not yet arrived.

A gentleman, a friend of the family who was staying in the house (*presumably Joseph Gratton*) said that, as was going up to the town during the morning, he would call at the station and find out if he could discover the reason for the delay in their arrival. I believe my sister Lillian and he were going up together – at any rate, that was the arrangement during the morning.

We had an early lunch at twelve-thirty, and it was soon after lunch that, tempted by the fine weather and the excellent condition of the roads, I determined to go out for a run in the motor. There was nothing unusual in this, for, as I have previously explained, I was in the car pretty well every day, either on long or short journeys.

I turned to my sister and said, "Lillian, would you like to come too?"

She replied, "I would very much."

"Very well," I said, "then we will just run as far as Colwyn Bay and back."

I sent out for Watts, the chauffeur, and told him to get the car ready by three o'clock, intending to start about that time. As a matter of fact it was about half-past three when we set out. Watts was driving, I was by his side, and Lillian was in the covered part of the Landaulette, with the window separating us let down so that we could talk together. The front seat was always a favourite of mine unless it was raining hard or unless there as a cold wind and the windscreen was not in place. Then I would ride inside like Lillian. However, as I have explained, I was by the side of the driver.

Groundless Accusations

Now I must explain the geography of our area. Look at the map of North Wales and you will see that St Asaph lies about six miles inland, south of Rhyl, on the coast. Run your eye westwards along the map and you will come to Conwy, Penmaenmawr, Colwyn Bay, and finally, right down in the Menai Straits, Carnarvon. Taking the road in a south-westerly direction from St Asaph we came to Colwyn Bay on the coast. Then, after, travelling about nine miles more, on we went. It was a lovely day and we enjoyed it very much. I spoke to Watts sometimes about the motor, and occasionally turned round and exchanged a word with my sister in the back of the car.

Before I go any further it would be well for me to address the sundry accusations and in so doing make a blunt statement. We went out for that ride solely with the idea of enjoying ourselves. I had no more idea that an accident was going to happen than anyone else driving a car that day. I believed that I should be home again, happy and comfortable, quite early in the evening.

We reached Colwyn Bay somewhere about four o'clock, and Watts came to a stop near the middle of the town with the idea of turning round for the return journey to St. Asaph.

"It has been a splendid ride," I said to Lilian, "shall we go on further?"

"Yes," said Lilian, "the roads are good. and a little further run will make but a small difference in the time we get back."

So I instructed Watts to drive on, and he did so. We passed along the coast through the various towns without incident. Of course, we went by the very spot where later in the night there was to be so serious and so dramatic an occurrence. Little did I think as we sped by the tiny gap in the wall that some four hours later I should be standing there half-dazed and almost distraught with terror, believing that I had caused the death of my sister.

We reached Bangor about twenty past five, or thereabouts, and we came to a halt just in the town, and my sister and I got out of the motor-car. I asked Watts if he would like to go to an hotel for tea, and he said he would prefer to have it at some restaurant. I replied that I didn't care where he had it.

but that he must keep the car within sight. I told him to be back in the same place waiting for us in about half an hour. Then my sister and I strolled up through the town, looking at the shops, until we came to the Castle Hotel. Here we went in to get some tea. It has been pointed out by those who see a grim significance in every trifle that I did not eat very much. This is perfectly true. For one thing. I was not very hungry. and for the other, the bread and butter was rather thicker than I liked it.

While we were in the hotel I asked for a Bradshaw, and at the same time Lilian asked for another time-table, and these innocent requests of ours have set a good many pens going and good many tongues wagging in the last week or two. As a matter of fact, they were the most innocent and natural requests. I had intended to go to London in my motor-car on Monday in order to see my solicitors, and, finding that the tyres would not allow me to do so, I was desirous of ascertaining how the trains ran. I had some idea of catching a train on Sunday night and arriving in town on Monday morning. That is the sole explanation of the time-table and the Bradshaw.

Our walk in the town to the hotel and our tea took up longer time than we had reckoned on. and it was after six when I called Lilian's attention to the fact that we must be keeping Watts waiting with the car. We paid for our tea, and then went on down through the town to meet him. It would now be about twenty past six. The nose of the motor-car was pointing in the direction of St Asaph, but when we had entered and taken our seats I had an idea and said,

"Let's go a little way on the Carnarvon road. The weather is so delightful. I could spend the whole night out of doors."

My sister agreed about the extra run, so we turned the motor-car around and went, not in the direction of home, but in the opposite direction towards Carnarvon. We travelled no great distance - a mile or two, perhaps, out of Bangor - and then we swung round for the return journey, and travelled back by another road, past Bangor and onto the main road for home. We had covered a couple of miles or so on the St. Asaph side of Bangor when we noticed that the car was not pulling properly. After a few minutes Watts brought the car to a standstill, and got down to see what the matter was. Lillian and I kept our places in the car. Travelling a great deal by motor, we were used to these halts, and paid comparatively little attention to them, except in so far as they caused inconvenience in delaying us on our journey anywhere.

Watts lifted both sides of the bonnet of the car and examined the machinery within. I can't remember what he did. I only know that he was probing and examining and adjusting for quite a long time. It may have been half an hour, it may have been a good deal longer, that we were stationary in this road. Eventually, however, Watts managed to fix things up, and we started once more on our homeward journey.

The night was exhilarating, the moon shone brightly, the air was crisp and clear. We sped on at a moderate pace along the road, parallel with the coast as far as Penmaenmawr. It was after passing Penmaenmawr that there began the series of events which led up to the recent great commotion. I asked Watts to let me take the wheel,

"I think you had better not," he said; "the road is none too wide. I think it would be well if you let me continue to drive for the present."

I insisted. It must be remembered that I have driven very frequently, and rather flattered myself on the idea that I had more than once been called a very good driver. The clear road, the moonlight night, the invigorating air, the sense of motion had set me in high spirits. Nothing would satisfy me but that I, and I alone. should control the car. Once more Watts protested; I overbore him. The car was brought to a standstill, and we changed places. We were now at some point between Penmaenmawr and Conway, four or five miles distant.

It could not have been very many minutes after I had taken the wheel that we approached the upward slope leading to Pennmaenbach Point, where the accident occurred. Let me explain the position. The road, which was of moderate width, was practically cut in the face of a great, towering cliff. As we sped along it the rocks on our right hand rose almost sheer for a distance of hundreds of feet above our heads, while on our left a wall three or four feet high was our only protection from a precipitous drop straight into the sea. In effect, therefore, we were some distance up the face of the cliff on a ribbon of road, the edge of which, but for the wall, would have formed a precipice above the sea. There were undulations in the road itself. Some few hundred yards before reaching Penmaenbach Point the road began to rise, and went up at a fairly stiff gradient until we were within about a hundred yards from where the accident occurred. From the summit of this gradient the cliff face and the road bend slightly to the right, the curve becoming more pronounced at the point where the accident happened. I should not omit to say that just at this point the low cliff wall has an opening in it, about three or four feet wide. This, then, is the position: I have reached the top of the up gradient, and have before me a slight down gradient of eighty or a hundred yards, with a road gently turning to the right, and at the end of that, eighty or a hundred yards ahead, just where the curve is sharpest, there is a small opening in the sea-wall. I came down that eighty or a hundred yards at a good speed – say something between fifteen and twenty-five miles an hour. I had not the ghost of a fear in me. The car was running well and smoothly. Nothing was farther from my mind than an accident or disaster of any kind. We swept down towards the curve, and with both hands on the wheel I gently inclined the car to take it, as was usual. We were nearly opposite the gap in the wall when I felt the wheel tremble under my hand. I had one horrid moment of tremulous doubt and wonderment. In the fraction of a second there crossed my mind the thought that a portion of rock or a large stone, fallen from the cliff side on to the road, had suddenly deflected our course. I was on the right hand side of the road, and almost simultaneously with the spasmodic trembling of the wheel the car swerved and plunged to the left towards the sea wall. Never to the day of my death shall I forget that agonised moment. We were speeding towards a precipice 20ft or 30ft away, with only a low wall between us and death. In that terrible second my senses left me. I released the wheel; but did not touch either the brake or the clutch lever. To put on the brake or to put out the clutch did not come to my mind at all. All that I was conscious of was the yawning precipice in front of me, and that within a second or two we should be thrown over.

I remember making an instinctive effort to rise from my seat and screaming out incoherently in fright. I think I heard my sister Lilian screaming behind me in the car. But the shock and terror of the whole thing was such that it is difficult to recall the details of what happened with any precision. I remember the car going with a tremendous crash into the wall. I had one fearful glimpse of the cliffs and the water beneath. My arms were lifted. Watts at the crucial moment was either flung from the seat of the car or jumped from it.

He caught hold of my arm and dragged me from the car. As he did so, my other arm flew out and struck the glass windscreen, smashing it. For a few seconds after that I do not remember what happened. I was literally stunned by the shock of the whole thing. I came to myself, and found that I was standing near the car, and that Watts and my sister had disappeared.

The awfulness of the whole scene thrills me now when I think of it. At that time I felt myself consumed with paralysing terror. Here was the car partly through the wall, on the very verge of the cliff. There were only a few inches of space between the front wheels and the drop into the water. Part of the wall was shattered presumably by the impact of the car. Watts, who had a few moments ago tried to save me and my sister in the back of the car, had both vanished utterly. The one fearful thought that held me was that both had been thrown over the cliff and killed.

I looked at the sea beneath me and found myself trembling. I cannot possibly explain the emotions that chased through me in the course of a few seconds. One thought dominated everything. That was that by my obstinacy in taking the wheel I had caused an awful calamity and killed two people, one of them my sister.

The moon was still shining brightly; but there was no soul to be seen up or down the long, lonely road on either side. I was alone on the edge of the cliff with the wrecked motor-car. Repulsion for the whole scene filled me. I was seized with a mad desire to get away from it, to go anywhere, anyhow, to escape from the site of the disaster and the thought of all it meant. It was a desperate mental crisis for me. I had completely lost my balance. No thought that my sister and Watts might conceivably be lying on the cliff face or at the foot of the cliff came into my mind. A few moments sane reflection would have shown me that Lillian could not have been thrown out of the car over the cliffs in the way that Watts might have been, and I should then have considered whether it was not possible to go for help.

But none of those ideas came to me. I simply had to get away from the results of what I had done. I know now that it was cowardly and wicked. I ought to have thought of the others. But I was beside myself. I remember giving one wild look round, and then, hatless and in my crimson motor-coat, I went up the road towards Conway, a mile and a half away.

Excited, panting for breath, I hurried along on the right-hand side of the road towards Conwy. I kept to the right because the rocks protected me in some measure from the moonlight. The last thing I wanted now was to be observed or recognised. I did not meet anyone until nearing Conwy, and then I passed a youth and a women, neither of whom, I am glad to say, paid any attention to me.

Directly I got into the streets of Conwy I, of course. met a lot of people, but repressing my excitement, I showed no undue haste, and managed to get to the railway station without drawing attention on myself. Hurrying through Conwy. I remembered that there a train going up to Crewe at about half-past nine. Fearful lest it had already gone, I ran on the platform and asked a porter about it. He said the train was due in two or three minutes. I have learned since, that the train is timed at Conwy at 9.23, although on this occasion I think it was a little late.

While waiting for the train I remembered that I had in my pocket a silk mackintosh hood which I usually wore over my motor hat. This was a great good fortune. I adjusted it on my head, the absence of my cap was not then noticeable.

My Plight in the Night

The train steamed in, and I noticed several empty third-class carriages. I entered one of them, and as soon as the train had started I pulled down the blind so that at subsequent stations I might, as far as possible, escape observation. My greatest anxiety was with regard to Rhyl, which we were soon to reach. Rhyl is the main line station for St Asaph, and there might easily have been some people from St Asaph there. Apart from that, I was very frequently in Rhyl and might be known there, and the chances were, therefore, about level that if a resident of St Asaph or Rhyl entered my carriage I should be immediately recognised. The train was due at Rhyl at 10.40, and whether it was punctual or not, I am not quite certain, but this I do know: that it stayed seven minutes in the station before it went on again. They were seven terrible minutes to me. Every footstep that went past the carriage door might have been that of a person who was to bring discovery upon me. I have not the least idea what I should have done if some person who knew me had got into the carriage. Fortunately, no one did so.

Filled with burning thoughts as to what had happened, I travelled on in the train to Chester. My mind was in a whirl. I have heard it said somewhere that tickets are usually collected on this train at Flint. All I can say is that they were not collected on this occasion, or at any rate no demand for a ticket was made from me. Between Chester and Crewe I sank into a muddled, hazy dose. Through it all, I could see the scenes of Penmaenbach Point, the wrecked wall, the broken motor-car, the threatening precipice, and the sea beneath, with the moonlight shining on the ghastly loneliness. It was a terrible sleep for me.

I reached Crewe some time before midnight. I could get no train for the north till four minutes past one. By this time I had decided to make for Scotland, somewhere in the Highlands. My sole idea was to escape notice for the time being. I had formulated no definite plans. I only wanted to get away from the whole world and from everybody who knew me. I would return home later; I thought to myself. If I could get to Glasgow, I would be able to book to somewhere further north from there.

So, at Crewe I took a ticket for Glasgow and journeyed by the train leaving at four minutes past one. I travelled third-class, having, naturally, only a few sovereigns in my pocket. It was a long, dreary journey, and I eventually arrived at Glasgow about seven o'clock on Sunday morning. I was, so may be guessed, extremely tired and very dejected and very frightened. I had sense enough to know that the first thing I must do was to get some sleep, in order to refresh myself. I went to the North British Hotel and booked a room in the name of McKay. Then I had a good sleep.

When I awoke later in the day I was able to think a little more clearly of all that had happened and to lay out my future course with a little more precision. I still had an undefinable repulsion against letting my people know where I was, for the horror of Saturday night still held me in its grip. Where can I get away till the first shock of the thing has blown over? That was my thought. I tentatively decided on one of the islands further north. Mull occurred to me, although I did not know the name of any place there. As I had previously been to Oban,

I was aware that boats ran from there across to Mull, and so I decided first of all to get to Oban. Then I had to think of practical details of course. I brought nothing with me in the shape of luggage, and it is awkward in more ways than one to go to an hotel without baggage of any kind. Then I remembered that by a piece of great good fortune I had, some little time before, left a trunk with some clothes in it at one of the railway stations in Glasgow.

Pangs of Conscience

I had been staying in Scotland last year, and during my journey had left a trunk at the station and neglected to collect it. To my joy I remembered I had the ticket in my purse. I made up my mind that I would get the trunk in the morning and go on to Oban with it. I had a good night's rest on Sunday, and on Monday morning I went out into the streets of Glasgow to begin my preparations. I was naturally extremely curious as to what was known of the accident, and so I made my way to the railway bookstall and bought a Daily Mail. Rapidly looking over the columns, I came upon an account of the accident, and learned for the first time that my sister was safe. For that moment a great gush of feelings took possession of me, and it is easy to imagine my relief. Then, after the first great burst of gratitude, there came a reaction. My cowardice came upon me like a flood. I had basely deserted my sister and my servant when they might both have been in deadly peril and both very seriously in need of my help. I pictured myself going back to St Asaph and the reception I should get there. I had run away from danger and left those connected with me to take care of themselves. It was a horrible thought. So, it came about that I decided that, being away, I would stay away for a little longer and not communicate with my friends for a while. This decision, however, was only reached after a lot of anxious thought and some hours of pondering. Of course, the proper thing to do would have been to send a wire at once to mother telling her of my safety but like a cowardly girl I could not bring my mind to it. I determined to postpone the evil day.

So, then I went on to proceed with the plan I had already formed. I secured my trunk, and I left by the two o'clock train from Buchanan Street Station. I booked to Perth. At Perth I changed and booked again for Oban, and had to wait three-quarters of an hour before I could get on a train. In that three-quarters of an hour I walked out into the street and got some more papers, and read the accounts in all of them as to what happened at the scene of the accident. They differed considerably, but none of them was uncomplimentary: indeed, it seemed to me that they only differed in describing the degree of popularity which I enjoyed.

I must retrace my steps here for a moment and explain that on the way from Glasgow to Perth I had been in a carriage with other passengers, among whom were two soldiers who discussed the Penmaenbach accident with much interest. One was very sympathetic,

"It is a bad business," he said. "Fancy the poor girl being thrown right out of the car over the cliffs into the water."

The other soldier was doubtful, "It is not so certain she is dead," he said, "perhaps she has escaped and is alive after all."

He was a careful man, that second soldier. I was a good deal too upset to be amused, but I was certainly very much interested in their conversation. You may be certain that I did not join in the discussion or manifest that it had any attraction for me.

The train had got as far as Stirling when I learned that I ought to have changed at Dunblane, an intermediate station. There was no train on from Stirling until 5.30 in the morning, so I went to an hotel, stayed the night, got up at a quarter to five. and caught the 5.30 to Oban. I reached Oban at a few minutes to nine, and quickly ascertained that there was a boat over to Tobermory in Mull in a few hours' time. I had some breakfast in the station hotel, and then went down and joined the boat. We reached Tobermory at about half-past three and I went to the Mishnish Hotel, where I engaged a room as Miss MacLeod.

I used to have one or more of the Scottish newspapers every day, and the indications of the hue-and-cry both frightened me and hardened me. What had I done, I asked, that I should be treated like a wild beast? Here was I, a girl innocent of any crime, who was being desperately hunted both by Press and public. Anger and rebellion were mingled with fear. With many emotions fighting each other, I saw that to return at that time or to give any indication of my whereabouts would simply add to the notoriety. There would be another great outburst as soon as I reappeared.

It was the newspapers alone that induced me to keep myself in hiding for another period. Naturally I took what precautions I could to prevent the disclosure of my identity, and I had done so from the first. On reaching Glasgow some days before, realising that my crimson coat, might attract attention. I had carried it on my arm when I entered an hotel. Before I left the city I took the crimson coat to a firm of dyers and asked them to dye it blue.

I left Tobermory on the 13th to come back to Oban. On the steamer I saw a man watching me very carefully, and I am convinced that this man, whoever he was, first set in motion the inquiries which resulted in my discovery. On reaching Oban I went to the Palace Hotel and engaged a room. I had not been in the place more than twenty minutes, when the landlady quite unsuspectingly brought up the topic of the missing lady motorist.

"She's a wicked girl," said the landlady, "we have heard a lot about her."

"Oh," I said, "there may be another side to the story."

"No," persisted the landlady, "I have even heard that she goes horse-racing!"

An Amusing Anecdote

Neither then, nor at any time during the next few days would the landlady have any mercy on the character of the missing lady motorist.

I have explained that I knew Oban pretty well, having stayed there for a holiday eighteen months or so ago. Out of this arose a rather amusing incident. On the day after my arrival, I went along to the local photographers to get some plates for a small camera of mine. The photographer like everyone else, was full of talk about the missing lady.

"They say she has been seen around here," he said to me.

"Indeed," said I, "perhaps you know her?"

"Oh, yes," he explained, "I know her, because she has been in here to have her photograph taken."

"You took it?" I asked.

"Yes." he said. "She was in here with her sister. Here's the photograph of them."

He produced a portrait and handed it to me. I expressed some little interest is it.

"I remember her well," said the photographer, "very demure she looked. Never a girl who you would think would be up to tricks like this."

"She was very quiet, was she?" I asked.

"Yes," said the photographer, "but she had a touch of temper. I could see that even when she was in here."

I smiled over the anecdote and left him with my photo; his hands quite unaware that he had been talking to the original.

This was Thursday. Events developed rapidly. On Sunday I began to feel that I was suspected in the hotel. On Monday a pack of eager, hunting journalists arrived at Oban, almost at the same time as my sister Lillian and Mr Gratton, who had come from Wales. I had lain in bed very late, up to noon in fact, as had been my practice since I had been at Oban. The first indication I had that people were definitely on my trail was when a man opened my bedroom door, and exclaimed, "Your sister and father have come."

"How dare you," I exclaimed. "Close the door!'

My Sister Lilian Arrives

Within a few minutes my sister was shown into my room where I lay in bed. Now I was quite convinced that people were listening outside, and probably in the next room, in order to ascertain what our meeting would be like. Directly Lillian came in, I indicated to her by a sly gesture to say nothing, and then smilingly we conversed as well as we could in a dumb show. She was there but a few minutes and then went downstairs to lunch in the coffee-room. While she was there, I sent down a message that I should like to see her, together with the police inspector who had previously called upon me, in order to ascertain whether I was really Miss McLeod or Miss Charlesworth. The Inspector and Lillian came to see me together. The. inspector had a photograph of myself taken as Miss Charlesworth.

"Do you think that this portrait is like you?" he asked.

I was out of bed and dressed by this time. I took the photo in my hand, crossed over to the mirror, looked at myself, and then at the photo, and said, "Yes. I think there is some small resemblance."

"Yes," he replied, in his genial Scotch way, "I think there is, too."

But all this time I was, of course, Miss MacLeod. Miss MacLeod I remained throughout the day. In the afternoon journalist after journalist opened my door and tried to extract admission from me. By this time, I was thoroughly roused, and nothing on earth would have caused me to have admitted to any one of those journalists that I was Miss Charlesworth. They tried all kinds of methods, persuasion, bluff, and denunciation. I made up my mind that I would not be bullied, not admitting anything.

At the time I was very much annoyed and angry at the things I had put up with, but able to see that they had their humorous side. For instance, after I had been for an hour or two explaining that I was Miss MacLeod one reporter walked straight in and, disregarding my cold air, said in loud tones, "Miss Charlesworth, why don't you go home to St Asaph?"

Of course, I did the only thing possible – I walked to the bell, rang it, and asked that he should be shown out.

In London at Last

Altogether it was an exciting and unpleasant afternoon for me, but the reporters, in spite of their waylaying me and their forcing themselves into my room, could extract nothing from me. I should add that there were one or two among them who, finding legitimate enquiries from me useless, endeavoured to protect me from farther annoyance.

With my sister and Mr Gratton I left Oban for Glasgow by a train between four and five o'clock in the afternoon. When I and my sister reached King's Cross next evening there was a crowd of Pressmen and photographers on the platform to meet us. We kept our blinds down, and made no attempt to emerge. Presently, the door on the other side of the carriage was opened and two station officials standing on the line asked us to get out that way and escape the crowd. We hurried down on to the metals. An approaching engine was stopped, so that we might cross in front of it, and we were helped up on to the opposite platform. A fast motor-car was in waiting for us. and we were soon away from the pursuing crowd of taxicabs.

Before I conclude, I would like to say one word of deep gratitude to all who have sent kind letters and telegrams to me and to my people during this time of great trouble. The kindness of a great many of these ladies and gentlemen has been extreme. I cannot say how much I appreciate all their goodness at a time when so many have been engaged in vilifying me.

THE END

Miss V. Charlesworth

Appendix G: Thérèse Humbert – The Lady That Inspired Violet?

The inspiration behind Violet and Miriam Charlesworth's original plan to invent an imaginary benefactor, seems to have been derived almost entirely from the story of a female French fraudster named Thérèse Humbert.

In fact, both stories were so remarkably similar, and the escapades of Thérèse Humbert so well known, it is astonishing that those who succumbed to Violet's scheme did not tumble her ruse earlier. Perhaps it was a testament to her abundant charm and persuasive skills.

Thérèse Humbert

Thérèse Humbert was born Thérèse Aurignac in 1855; a simple peasant girl in the small French village of Aussonne. As a child, she somehow managed to convince her friends to lend her their jewellery; thus allowing her into fooling others that she was the child of wealthy parents.

In fact, Thérèse's father was a notorious drunkard, who often claimed to be of noble ancestry, even calling himself the Count d'Aurignac. As so many aristocratic families had been ruined by the Franco-Prussian war, it was not unusual to appear both impoverished and yet claim to be of noble birth. With considerable ease, he managed to convince a surprising number of acquaintances that he was, indeed, of royal birth. As he grew more confident, he even elaborated his story, proudly showing his neighbours an old wooden chest, which he had carefully sealed and locked. He informed everyone that the chest contained the title deeds to a vast estate in Auvergne called Chateau d'Aurignac. Following his death in 1874 the family opened the chest – only to find it contained nothing more than a solitary house brick.

Upon reaching adulthood, Thérèse became a laundry-maid to

the family of Toulouse Mayor Gustave Humbert. She seems to have inherited her father's talent for fantasy. Not only did she continue her fable of noble ancestry from a once-mighty family, she embroidered the story still further. Thérèse announced to the mayor's family that she had been made sole heir to a fabulous ancestral estate in the Tarn region of France, known as the Chateau de Marcotte. She claimed that the previous owner of this estate, a wealthy spinster named Mademoiselle de Marcotte, had made a will endowing the chateau and her entire fortune to Thérèse. The tale was repeated so confidently, and so often, that everyone she encountered seems to have accepted her story without question. Her employers, the Humbert family, even seemed to be suitably overawed by their laundry washing heiress. Indeed, the Humbert's son, Frédéric, was so taken with the story that he eloped with Thérèse, who he believed would soon become hugely rich, and the couple married in 1878.

The story, of course, transpired to be a complete fabrication.

In 18979, in yet another version of her inheritance scam, Thérèse Humbert claimed that, while travelling on the Ceinture Railway, she overheard groans of pain coming from the adjoining compartment. Upon going to investigate she found an elderly gentleman who appeared to be having a heart attack. According to Thérèse, she gave the man some smelling salts and did what she could to make him comfortable. He recovered sufficiently, and was able to leave the train at the next stop, but not before requesting her name and address. He thanked her profusely for her kindness; and swore he would never forget it.

The gentleman, Thérèse claimed, was a billionaire Chicago business tycoon named Robert Henry Crawford. After they parted at the train station, Thérèse claimed, she forgot the entire incident until, in 1881, she received a letter from a New York law firm, informing her that Robert Crawford had passed away, leaving her £4 million (approximately £600 million today!). Thérèse even claimed to be in possession of Crawford's death certificate and a copy of his will to prove the legitimacy of the story. According to the latter document, Crawford's fortune was to be divided between Thérèse, her younger sister Marie, and the dead man's nephews, Robert (Junior) and Henry Crawford. The three other beneficiaries were to pay Thérèse £14,000 a year. However, the deceased man's American lawyers had stipulated, - according to Thérèse - that the entire Crawford fortune should remain in the family. Thérèse was instructed to keep the entire £4 million (in cash) in a safe. Then, when her sister Marie came of age, one of the Crawford nephews was instructed to marry the girl, thus keeping the estate undivided.

After her previous escapade, regarding the imagined estate at Chateau de Marcotte, one might be tempted to think that her husband's family would treat this story with a certain scepticism. Instead, they seemed to embrace it. Perhaps, the most peculiar feature about the entire affair is just how easily the Humberts appear to have accepted everything Thérèse told them. In fact, they eagerly informed everyone that their daughter-in-law would soon be an exceedingly wealthy woman, perhaps the richest in the world.

After all, no one in Paris dreamed that the powerful Minister of Justice, Gustave Humbert, could possibly be mistaken, so Thérèse's story went largely unquestioned. Almost instantly, she became the most famous woman in the city, and she lost no time capitalizing on her new renown as a romantic heiress. She rented a country estate and a grand mansion in the fashionable *Avenue de la Grande Armée*, in the heart of Paris. In the downstairs parlour she had a large safe installed, in which she claimed to keep the famed Crawford millions. At the height of *La Belle Époque*, Thérèse became the star of Paris society. She threw lavish parties, at which she impressed everyone with the expensive dresses, glittering diamonds, and other fabulous jewels (all purchased on credit, of course). Outwardly she appeared to live like a queen. France's wealthiest financiers and businessmen fell over themselves to lend her huge sums of money, based entirely on the promise that she would one day inherit a fortune, and would then happily repay these sums with interest. If any lender displayed the slightest doubt in her story, she would simply take them aside and show them a bundle of official letters, all supposedly written by the Crawfords. This seemed to be enough to satisfy their fears, and the matter was soon dropped.

Thérèse's wealthy lifestyle continued for two years, until an exposé appeared in a French newspaper which, for the first time, raised doubts about the legitimacy of her story. It would later transpire that the journalist who wrote the article had been raised in Thérèse's hometown and he, no doubt, remembered her father's fable about his noble ancestry, his safe, and the infamous brick. The journalist speculated that history was about to repeat itself.

Thérèse realised that if any doubts began to spread in Parisian society, she would be uncovered. She decided to go on the offensive, backing up her lies with yet more lies. Firstly, she invented a quarrel with the fictious Crawford nephews in which, she claimed, the other beneficiaries were no longer happy with the family fortune being left in her care. The Crawfords, according to Thérèse, insisted that the £4 million should now be transferred to a bank for safe keeping; but that she had objected to their plan. So convincing was Thérèse that she took the entirely imaginary Crawford family to court. Lawsuits were filed, some of them apparently originating from the fictious Crawford family, others from Thérèse. Both sides even hired some of the most expensive lawyers in France, although, of course, the Crawford family never appeared personally in court! Thérèse filed lawsuit after lawsuit on a host of petty issues relating to the fictional estate, ensuring the case remained in the courts (and in the news) for two decades.

This flurry of legal activity erased any doubt in Thérèse's claims regarding the genuineness of the Crawford fortune. After all, the French newspapers reasoned, non-existent people could not file a lawsuit.

During this time Thérèse's younger sister, Marie Aurignac, had graduated from school. It seems that Marie was entirely innocence and genuinely believed she was destined to marry 'Henry Crawford.' She happily bragged to her friends about the wealthy, charming and handsome young American who would soon become her husband.

However, by 1900 one of Thérèse's creditors, a banker named Delatte, began to grow impatient for repayment of a substantial line of credit he had advanced to Thérèse. He demanded that she open her now-famous safe and begin to pay back the huge sums she owed. Thérèse naturally stalled Monsieur Delatte, which only increased his suspicions and his level of anxiety. He engaged Thérèse in conversation and casually enquired where Henry Crawford lived. Astonishingly, he appears to have been the first person to do so. However, Thérèse was well-prepared and told him that the Crawford family lived in Somerville, a wealthy suburb of Boston.

Monsieur Delatte took the first available steam ship to America, determined to see this mysterious heir for himself. However, on arriving in Boston, he was unable to trace anyone by the name of "Henry Crawford" living in Somerville, or anywhere else in the Boston area. Not a single person he spoke to had ever heard of the family. Next, Delatte hired a team of private detectives to trace the Crawford family; but they also failed to locate anybody of that name. In fact, there was no evidence that any person matching that description existed anywhere in the entire United States. Delatte angrily wrote to a colleague in Paris, informing him of his findings. Delatte declared that he would return immediately to France and expose Thérèse Humbert's entire fraud.

Sadly, Monsieur Delatte never had the opportunity. Before he could sail back from New York, his body was found floating in the East River. Was his death an accident or suicide – or perhaps something more sinister? The cause of his death remains a mystery to this day.

Delatte's death merely acted as a catalyst to Thérèse's other creditors, who became more and more anxious. Surely, they insisted, it was now time for her sister Marie to marry Henry Crawford and finally open the famous safe containing the Crawford millions? Predictably, Thérèse attempted to extricate herself from this predicament by perpetrating a further fraud. She launched a scheme to obtain yet more funding from a series of new investors, which she then hoped could be used to pay off her existing creditors.

She opened a suite of impressively luxurious office buildings in the heart of Paris' business district and began what was called a *rente viagère* (life annuity) scheme. Thérèse informed the public that a large insurance company had promised to provide an impressive retirement annuities, with the potential of huge returns, should they wish to invest immediately in the new company.

Bizarrely, this scam proved to be even more profitable than Thérèse's previous schemes. With the help of her brothers, she drew up a prospectus that was so enticing that throngs of investors from all across France queued to purchase annuities or insure their lives, with an entirely fictious insurance company, all firmly believing that they were making a once-in-a-lifetime investment with a guaranteed substantial return on their money. Millions of francs poured into the coffers of the make-believe insurance company and Thérèse's was able to repay her existing creditors just enough money to allay their suspicions.

For a short time, it seemed, Thérèse was safe. However, it was not long until her creditors again became impatient for the opening of the infamous safe. In addition, everyone agreed, it was now time for Marie (who had been nicknamed *'the eternal fiancée'* by the French newspapers) to marry Henry Crawford. In the spring of 1901, a large group of Thérèse's creditors who were now close to bankruptcy, held a meeting to agree on a course of action. They all arrived at the same grim conclusion - Thérèse Humbert had swindled them.

The aggrieved group of creditors decided to employ one of France's leading lawyers, Rene Waldeck-Rousseau, a man who had already crossed swords with Thérèse in court on several occasions.

He instinctively disliked her, and was more than ready to believe she was a confidence trickster. Indeed, his own son-in-law had been swindled by her - giving him a personal motive to ensure that *'La Grande Thérèse'* was finally brought to justice. Rene Waldeck-Rousseau met with the editor of *Le Matin* newspaper, who agreed to publish a series of damaging articles blatantly accusing Madame Humbert of fraud.

These articles had the immediate effect of further emboldened Thérèse's creditors to demand that the French courts order her to open the infamous safe. The presiding judge sided with the creditors and agreed that opening the safe was the best and only way to settle their grievances. Although Thérèse and her lawyers vigorously fought this decision, they were finally forced to concede. Thérèse handed the keys of the safe to the French courts, and Friday 9th May 1902 was set as the official day upon which the safe would finally be opened.

Meanwhile, on the previous evening (Thursday 8th May), and unknown to the authorities, Thérèse and her family quietly slipped away.

The next morning, the safe was finally opened. Inside lay a single penny coin and one solitary brick.

Arrest warrants were immediately issued for Thérèse and her brothers. Finally, in September 1902, they were eventually tracked down in Madrid and brought back to Paris to face the angry public.

In a similar vein to Violet Charlesworth, Thérèse, continued her charade. She refused to admit any wrongdoing whatsoever. Instead, she manufactured a new legal defence that surprised everyone. Thérèse now conceded that the American billionaire Robert Crawford had never actually existed. She now claimed that the man who had actually bequeathed his fortune to her was François Achille Bazaine, the French officer who had given distinguished service to his country during the Second Empire. Although promoted to Marshal Bazaine, he was sentenced to death for his surrender of the town of Metz, along with over 140,000 men, to the Germans during the Franco-German War of 1870-71.

Although granted a stay of execution, Bazaine eventually passed away in 1888.

Thérèse testified that the £4 million fortune left to her by Bazaine, had been Germany's reward to him for the betrayal of his men at Metz. She also insisted that had never been made aware of the money's provenance. Conveniently for Thérèse, of course, Bazaine was no longer able to disprove her claim – in an identical fashion to Violet Charlesworth's story regarding the fortune left to her by General Gordon.

Thérèse added that, as soon as she had realised the money had been a German bribe, it had seemed morally wrong to keep such tainted money and, in a fit of patriotic fervour, she had burnt every single franc, thus explaining why the safe was completely empty.

Unsurprisingly, Thérèse and her brothers were found guilty of fraud. Thérèse was sentenced to five years in jail, with hard labour. Her brother Romain, three years, and Emile two. Her husband Frédéric was also sent to jail, although many onlookers at the time believed he was yet another victim of his wife's persuasive tale.

Similarly to Violet Charlesworth, following her prison sentence, Thérèse managed one more trick, by effectively disappearing. It was generally believed that she emigrated to America, where she was widely thought to have died in obscurity in 1918. However, in 1930, the investigator who brought Thérèse back from Spain in 1902 to face trial wrote an article in which he claimed to have found her living in poverty and obscurity in Paris. Underneath a picture of a rundown hovel in the *Boulevard des Batignolles* he declared, '*Here lives today, she who was "la Grande Thérèse". Behind these windows with the white curtains, Thérèse Humbert meditates on her past*.'

The story of Thérèse Humbert was widely reported in the English newspapers during 1902, at the exact time Violet and her mother first plotted their tale of an imaginary inheritance. Their respective frauds seem so similar, that it seems Violet and Miriam must have found inspiration in, not only, the original idea but also in the length of time Thérèse was able to maintain the façade.

Perhaps the key question that remains, is why both women's victims were not more suspicious, and why they made so little effort to check the validity of her story. There are two probable answers to both cases. Firstly, both women had created a fable in which the 'proof' of their inheritance lay abroad, thus making it difficult, or nearly impossible, to verify, especially more than a century ago. And secondly, both ladies were not only charming and utterly believable, but had both created such a romantic and layered fantasy, coated with such conviction and certainty, that they both went to prison suffering from a degree of incredulity and injustice - almost believing their own invention.

Bibliography

Newspapers and magazines

Airdrie and Coatbridge Advertiser
Australian Women's Mirror
Bath Chronicle
Belfast Newsletter
Beverley Independent
Central Somerset Gazette
Chicago Tribune
Cornwall Advertiser
Daily Arkansas Gazette
Daily Express
Daily Mirror
Daily Telegraph
Derby Daily Telegraph
Derby Evening Times
Derbyshire Courier
Echo Magazine
Evening News
Evening Standard
Evening Times
Fermanagh Herald
Glasgow Herald
Good Morning
Graphic Magazine
Highland News
Illustrated Police News
Kilkenny Moderator
Leeds Mercury
Leicester Evening Mail
Manchester Courier
North Wales Weekly News
Northern Chronicle
Nottingham Evening Post
Oban Times
Perthshire Advertiser
Press and Journal
Ross Gazette
Sheffield Daily Telegraph
Somerset Standard
Staffordshire Sentinel
Sunday Dispatch
The Courier
The Echo
The Scotsman
The Sketch
The Sphere
The Times
Weekly Dispatch
Weekly Freeman
Weekly Irish Times
Wellington Journal and Shrewsbury News
Yorkshire Telegraph

Books and articles

The Fall of Miss Violet Charlesworth (1983) R.L. Jones, in conjunction with Rhyl Library.

'History of the Charlesworth Case' – supplement produced by the Derby Mercury (1910)

'The Lady Vanishes' – North Wales Life article (1986)

Violet's Leap: the Story of Violet Charlesworth – booklet produced by the Penmaenmawr Museum (2023)